MODERN PRACTICAL
STAIRBUILDING
AND HANDRAILING

Late Stuart Open Well Newelled Stair, Dunster Castle, Somerset, *circ.* 1681.

MODERN PRACTICAL STAIRBUILDING AND HANDRAILING

FOR THE USE OF WORKMEN, BUILDERS, ARCHITECTS, AND OTHERS

BY

GEORGE ELLIS

Author of "Modern Practical Joinery," "Modern Practical Carpentry," "Lessons in Carpentry," "Modern Technical Drawing," etc., etc.

Fully illustrated by Working Drawings and diagrams, and photographic reproductions of old and modern types

STOBART DAVIES, LTD.

STOBART DAVIES LTD.
Publishers & Booksellers
STOBART HOUSE, PONTYCLERC
PENYBANC RD, AMMANFORD SA18 3HP
Tel: 01269 593100 Fax: 01269 596116
www.stobartdavies.com

4689753

MODERN PRACTICAL STAIRBUILDING AND HANDRAILING

BY

GEORGE ELLIS

First published 1932
With new additions.
Copyright © 1990, 1999, 2001 Stobart Davies Ltd. Hertford, England

British Library Cataloguing-in-Publication Data

Ellis, George, 1854-1930
Modern practical stairbuilding and handrailing.
I.   Title
694'.6

ISBN 0-85442-046-0

Printed in the United States of America

Cover Artwork by James Goold

STOBART DAVIES LTD
Publishers & Booksellers
Priory House
2 Priory Street
Hertford SG14 1RN

FOREWORD

AS I WRITE, the trade of wooden stairbuilding and handrailing is undergoing something of a nationwide rebirth. Craftsmen have been asked to build stairs and rail systems that are beyond the scope of common knowledge in today's woodworking for trade schools and custom shops. A few enclaves of traditional stairbuilding knowledge do remain, but stairbuilding and handrailing as a trade—as a nationally identifiable group of shops, craftsmen, techniques, tooling, and literature—have all but disappeared from the landscape. Although still taught in the trade schools of Europe, the techniques found in this rediscovered work by George Ellis have largely been lost in the fast-paced drive toward a modern world.

A resurgence of demand for expert woodworking today, coupled with a void in the experience of most craftsmen, has created a particular need for knowledge and information. *Fine Homebuilding Magazine* has done numerous articles on stairbuilding techniques, and such articles are becoming a regular feature in their issues. *This Old House*, the well known PBS program, recently aired a special program devoted to the work of stairbuilding. The publisher of this current work has already been back to the printer several times to print more copies of the successful 1985 version of William and Alexander Mowat's *A Treatise on Stairbuilding and Handrailing*. These events are all evidence of the increasing awareness of the demand for information on the subject and a lack of expertise in the trade as a whole.

Yet with all this activity, good information on stairbuilding and handrailing is still very hard to come by. The collective literature that deals comprehensively with the twin subjects for the entire century can be counted on one hand.

This particular work by George Ellis is the most lucid, coherent work in the field that I have found in over 15 years in the trade. *Modern Practical Stairbuilding and Handrailing* was written by a man who spent years in the shop practicing, perfecting and teaching his methods. He understood wood, tools, and the shop environment and this understanding shows through in the text. It gives the book a readability and practicality uncommon to technical works. The author's sense of humor is even given an occasional chance to show itself. Unlike so many of his predecessors, Ellis writes in a style that is clear, logical, and easy to follow. Because Ellis is British, some thought and occasional reference to the glossaries will help with unfamiliar terminology. But the simple fact that this was written in the 1920's and 1930's makes it eminently more readable than most works on the subject that predate it by 30 to 100 years. Ellis' career spanned the heyday and evolution of stairbuilding and he has the advantage of a much broader perspective than his forebears and their attempts at perfecting the art. Of course, when he refers to "the sixties," he refers not to our times but to the way things were in the 1860's when he first entered the trade.

It is well to comment at this point on the purpose of most literature on the subject of handrailing. In the decades since the zenith of stairbuilding some 90 years ago, much has been lost both in commonly recognized terminology and in what an author may assume of his readers. The reader will be assisted in his attempts to understand the second half of this book, but he must be aware of some of the assumptions that were made at the time of its writing. They are as follows:

  1) That readers would understand what is meant by the term
    "handrailing."

Handrailing is the science of performing geometrical layouts, producing precise templates and creating with their assistance any combination of curved and straight rails with any variety of radius and pitch, and creating them with exactly predetermined and pre-cut joints in a beautiful and functional manner over any staircase. Handrailing as taught in this and all other books of its era lead a workman through the necessary steps to produce a twisted piece of handrail from a solid block of wood—not from strip laminating. Strip laminating has its proper place and is simple to understand by comparison. But the layouts in the "Handrailing" section of this book are limited to making twisted rail pieces from a solid block. Twisted pieces of railing, or rails of double curvature, are commonly called wreaths. Thus, the section of the book entitled "Handrailing" might better be called "Wreath-making and Handrail Construction." The simple term handrailing understates the complexity of the task to no small degree.

However termed, handrailing must never be studied alone, or divorced from the study of stairbuilding. The two are inextricably linked and it is common for decisions made by the handrailer to determine the final design of the staircase itself. Without proper stair design, a handrail may be unsightly and even dangerous, and without a thorough understanding of the principles of handrailing, even a competent craftsman will be at a loss to satisfactorily design a staircase. And should he chance upon a satisfactory stair design, the handrail will most certainly lack the beauty, precision, and visual flow that marks the work of the masters of Ellis' time.

  2) That readers would understand what they are looking at when
    viewing the drawings and geometrical layouts that accompany the
    text.

This poses no great problem in the section on stairbuilding where drawings are a representation of the object to be built. However, it must be understood at the outset that the purpose of the drawings in the section on handrailing is quite different. Their purpose is simply to lead the craftsman through the layout process to the creation of templates—commonly refered to as face moulds and falling moulds. These moulds are then applied to a wood block in various ways (which are described but rarely shown well in the drawings) and their lines traced onto the wood. These lines create the form that is to be cut out, smoothed and squared up before it is shaped to any profile.

  3) That readers would understand the sequence by which a given
    drawing arrived at the state shown in the book.

In the section on handrailing, many individual steps are shown in a complete layout, and the means by which the drawing progressed is not clearly evident. In some cases it is necessary to reconstruct the drawing oneself to understand its course of development and the significance of each line. However, Ellis is much more helpful than most authors in his ability to walk a reader through a drawing without getting lost forever, and in pointing out what is essential and what is not in the process of developing wreath patterns.

These are some of the unspoken assumptions of most books on handrailing from Ellis' time and before. Keeping them in mind will spare the handrailing craftsman many hours of uncertainty and frustration. It is also good to keep in mind that the bulk of the section on handrailing is simply case study applications of the same system. Once the system is explained, Ellis merely applies it case by case to a wide variety of likely situations with additional comment and refinement given as needed.

For those familiar with the reprinted work by Mowat, this book will be received in one of two ways: either Ellis will be seen as unscholarly and incomplete in his approach to stairbuilding and handrailing, or he will be welcomed as a clear thinking master of the trade who understood the geometry and the shop enough to explain the subject in plain English. His system varies only slightly from Mowat's, the key point of difference being the use of falling moulds. Ellis uses them, Mowat does not.

Beyond that, the differences lie more in style than in substance. Though the primary principles will be found to be similar, Ellis' system provides more explanation in each case study, and the subject as a whole is set forth in much plainer language. Mowat is more technical and theoretical; Ellis is more practical and shop-oriented. Mowat's work is slightly more complete in that he deals with the "normal sections" method of handrailing. The normal sections method is a system of wreath making that arranges the sides of a wreath in such an attitude as to allow much easier detailing with a router or shaper cutter. It has advantages and limitations that are adequately spelled out in Mowat's work. This is an element of some significance that is lacking in Ellis' work. Nevertheless, given the nearly "lost art" status of our trade, I would recommend gaining a fundamental understanding of the system through Ellis. That can be used as a platform for more in-depth work with Mowat.

I view the publishing of this book as an important event. This is a breath of new life for a trade that suffers from being orphaned from its past. It is a resurrection of George Ellis, W. and A. Mowat, and other masters whose voices ceased to speak years ago. It is a down payment on all the hopes and aspirations of today's stairbuilders who are trying to recapture our past from extinction. Simply to have a text written in an English 30 years closer to our time than any other work is to have many of the scales peeled away from our eyes. This represents a significant step in our movement today to reconstruct the methods and techniques of the past.

Shawn Christman
Seattle Stair and Millwork
1989

SAFETY REGULATIONS APPLICABLE TO STAIRBUILDING AND HANDRAILING

Part One

*

STAIR CONSTRUCTION AND DESIGN

CONTAINING A FULL DESCRIPTION OF THE METHODS OF CONSTRUCTING AND
ERECTING VARIOUS TYPES OF WOOD STAIRS FOR COTTAGES, MANSIONS, MODERN
STORES, RAILWAY STATIONS, ETC., WITH EXAMPLES OF IRON, STONE, CONCRETE,
AND MARBLE STAIRCASES, ALL KINDS OF CURVED, MOULDED AND SHAPED
STEPS, INCLUDING CLEAR AND PRACTICAL DIRECTIONS FOR TAKING DIMENSIONS,
SETTING-OUT, PLANNING, FIXING AND FINISHING, ALSO THE CONSTRUCTION OF
SIMPLE AND COMPLICATED, TWISTED, WREATHED AND FRAMED-AND-MOULDED
WOOD SOFFITS, BOTH RECTANGULAR AND SPIRAL, ETC., ETC.

PREFACE.

MR. GEORGE ELLIS long had the intention of expanding the chapters on Stair-building and Handrailing, which appeared in the earlier editions of "Modern Practical Joinery," into a comprehensive treatise, by the inclusion of his lessons on these subjects, and the incorporation of his wide additional knowledge.

It was the author's purpose that the work should be primarily a practical treatise on the art of Modern Stair Construction and Handrailing as it had been evolved during his long practical acquaintance with the subject, when he had opportunities of taking part in, or directing, the construction of stairs of almost every class to be found in the country.

The execution of this important project was steadily proceeded with, although its final completion was hindered by the frequent attacks of severe ill-health to which the author was long subject.

It is a matter for deep regret that Mr. Ellis was not spared to see in book form the result of his long and arduous task, having died suddenly while the work was still in an advanced stage of preparation.

The work of giving the book its final overhaul and seeing it through the press was, with the approval of the executors, entrusted to Mr. Ellis's old friend and colleague, Mr. William Cox, Vice-President, Incorporated British Institute of Certified Carpenters, Lecturer and Head Instructor at The Polytechnic, Regent Street, London, who has spared neither time nor trouble in completing the work in conformity with the author's views. The grateful thanks of every one must be accorded to Mr. Cox for his invaluable co-operation.

Acknowledgment is due to the following who have generously placed at the publishers' disposal a full selection of drawings and photographs of certain examples illustrated :—

Sir Richard Allison, C.B.E., F.R.I.B.A., of H.M.O.W., Plates LXXIV., LXXV., and Illustration 19 ; *Architect and Building News*, Plate LXXVI. ; Maxwell Ayrton, Esq., F.R.I.B.A., Plates LVIII., LXIII., LXIV., LXV., LXVI., LXVII., Illustrations 17, 18 ; Louis Blanc, Esq., Lic.R.I.B.A., Plates LXVIII., LXIX., LXX., LXXI., LXXII. ; Messrs. Clayton & Black, AA.R.I.B.A., Plate LXI. B ; Messrs. F. Frith & Co. of Reigate, Plate XLIX. ; E. Stanley Hall, Esq., M.A., F.R.I.B.A., Plates LX., LXI. (top), Illustration 16 ; Messrs.

Harrods, Ltd., Plates LXVIII., LXIX., LXX., LXXI., LXXII.; Messrs. Henry & Maclennan of Edinburgh, Plate LXII.; the late J. Weymouth Hurrell, Plates XXXII. E, H, K, XXXIV. D, E; Sydney R. Jones, Esq., Illustrations 4, 5 and 8; A. E. Martin Kaye, Esq., Plate LIX.; H. Nelson King, Esq., Plate VIII.; A. Marshall MacKenzie, Esq., LL.D., F.R.I.B.A., Plate LXXIII.; Roland W. Paul, Esq., F.S.A., Plate XXXII. A, B; Frederick W. Pratt, Esq., Plate LXI. B; The Victoria and Albert Museum, Plate III. The Joint Publishing Committee representing the London County Council and the Committee for the Survey of the Memorials of Greater London must be thanked for Plate XL., No. 10, taken from L.C.C. Survey of London, Vol. III., Plate 16; Plate XL., No. 11, *ibid.*, Vol. IV., Plate 63; Plate XL., No. 12, *ibid.*, Vol. V., Plate 13; Plate XL., No. 13, *ibid.*, Vol. VI., Plate 121; Plate XL., No. 17, *ibid.*, Vol. VI., Plate 77; Plate XL., No. 14, taken from the Fourth Monograph of the Committee for the Survey of the Memorials of Greater London.

To Messrs. Higgs & Hill, Ltd., Messrs. Holland & Hannen, and Messrs. Trollope & Colls, Ltd., thanks are also due for advice and helpful information.

Certain of the illustrations have been taken from the following of their publications, to the authors of which the publishers are much indebted: "Later Renaissance Architecture in England," by John Belcher, R.A., and Mervyn E. Macartney, F.R.I.B.A.; "Architecture of the Renaissance in England," by J. Alfred Gotch, F.S.A., F.R.I.B.A.; "Some Architectural Works of Inigo Jones," by H. Inigo Triggs and Henry Tanner, FF.R.I.B.A.; "The English Staircase," by Walter H. Godfrey, F.S.A., F.R.I.B.A.; "The English Interior," by Arthur Stratton, F.S.A., F.R.I.B.A.

THE PUBLISHERS.

January, 1932.

INTRODUCTION

George Ellis was one of the premier English writers on carpentry and joinery and his works have been in demand for many years on the rare book market. Ellis, along with such writers as Nicholson, Radford, Hewitt, Riddell, Mowat and others performed a great service by bringing new ideas and methods of work to their respective fields.

Modern Practical Stairbuilding and Handrailing was the author's last book, and in fact he did not live to see its completion. The work was originally issued in two volumes, one on Stairbuilding and one on Handrailing. These were made available in a one volume edition in 1932 and it is this work which has been republished.

The present edition is a facsimile of the 1932 edition except for minor changes. The numerous fold-out plates have been re-arranged to fit modern book production methods and the overall size of the book has been slightly reduced.

The original photographs have all been retained throughout the new edition but a minor loss of clarity was unavoidable.

Readers are advised that this is a republication of a 1932 edition and is intended to show how staircases and handrailing systems were produced at that time. The methods illustrated here may not conform with local regulations and safety standards. Be certain to consult your local building codes for guidance.

CONTENTS.

CONTENTS

CHAPTER I.

TYPES OF STAIRS AND THEIR CLASSIFICATION.

(Plates ii.–vi.)

EARLY FORMS OF STAIRS AND THEIR DEVELOPMENT.

Short Historical Review of Early English Stair Construction—Evolution of Stairs—Early Forms of
Dogleg Type—Double Newels, Elizabethan Examples—Influence of the Smith—Modern Stairs—
Classification, Definitions—Close Newelled Stairs—Cottage Types—Situation of Winders discussed
—Dangers to avoid—Forms of Strings—Dogleg Stairs—Half-space Landing—What Constitutes
a Dogleg Stair—Use of Carriages—Spandrel Framing—Variety with Quarter-pace Landing and
Quarter-space of Winders—Hand of a Stair—Objections to Four Winders—How to avoid them—
A Four-flight Dogleg Stair—Balanced Winders to be avoided in Newel Stairs—Spacing Steps—
Open String Dogleg Stair—Open Newelled Stairs—A Two-flight Close String Open Well Stair
—Large Open Well Newel Stair with Quarter Landings with Side Entry—A Quarter Turn Open
Newel Stair—Skew Stairs—Three-Flight Grand Stairs—Octagonal Open Well Stair—Geometrical
Stairs—Why so called—Open Stair with Reverse Flights—A Continuous Open Well Stair—Different
Planning of Winders—A Large Open Well Stair with Reverse and Return Flights—A Right Angle
Return Flight Stair with Continuous Rail and Mitre Cap to Newel—An Obtuse Angle Continuous
Stair—A Georgian Quadrant Stair.

THIS being primarily a practical book for workshop use, it would not be in keeping with its
character to treat the subject with any degree of fullness from the historical point of view;
moreover, this side has been adequately presented in a useful standard work issued by
the same publishing house,[1] but it may be interesting to note that the type of wood stair,
now considered the most difficult of construction, would appear to be, if not the first form
used (if the inclined planes formed of rammed earth as used by Egyptians, Romans, etc., in
early times are disregarded), for interior stairs, at least the earliest form of which any examples
still exist, viz. the spiral or " winding " stair.   The reasons for the adoption of this form of
construction in early times are fairly well known to students of architecture, but it is a remarkable refutation of the generally accepted view, that progress in the constructive arts is made
by the slow and tentative process of evolution, when a type calling for the highest degree of
skill on the part of the workman should have been boldly attempted, and its difficulties suc-
cessfully overcome, at a period when those arts were comparatively young, at least in England.
Succeeding the winding stair, the next earliest type of which examples remain is that now
known as the dogleg stair, wherein the carpenter, following the usual custom of the craftsman not yet realising the limitations and possibilities of his own material, copies broadly
the designs and constructive methods of his fellow workman, the mason, who was the
leading constructor of the mediæval period, and we find these first straight stairs with, in
the earlier forms, wall-like balustrades, which were later pierced with tracery, for the purpose of reducing both actual and apparent heaviness, supported at each end by massive piers,
and surmounted by heavy copings, forerunners of the newel post and handrail.   But before

[1] " The English Staircase," by Walter H. Godfrey.

these latter devices had dawned upon the carpenter, the worker in wood who had not yet developed to a joiner, his attempts to deal with the difficulties brought about by the use of methods appropriate enough in stone, but unsuitable for wood, occasioned sundry odd contrivances ; one of these is to be seen in the double newel dogleg stair at the Castle House, Deddington, Oxfordshire, shown in the photo (Pl. II.). This stair was erected fairly early in the seventeenth century, and is typical of that period. It is devised to overcome the difficulty met where the heavy handrails cross the strings, but doubtless the clumsy appearance of the twin newel soon suggested their separation by a landing, and forthwith the opened newel stair was born, and it is not far fetched to add, with it the art of joinery, for in the early and first later Renaissance periods, those specialists in woodworking, the carver and the turner, attained their highest development in conjunction with the joiner, the craftsman that provided the constructive framework for their embellishments. It is generally conceded that the open newel stairs of the late Stuart period are the triumph of the joiner's art, as in the beautiful example at Dunster Castle (frontispiece), just as, at an earlier period, the ornate hammer-beam roof marked the climax of the art of carpentry. Later, another craftsman was to exercise great influence on stair design : during the Georgian period the art of the smith acquired pre-eminence. The wrought-iron balustrading, current in the eighteenth and beginning of the nineteenth centuries, gave rise to the science of " geometrical " handrailing, and for the production of the slender continuous rolls considered a sufficient foil for the light, elegant, but rigid constructions of the smith, with its open wreathed string to match ; a fashion which has held sway to our own times. A typical example of this style is given in the photograph of the geometrical stair at Sheen House, Richmond (Pl. III.). There are, however, signs of revival of the taste for the heavier newel stair, with its more substantial handrail, typical of the earlier period, with the addition of such modern refinements as square-turned balusters (see Pl. LVIII.), inlaid strings, and newels.

Modern Stairs, in regard to their principles of construction, may be broadly reduced to three main types, viz. the close newel, the open newel, and the newel-less or geometrical stair, but the details of each type are made so interchangeable in practice that no definite standard types of construction can be asserted, and such classification as is herein made is rather for convenience of reference than for any practical utility that arises from such classification.

For instance, we may have an open string " close " newel stair, and a close string " open " newel stair, and vice versa a close newel stair having a close string, or an open newel stair with open string : the terms open and close, in reference to the strings, signifying that the ends of the steps are visible in the one case, and hidden by the string in the other, also the term " close " is applied when the balustrade above the string is solid or panelled, as in the photos (Pl. LIV.-LVII.). Similarly the same terms in reference to the stair mean that there is an open space or well between the strings in the one case, and an absence of the same in the other ; the conjunction of the word newel with these terms differentiating the stair from the geometrical or non-newel class. It must also be understood that it *is* possible to have geometrical stairs with newels, and stairs in which the newel is an essential feature of the construction, in conjunction with continuous handrails, a feature which is, however, usually associated with the absence of newels (see Pl. X.). Therefore, the grouping of certain typical plans in the adjacent plates is merely for the purpose of comparison.

CLOSE NEWELLED STAIRS.

The simplest form of this variety is the common straight stair, which differs only from a step-ladder in having *risers* framed between the treads, or steps, the latter of course being

PLATE II.

CASTLE HOUSE, DEDDINGTON, OXON, WITH DOUBLE NEWELS (Early Seventeenth Century).

PLATE III.

GEOMETRICAL STAIR, SHEEN HOUSE, RICHMOND (Late Eighteenth Century).

(Now demolished.)

open between the treads. It has not been thought necessary to illustrate specially this type, as all its constructional details are included in the illustration of a **small, straight stair with winders at the start**, suitable for a cottage, as shown in Figs. 1 and 2, Pl. IV. As the details of construction will be fully dealt with in a succeeding chapter, only the general principles will be reviewed in these remarks upon types. This example consists of ten straight parallel-edged steps or " flyers," and three winders at the bottom, for obvious reasons ; the stair is placed in the angle between a partition and a party wall, therefore must be entered from the side. The best position for winders is a disputed point, and, like most matters about which there are differences of opinion, it largely depends upon circumstances. Winders are generally considered dangerous, but this is less on account of their narrowness of tread at the outside end than for the abrupt change in going which they occasion when introduced into straight flights. A spiral stair, which consists *entirely* of winders, is no more dangerous to the user than are straight stairs, though undoubtedly descending them quickly causes vertigo to some persons, the writer among them ; the tendency may be reduced by partially closing the eyes, or by avoiding looking at the side walls ; but the change of going from a straight step to a winder is a very considerable danger, and for this reason, it is an invariable rule in stair construction not to alter either the rise or the going in any one flight, and to avoid doing so, if possible, in contiguous flights, for the users seldom look at their feet when descending, but intuitively feel their way. Probably, in most instances, winders at the top of a flight offer the least danger, because a person descending a stair invariably goes carefully at the commencement, and, finding winders, will use caution until he is past them, but when descending in the straight, then coming suddenly upon winders at the bottom, he is liable to stumble. The argument for placing them at the bottom is, that if children have to use the stairs they will inevitably fall at the winders, therefore if these are at the lower end the fall will be a short one (of two evils choose the least). This stair has close strings on both sides, the wall strings are grooved and tongued together at the angle, and the outside string, like the handrail, is framed into the newels. Wall strings, except in very rare instances, are invariably " close," that is to say, they extend above and below the steps, thus enclosing their ends, which are housed into the string, but outer strings may be either " close " or " open " ; a more expressive term for the latter type is " cut." In these, the string extends *below* the steps only, and is cut or notched out upon the top side to the outline of the steps, which they thus reveal, as shown in Fig. 2, Pl. XI., and Fig. 2, Pl. XXI. ; these are also known as " stepped strings." For more explicit definition of these and other technical terms employed in this book see the " Glossary " at the end.

The example under consideration being a small stair, no carriage piece is shown underneath ; as a matter of fact, carriages are seldom used in cottage work, whatever the type of stair ; the necessary stiffening for the outer string is obtained in these by either spandrel framing beneath the string, or match-lining nailed on its face to form an enclosure (see Fig. 2, Pl. XII.). The wall string is stiffened by driving one or two joint-plugs into the brickwork, hard under the lower edge of the string. The dotted lines in the plan, Fig. 1, Pl. IV., indicate the position of the joists and trimmers of the floor above, to which the stair gives access, and the dotted dimension line between arrow-heads indicates the " going " of the stair, to which further reference will be made presently. Next, in order of simplicity of construction, is the **Dogleg Stair**, with half-pace landing (Figs. 3 and 4, Pl. IV.). A dogleg stair has two or more flights in reverse direction ; the alternate forward and backward outer strings and handrails are framed into the same newel post, at the change of direction, as shown in the drawings. It is the consequent absence of any space between the two strings that constitute the " close " stair, and as a corollary, there never can be a *return* or cross flight in a dogleg stair, for directly this feature is introduced, the stair becomes an open newel one. The lower flight, in this

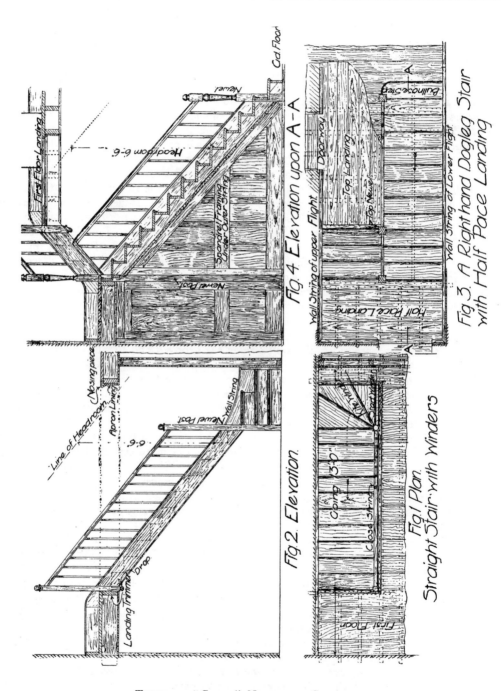

Fig. 4 Elevation upon A–A

Headroom 6-6

First Floor Landing

Newel

Spandrel Framing
Under Outer String

Newel Post

Cd Floor

Nosing piece

Line of Headroom.

Apron Lining

6-0

Newel Post

Wall String

Landing Trimmer Drop

Fig. 2. Elevation.

Fig. 3. A Righthand Dogleg Stair
with Half Pace Landing

Wall String of Lower Flight

Bullnose Step

A

Top Landing

Top Newel

Half Pace Landing

Wall String of upper Flight

Door way

A

Going 13'-0"

Close String

First Floor

Fig. 1 Plan.
Straight Stair with Winders

TYPES OF "CLOSE" NEWELLED STAIRS.

PLATE **IV.**

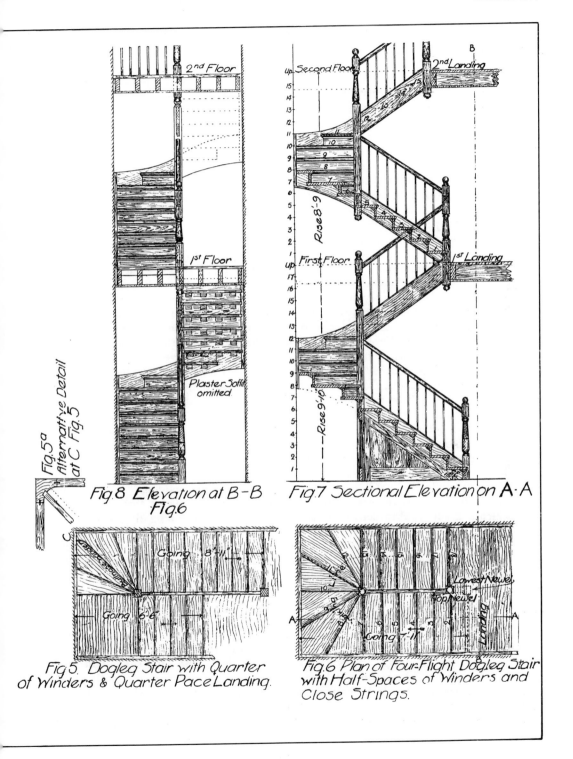

2nd Floor

1st Floor

Plaster Soffit omitted.

Fig.5ᵃ
Alternative Detail
at C Fig.5

Fig.8 Elevation at B-B
Fig.6

up Second Floor
2nd Landing
B
15
14
13
12
11
10
9
8
7
6
5
Rise 8-9
4
3
2
up First Floor
1st Landing
17
16
15
14
13
12
11
10
9
8
Rise 9-0
7
6
5
4
3
2
1

Fig.7 Sectional Elevation on **A·A**

Going 8-11

Going 6-6

Fig.5. Dogleg Stair with Quarter
of Winders & Quarter Pace Landing.

Lowest Newel
Top Newel
A
A
Landing
Going 7-11

Fig.6 Plan of Four-Flight Dogleg Stair
with Half-Spaces of Winders and
Close Strings.

case, is shown with a single " solid notched carriage piece " in the middle, to stiffen it, as the flight is a long one, containing twelve steps, consequently the strings would be liable to " give " and cause squeaking without such support. These solid notched carriages are now seldom used, as the " bracketed carriage " shown in connection with other examples is more quickly fixed and requires less skill in construction. The short upper flight obviously does not need a carriage. The two flights finish at a landing, carried right across the stairway. This is known as a half-pace, or sometimes incorrectly as a half-space landing, and, as shown at A, Fig. 3, Pl. IV., in the plan, it gives access to a room beyond the partition wall at a lower level than the first story. The top flight terminates at the first floor, with a doorway, as shown, a few feet beyond. The spandrel framing to be seen in Fig. 4, Pl. IV., closes in the space below the outer string, which may either be a cupboard or stairway to the basement. This type of stair is much used in the class of house known as the " suburban villa "; both open and closed strings are used with it, and the bullnose-step at the start facilitates entry from the passage or lobby at the side.

Another variety of dogleg stair is given in plan at Fig. 5, Pl. IV. In this case the stairway is divided into two quarter-spaces, one fitted with winders, the other with a landing, or, as termed in the United States, a platform; the determining factor (as we shall see presently), whether winders or landings are to be used, is the number of " rises " we are compelled to obtain with the available " going." This plan, Fig. 5, Pl. IV., shows a left-hand stair, and is the opposite hand to the previous example. The " hand " of a stair is determined by the relative position of the handrail when ascending the stair, thus, if the right hand grasps the rail, the stair is a " right-hand " one, and vice versa. The arrows on the plans indicate the upward direction of travel. Four winders are placed in the quarter-space, and although this is often found necessary, there are objections both constructive and hygienic to the arrangement. The riser that is taken into the angle cuts away the joint in the strings, also dirt is removed with difficulty from the corner. Alternative modes of construction to avoid these evils are shown. First, as in Fig. 5, Pl. IV., the riser and tread may be rounded off into the return string, so avoiding housing in the angle; secondly, as in the enlarged detail, Fig. 5a, Pl. IV., a hollow corner block may be interposed between the strings, and the riser taken straight into this, thus occupying its normal position without detriment to the strings. The third variety of dogleg stair is shown in plan, Fig. 6, and in transverse elevations, Figs. 7 and 8, Pl. IV. Here we have a stair of four flights connected by half-spaces of winders and landings, the said " landings " being the respective floors of the building. The side elevation, Fig. 7, Pl. IV., clearly shows the peculiar " kink " characteristic of this type of stair, from which it is supposed to derive the name " dogleg," as resembling the hind leg of a dog. The chief difficulty to be overcome in these stairs is the interruption of the handrail of one flight by the string of the flight above. As stated elsewhere, the old stairbuilder sometimes avoided this break by placing two newels side by side, one for each handrail and string, but more frequently forming the double newel in one large balk of timber. An example of this is shown in the photograph, Pl. II. Apart from the unpleasing effect, the additional expense in material and space required at the landing make this expedient unsuitable to modern requirements. A compromise is shown on the plate (No. XI.), at Fig. 8, which is dealt with in the description of that plate. A good deal of nonsense has been written about the winder " difficulty," and various more or less impracticable suggestions made about " balancing " the stairs to overcome this. The latter suggestion was, I believe, first made by Colonel Emy, a French writer on the art of carpentry, early in the nineteenth century, and his drawings have been consistently copied by architectural writers since, generally without acknowledgment. Balancing, or " dancing," as it is also called, is in some cases suitable for geometrical stairs, but in newelled stairs this merely accentuates the supposed evil, the process simply meaning that the winders are brought out of the true turning space into the straight flights, which in effect is making more winders, and so increasing their drawbacks. The few fractions of an inch in width of step which accrues at the newel by this arrangement is not worth consideration, for, as stated in a previous paragraph, it is not the narrowness of the winder which constitutes its danger, but the sudden change in " going " from that of the flyers. This defect, however, may be minimised by spacing the steps equally throughout upon a general walking line, as shown in Fig. 6, Pl. IV., thus securing an equal rise and going along a particular path over the entire stair. This " walking " line is usually placed at 15 ins. from the centre of the handrail in ordinary width stairs and at 18 ins. for very wide stairs, which is about the distance an average person keeps from the rail when descending stairs (the ascent is never considered in this connection); none but children would cling around the newel, and this danger would be better met by either a lower safety rail around the newel or a plinth block on each winder. In certain confined situations raking risers are used, as shown in Fig. 5, Pl. IV. This being a narrow stair, with very short flights, no carriages are used, but the lath-and-plaster soffit is secured to 1½-in. firring pieces, cut between the strings about every 20 ins. The soffit of the second flight is removed in Fig. 8, Pl. IV., that the underside of the stair may be seen, also the method of blocking the steps. A photograph of an Elizabethan close string dogleg stair is given on Pl. XLVIII. All the examples on this plate have " close " strings. A dogleg stair with an *open* or cut string is shown on Pl. XI.

OPEN NEWELLED STAIRS.

A **Close String Open Well Newel Stair**, of two flights, with half-pace landing, is shown in plan and elevation, Figs. 1 and 2, Pl. V. The space beneath the landing, being too low for a passage, scarcely yielding 5 ft. 3 ins. of headroom, is closed in with a panelled screen and may be utilised as a cupboard. In this event it will not be necessary to take the second newel post down to the floor, as sufficient support for the stair can be obtained from the landing trimmer. Details of construction of this and other types are dealt with in succeeding chapters. The plan of an **Open-string, Open Well Newel Stair**, having two flights with two quarter-spaces of winders and a half-landing in the well, is shown in Fig. 3, Pl. V. A " tower " or return step is introduced at the start (details of this step will be found on Pl. XVIII., Figs. 3 and 4), and at the finish; the balustrade is carried around the well with a short newel in the angle to support it. It may be remarked that the various minor details shown in these plans are not necessarily confined to the type of stair upon which they are drawn, but may be utilised where deemed suitable in other situations.

A **Large Open Well Newel Stair** with return flights, having quarter-pace landings at their junctions, is shown in Fig. 4, Pl. V. The upper return flights are not drawn, but their plan would be a repetition of that shown. Two commode steps are shown at the bottom with a turn-out handrail and newel, the object, of course, being to facilitate side entry.

A **Quarter-turn Open Newel Stair**, with a quadrant of winders and quarter-pace landing, is shown in plan, Fig. 5, Pl. V. This variety is sometimes called a " square," or right-angle stair, to distinguish it from **the Skew or Acute-angle Stair** shown in Fig. 6, Pl. V. There is little difference in the construction of these two kinds of stairs, save that the strings and landings must be fitted to the given angles in the plan. They are erected at the end of an apartment, consequently follow the shape of the enclosing walls. To improve the appearance of the acute angle on the landing it is usual to construct a seat, or shelf, with

PLATE V.

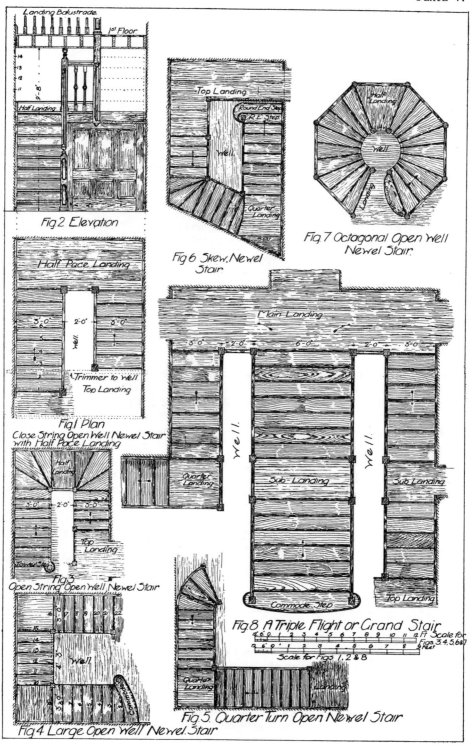

Fig 2 Elevation

Fig 6 Skew Newel Stair

Fig.7 Octagonal Open Well Newel Stair.

Half Pace Landing

Fig 1 Plan
Close String Open Well Newel Stair with Half Pace Landing

Fig 3
Open String Open Well Newel Stair

Main Landing

Fig.8 A Triple Flight or Grand Stair

Scale for Figs. 3.4.5.6&7

Scale for Figs 1, 2 & 8

Fig 5. Quarter Turn Open Newel Stair

Fig 4 Large Open Well Newel Stair

TYPES OF OPEN NEWELLED STAIRS.

a riser to correspond with the dado over the flyers. Two semi-circular or round-end steps are provided at the start of the first flight.

A **Triple Flight or " Grand Stair,"** as used in public buildings, stores, etc., is shown in plan, Fig. 8, Pl. v. The details of these stairs vary greatly, and they are among the handsomest and most costly of these constructions; the richest woods, and even marble is sometimes employed in their construction; often each newel will involve a larger expenditure in its preparation than many entire stairs of the common class. Examples of possible newels will be found on Pl. xxxvii. and of balusters on Pl. xxxviii.

An **Octagonal Open Well Newel Stair** is shown in plan, Fig. 7, Pl. v. This is an independent stair, and embodies characteristics of two distinct types, the newel and the geometrical; as these are both dealt with fully in succeeding chapters we need not repeat here. It will suffice to explain that the two inside newels at the half-landing are introduced to avoid a crippled appearance which the continuous rail would otherwise have, consequent upon the interruption of the true helical curve produced by the falling line of the winders, and broken by the level line over the landing. Carriages about 18-in. centres, according to the width of stair, are framed in under each step, and the well string is built up in several laminæ.

TYPES OF OPEN GEOMETRICAL STAIRS.

Geometrical Stairs (so called because some acquaintance with solid geometry is required to set them out and to obtain the moulds and templets for the handrails and wreathed strings) are of two distinct types : the earlier has continuous strings and handrails on both sides, as seen in Figs. 4 and 8, Pl. vi., and the later type continuous string and handrail at the outside only. This type, it may be added, is practically the only one used at the present time, and most of the varieties shown on Pl. vi. are in this style.

A **Geometrical Stair with Reverse Flights** and two quarter-pace landings, one stepped —that is to say, the half-space is divided and one-half raised a step above the other (not a desirable arrangement, but often necessary through exigencies of space)—is shown in Fig. 1, Pl. vi. This stair has a narrow well between the strings just sufficient to make a convenient turn in the handrail. The treads in this instance are drawn in full lines and the risers in dotted lines. A portion of the handrail is broken away to reveal the return nosings of the treads beneath, and the return handrail over the landing above is also indicated in dotted lnes. A part of the first floor is shown, broken away at *a-a-a* to reveal the starting of the stair below, which is of the right-hand variety.

A **Reverse Flight, Open Well Stair,** with half-pace landings and a half-space of winders, are shown respectively in plans, Figs. 2 and 3, Pl. vi. The steps in the latter are divided equally upon the walking line, and radiate from the centre of the well, as indicated by the dotted projectors. This stair, like No. 1, Pl. vi., has a curtail step and scroll, but no newel post. Fig. 2, Pl. vi., has a round-end step, a newel post, and mitre cap to its handrail, indicated by dotted lines. Both of these stairs are of the left-hand variety, and start farther back than the face of the landing above.

A **Continuous Open Well Stair,** with the winders separated by a wide step, or quadrant landing, is given in plan, Fig. 4, Pl. vi. The two sets of winders are differently spaced, although set out equally along the walking line. On the right hand, the risers radiate from the centre of the well, as indicated by the dotted projectors, whilst on the left the face of each is made tangent to a small circle struck upon the centre of the well; a slightly better falling line for the outer string and handrail is obtained by this method, but the chief advantage is the more regular going of the steps at the wall string, and consequent better

PLATE VI.

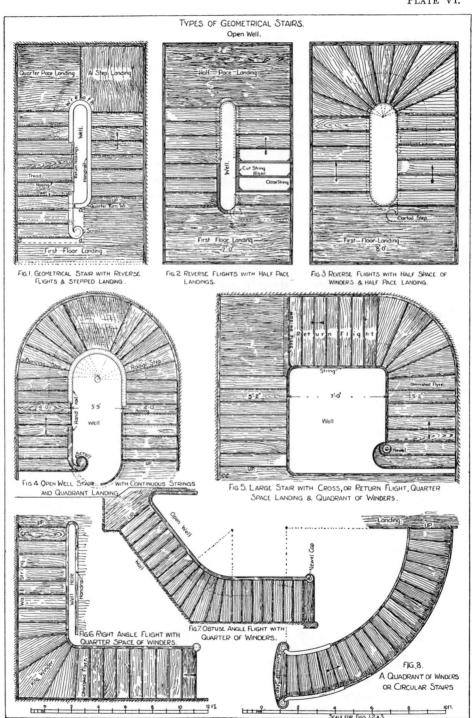

TYPES OF GEOMETRICAL STAIRS.
Open Well.

Quarter Pace Landing. A Step Landing.

Wreath

Well.

Return Nosings.
Handrails.

Tread.
Nosing
Riser.

Quarter Turn Wr.

UP.

Scroll.

First Floor Landing.

FIG.1. GEOMETRICAL STAIR WITH REVERSE
FLIGHTS & STEPPED LANDING.

Half Pace Landing.

Well.

Cut String
Riser.
Close String.

First Floor Landing.
7' 0"

FIG.2 REVERSE FLIGHTS WITH HALF PACE
LANDINGS.

Curtail Step.

First Floor Landing.
8' 0"

FIG.3 REVERSE FLIGHTS WITH HALF SPACE OF
WINDERS & HALF PACE LANDING.

Dancing Step.
Radial Step.

Hand rail.

4' 0"
3' 9"
Well
4' 0"
Nosing.

Scroll.

UP.

FIG.4 OPEN WELL STAIR WITH CONTINUOUS STRINGS
AND QUADRANT LANDING.

Return Flight

String.
5' 2"
7' 0"
5' 2"
Diminished Flyer.

Well

Newel.

UP.

FIG.5. LARGE STAIR WITH CROSS, OR RETURN FLIGHT, QUARTER
SPACE LANDING & QUADRANT OF WINDERS.

UP.
Open Well

UP.

Well

Well Hole

Wall String.

Handrail.

Kite Winder.
Diminished Flyer.

FIG.6 RIGHT ANGLE FLIGHT WITH
QUARTER SPACE OF WINDERS.

Newel Cap.

FIG.7. OBTUSE ANGLE FLIGHT WITH
QUARTER OF WINDERS.

Landing.
UP.

FIG.8.
A QUADRANT OF WINDERS
OR CIRCULAR STAIRS

12 FT.

10 FT.
SCALE FOR FIGS. 1.2.& 3.

TYPES OF GEOMETRICAL STAIRS.

falling line of that string, which is frequently surmounted by a framed dado and moulded capping. The quadrant landing is a common feature of the continuous stair.

A Large Open Well Stair, with reverse and return flights, a quarter-space of balanced winders and a quarter-pace landing, is given in Fig. 5, Pl. vi. This is an example of the geometrical stair which is *not* continuous, notwithstanding it has a continuous handrail, for the stair is made in two distinct flights separated by the landing, also it has a newel which may, or may not be a structural feature, according to treatment. The newel rises from a double, round-end step. Another method of dividing the winders is here shown. The two flyers adjacent to the winders are diminished at the outer end by, in this case, 3 ins. each; this amount is added to the quadrant on the face of the string, and the total length divided by the number of risers required. A similar division is made on the walking line and the risers are drawn through these two sets of points.

A Right-angle Return Flight, with quarter-space of winders, a continuous rail and newel with mitre cap, is shown in Fig. 6, Pl. vi. This stair has a narrow well between it and the landing which will run across the lower flight.

An Obtuse-angle Continuous Stair, with return flight and quadrant of winders, is shown in Fig. 7, Pl. vi. This plan, with the last described, are also common forms of stone stairs.

A Quadrant of Winders or Circular Stair, as it is indifferently termed, is given in Fig. 8, Pl. vi. This is the original type of the Georgian geometrical stair with stepped strings and long, thin sweeping handrails (see Pl. x., Stratford House stairs).

Spiral Stairs, both circular and elliptic, are considered in the next chapter, as also are some miscellaneous examples that cannot conveniently be grouped under standard types.

In all the preceding examples shading or " graining " is used to indicate the best direction in which to arrange the grain of the boards in steps and on landings.

CHAPTER II.

GENERAL PRINCIPLES OF PLANNING AND DESIGN OF STAIRS.

(Plates VII.–X.)

Scope of the Chapter—Planning—Comparison of Early Examples with Modern Practice—Lighting—Position of Windows—Suitable Types of Stair for Cottages, Large Houses, Public Buildings—Spiral and Elliptic Types—Details—Where Winders are Unobjectionable—Stepped Landings—Width of Stairs—Requirements of Building Acts—Exceptions—Headroom—Minimum Allowed—How Obtained—Fitting Stairs to Old Buildings—Proportions and Pitch of Stairs—Ratios of Going and Rise—Evils to Avoid in the Pitch—Minimum and Maximum Pitches—Difference in Effort of Ascent in Various Pitches—Methods of Proportioning Rise to Going—The French Method, its Basis—The English Standard—Method of Calculating Number of Steps to a Given Height—The Universal Riser Chart, its Uses—The *Two to One* Chart, How to Make it—Calculations to be Made on the Building—A Comparative Diagram of Stair Pitches—Showing Floor Space Covered, and Appropriate Pitch-boards.

NOTWITHSTANDING that this book is written chiefly for the instruction of workmen who, under modern conditions of building, have but little opportunity for widening the knowledge obtained in their local practice by observation, either of the methods of other skilled workmen or of the more elaborate productions of high-class workshops in distant towns, it is felt that no apology is needed for the introduction of the theoretical matters of this chapter, which it may be contended lie outside the province of the workman. That is to say, the chief aim of the book is to make the reader familiar with the various details of present-day construction. Therefore, although the matters dealt with in this chapter may seem outside the scope of a workman's requirements, the author believes that some acquaintance with the problems to be solved by the stair-designer, though it may seldom fall to the lot of the stair-builder to deal with them, cannot fail to widen his grasp of the subject and tend to further efficiency in his own particular sphere.

Planning.—By this term is meant the general disposition of stairs according to the class of building they are to occupy, the type, or form of stair to be adopted, methods of lighting, proportions, etc. Drawing the conclusion from the magnificence of detail shown in such stairs as that illustrated of Dunster Castle, Somerset (frontispiece), or in the bold expanse of the apartment and sweeping lines of the staircase at Belton House, Lincolnshire (Pl. VII.), it might be asserted that in earlier times the house was planned chiefly to accommodate the staircase, a conclusion strengthened by the wealth lavished upon the celebrated marble and iron staircase of the Earl of Chesterfield's house, Mayfair, London (Pl. VIII.) (originally built for the Duke of Chandos' house, "Canons," Edgware), the cost of which is said to have equalled that of the remainder of the building. But in more recent times, with a few exceptions, it might be more exact to say that any otherwise useless corner in the building is utilised for the staircase. In town houses, where land is valuable, it is not to be expected that a large apartment can be devoted to the staircase, but such glaring defects as stairs placed in a narrow enclosure, unlighted at top, and obtaining only a borrowed light at bottom, or of long flights starting from an entry, a few feet from the street, could easily be avoided by

PLATE VII.

The Staircase, Belton House, Lincolnshire, 1689.

PLATE VIII.

THE GRAND STAIRS, CHESTERFIELD HOUSE, 1749.

Marble Steps, and Staircase with Wrought-iron Balustrade of 1720.

By Isaac Ware, Architect.

a little consideration when planning the apartments.   Lighting from the top is to be preferred, if possible of attainment, either by means of a lantern, a skylight, or overhead window,
as the class of building may determine.   Failing this, a window upon a landing at the top
of a flight in an outer wall is the best arrangement.   A turning stair lighted from the bottom
is a constant danger to the users, unless, of course, artificial illumination is provided.

Suitability of Types.—For town houses of moderate dimensions the open newel stair
seems the most suitable.   For larger houses and semi-public buildings the open geometrical
stair is the simplest and most convenient, with possibilities of elegance and elaboration to
harmonise with any surroundings.   For the small cottage and the " workman's dwelling "
class of building, the close newel or dogleg types are obviously the most suitable, both on
the score of low cost of construction and economy of space.   Spiral stairs are eminently
suited for restricted ground space, but are unsuitable for public buildings where there is
much crossing traffic, although it must be conceded they serve this purpose fairly well on
the underground railways of the Metropolis.   Elliptic stairs are suitable only for large
buildings and, given symmetrical surroundings, with such concomitants, they represent
perhaps the most graceful and impressive examples of staircase work, either in wood or
stone.

Details.—Landings are to be preferred to winders when altering the direction of newel
stairs ; it is seldom that in this class of stair winders are introduced, unless unavoidable,
owing to restricted space.   Three to six risers can be obtained by their use over the same
ground-space which is occupied by one landing ; and this advantage often outweighs the
objectionable features which have been referred to at page 3.   In geometrical stairs,
winders are less detrimental, and, from the point of view of the handrailer, are to be preferred,
for a much better falling line is to be obtained with winders than can be produced with a
landing.   Stepped landings are to be avoided if possible : they are so uncommon that when
used they often prove traps for the unwary.   It is much better to distribute the amount of rise
gained by the single step over the whole number of steps.

Landings may exceed the width of the stair without ill effect, but should never be less
in width in relatively narrow stairs, in view of the difficulty of large pieces of furniture
being turned in the angles.

The Width of Stairs is of course determined by their purpose or position, but the
minimum width between the strings for cottage stairs should be 2 ft. 8 ins., and in this case
the landings should be at least 4 ins. wider, to permit the passage of furniture.   Public
buildings are, under the requirements of the London Building Act, 1894, compelled to
provide a minimum width in the clear of 4 ft. 6 ins.   Exceptions to this are made in the
case of chapels, lecture rooms and the like, with accommodation for less than 200 persons,
when the stair and its approaches may be of a width of 3 ft. 6 ins. at least.   Where accommodation is provided for more than 400 persons, an additional 6 ins. must be given to the
width of stairs for each 100 persons, until a maximum width of 9 ft. is reached ; also all
staircases of 6 ft. width and upwards must be divided longitudinally in the middle by a handrail.
Although not specifically condemned in the Act, winders are ruled out by the clause requiring " the treads of each (and every) flight of stairs shall be of uniform width."

Headroom.—Difficulties often arise in regard to the clear-way to be obtained over the
stairs, especially in the case of the cottage class of stair, where the heights of the stories
rarely exceed the minimum prescribed by the Building Acts.   This is, of course, a matter
for the building foreman to carry out, but the stair-builder should early ascertain his requirements in this direction and forward them to the building.   Not less than 6 ft. 6 ins. vertical
height must be allowed between the lower edge of the well trimmer and the nosing line of
the stair.   The method of ascertaining this is shown on Pls. XI. and XII.   In the case of fitting

a new stair to an old building, it is very important that the exact position of the floor trimmers is ascertained previous to the setting out of the stair, also, in planning " spiral " stairs, caution must be exercised in setting the pitch, or insufficient headroom may occur.

Proportion and Pitch.—The proportion which the width of the tread must bear to the height of the riser, commonly termed, in the workshop, ratio of " going " to " rise," is so intimately connected with the pitch, or inclination of the stair, that it is proposed to consider them together. The respective parts played by the architect and the joiner in the preparation of stairs might be summarised thus : the architect decides the pitch, and the staircase-hand decides the rise and going, or the proportions, of the steps. Certainly the pitch of the stair has a most important bearing upon its appearance, because the pitch of the steps governs the inclination of the handrail, the dominant feature in all stairs. Steeply pitched stairs are laborious to ascend and dangerous to descend ; on the other hand, stairs of too low a pitch are irritating to travel over, and tempt the user to take two or three steps in a bound. The usual extremes of pitch that are adopted for interior stairs, which are those chiefly considered in this book, are from a minimum of 17° to a maximum of 45°, and the average stair approaches the higher limit more often than the lower.

Were appearance of the stair the only consideration, it would not be difficult to decide upon a standard pitch and to make all steps conform to that pitch, but there are other considerations, as we shall see. It is sometimes assumed that no matter what the pitch of the stairs, the same amount of energy must be expended by a person to reach a given height, but this is only partially true. It is quite correct that so many pounds and no more have to be lifted a specified height, but the *time* taken to do this is a factor also to be considered ; that is to say, it is more exhausting to lift, for example, 150 lbs. 10 ft. high in twelve steps, than it would be in fifteen steps. In the first instance the load would be lifted 10 ins. each time, whilst in the second, 8 ins. would suffice. The difference between the effort to move forward on a level and to lift vertically varies largely in individuals, and, of course, as no stair could be constructed exactly to suit every one, a mean or average ratio must be taken. Numerous proportions have been suggested, but as any arbitrary rule can only be taken as a guide in setting-out (for the actual determining factors are the available space in length and height of the stairway), only the two principal standards in use are quoted here.

The French Method of Proportioning Rise to Going shown in diagram form in Fig. 1, Pl. IX., is based on two assumptions : first, that the average step taken in walking on the level is 24 ins. ; second, that it requires double the effort to move vertically than it does to move horizontally. Taking these assumptions as data, a chart may be constructed upon which can be shown the proportionate rise, for any given going, or vice versa. This chart is drawn in Fig. 1, Pl. IX., and to increase its usefulness the respective pitches and their degrees of inclination from the horizontal are shown. Thus, if a drawing is presented to the stair-builder showing the desired pitch of a stair, he can readily, by inspection of the chart, ascertain a suitable rise and going that will approximate thereto. Set off on the horizontal line A-B, 24 ins. Erect the perpendicular B-C, and make it 12 ins. high. Join A-C, which becomes the standard pitch. Next, set off from B, along the horizontal line, any desired going, for instance 10 ins. At the point marked 10 erect a perpendicular, and at the intersection with the line of pitch *d* draw the line *d*-B. Then 10-*d* will be the proportionate rise, viz. 7 ins., and the triangle B-10-*d*-B is the pitch-board for that step. Various goings and their appropriate rises within the maximum and minimum width of steps are shown, viz. 15 ins. and 8 ins.

The English Method of Proportioning Steps is shown in Fig. 2, Pl. IX. It is not usual to make a chart of these, as the appropriate rise or going can be quickly ascertained by calculation ; but the chart is shown for graphic comparison with the former method.

PLATE IX.

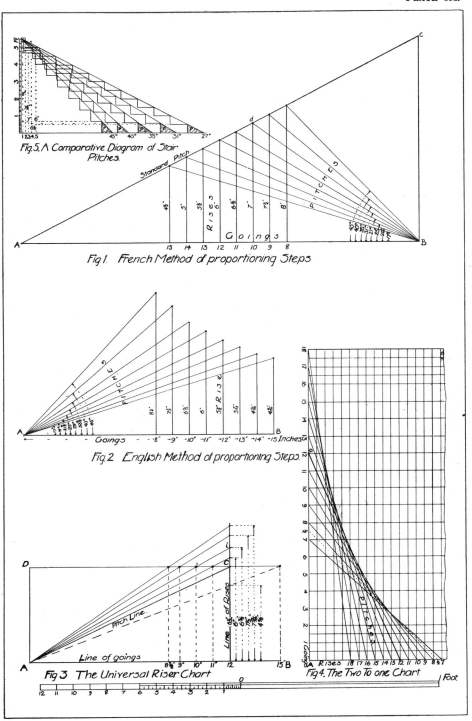

Fig.5. A Comparative Diagram of Stair Pitches.

Fig 1. French Method of proportioning Steps

Fig.2 English Method of proportioning Steps.

Fig 3 The Universal Riser Chart

Fig 4. The Two To one Chart

THE STAIR-BUILDER'S PITCH CHART.

This method is based on a standard proportion, found by experience to provide an "easy" stair, which is, going 12 ins., rise $5\frac{1}{2}$ ins. The sum of these two dimensions is 66, and any corresponding dimensions can be proportioned to equal that sum, and so obtain a step similar to the standard, for example, a given "going" of 8 ins. divided into $66 = 8\frac{1}{4}$ ins.—the proportionate rise. In like manner, a given "rise" of 6 ins. divided into $66 = 11$ ins.—the proportionate going. To draw the chart, Fig. 2, Pl. IX., set off on the line A-B from A a series of "goings" in inches, as shown. Erect perpendiculars at the points 8 ins., 9 ins., 10 ins., etc., make them equal in length to the figures found by dividing 66 by the respective goings, e.g. $\frac{66}{15} = 4\frac{2}{5}$ ins., and 66 divided by 9 ins. $= 7\frac{1}{3}$ ins., and so on. Join the extremities of the lines so found to point A, and the triangle thus constructed upon each rise gives the pitch for that proportion as shown.

The Universal Riser Chart, Fig. 3, Pl. IX., I have so called because the proportionate rise for *any* going can be ascertained by its aid without calculation; it is based on the standard going and rise of 12 ins. and $5\frac{1}{2}$ ins. To construct it, draw the line of goings A-B, set off from A 12 ins., and erect a perpendicular at this point. On this line mark point C $5\frac{1}{2}$ ins. from the base line, and join the point C to A, thus obtaining the pitch of the standard step. Next, produce the line 12-C indefinitely. Form a rectangle upon the sides A-12 and 12-C. Set off from A, on the line of going, any desired going, as, for instance, 10 ins.; erect a perpendicular at point 10, intersecting line D-C in point O', through this point draw the pitch line from A and continue it to intersect the line of rises in point i. The height thus obtained on the line 12-C will be the proportionate height for that rise, viz. $6\frac{3}{5}$ ins., as indicated in the diagram. Several other rises are found in the same manner, which will be clear on inspection of the diagram. The advantage of this method is that any odd fraction of an inch in the width can be readily plotted without calculation, as in the example, a going of $8\frac{3}{8}$ ins. yields a rise of $7\frac{13}{16}$ ins. If the diagram is drawn full size, and the width of tread set off along the base, the pitch-board can be constructed without even considering the derived figures. By reversing the process, the necessary going for any given rise can be ascertained.

The Two-to-One Chart, Fig. 4, Pl. IX., so called because the division lines on the riser side are in the proportion of two to one on the tread side of the diagram. This arrangement, although based on the usual English standard of 12 ins. by $5\frac{1}{2}$ ins., yields a different series of proportions to the other methods that have been described. The chart may be constructed on half inch "squared," or sectional paper, or the divisions may be ruled on a piece of board as follows: Let the length equal 18 ins. and the width 8 ins. Divide the longer side into 18 equal parts, which will, of course, measure 1 in. each. Divide the shorter side into sixteen equal parts measuring $\frac{1}{2}$ in. each. Counting in each instance from the corner A, number on the longer side each division consecutively from 1 to 18. Number on the shorter side the eleventh division, 12, and draw a line to number 12 on the other edge, as at a; this line gives the pitch of the standard step; it is more heavily marked in the diagram. Next, complete the numbering on each side from No. 12 consecutively. Now if the corresponding figures on each side are joined, the triangles so described indicate the proportionate rises to goings, and vice versa; also the corresponding pitch for taking bevels. Any fractional part of an inch in going will in like manner indicate the proportional rise, as shown in the dotted line, for $7\frac{1}{2}$-in. tread. It will be seen that only the squares numbered between 7 and 18 are used, as these are the practical limits, for treads. For workshop use, it is advisable to draw the several pitches in different coloured inks, by which means they can be traced more easily.

In the case of buildings already erected, the actual dimensions of the stairway must be ascertained and dealt with by the following rule, to obtain the exact proportions. Reduce

PLATE X.

STRATFORD HOUSE STAIRCASE, LONDON.
Example of Late Georgian Geometrical Stair.

the total height to inches, and divide it by the proposed rise.   Should there be no remainder the divisor will be the exact rise, and the quotient the number of risers required ; but if there is a remainder, then divide the sum by the quotient, discarding the fraction, and the result will give the exact rise.   For example, suppose the height from floor to floor to be 10 ft. 3 ins., the available length of going for the stairs to be 11 ft., and the desired pitch to be about 40° ; by reference to chart No. 1 it is seen that the standard proportions for this pitch are $7\frac{1}{2}$ ins. rise, 9 ins. going.   The floor height, 10 ft. 3 ins., reduced to inches = 123 ins., divided by $7\frac{1}{2}$ ins. gives 16, with a remainder of 3, therefore again divide 123 by 16 = $7\frac{11}{16}$ ins., which will be the net rise with sixteen steps.   Now, as the last step in a flight is always the landing, it follows that there will be one going less than the number of rises ; so, to ascertain the exact going, divide the available space, 11 ft., by 15 = 132 ins. ÷ 15 = $8\frac{4}{5}$ ins., the exact going ; this is as near the standard proportions as it is possible to get, and will give a tread of just over 10 ins., including the nosing.   The method of using these data in setting-out is fully detailed in subsequent chapters.

A **Comparative Diagram of Stair Pitches,** showing their appropriate rises and goings, to reach a given height, is drawn in Fig. 5, Pl. IX.   The proportions are taken from No. 1 chart, and the necessary variation in the steps and the variable floor space occupied by the several pitches is thus readily seen.   Also, the diagram makes clear the importance of the pitch-board in setting out stairs.   The respective pitch-boards are shown in the first step of each flight, marked P.

CHAPTER III.

TAKING DIMENSIONS AND SETTING OUT.

On the Setting-out of Stairs—Differing Procedure According to Class of Shop, Hand Shops, Machine Shops—According to Class of Work—What "Rods" should Contain—Limitations of the Workman —Taking Dimensions, on the Building—Preliminaries—The Story Rod, How to Set it Out— Precautions, as to Plaster, Irregular Openings, etc.—The Pitch-board, Its Use and Preparation —Reference to Charts and their Use.

It is very amusing to the practical men to read some of the dogmatic instructions given in books for the setting-out of stairs; as a matter of fact, there is more diversity of method employed in this branch of joinery than in any other, the reason for which lies more in the organisation of the particular workshop than in the class of work. In large shops where most of the work is done by machinery a great deal of the stuff comes to the joiner ready prepared, and the "setting-out" of this is quite different from that required in a small hand shop, where the stuff comes in, either in the rough from the saw, or at best, roughly planed on a four-cutter. Therefore, any attempt to indicate a universal mode of setting-out would be doomed to failure.

At the most, broad principles can be given which the reader must adapt according to circumstances. In the ordinary class of work, whether of newel or geometrical stairs, no setting out on "rods," as is usually understood by the term, is attempted. In most cases the foreman, or leading hand, prepares a pitch-board from the scale drawings supplied by the architect, gives written or verbal instructions as to number of steps in the flights, height of the handrail and newels, number of winders, and similar details, and, with this data the "staircase hand" proceeds to set out direct upon the stuff itself in the manner indicated in the several examples shown elsewhere in this book. Given an accurate pitch-board it is next to impossible to build a stair wrongly. More elaborate work, such as grand stairs, or smaller stairs with intricate detail in the strings, balustrades, newels, soffits, etc., do require setting out upon rods, just as other items of joinery require to be, where there is much detail that might be overlooked, or where the work is divided up among several workmen. In the latter case, which is the usual one in large shops, "rods" are an absolute necessity if mistakes are to be avoided; but as to how far this should be carried out depends upon the organisation of the shop and the class of workmen employed. Some men can be trusted to use their own brains, others require almost every nail and tenon set out for them, not because they do not know what is wanted, but simply because it saves them thinking if they wait to be told.

Such rods as described above would show (of course full size) the length, thickness, width, and all details of moulding, sinking, etc., of strings, but *not* housings or steppings for the treads and risers, it would simply be waste of time to set out these, as the setting out could not be transferred to the stuff. The size and position of the newels should be indicated on the string-rod, that the amount required for tenons may be seen. Should the newel be shaped, framed, or moulded in similar manner to the designs on Pl. xxxvii. it will be necessary to set out one face or side, and in the case of turned newels or balusters a templet will be required for the guidance of the turner, which will be a profile of one side only of these respectively. Winders must always be set out full size. This rod is required by the cutter-out to line out the stuff for jointing, and subsequently by the staircase hand with which to set out the treads. The handrail is usually shown by a couple of parallel lines, indicating its thickness on the string rod. The length and a section are also required. The length of balusters can, in most cases, be shown on the newel rod, between the handrail and string, but in cut string stairs they are frequently fitted on the job after the rail is fixed, in which case it is necessary only to set out the turned portion, leaving sufficient square at each end for fitting purposes. A method of obtaining the lengths of these is described at page 34.

As we have remarked elsewhere, the planning of stairs under modern conditions of building is the work of the architect, and the stair-builder has not much concern with it; the latter generally has to work to drawings supplied, from which he can make but slight departure, unless of course some obvious error in dimension or position has been made; but in that smaller class of work which does not come within the purview of an architect it is usual to obtain the required data from the building itself, as seldom in such cases are any drawings available.

Taking Dimensions.—Having decided where the stair is to be placed, and its type, whether newelled or geometrical, also if to be " open " or " close," etc., we can proceed to take the dimensions and enter the same in a note-book, or, as was formerly a common procedure, take them directly upon a rod, which should be a planed square staff of about 1¼ ins. side, long enough to reach from one floor to the next. A separate rod should be used for each storey, and marked distinctly to which " floor " it refers.

The Story Rod, as it is termed, is indicated upon several of the plates herein, including Fig. 7, Pl. iv., and Fig. 2, Pl. xv. Cut one end of this rod square, then place it plumb against the first floor trimmer, and mark the upper surface of the flooring thereon. Write the word " up " against this line, which gives the total height of the stair, including any winders or landings that may be necessary. Write the word " height " or " rise " as preferred, upon the side just marked, we can then take the length, or *going*, of the stair upon another of its sides. The " going of the flight " is the horizontal distance between the first riser and the end wall of the staircase, or, more correctly, the stairway, i.e. the opening or apartment in which the staircase is erected. In many instances this going has to be determined on the spot, taking into consideration adjacent door or window openings, or anything else that may influence the position of the first step. Assuming this point determined, place the square end of the rod against the end wall, or face of trimmer, as the case may be, then mark upon it the position of the first riser and of any landing trimmer that may be in the opening, as for example, that shown in Fig. 1, Pl. iv. In this particular instance, the first riser to be marked would be that of the fourth step, because there are winders at the bottom, but the actual *going* would be the length between the two walls as shown. This side of the rod should be marked " going," and in the case of a stair similar to Fig. 5, Pl. iv., it should be marked also " first flight." Then a third side of the rod should be used to set off the going of the upper flight, with its landing, as shown, the position of the last riser being determined by the trimmer at the top. Relating to the position of this, see remarks under " headroom." Having taken the height and length of the stair upon the rod, we may, upon the fourth side, set off the width, if practicable. It is not always so, and we may have to use another rod, which must be cut in neatly between the walls; this would be the procedure in the case of Fig. 5, Pl. iv. It must be borne in mind that stairs are generally placed in position after the plastering is done, therefore, though the clear length between the brickwork is taken on the width rod, the thickness of the plaster must be marked upon each end, and these lines will give the position of the outsides or back of the wall strings. Care should be taken to apply the rod at each end of the opening, also at the point where the flights join or change their direction, in case there may be differences in the width, which, if so, must be duly noted upon the rod. We have now obtained all the data required, and can proceed to space out the steps. It is generally more convenient to divide up the height rod first, to determine the number of steps or rises required to reach the top of the flight. Having decided upon a suitable " rise " for the step, based upon the rules given in the article upon Planning, pages 12 and 14, the compasses should be set to this approved dimension, and stepped along the rod, to see if it works out exactly to the landing height, or " up " mark; if so, the trial dimension will do; if not, alter the compasses until an equal division can be obtained. This rise may of course be ascertained by computation instead of trial, as described on page 14.

Next, divide up the going-rod in like manner into the same number of parts that have been obtained in the height, less one. As before remarked, these points of division will be riser lines and not tread lines, for though each riser, excepting the last one, will have its corresponding tread, the nosings will project more or less over the risers, therefore cannot be considered in the setting out. The top riser, of course, comes under the landing, therefore, when counting the number of treads from a plan remember there is one less than the number of rises. Having now spaced out both story and going rods, the pitch-board may be made to suit their dimensions of rise and going. This templet is the chief setting-out appliance used in stair construction, as by its aid we determine the pitch or inclination of the stair, and ensure that when the strings are erected to this pitch the treads will be horizontal and the risers vertical. **The Pitch-board** (Fig. 10, Pl. XI.) must be made of a thin piece of dry hardwood or zinc, the angle at *a* must be a right angle or " square," the edge *a-b* must exactly equal one of the divisions or " goings " on the going-rod, and the side *a-c* must equal one of the divisions on the height-rod. Then the side *c-b* will equal the pitch of the stair, and in setting out the strings this side is kept flush with, or parallel to, the top edge of the string, as will be more specifically explained when describing its use with the several examples.

When setting out " close " or housed strings, the pitch-board needs three other templets for use with it; one, the margin templet, equal in width to the required distance of the nosings within the edge, and two wedge templets for tread and riser respectively; these are shown in position in Fig. 10, Pl. XI.

NOTE.—The above description of setting out and obtaining the pitch-board is that of the method commonly pursued. A more scientific method by aid of charts is described in Chapter II.

CHAPTER IV.

A SMALL DOGLEG STAIR.

(PLATE XI.)

Suitable for a Small Villa — Description — Position — Trimming of the Landing — Headroom —Treatment of Landings—Margin Nosings—The Method of Setting Out—Pairing the Strings—Different Methods for "Cut" and "Close" Strings—Using the Pitch-board—Difference between Nosing Line and Line of Nosings—Marking the Housings—Where to Commence—Wedge Templets, Where to Use—Making the Easings—Machine Housing—Housing by Hand—Lines that should be Knife-cut—Setting Out the Cut String—Variations in Practice—Setting Out the Newels —How to Mark for Turning—Position of Mortises—Position of Handrail—Portion to Cut Away.

Example I. A Dogleg Stair for a Small Villa (Pl. XI.).—This stair would be specified as a cut-string dogleg stair, of two flights, having a quarter-space of three winders and a quarter-pace landing, with turned newels and balusters, moulded handrails, and a veneer-bent-and-solid-blocked bullnose step at start. For a quarter-landing see Fig. 5, Pl. V.

The plan, Fig. 1, Pl. XI., shows the lower flight of nine flyers and three winders, without the treads, save one, which is given that the position of the balusters and return nosings may be indicated thereon. The landing and the upper flight of three steps shows treads and floors, the riser and joists beneath are indicated by dotted lines, as also are the joists of the first floor, with the binder carrying the ends of the joists over the passage at the side. This stair is supposed to be placed at the end of a passage or "hall," between the party wall of the house and a stud partition, lathed and plastered, in which are doorways, as indicated in the plan and elevation. The elevation, Fig. 2, Pl. XI., is taken on the line A-A, Fig. 1, Pl. XI., showing the lower flight in section, with the winders, landing and upper flight in elevation. No. 2 newel post runs down to the ground floor and rests either on a joist or upon a trimming piece framed between two joists, as they may happen to come. The space under the stair is to be used as a cupboard, therefore is shown with match-lined soffit (see Fig. 2, Pl. XI); one carriage piece is all that is required, the ends of the match-lining nailing to the under edges of the strings.

The headroom, shown under the trimmer, is 7 ft. 1½ ins., which is ample for a house of this class. The position of the studding is indicated by dotted lines on the plaster facing.

A Transverse Elevation on line B-B is given in Fig. 3, Pl. XI., showing the arrangement of the trimmed opening for the stair, the landing balustrade and the underside of the upper flight uncovered, that its construction may be better seen. No angle blocks are shown under the landing because, in good work, the landing floor would be tongued and glued-up in one piece, then secured to the joists with screw buttons. In common work it is simply nailed, like the upper floor boards, but in either case it would be a mistake to block it, as to do so would prevent equal shrinkage, which is essential to permanence.

The remaining figures on this plate are details of the several parts, drawn separately, chiefly to indicate methods of setting out, and they are referred to as the occasion arises. Returning to the plan, Fig. 1, Pl. XI., the margin nosings shown grained are pieces about 3 ins. wide and equal the treads in thickness, also fitted with Scotias to match, which finish

(19)

off the floor at openings and landings ; they are especially necessary where the landing floors would display end grain, and frequently the floor boards are of a less thickness than the treads, hence the nosing pieces must be rebated over the trimmers, as shown in section in Fig. 2, Pl. xi. These pieces should be mitred at the returns, as shown near Nos. 1 and 3 newels in the plan. The balusters on the landing are housed into these pieces.

The Setting Out.—In Fig. 4, Pl. xi., the two strings of the lower flight are laid out in " pairs," that is to say, the faces are arranged in the same relative position they will occupy when the flight is put together ; the object being to render clearer to the beginner the differences required in setting out a " cut," or " open " string, and a " close," or " housed " string. Taking the housed string first, the top edge is shot straight, and a pencil line gauged on the face for the nosing line as marked. The experienced hand will not require this, as the margin templet shown at M.T., which is used in conjunction with the pitch-board, would give him the position of the nosings, but it will render the explanation clearer if the nosing line is drawn. It may here be explained that the nosing line of a stair is *not* a line touching, or tangent to, the nosings of the *treads*, as is sometimes stated in books, etc., not written by craftsmen, but is the line touching the salient angles of the steps just as a straight-edge would do, if laid on stone or other solid steps. The reason for using this line in preference to the line of nosings (see page 21) is, that the housings for the nosings are not cut until each step is fitted singly into its place. Before the housings can be marked it will be necessary to prepare wedge templets for the riser and tread respectively. These are thin slips of wood rather longer than the width of a tread and of a riser, and equal in width to the thickness of these, plus the space required for the wedge, which should be kept as narrow as possible, consistent with providing sufficient substance in the wedge itself to enable it to be driven home ; the templets are shown in position to mark the fourth step ; although both are there shown, one must be removed before the other is applied.

Commence setting out the housings at the bottom, placing the pitch-board as near the end of the stuff as possible, with its pitch edge tight to the margin templet, mark along the "going" edge for the floor line, and along the " rise " edge for the first riser. These lines should be knife-cut. Before moving the pitch-board, lay the riser wedge templet against it and pencil in the housing for same. Move the pitch-board upwards until its lower point coincides with the riser line just drawn, and mark the tread and riser of the second step, which, after the application of the wedge templets, will appear as drawn at No. 2 step. Continue this process until the top flyer, No. 10, is reached, when the first winder tread is marked, by taking the measurement from the winder rod, which will be a replica of the quarter-space of winders shown in Fig. 1, Pl. xi., but set out full size. It is not worth while to make wedge templets for the winders, but draw in the back of the housing with a straight edge. Mark the shoulder against the return string by measurement from the winder-rod ; the riser edge of the pitch-board gives the shoulder. Note that if the string is moulded in the solid, a piece must be left on as shown, long enough to form the mitre on it, also the tongue must be set off. The pieces to be added to form the easings at each end may now be considered. The sizes of these pieces, which are tongued and glued on the main board, are ascertained by a preliminary run over with the pitch-board. The amount of easing is a matter of taste. At the lower end, the height of the adjacent skirting must be set up as shown at *b*, Fig. 6, Pl. xi., and the joint marked with the rise edge of the P.B. ; the easing may be struck from a centre, found as shown at *a*, Fig. 6, Pl. xi. The top end has its easing taken by an easy sweep into the height of the return string at C, Fig. 5, Pl. xi. It is impossible to carry regular margins over the winder nosings, and the curves of the strings are adjusted to taste. Some of the housings on the string (Fig. 4, Pl. xi.) are shown cut through to the lower edge ; this is the usual way in common work, as it saves time in sawing when the housing is done by hand, but the string is weakened thereby, and in machine shops the tread housing is stopped just beyond the back of each riser, sufficient to give space for the insertion of the wedge. Strings are housed by boring machines of the " elephant " type, consequently the housing can be stopped wherever the operator desires, also in such cases a preliminary sinking for the nosings is made by the machine, but it should be left tight for final fitting by hand individually. When the strings are housed by hand, that is to say, by sawing in the knifed lines and clearing out the core with chisel and router, the nosing sockets are not cut until the fitting up of the steps, because the nose of the tenon saw would damage the recess, also the projection over the riser is likely to vary. A few centre-bit holes are sunk in, as shown at No. 3 step, to provide a start for the tenon saw. We may now consider the outside or cut string (Fig. 4, Pl. xi.). The first riser that enters this string is No. 3, for the reason that the first two enter the newel, as shown in the plan, Fig. 1, Pl. xi. A projector has been drawn at each end from the nosing lines of the wall string to illustrate their correspondence, but of course this is unnecessary in practice. Start the pitch-board from the centre line of the newel, which will be the position of the second riser, and mark the second tread. A variation in practice of setting out cut strings may now be referred to. Some joiners set these out similarly to housed strings, that is to say, line out the tops of the treads and faces of the risers with the pitch-board, then mark down the thickness of the tread for the cut, because in the case of a cut string in which the treads run over to the face, it will be obvious that the notch must be cut to the underside of the tread. The above-mentioned method ensures good results when the undersides of the treads are not planed or thicknessed, but involves a loss of time in setting out, and a waste of material in the string, because a nosing line must be run on as indicated in the dotted lines at the second and ninth steps, and this amount of stuff must be afterwards cut off. My own method is to line out the undersides at once from the edge of the stuff, as shown in full lines in Fig. 4, Pl. xi., making due allowance at the shoulder lines of the newels for this. The procedure will be readily understood by reference to the drawing. There is a third method sometimes adopted, of lining out from the bottom edge of the string by using a margin templet equal in width to the amount required for covering the carriage and soffit. The same result is obtained as in the last-mentioned method, but the procedure breaks the chief rule of setting out, viz. always to work from the *face* edge, and is not to be recommended to beginners.

The setting out of the strings of the upper flight is shown in Fig. 6, and should be clear. The dotted lines indicate the size of the stuff in the rough and the full lines the finished string. The line marked " cut " is the abutment against the landing trimmer, and should *not* be cut until fitting-up on the job, for obvious reasons.

The Setting Out of the Newels is shown to same scale in Figs. 7 and 9, Pl. xi., with an enlarged detail of parts of No. 2 newel in Fig. 8, Pl. xi. It is advisable to set out and mortise the newel before sending it to the turner, there can then be no chance of mistakes as to the position of the " squares," but whether this is done before or after turning, the setting out will be practically the same. The parts to be turned should have the extremities only of the turned part marked, as shown in Fig. 9, Pl. xi., and the portions to be turned indicated by drawing lines diagonally across them. Usually this is done with red pencil, and need not be so carefully shown as in the drawing. Either a tracing or a wood " profile " must be sent to the turner ; it would be useless to draw it upon the stuff, for it would be cut away at the first turn. The relative position of the mortises, etc., can be seen in Fig. 7, Pl. xi., and the sizes of the details in Fig. 8, Pl. xi. It will be noticed that the position of the strings is not vertically over each other, but is subordinate to that of the handrail, which is first drawn in section in the middle of the newel, then a baluster (shown in dotted lines) is drawn under the middle of the rail, and this baluster locates the position of the face of strings, which are placed respectively flush with opposite sides of the baluster. The mortise gauge is set to the distance marked " gauge " in Fig. 8, Pl. xi., and applied on opposite sides of the newel as indicated. The tenons are made equal in thickness to half the substance of the string, and must be cut as shown in Fig. 7, Pl. xi.   This is to preserve straight grain ; the portions cut away would be useless, as the grain would be cut across at the root.   The pitch-board gives the bevel for the mortise.   The portion of handrail, shown in section on Fig. 8, is cut off the rail and planted on the top string for a return, as drawn in the elevation, Fig. 2, Pl. xi.   The long rail should be taken through, lapped on the string, and rounded off after the return piece is fixed.   In common work the two are simply mitred together, as this method saves trouble in returning the bead in the solid.

A sketch of the front newel as set out ready for the turner is shown in Fig. 9, Pl. xi., with the housings for the second step ; these, however, are not really made until the stair is fitted together, by which time the turning will have been done.

PLATE XI.

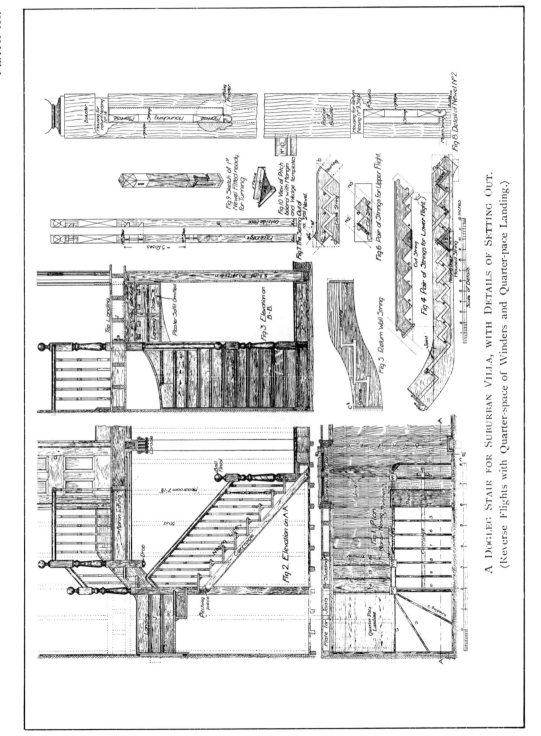

A DOGLEG STAIR FOR SUBURBAN VILLA, WITH DETAILS OF SETTING OUT.

(Reverse Flights with Quarter-space of Winders and Quarter-pace Landing.)

PLATE XII.

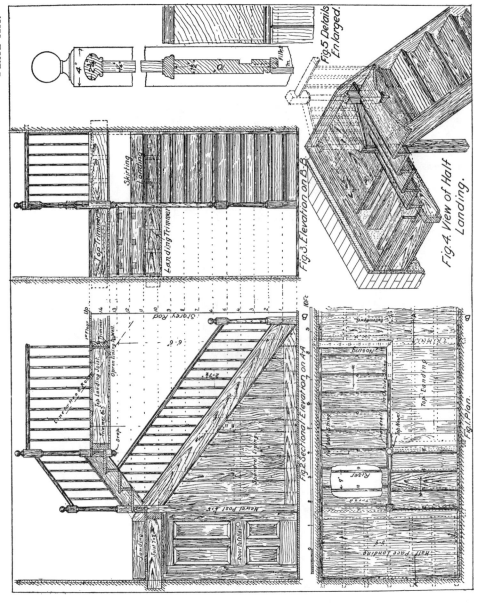

Fig.5 Details Enlarged.

Fig.3. Elevation on B-B.

Fig.4. View of Half Landing.

Skirting Landing.

Top Trimmer

Landing Trimmer

Line or die of Trimmer

Top Landing Joist

Apron Lining Newill

Trimmer 6.5

Drop

Spandrel Lining

Storey Rod

6' 6"

Newel Post 4×4

Joint Top

Fig.2. Sectional Elevation on A-A.

Door to Cellar

10 Ft

Trimmed

Bullson

Top Landing

Half Landing String

Top Newel

Riser

Tread

TRIMMER

Fig.1. Plan.

Half-Pace Landing

A SMALL DOGLEG STAIR, WITH HALF-PACE LANDING AND DETAILS, SUITABLE FOR A COTTAGE.

CHAPTER V.

A COTTAGE DOGLEG STAIR.

(PLATE XII.)

Description—Usual Methods of Fixing—Provision of Headroom—How to Obtain—Spandrel Linings
—How Fixed—How to make the Drawings, Plan, Elevation—Setting Out the Story Rod—What
to Omit—Method and Details of Fixing this Type—Order of Procedure—Carting to the Job—
Treatment of Landings—Finishing Up—Isometric View of the Complete Stair with Landing.

PL. XII. is of a small dogleg stair suitable for a cottage. The drawings are so complete that it is considered little explanation will be necessary for their understanding, and the chief con-structional instructions, as given in the preceding examples, apply generally to this one.

The stair is of the " close string " type, with reverse flights meeting at a half-pace landing. The top landing is at the first floor, and the well-hole is enclosed by plain balusters and a simple " toads-back " handrail which returns at the well-end, where it is fixed to the wall, as shown in Fig. 3, Pl. XII.

The enlarged details shown in Fig. 5, Pl. XII., will make this clear. An isometric view of the stair at the half-landing is given in Fig. 4, Pl. XII., and to simplify the reading of this, the wall string, newels and balustrade of the short reverse flight are indicated in dotted lines, as less likely to obscure the parts beyond. Part of the half-landing floor is omitted to obtain a clear view of the tailing into the wall of the joists, and a part of the top landing is shown cut away to reveal a portion of the lower flight of stairs.

Fig. 1, Pl. XII., is the plan of the entire staircase, with portions of the handrail cut away to reveal the string beneath.

Fig. 2, Pl. XII., is a sectional elevation on line A-A, showing the spandrel match-lining enclosing the clear way to the cellar, to which access is gained by a framed four-panel door. The method of projecting the steps from the story rod to both elevations is shown on Figs. 2 and 3, Pl. XII., also the method of locating the position of trimmer to secure headroom.

Fig. 3, Pl. XII., is a front elevation on B-B, Fig. 1, Pl. XII., wherein can be seen the face of the trimmer just referred to ; of course this is covered by an apron lining, as shown in the transverse section, Fig. 2, Pl. XII.

Fig. 4, Pl. XII., has been alluded to in a previous paragraph, and probably needs no further explanation.

Fig. 5, Pl. XII., is, on the left hand, a much-enlarged vertical section through the lower string, showing the match-lining at M, the fillet to which it is fixed, and the planted capping to the string, with the housing of the baluster indicated by dotted lines. At the upper part of this drawing is shown the toads-back handrail and the turned finished head of the newel with an alternative profile of the terminal.

At the right-hand of Fig. 5, Pl. XII., is shown a front elevation of the several parts to same scale as in the section.

Note that the match-boards must be cut long enough to run up to the bead, and be mitred back to the chamfer seen in the section.

(23)

PLATE XIII.

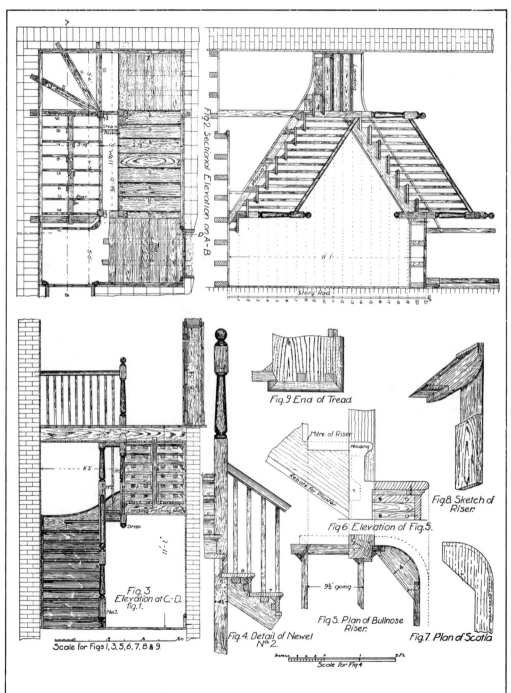

Fig 2. Sectional Elevation on A–B

Fig 9. End of Tread.

Fig 3. Elevation at C–D. fig. 1.

Fig. 4. Detail of Newel Nº 2.

Fig 6. Elevation of Fig. 5.

Fig 5. Plan of Bullnose Riser.

Fig 8. Sketch of Riser.

Fig 7. Plan of Scotia.

Scale for Figs 1, 3, 5, 6, 7, 8 & 9.

Scale for Fig 4

A SMALL OPEN WELL NEWEL STAIR WITH CUT STRING HAVING A QUARTER-SPACE OF
WINDERS, A STEP IN THE WELL AND A QUARTER-PACE LANDING.

CHAPTER VI.

A SMALL OPEN WELL NEWEL STAIR.

(Plate XIII.)

With a Quarter-space of Winders, a Step in the Well, and a Quarter-pace Landing with Cut Strings and Bullnose Step—Description of the Drawings—Modern Method of Making Working Drawings as differing from the Pedantic School, Awkward Results Occasioned by the Latter Methods —What a Plan should Show—Discretion to be Exercised according to Type of Workman— Procedure in Bending a Bullnose Riser—Method of Securing Nosing in Common Work.

THIS is an example of a modern open newel stair of small dimensions, suitable for the " villa " type of house, that would be specified as a reverse flight stair with a quarter-space of winders. A step in the well and a quarter-pace landing in the half turn (the top landing, of course, being the first floor of the house) having cut-and-mitred strings, plain turned newels and moulded handrails.

Description of the Drawings.—Fig. 1, Pl. XIII., is the plan, such as is used in the larger workshops and prepared by practical architects, but it is not in accord with the tenets of the pedantic school of geometrical draughtsmen of a past age, whose aim was to make precise geometrical projections rather than working drawings that would be intelligible to the layman. These precisians will stop their drawings dead level on the arbitrary line of section selected, then make another projection to show the parts lying a foot or so above or below the same arbitrary line, with the result that a stair, for instance, is shown with a break in its length that does not, or at least should not, exist in the construction itself, which, however, has sometimes induced an inexperienced workman to make the stair in two parts, as shown on the misleading drawing provided. The latter, of course, is rarely shown an elevation to enlighten him. When the workman does receive a drawing it is usually confined to the plan, and this, as shown in the example, *should* be a complete view of the whole construction as would be seen if viewed from the highest point of the structure. Naturally, all the minor details herein given for the benefit of the beginner would be unnecessary for the experienced workman, therefore the supervisor will exercise his discretion in preparing plans to meet the needs of the class of craftsman with whom he has to deal. Generally, a plain outline plan, showing position and number of newels, strings and steps, with exact location of starts, landings, winders and floor openings will be found sufficient.

All the items in this drawing being named and numbered thereon, it will be necessary only to refer to them in passing.

The sectional elevation, Fig. 2, Pl. XIII., placed in its appropriate position above the plan, reveals the heights of the several parts whose widths and lengths are shown in the plan beneath, from which they are projected.

The transverse elevation, Fig. 3, Pl. XIII., shows the faces of the steps in the lower flight and as much of the winders that cannot be seen in the longitudinal elevation ; also the front end of the step with string that forms the end of the well between the flights.

In Fig. 4, Pl. XIII., is seen an enlarged detail of No. 2 newel, as it is shown in the elevation, Fig. 2, Pl. XIII., with the various joints connecting the several parts to the newel indicated in

(25)

dotted lines.   The housing and tenon for the handrail over the well step is also in dotted lines, because these occur at the *back* of the face shown.

Fig. 5, Pl. XIII., is an enlarged plan of the bullnose step with the tread removed to make the connections visible ; the position of the tread, also of the return nosing of the next step, is indicated in dotted line.   A sketch of this riser at the start of the procedure in bending the veneer around the shaping block is shown in Fig. 8, Pl. XIII.   As this process is fully described on page 65, it need not be further dealt with here.

Fig. 6, Pl. XIII., is an enlarged sectional elevation of Fig. 5, Pl. XIII. ; and Fig. 7, Pl. XIII., is a plan to same scale of the Scotia piece seen in section in Fig. 6, Pl. XIII.   Fig. 9, Pl. XIII., is a plan of the outer end of a tread showing position of the balusters and the mitres of the riser and of the return nosing, also the method of securing same in common work by means of a brad.   A superior method of fixing these is shown in Fig. 13, Pl. XVIII., and Figs. 4 and 5, Pl. XXVIII.

CHAPTER VII.

A SMALL OPEN WELL NEWEL STAIR.

(Plate xiv.)

An Open Newel Stair of Heavier Construction, having Two Quarter-spaces of Winders, a Step in the Well, with Close Strings, also Enlarged Details of Construction, Reverse Flights—Description of the Drawings—Purpose of a Step in the Well—Wall Fillets, Why Used—Pitching Pieces, Uses of—Fitting Balusters to Handrail—Method of Obtaining Bevel for Housed Balusters—Enlarged Section through both Strings—Method of Fitting and Fixing the Stair—How Dispatched to Building—Precaution to Take in Tongueing Strings.

Another example of a small open newel stair, compact in plan, plain but substantial in construction, and economically designed, with the least possible amount of ornament (this feature being confined to the newels, handrails, and the moulded edges to the strings) is shown on Pl. xiv.

Description of the Drawing.—Fig. 1, Pl. xiv., is a plan of the staircase, showing only the naked or constructive timbering and the risers of the steps. The complete stair consists of two reverse flights of nearly equal length connected at near mid-height by two quarter-spaces of winders; these are separated by a single parallel step at the end of the well, which to some extent fulfils the object of a landing by giving the user a welcome rest in the travel up or down the eight winders. The carriage pieces are lettered R, and the rough brackets, or cleats, C; these can also be seen in elevation in the projection above (Fig. 2, Pl. xiv.), which is a section taken on the line E-F close to the wall string. The wall fillet, seen in the section, is used to make up the wall string to same depth as the outside string, to provide a level fixing for the soffit lathing. The bearers under the winders are marked *b*, and the timbers marked P are the pitching pieces to take the ends of the carriages.

Fig. 3, Pl. xiv., is a transverse section taken on the line G-H in the plan showing the winder wall string, etc., and the method of obtaining this should be clear, as the projectors are drawn from the same parts in the plan, where they are cut by the line of section. Fig. 4, Pl. xiv., is a sectional elevation taken on the line I-K parallel with the preceding section, but passing through the two flights, also the well. Owing to exiguous space it was not possible to project the section directly from the plan, but the correspondence of the numbering and letter references should make the drawing fairly easy to follow; the only letterings not yet referred to are: O.S. for the outside string, and S. for soffit at the end of the well.

Fig. 5, Pl. xiv., is a sectional view taken on the line C-D, showing the upper flight and winders in elevation, with the top landing lower handrail, strings, etc., in section. Two projectors, from Nos. 3 and 4 newels only, are shown to avoid confusion with the projectors from other figures.

Fig. 6, Pl. xiv., is a section through the lower flight.

Fig. 7, Pl. xiv., is an enlarged detail at the head of the top flight and landing.

Fig. 8, Pl. xiv., is a similarly enlarged detail of the outside string and capping, showing housing for balusters in dotted lines.

Fig. 9, Pl. xiv., is an enlarged detail through the winders and well step shown at S in Fig. 1.

PLATE XIV.

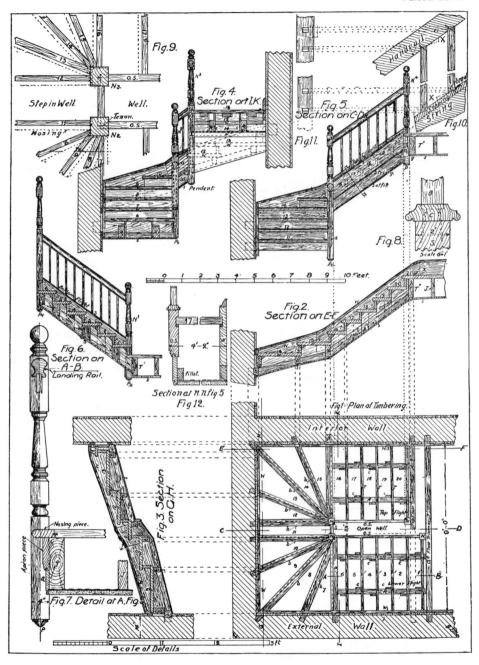

A SMALL OPEN WELL NEWEL STAIR WITH TWO QUARTER-SPACES OF WINDERS,
A STEP IN THE WELL AND A PAIR OF CLOSE STRINGS TO REVERSE FLIGHTS.

Fig. 10, Pl. xiv., is a detailed section through the handrail, balusters, capping and string, showing how the balusters are cut and fixed. The method of obtaining the bevel is indicated in dotted lines at X, and a projection is taken across to Fig. 11, Pl. xiv., which shows the housings in the capping and the under-side of rail. For a plain bevel-cut without sinking, the bevel can be set as shown at top of the last baluster in Fig. 5, Pl. xiv., by holding the stock to a plumb line and the blade to the pitch line.

Fig. 12, Pl. xiv., is an enlarged section through the seventeenth step, giving details of the two strings, etc.

Fitting and Fixing.—This stair would generally be fitted together on the bench, each portion complete in itself, as all the newels are relatively short and of the " drop " or pendant variety—strings and handrails first fitted, as shown in Fig. 9, Pl. xiv., then taken to pieces for the fitting in of the steps which would be blocked and nailed to the strings, and eventually the newels draw-bored upon the string tenon. For convenience of transit the two flyer flights could be attached to their newels and sent separate from the winders, the wall strings being grooved and tongued together as shown in the plan, Fig. 1, Pl. xiv.; thus the lower flight would be set up first, resting on the pitching-piece, then the winder string brought down and its tongue glued to the lower string, the steps worked into their respective housings in the strings and newel, due clearance being effected at the backs of the risers, as detailed in a previous example.

Next the well step is inserted, then the top set of winders ; previously bringing down into position upon the top pitching piece seen in Fig. 2, Pl. xiv., at P, the top flyers. Note, that the tongues on the strings must be as shown in the plan, one on lower end of winder string and one on lower end of top string, otherwise they cannot be got together.

CHAPTER VIII.

A LARGE OPEN WELL NEWEL STAIR.

(PLATE XV.)

Including Two Straight and Reverse Flights, a Quarter-space of Winders and a Three-quarter-pace
Half-landing; a Round-end Step at Start, Carriage Pieces, Rough Strings and Rolled Steel Joist
used in the Construction—Description of the Drawings—How the Landing Trimmers are Framed-
in—Practical Details of the Newels—Methods of Avoiding Differing Heights in the Newels—
Sizes of Parts—General Method of Fixing these Stairs—Order of Procedure—Testing for Level—
Adjustments—How to Fix the Winder String—Fixing the Lower Flight—Fixing the Balusters—
Method when Tenoned or Dowelled at both Ends; Alternative when Housed—Fitting in the
Winders—How to Avoid Trouble with the Kite Winder—Buttoning the Landing Floor—Fixing
the Top Flight—Method of Fixing the Apron Linings around the Well.

A Large Open Well Newel Stair, having reverse flights, a quarter-space of winders, and
a three-quarter-pace landing, is shown in plan, elevation, and section on Pl. xv.

Description of the Drawings.—In the plan (Fig. 1) the treads of the steps and floor of
the half-landing are omitted, the better to show the constructional parts beneath, but their
nosings are indicated by dotted lines. These should not be confused with the joist lines, also
dotted, which are in pairs. The flight starts with a " semi "-circular or round-end step,
through the block of which the 5-in. square newel is tenoned. There are eleven flyers in
this flight and three winders in the quarter-space, from which the landing is reached; this
crosses the well to the opposite wall, thence the reverse flight of six steps brings us to the
first-floor landing, which runs completely across the well, the fifth newel indicating the
start of the next flight above. The floor joists are indicated in dotted chain lines, as also is
the rolled steel joist carrying a partition wall above. One carriage piece, and two rough
strings of less scantling, are used in each flight; the former are framed between pitching
pieces and the trimmers, the latter are fixed by screws or nails to the wrought strings for the
dual purpose of stiffening them and to provide fixings for the soffits. Rough bearers are
placed under the riser of each winder; these enter the wall at one end and are fixed to the
newel at the other. The trimmers carrying the landing joists are framed into the newels and
wedged into the wall.

The Sectional Elevation (Fig. 2, Pl. xv.), taken on line A-A in plan, shows the first or
main newel as sunk panelled, moulded and carved in the solid, with a turned and carved finial.
The second and third, or landing newels, are less elaborately ornamented, and run down to
the ground floor, as they have to carry half the weight of the landing in addition to the
stairs. The moulding of these, below the soffits, will be in character with the surroundings
of the staircase or, alternatively, turned as columns.

A Transverse Section on B-B is given in Fig. 3, Pl. xv., showing the winders in elevation
and the underside of the upper flight; this drawing, in common with the plan, had to be
broken, owing to the limitations of the plate, but the missing portions can be gathered from
the elevation of the landing (Fig. 4, Pl. xv.). It will be observed that the newels differ in
height, this necessity arising through the rise of the handrail in the upper flight; if this is

objectionable a ramped easing to the rail could be made, and the newels kept at the same height. (See ramped easings, Pl. XVI.)

The construction of this stair is fairly obvious from the drawings. The strings are of the " close " variety, the outside pair 2 ins. thick, twice tenoned, and drawbore pinned to the newels. A 2¼-in. × 4-in. capping covers the strings, and is housed into the newels ; the turned balusters are housed into the capping, with a square seating, as shown in the details, Fig. 1, Pl. XXVIII., and are tenoned or dowelled at top into the handrails, which are 3 ins. thick and 4½ ins. wide. The wall strings are 1½ ins. thick, solid moulded, to match the capping. The setting out of this stair is so similar to those previously described that there seems no need to repeat the instructions relative to that part of the work.

The Fixing of this Stair will to some extent depend on circumstances, but generally the procedure would be—assuming that all the parts have been previously fitted up dry at the shop, and the two straight flights put together, minus the newels—fix the landing and its two newel posts, inserting the rail over the landing at the same time. Next cut in, and fix, the pitching piece P (Fig. 2, Pl. XV.), and offer up the lower flight ; the wall string will need scribing up to the end wall until the shoulder of the outside string comes to its place at the face of No. 2 newel. During this fitting the steps should be tested for level, in both directions, and the bottom step, or the newel, adjusted accordingly. Having accomplished this satisfactorily, cut in the winder string in the clear, between the landing and opposite wall, fix it temporarily with wedges parallel to the newels and at the proper distance, as measured on riser 15. Then mark down its face on the lower wall string, draw back this flight, and cut in the groove as shown in the plan. The lower flight can now be fixed permanently, by gluing and drawboring the tenons, and fixing two screws through the back of the first riser and riser block. Some might prefer to fix the carriages first ; personally I have always fixed them up under the stair, after it was placed in position, cutting away the back of the treads until a solid seating throughout was obtained. This method is a little more troublesome than the other, but there will be no risk of " squeaking " when it is done. Slip in the first newel and tread, also the handrail (of course all previously dry-fitted), pin the tenons, and glue-block the tread underneath. Should the balusters be tenoned or dowelled at both ends, these would need inserting *before* the handrail is fixed, but if housed at the bottom ends, as shown in the detail A, Fig. 1, Pl. XXVIII., they can be inserted at any time, and as a matter of fact would be better left out until all the rough building work was over. The end of a scaffold board swung around against one may introduce undesirable members in its moulding. The next thing to be done will be the fitting-in of the winders ; these may, or may not, have been previously fitted in, but anyway they should have been cut to exact size and shape upon the winder board, and the steps glued and blocked in the same manner as the flyers ; not much difficulty will be experienced in the insertion of the first and last winders, but the kite winder is apt to cause trouble ; the extreme edges of the tread and riser should be " dubbed " off and the wood at the backs of the riser housings in the newel should be cut away, as shown in the sketch of a newel on Pl. XI., Fig. 9, and Pl. XXVIII., Fig. 4 ; then insert the wide ends in the strings and by careful levering up they can be got into their seatings all right and nailed there. If the landing is glued up into one slab, as it should be, button-holes must be cut in the joists—about two in each joist, but arranged hit-and-miss fashion, will suffice. Having fixed the landing, also its skirting temporarily, proceed to fix the top flight. This will have No. 4 newel already fixed and the birdsmouth over the trimmers being cut, the flight can be eased down into place at top, as the tenons on string and handrail are entered in the landing newel. The housings for the apron lining to the well will be cut from a scaffold, which it will be necessary to erect to fir-out from the trimmer and to fix the linings straight and plumb.

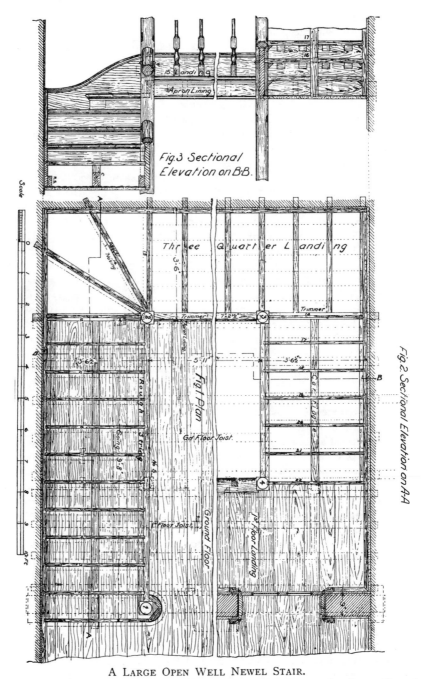

Fig.3 Sectional
Elevation on B.B.

15 Landing

Apron Lining

17

16

Three Quarter Landing

3-6

Trimmer 7-2½

Trimmer

Nosing

Scale

0

1

2

3

4

5

6

7

8

9

10 Ft

B

B

13-6¼

Rough String

Going 3-8

16-5 C

Fig.1 Plan

Gd Floor Joist

1st Floor Joist

Ground Floor

Ground Floor Joist

5-11

3-6¼

Corridor

1st Floor Landing

Fig.2 Sectional Elevation on AA

A LARGE OPEN WELL NEWEL STAIR.
(With Reverse Flights, Quarter-space of Winders and Three-quarter-pace Landing.   Close Strings.)

PLATE XV.

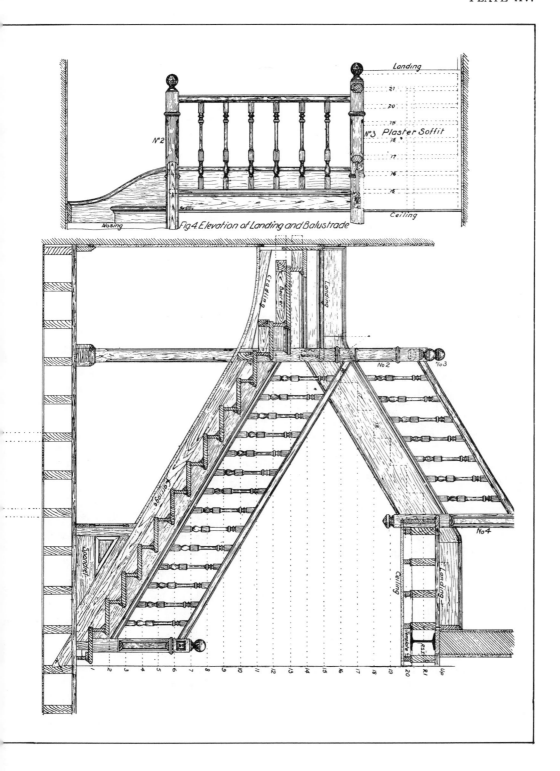

Fig 4. Elevation of Landing and Balustrade

CHAPTER IX.

AN OPEN WELL NEWELLED STAIR IN EARLY GEORGIAN STYLE.

(PLATE XVI.)

Including Ramped and Kneed Handrails, Panelled and Moulded Dado, a Doorway on Half-landing
—Description of the Staircase—Details of Carved Brackets—Method of Setting Out and Fixing these
—Duplicating Carving Details—Characteristics of Old World Balusters and Brackets—Detail of
Fluted Newels—Spiral Turned Balusters and other Mediæval Balusters—A Selection of Suitable
Woods for these readily Obtainable—Section of Handrail—Section of Dado—A Buttoned Landing
—Method of Forming Easings in Rail to avoid Wreathing—Treatment of Landings.

A Small Open Well Newelled Stair with Cut and Mitred Steps and String, fitted
with carved brackets, turned and fluted newels, with similar responds and ramped and kneed
handrails, is shown on Pl. XVI. A framed and moulded panelled dado, with a moulded capping
to correspond with the upper section of the handrails lines the staircase, and follows the line
of ramps and knees in the latter. This dado framing is indicated in dotted lines upon the
respective elevations, but is shown in full lines upon the landings, and an enlarged section
through a part of the dado, with one of the pilasters or responds that are placed opposite
each newel, is shown in Fig. 2, Pl. XVI. Fig. 1, Pl. XVI., is a complete plan of the stair, which
consists of one forward and one reverse flight, connected to a return flight at right angles by
two quarter-pace landings, and finishing at the first floor, which is reached by twenty-four
rises of 7 ins., with a going of 9 ins. The treads are shown in full line in this plan, and the
faces of the risers indicated in dotted lines, as are also the carriages, the landing trimmers and
the dado framing, with its capping. The handrail is drawn in full line, as also all the bases
of the newels. The various elevations and sections are taken on transverse broken lines,
the better to show salient features of the construction. Thus Fig. 2, Pl. XVI., is a sectional
elevation, taken on the line B-B-B-B ; by this procedure a front elevation of the lower flight
and first landing is obtained, also an outside elevation of the return flight, showing the ramped
and kneed rail, the second newel, the window on the landing, and a section of the upper
flight, with the doorway on the second landing, in elevation. Owing to exigencies of space,
a portion of this drawing is broken away to provide space for the transverse section, which
is also broken in like manner ; and it may be explained that the intention was to make these
stairs 3 ft. 6 ins. wide between the strings ; but in the drawing they are shown as 3 ft., to
avoid reducing the whole to a very small scale. No difficulty should be found in extending
the width as required, when copying the drawing. Fig. 3, Pl. XVI., is a section on line A-A-A-A,
showing the lower and upper flights in section, and the return flight in elevation, also a portion
of the dado above the stair is seen in elevation ; the position of the dado to the first flight is
indicated in dotted lines, but is of course behind the line of section taken. Fig. 4, Pl. XVI.,
is an elevation on the line C-C-C, showing in elevation the flight that is seen in section in
Fig. 3, Pl. XVI., where there is insufficient space to complete the top landing, etc. ; the handrail ramps down at each side of the landing newel, as does in a like manner the wall dado.
This section is broken on the seventeenth step, so that it may pass through the doorway
leading from the second landing into an ante-room. The position of this doorway relative
to the landing is indicated in dotted lines in Fig. 3, Pl. XVI., as the main section in that figure

is taken through the window opening. Fig. 5, Pl. XVI., is an enlarged detail of the carved brackets at the ends of the steps. The method of mitreing and fixing these brackets to the string is shown in the plan below, the dotted lines indicating the position of the return nosing and scotia, shown above it. These brackets should be cut out to the curved outline, mitred at the front end, and glued on to the face of the string board, after the latter is fixed to the risers. Usually the carving is done after the stairs is fixed in the building, so that it may be preserved from damage. One bracket should be set out full size and the details taken off upon tracing cloth, and, by means of carbon paper, transferred to the bracket-blanks. Carvers do not aim at absolute repetition, they merely keep the design uniform generally. Some old-world stairs have the brackets, also the balusters, each one slightly different in detail. These differences are not obtrusive, but just sufficient to give interest to the careful observer, without impairing the general effect, and arose through the desire of the craftsman to identify his own work. Details of the newel post and baluster are shown in Figs. 6 and 7, Pl. XVI. The cap and base of the newel are square, the intervening portions turned, moulded and fluted. The shaft and moulded portions of the balusters are turned; the two ends and mid-fillet are square. In the elevations, a plain and a spiral turned baluster is used alternately on each step, but, if preferred, one or other pattern may be adhered to throughout. Balusters turned to the section shown in Fig. 7, Pl. XVI., should be of hard wood, such as oak, beech or mahogany, and even these must be free from cross-grain; they would be too fragile in soft or white pine. Suitable " Colonial " and foreign woods that are effective and accessible in British timber yards are : Japanese white birch (Alba vulgari). Bombay, Bija-Sal (peterocarpus marsupium), trade name Malabar Kino. Philippines, Calamansanay (Nauclea nilida), colour orange red. Ceylon, walnut (Albizzia Lebbek). Canadian cherry birch (Betula rubra). Queensland, black bean (Castanospernum Australe). Jamaica, Yacca from the Blue Mountains (podocarpus urbamii). Fig. 8, Pl. XVI., is a section of the handrail; to double the scale of the other details the outside of the rail has an additional sinking. Fig. 9, Pl. XVI., is a section of the outside strings, showing the bracket and the stuck and planted mouldings thereon. Fig. 10, Pl. XVI., is a similarly enlarged section through the wall string and dado framing, taken on line E (Fig. 4), perpendicular to the pitch. Fig. 11, Pl. XVI., is a horizontal section through a pilaster, and the two adjacent dado stiles, showing the skirting below. Figs. 12 and 13, Pl. XVI., indicate an alternative method of forming easings to the rails, which is considered by some less objectionable than the sudden breaks at the mitres shown in Fig. 1, Pl. XVI. A mitre cap is placed over the newel, and the two rails eased into this, so avoiding a wreath, these easings being of single curvature. For details of construction of ramps, etc., see Chapter I., Volume II. The quarter landings are tongued-and-glued together and secured to the joists by screwed buttons, as shown in Fig. 3, to allow for shrinkage and expansion.

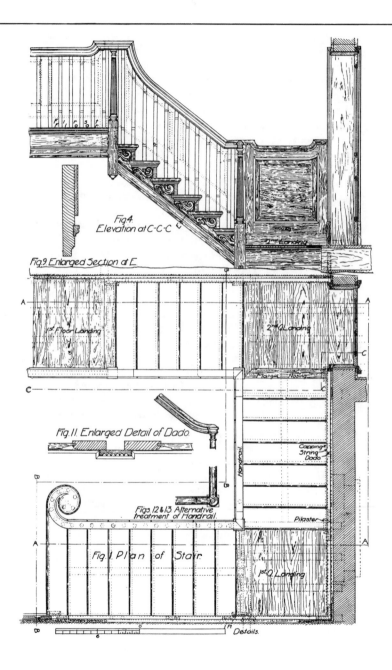

Fig.4.
Elevation at C-C-C

Fig.9. Enlarged Section at E.

2nd Landing

1st Floor Landing

2nd Q. Landing

Margt. Nosing

Fig.11. Enlarged Detail of Dado.

Capping & String Dado

Handrail

Figs.12 & 13. Alternative treatment of Handrail.

Pilaster

Fig.1. Plan of Stair.

1st Q. Landing

Details.

AN OPEN WELL NEWEL STAIR IN EARLY GEORGIAN STYLE.

PLATE XVI.

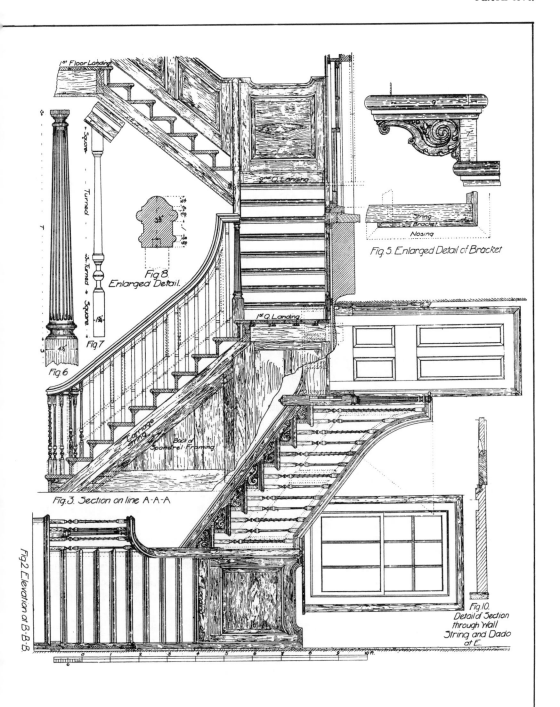

Fig. 5. Enlarged Detail of Bracket

String
Bracket
Nosing

Fig 8.
Enlarged Detail.

Fig 7

Fig 6

1st Floor Landing

2nd Q. Landing

1st Q. Landing

Carriage String

Board

Spandrel Framing

Fig 3. Section on line A-A-A

Fig 10.
Detail of Section
through Wall
String and Dado
at E.

Fig 2 Elevation at B-B-B.

CHAPTER X.

A THREE-FLIGHT GEOMETRICAL STAIR.

(PLATES XVII. AND XVIII.)

Description of the Drawings—Continuous Rail and String Construction—Details of the Construction—
Locating Position of Carriages, Strings, Pitching Pieces, and Method of Inserting them in Wall—
Stepped Balusters, their Requirements—Proper Method of Marking for Turning—Circular Nosing
Piece at End of Well—How to make the Joints in Wall String—Which Side of the String to mark
"Face Side"—Points to Note in Setting Out the Strings—Setting Out the Curtail Step—What a
Curtail Step is Used for under a Handrail Scroll—How to make the Development of Wreathed
String to Obtain the Covering of the Cylinder—Workshop Method of Locating Position of Risers
in the Curve—Planting the Return Bead on the Wreathed String—How to Keep the Veneer to
Correct Pitch on the Cylinder—How to Prevent Damage to Wreath Piece—Isometric View of a Cut
and Mitred String, etc.—Method of Reducing Shape of Brackets to the Winder Steps.

A Geometrical Stair of Three Flights, with open well, cut and bracketed strings, half-spaces
of winders and half-pace landings at the turns, is shown in plan and elevation on Pl. XVII.,
and a complete set of enlarged details of various parts of the same, with their setting out, on
Pl. XVIII. This example is fairly typical of the modern continuous-rail stair. There are no
newels, the rail finishing with a horizontal scroll, supported by a group of balusters. The
outside string is of the form termed cut-and-bracketed, and it is wreathed at the winder ends.
The wall strings are " close," or housed, ramped into each other at the turns, and the entire
staircase fits within rectangular walls. The plan in this instance shows the tops of the steps,
or treads in full line, with the risers in dotted lines, except upon a portion of the lower flight,
where the treads are broken away to show the construction beneath. The flooring of the
first landing is drawn in full lines, the joists, trimmers, etc., in dotted lines, as also are the
carriages, rough strings and pitching pieces (P) under the winders. These are shown in their
approximate position on the drawings, but their exact position is always located at the time
of fixing, as they must be got into convenient header holes cut in the brick walls. They are
got in by cutting the upper hole deep enough to allow the lower end to enter its hole, then
the timber is brought back, wedged up tightly to the angles of the steps and the holes filled
in with cement and pieces of brick. The pitching pieces must be first fixed, then the carriages
and rough strings fitted to them, as shown in the illustrations. The elevation (Fig. 1, Pl.
XVII.), taken on a stepped line A-A for the purpose of including a greater number of parts,
shows a lower flight, also the corresponding flight on the second floor in section, and the
second flight with most of the winders in elevation. The balusters are stepped to correspond with the treads, which necessitates two patterns of turning, a common practice with
" stepped " or cut strings. The parts covered with a straight line indicate the turned
portions, the squares being defined by squared-over lines. This is the proper method of
marking for turning, when stock patterns are not used. A dwarf cupboard is constructed
under the stair, up to the portion filled in with the small spandrel framing, this portion being

PLATE XVII.

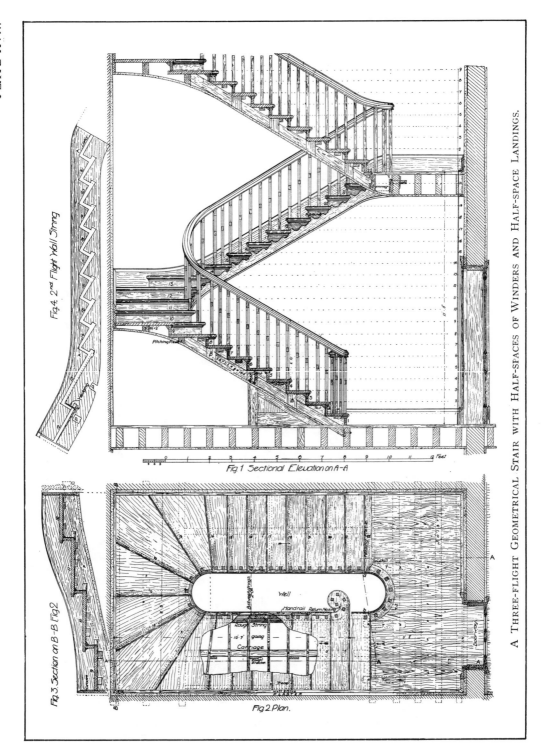

Fig.4. 2ⁿᵈ Flight Wall String

Fig.3. Section on B-B Fig 2

Fig 1 Sectional Elevation on A-A

Fig.2. Plan.

A Three-Flight Geometrical Stair with Half-spaces of Winders and Half-space Landings.

PLATE XVIII.

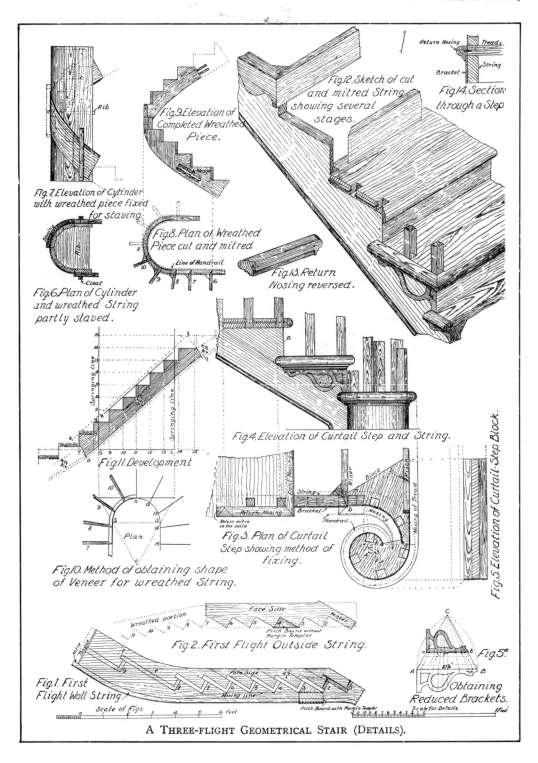

Fig.12. Sketch of cut and mitred String showing several stages.

Fig.14. Section through a Step

Return Nosing   Tread

Bracket   String

Fig.9. Elevation of Completed Wreathed Piece.

Head

Fig.7. Elevation of Cylinder with wreathed piece fixed for staving.

Rib

Fig.8. Plan of Wreathed Piece cut and mitred

Line of Handrail

10   9   8   7   6

Fig.6. Plan of Cylinder and wreathed String partly staved.

Rib

Cleat

Fig.13. Return Nosing reversed.

Springing line

Springing line

Fig.11. Development

Fig.4. Elevation of Curtail Step and String.

a

Fig.10. Method of obtaining shape of Veneer for wreathed String.

Plan

10   11   12   13

9   S   14

8   15

7

Fig.3. Plan of Curtail Step showing method of fixing.

Return Nosing

Return mitre in the solid

Bracket

Front Nosing

String

Riser

Block

Tread

Handrail

Nosing

Nosing of Tread

Fig.5. Elevation of Curtail-Step Block.

Fig.2. First Flight Outside String.

Face Side

Wreathed portion

Veneer

Pitch Board without Margin Templet

11   10   9   8   7   6   5

Fig.1. First Flight Wall String

Mitre

Face Side

Nosing line

Pitch Board with Margin Templet

C

a   b   Fig.5ᵃ

A   B

Obtaining Reduced Brackets.

Scale of Figs
0   1   2   3   4   5   6 Feet

Scale for Details.
1 Foot

A THREE-FLIGHT GEOMETRICAL STAIR (DETAILS).

useless. It will be noticed that the two trimmers at the ends of the flights are carried by return trimmers, marked T, in the plan ; which are themselves framed into the main trimming joist (T.J.) at the crown of the well. A semi-circular nosing piece is required to finish off the flooring of the landing to which it is tongued, this can be better seen in the plan. A transverse section on the line B-B, through the winders and showing the end wall string in elevation, is given in Fig. 3, Pl. xvii., which shows also, in dotted lines, the third pitching piece P running from B to C. This will conclude the general description, and we may now consider the various details of the construction shown on Pl. xviii.

The wall string of the lower flight is shown in Fig. 1, Pl. xviii., as it would appear after setting out for housing, easings made, top edge lined for moulding and the joints cut at each end. The joint for the skirting at the lower end should be ploughed and tongued, the top end grooved and tongued, stopped at the moulding mitre. This mitre would not be cut until actually fitting up at the building, but sufficient stuff must be left on to make the mitre. The pitch-board with margin templet is shown in position for marking, at the second step, but as all details for use of this have already been given in connection with the previous examples they need not be repeated here. The dotted rectangles marked P indicate the places that the pitching pieces pass through, but for reasons previously stated they are not cut until fixing. The opposite string, which is a cut one, is shown in Fig. 2, Pl. xviii., arranged in pairs for the purpose of indicating which side should be set out. Note should be taken that the "face" side of the cut string is its outside, but the wall string has its face inside, and the stuff should be picked accordingly. I have already remarked on the objection to setting out cut strings from the under edge (see p. 21) ; the best method is shown in Fig. 2, Pl. xviii. The long riser piece shown under the first step is the veneer, to cover the inside of the curtail block, which is shown in the enlarged detail (Fig. 4, Pl. xviii.), and to be described presently. The dotted lines in Fig. 2, Pl. xviii., indicate the size of the plank, also the size of pieces to be glued on. The dotted outline at the upper end indicates the wreathed part of the string, which is shown fully in Fig. 11, Pl. xviii., but is placed here to make clear its position relative to the flyer portion. One further small detail in setting out this string must be noted ; after the steps have been marked in pencil, by the pitch-board, a second parallel riser mark must be knife-cut in, as seen at a, Fig. 4, Pl. xviii. ; the reason of this can perhaps be better seen in the plan, Fig. 3, Pl. xviii., at the point b. When a string is bracketed, the bracket must run over the face of string to mitre with the riser face, a distance equal to the thickness of the bracket. In setting out, a piece of the bracket stuff should be used as a gauge. Alternatively, the second marking can be avoided by considering the string moved upwards by the desired amount, and an equal amount added at the lower end, and a similar amount set back at the top joint, but there are risks with this method, which perhaps more than offset the time saved. Enlarged details of the curtail step and adjacent parts are shown in Figs. 3, 4, and 5, Pl. xviii. The plan, Fig. 3, Pl. xviii., is reversed, owing to exigencies of space, but this in no way affects the construction.

To Set Out the Curtail Step.—The handrail scroll must first be drawn because the balusters must range along its centre line, also one side of the balusters must line with the face of the string, and the other side with the face of the riser ; hence it follows that the "neck," or narrowest part of the curtail step, must exactly equal a baluster in thickness to comply with these conditions. As the block upon which the riser veneer has to be bent and glued is necessarily two veneers thinner than the finished riser, it is very weak at the neck, consequently has to be built up in three or more layers, with the grains crossing each other to strengthen it, as shown in Fig. 5, Pl. xviii. This is the chief reason for building up blocks, and is not necessary in the case of small blocks that are not much cut away, or will have their strength reduced by mortises, as in the case of Figs. 3 and 4, Pl. xviii. The method of drawing scrolls is fully described at page 75, and need not be repeated here. The diagram of centres is shown in dotted lines numbered in their order of use. Having drawn the scroll, strike from the same centres the middle line of the handrail and space out equally upon it the six balusters, arranging them tangentially to the curves at the point at which they occur. The string is made to coincide with the face of the balusters and its face carried around for the first quadrant, where the block starts. The nosing of the tread is also struck out from the same centres. The block usually starts at the first quadrant; this stoppage, or curtailment of the scroll curves in the step, gives rise to its name, the object being to avoid a confined space on the floor, which could not be kept clean. Note that the scotia in this case is got out in the solid, and covers the block, therefore the curtail riser must be the thickness of the scotia, less in height than the other risers. Full details of making a curtail step are given at pages 75 and 76.

The Wreathed Portion of the String, containing the outer ends of the winders, is formed by reducing a clean, straight-grained piece of stuff, similar to that used in the straight parts, to a veneer between the springing lines, then bending it around a drum or cylinder, ·made to the required shape of the plan, as shown in Figs. 6 and 7, Pl. XVIII., backing up the veneered portion with " staves " or narrow slips of soft wood, glued to it and to each other, as shown in Fig. 6, Pl. XVIII. A plan and elevation of the wreath piece, after it has been staved, removed from the cylinder and cut to fit the steps, is shown in plan and elevation at Figs. 8 and 9, Pl. XVIII. The method of attaching the wreathed piece to the strings by means of counter-wedges is also shown in Fig. 9, Pl. XVIII. About a foot of solid wood is left on the veneer outside the springings for this purpose. It may be explained that the small projections of the risers to meet the brackets has not been shown on this small scale drawing, to avoid confusion of lines. The veneer must of course be bent before cutting out, and, as it would be difficult to mark after bending, it is necessary to set it out on the flat, as shown in Fig. 11, Pl. XVIII. For this purpose, a development of the end of the well (Fig. 2, Pl. XVII.) must be made full size on a board, in the manner now described. Let Fig. 10, Pl. XVIII., represent the plan of the wreathed portion of the stairs which must be drawn full size. In the actual setting out it will be necessary only to draw the *face* lines of the risers and string as on the right-hand side of Fig. 10, Pl. XVIII. They are drawn showing the thickness, on the left side, merely to render the explanation clearer. To obtain the stretch out of the semicircle, or " covering of the cylinder," draw the springing line S-S through the centre of the curve, and upon it describe an equilateral triangle as S-C-S, produce the sides C-S, to intersect a line drawn parallel to S-S, through the crown of the semicircle, or, in other words, tangent to the same. The distance between these points equals (approximately) the length of the curve in plan, and therefore represents the plans of the springings developed. Project them into the elevation as shown, and draw a ground line G-L. On this line must be spaced out the risers as they occur in plan. In this instance they are purposely arranged equally ; therefore as they rise regularly the " falling line " will be a straight line, but this arrangement does not always happen, and the method to be described is applicable to all cases. There are two methods of obtaining the positions of the risers on the development : the first, which is most suitable for small drawings, is to step a series of short chords around the face of the string in plan, with the dividers, noting how many steps are required to reach each riser, then transfer a like number of steps or distances to the line G-L, starting from the same springing, and number them correspondingly. In the second method—one usually preferred in the workshop—a thin templet is made to fit the plan exactly, extending beyond the springings sufficiently to cover about two risers ; this templet is laid on the plan, and the several riser lines and the springings marked upon its face. Then standing it on edge upon the ground line G-L, with point S upon the springing line, carefully roll the templet around until the opposite springing is reached, marking the points of the several risers 7-8-9-10, etc., as they reach the ground line. Draw projectors from these points parallel to the springing lines, i.e. perpendicular to the line G-L, and intersect them by horizontals from the rise lines numbered 7 to 15, previously set up on the springing line, and thus obtain the profiles of the steps. Draw the nosing line N over the winders, and parallel with it the bottom of the veneer. The proper depth of this is ascertained by drawing the thickness of a riser upon a tread line as at point *a*, which indicates the salient angle beneath the steps. Then two parallel lines, as shown, equal to the depth of the carriage or pitching piece, in this instance $4\frac{1}{2}$ ins.; another inch must be allowed to cover the soffit, but as in this example a bead is to be worked on the edge which would be impossible upon the veneered portion, the wreathed part must be made the depth of the moulding or bead, less than the straight parts of the string; the bead must be bent separately and planted on after the wreath piece is built up.

The dotted rectangle *d-e-f-g* indicates the size of the veneer required; the adjacent parts of the straight strings are shown in dotted lines with the treads in position. The joint lines at *d* and *g* are made square to the pitch of the straight strings, as shown in Fig. 2, Pl. XVIII., and the bevel of these in relation to the pitch of the winders must be carefully transferred to the veneer. All the marking (save the projectors) shown in Fig. 11, Pl. XVIII., should be transferred to the face side of the veneer, either by taking a tracing and pricking the angles through, or by laying the veneer on the board, over its draft, then lining in the steps by means of a straight edge, but *do not*, as is sometimes advised in books, knife-cut in any lines, for so sure as you do the veneer will break at the cut when bending it on the drum. The thickness of the veneer to which the string is reduced will depend upon the kind of wood to be used. For painted work yellow deal would be used, and generally a veneer of this wood will bend on a cylinder of 9 ins. diameter at $\frac{1}{8}$ in. thick; a quicker sweep than this would need the veneer to be thinner. Mahogany cannot be trusted to bend, if over a full $\frac{1}{16}$th of an inch, whilst oak will bend on easy sweeps up to $\frac{1}{4}$ in. thick. Of course in all cases the veneer must be either soaked in boiling water or placed in a steam chest; the latter method is by far the best. Great care must be taken to place the veneer at the right pitch on the cylinder; this is ensured by keeping the springing lines drawn on it coincident with the springings on the cylinder. Fix one end as shown in Fig. 7, Pl. XVIII., then bend slowly around fixing, as indicated in dotted lines, a cleat or two to keep it down, and proceed until the tangent piece is reached at the other side, which must be secured in like manner. Let the veneer dry thoroughly before staving, then glue on the staves one at a time as they are jointed. Staves should be narrow; theoretically their under edges should be hollowed to fit the sweep, but though I have seen scores of wreath pieces made, I have never seen this done. If the stave does not exceed $\frac{3}{4}$ in. on the face, a good joint can be made with the veneer. After the staving is dry trim it off regularly and glue a piece of " scrim " over it, when this is dry the wreath piece may be removed and cut to the lines. The mitres can be taken with a bevel from the plan. A piece of thin brown paper strained over the cylinder and glued at each side will preserve the face of the veneer from damage, should any glue accidentally get under it when staving.

Details of a Cut String are given in the isometric sketch, Fig. 12, Pl. XVIII., showing the fitting at different stages and treatments. The top step has the riser lip-mitred to the string, also to a bracket. The next step shows a plain cut-and-mitred string and riser, with the latter drawn back, that the notching-out of the back of the lower tread may be seen. The third step has the tread in position and showing the dovetail sockets for the balusters, also the tongue to hold the return nosing, which is shown separately in Fig. 13, Pl. XVIII. The rebate shown is to receive or cover the top edge of the bracket, which is thus secured in a better manner than when simply cut up underneath the nosing.

The mitre of the riser is bradded and covered by the bracket as indicated under the next step, which shows the end of the tread finished, with balusters in position. Fig. 14, Pl. XVIII., is a right section through the end of this step. A simple method of reducing the brackets for the wreathed portion of the string is illustrated in Fig. 5a, Pl. XVIII. Having drawn the flyer bracket full size, as at A-B, construct an equilateral triangle on the top edge, by striking intersecting arcs from the two ends as centres, as shown by dotted lines, join the ends A-B to the intersection C. From this point measure down, as at *a* and *b*, the length of the stretch-out of the winder bracket, 7 ins.; join points *a-b*, which becomes the top of the reduced bracket. Next divide the profile into as many parts as desired and project them to the line A-B. From these points draw lines to the apex C, and at the points where they intersect the line *a-b* erect perpendiculars and make them equal in height to the corresponding projectors on A-B. This method is applicable to any drawing or object to be enlarged or diminished, for obviously we might have obtained the larger bracket from the smaller by extending the sides of the small triangle until they contained the larger side. Any form of triangle will give like results, but none so readily as the equilateral, because the desired width can be set off upon the sides from the apex and the right proportion obtained immediately.

CHAPTER XI.

A CONTINUOUS STRING, OPEN WELL, GEOMETRICAL STAIR.

(PLATE XIX.)

Suitable for a Middle-Class House—Description of the Plans—Construction and Fixing—Usual Procedure with Rough Carriages—Details of Step Construction—Fitting the Strings—Rebate Mitred Risers, Advantages of Concealing the Nails or Brads for Polished Work—An Old Method of Setting Out the Handrail Section and Making the Joint—How to Draw the Stair—Projecting the Sections—Working from the Story Rod—Drawing the Handrail in Position.

A CONTINUOUS string, open well, geometrical stair with framed half-pace landings, cut-and-mitred strings blocked outside, housed wall strings, curtail step and scroll wreathed handrails, is shown on Pl. XIX. This stair is of substantial construction, suitable for a good class house, as will be seen in the details next to be discussed. Fig. 1, Pl. XIX., is a general plan showing the first two straight reverse flights, the first half-landing and the semicircular ends to the well in naked timbering. The second half-landing has only one side of its timbering shown, the other half of the drawing is occupied by the timbering of the ground floor.

As in previous drawings, to which the reader can refer, details of the surfaces of the steps are given, but are here omitted; the risers and their connection with the strings are shown, as also in the enlarged details. Fig. 2, Pl. XIX., is a section of both flights, taken near the wall strings in each flight on lines A-B and C-D respectively. The handrail and balusters are shown in the lower flights, but omitted in the upper one, the better to utilise the space on the Plate as the positions of these parts are similar.

Fig. 3, Pl. XIX., is a section through the half-pace landing, showing floor, joists, and skirtings.

Fig. 4, Pl. XIX., is the front elevation looking up the first flight. The upper flight has been drawn with the soffit omitted to show construction of the steps, fixing of the carriages, etc., underneath.

Figs. 6 and 7, Pl. XIX., are a plan and elevation to double scale of the end of the well at the landing, etc., showing the construction of the semicircular continuation of the strings, the nosing line of the landing and treads being dotted. The staving of the well end, which is in seven pieces, grooved and cross-tongued in the radial joints, may be connected to the strings similarly, or as shown in Fig. 7, Pl. XIX., with a solid tongue worked on the end of string. A carriage piece is also shown dotted in this Fig. Full details of construction and fitting of these " ends " are given in connection with other examples, therefore need not be repeated.

Construction and Fixing.—Solid bracketing is shown at *c-c* in the plan, but where economy is desirable it is not really necessary to bracket right across the step; equally serviceable work is obtained with only half the material, by bracketing as shown at *c-c* in Fig. 2, Pl. XIX. Two brackets are drawn on this section for convenience, actually they would not be visible in this section, as they lie outside it.

The Rough Carriages, two to each stair, are birdsmouthed against the pitching pieces and the trimmers, and would generally be fixed before the stairs are put up. Naturally the steps are not finished off underneath so neatly as shown, but the overhang would be scribed down and cut away to obtain regular seating on the carriages.

The Steps, first glued and blocked in the usual way, are fitted into the well string and marked, then the outer ends fitted to the cut strings and the treads, previously cut and mitred for the return nosing, and the mortises for the balusters sawn in and cut half through from underside, are attached by glued blocks in the angles as shown.

The Curtail Step is built up, as described in the previous example and on page 76, with a riser-block cut to shape to fit the scroll, made in three thicknesses with the grain crossing, to strengthen the neck, which of course must be of the same thickness as the balusters.

The Strings should be fitted dry on the bench to the circular ends at the landings, these being staved and veneered as shown in Figs. 6 and 7, Pl. xix. These circular pieces, after preliminary cleaning off, should be fixed by blocking or nailing, as the material decides, to the trimmer and the strings brought down tightly to the joints ; the weight of the flights will keep these up, but they would also be lightly glued to prevent shrinkage.

It will be noticed that in this case the risers are shown rebate-mitred to the string—this of course takes more time than plain mitres but enables the risers to be bradded through the front, which makes sure that the mitres will keep up. If the work is of hard wood, to be polished, or soft wood to be stained and varnished, the holes for the brads should have a small chip raised with the bradawl, then the hole bored and after bradding and punching the chip, glued and rubbed back in place, when the hole will be invisible. The dotted lines in Fig. 2, Pl. xix., indicate position of passage, floor and steps, down to basement entrance.

Fig. 5, Pl. xix., shows a method of **Setting Out the Handrail Section,** also method of keying the joints, which is sometimes preferred to dowelling. A semicircle, with a radius equal to the depth or thickness of the rail, is struck on the bottom edge of the rail, from a centre c, in the middle of a baluster ; through this centre erect a perpendicular, to the diameter line a-b. Next, at one-quarter of the depth of the rail from its back, draw a line parallel to the diameter of the semicircle, also a line parallel to the diameter line, tangent to the semicircle, at a point which coincides with back of the rail as shown. On this line, at each side of the centre line C, set off half the depth of the rail as at 1-2. Draw the lines 1-c and 2-c. Perpendicular to the centre line, and parallel to the diameter a-b, draw a line at one-third the depth of the rail, as at 3-4. Set off on this line, on each side of the centre, a distance equal to its distance from the back of the rail. This will give points 3 and 4, which are centres for the hollows. Where the first horizontal line intersects the lines C-1 and C-2 are the centres for the side rounds, and point c is the centre from which to describe the back curve, which falls neatly into those of the sides.

Drawing the Stairs.—Draw the plan first, set out the well-hole 1 ft. 11 ins. between the strings equidistant on each side of the centre line and the semicircular ends of the well, then set out size of stair-way, walls, plaster and wall strings, then the landings, with all the construction timbers first, such as joists, trimmers and pitching pieces. Next draw the first and the last risers and space out remainder equally between. Note that the *faces* of the risers are in line, at both sides of the well hole ; put these in first, that is to say, line straight across in pencil, but notice that the thickness of risers go the reverse way. Finally, draw-in the carriages to the pitch of the strings.

To Project the Section (Fig. 2, Pl. xix.). First draw the two floor joists, etc., projecting their position from the plan, then set up the story-rod and divide it into twenty-one equal spaces as shown. Project across the eleventh rise which is the half-landing and fill in details of this, excepting the skirting. Next project the various steps from face of risers in plan and the heights from the story-rod ; a few of these are dotted-in as indication.

Simply mark top of tread and face of riser until all are in, then put in the thickness of

PLATE XIX.

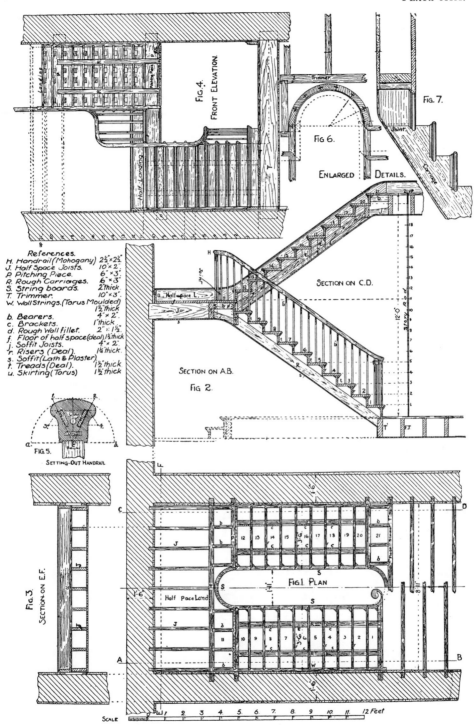

References.

H. Handrail (Mahogany)	2½"×2½".
J. Half Space Joists.	10"×2".
P. Pitching Piece.	6"×3".
R. Rough Carriages.	6"×3".
S. String boards.	2"thick.
T. Trimmer.	10"×3".
W. Wall Strings.(Torus Moulded)	1½"thick.
b. Bearers.	4"×2".
c. Brackets.	1"thick.
d. Rough Wall fillet.	2"×1½".
f. Floor of half space(deal)	1½"thick.
j. Soffit Joists.	4"×2".
r. Risers (Deal).	1¼"thick.
s. Soffit (Lath & Plaster).	
t. Treads (Deal).	1½"thick.
u. Skirting (Torus)	1½"thick.

FIG. 4.
FRONT ELEVATION.

FIG 6.

FIG. 7.

ENLARGED DETAILS.

SECTION ON C.D.

SECTION ON A.B.

FIG 2.

FIG 5.
SETTING-OUT HANDRAIL

FIG. 3
SECTION ON E.F.

FIG. 1 PLAN
Half Pace Land

Half-Pace Landing

Half-space L

SCALE   1 2 3 4 5 6 7 8 9 10 11 12 Feet

A GEOMETRICAL STAIR WITH CONTINUOUS OUTER STRING AND HANDRAIL
WITH CURTAIL STEP AND SCROLL, AND HALF-PACE FRAMED LANDINGS.

one tread and riser at top and bottom, and draw the carriage line, touching the angle of these, which will give the stop line for the rest.   A nosing line can be drawn, resting on the top— this is not shown ; make the wall strings parallel with this.   Fig. 4, Pl. xix., is projected similarly.   The wall face has been utilised for a story-rod in this instance.   All the cross dimensions should be taken from off the plan with the dividers.

To Draw the Handrail set up a baluster at each end over face of risers 2 and 11, and if it is intended to draw the top flight, also over Nos. 12 and 20 ; make them 2 ft. 1 in. high ; draw a straight line between, which will be the underside of handrail ; draw a parallel line to this, at 2½ ins. above, for the back of rail ; make this 2 ft. 8 ins. high over the landings, and join up by easy curves as shown.

PLATE XX.

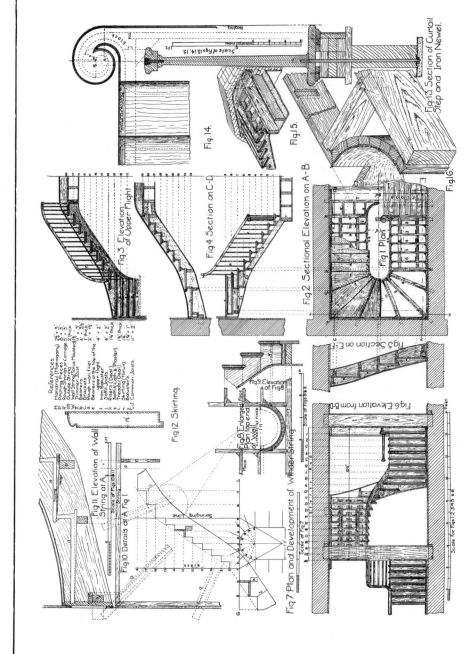

Fig.14.

Fig.15.

Fig.13 Section of Curtail Step and Iron Newel.

Fig.3 Elevation of Upper Flight

Fig.4. Section on C-D

Fig.2 Sectional Elevation on A-B

Fig.1 Plan

Fig.5 Section on E-F

Fig.6 Elevation from B-f

Fig.16.

References:
Handrail (Mahogany) 2½ × 3.
Pitching Pieces 8 × 3.
Rough Strings or Carriage 2 thick
Outside String 2 thick
Wall String (Torus Moulded) 1½
Bearers 4 × 2½
Bearers at the top of the upper flight. 11 × 1½
Rough wall Flight. 2 × 1¼
Brackets
Iron Baluster
Soffit Joists
Risers (Deal) 4 × 2
Soffit (Lath & Plaster)
Treads (Deal) 1¼ thick
Skirting (Torus) 1½ thick
Balusters 11 × 2
Ceiling Common Joists.

Fig.11. Elevation of Wall String at A.

Fig.12. Skirting.

Fig.10 Details at A Fig.1

Fig.9 Elevation of Fig.8

Fig.8 Enlarged Plan Top end of Wall String

Springing Line

Fig.7 Plan and Development of Winder String

Scale of Figs 14, 15.

Scale of Figs 14, 15.

RECTANGULAR OPEN WELL GEOMETRICAL STAIR WITH HALF-SPACE OF RADIAL WINDERS.

CHAPTER XII.

AN OPEN WELL GEOMETRICAL STAIR WITH REVERSE FLIGHTS.

(PLATE XX.)

Connected by a Half-space of Radial Winders and placed in a Rectangular Apartment—Description of the Drawings —General Plan of Entire Construction—Various Sections Projected from the Plan—Elevation of the Complete Structure —Isometric Views of Junction of the Stair and Landing—Isometric View of Details at end of Well Enlarged—Other Enlarged Details including Section of Curtail Step and Method of Fixing Iron Newel to Floor and Handrail—Tabulated List of Parts with their Dimensions—Precautions when Copying the Drawing—Practical Instructions for Connecting the Two Flights at the Wreath—Method of Trimming Floor at the Well End.

AN Open Well Geometrical Stair of Two Reverse Flights connected by a half-space of radial winders placed in a rectangular apartment. The stair can be continued through several floors. The handrail is continuous, wreathed at the turns and starting from a small scroll which is carried on a cast-iron newel post.

Description of the Plate.—Fig. 1, Pl. xx., is a general plan showing the first two flights. This stair is strongly constructed and is suitable for a good-class property.

The arrangement shown of two risers in the springing is not the best from the point of view of appearance of the handrail, but as this is a very common arrangement it seemed necessary to include an example in this treatise, which is intended to be comprehensive. The reasons for and against this arrangement are dealt with fully in Part II.

There are six flyers in each flight connected by eight winders, radiating from the centre of the well. In one-half of the plan the naked risers and the constructive carriages and bearers to the winders are shown; in the other half, part of the finished stair with treads is shown. Some of these treads are broken away, revealing return nosings and seats of the balusters, the rough strings, trimmer T and cross-bearers to the landing. This is done mainly to illustrate the variation in construction of the string at each end of the open well; one end of course is wreathed over the winders, the other end being level. Enlarged details of this are shown in Figs. 8 and 9, Pl. xx., and an isometric view at the head of the stair with adjacent parts in Fig. 15, Pl. xx. It will be understood of course that the floor timbers shown broken are merely so for convenience of illustration, and that in reality in each instance they continue to the opposite wall. Sundry dotted projectors are shown on the plan to which reference will be made presently; these are intended to carry the eye to the respective sections next to be described.

Fig. 2, Pl. xx., is a sectional elevation on the line A-B; in this the steps are seen in section and the near carriage, or rough string R, in elevation. The bearers (*b*) under each winder are seen partly in elevation and partly in section, due to their oblique positions, also the firring strips (*f.s.*) to which the plastering laths are nailed.

Fig. 3, Pl. xx., is an elevation of the upper flight from the top landing to No. 10 step, showing face of the outside string with return nosings to the treads; a part of the handrail and balustrade, also the complete wall string, can be seen in elevation, and the top edge only of the return string, which is shown full length in elevation in Fig. 5, Pl. xx. The parts shown in section are taken upon the centre line in the plan, Fig. 1, Pl. xx., and show the

(43)

first-floor landing with the nosing-piece which runs round the end of the well, also the staving and veneered string is seen, though these are shown more clearly in Figs. 8 and 9, Pl. xx.

Fig. 4, Pl. xx., is a section of the upper flight, taken upon the line C-D in the plan, close to the wall string. This view gives the true appearance of the wall string after it has been set out by means of the pitch-board, the only difference being that instead of the steps being shown in section the housings would be seen as shown in the enlarged detail, Figs. 10 and 11, Pl. xx.

Fig. 5, Pl. xx., is a section through the winders, taken on the line E-F, giving also the true shape of the return wall string. A few projectors are drawn to indicate from where the sections are obtained; naturally in copying the example every piece shown cut by the line of section in plan will have to be projected likewise into the elevation. This drawing also shows the notching for the bearers (b).

Fig. 6, Pl. xx., is an elevation of the stair as viewed from foot of the first flight. The commencement of the second flight immediately above is also shown, and, apart from the curtail step at start, each flight is a replica on the one below. To render the construction clearer, the plaster soffit is omitted below the upper flight; as is also the handrail, although the newel post is shown in position on the curtail step.

Fig. 7, Pl. xx., is the plan and development of the circular string around the winders. The method of its construction has been fully described in a previous example, so need not be repeated here, but all the lines necessary to obtain shape of the veneer or to set out in the solid are shown, therefore it is assumed the reader will readily follow the construction by reference.

Figs. 8 and 9, Pl. xx., are enlarged details at the landing end of the well, showing the method of connecting the circular end to the straight strings by means of folding wedges W, which tighten up the bevelled shoulder at the springings. This veneered end is driven down into position after the two flights are fixed; of course great care must be taken to keep the opposite shoulders out of winding, and personally the author prefers to make the shoulder very slightly tapering, this gives an opportunity to ease a shoulder when not exactly fitting. Also the circular end should be an $\frac{1}{8}$ in. wider than the finished size, to allow for driving; the overplus on either edge being planed off after glueing-in. Figs. 10 and 11, Pl. xx., are enlarged details at A (Fig. 1, Pl. xx), showing junction of the two wall strings, the housings for the steps, notching for the bearers, etc. The winders in the plan are dotted-in to avoid confusion with drawing 7, on which it is superposed to economise space.

Fig. 12, Pl. xx., is an enlarged section of the torus skirting. Fig. 13, Pl. xx., is an enlarged section through the iron newel with method of fixing the latter to the floor joist and the scroll cap to the newel.

Fig. 14, Pl. xx., is an enlarged part plan of the curtail and next two steps projected from Fig. 13, Pl. xx., to indicate the relative position of the parts, the construction of the curtail block and the connection to the string. Fig. 15, Pl. xx., is an isometric view at the top of the stair adjacent to the first floor landing, showing the construction at the well end. Fig. 16, Pl. xx., is an isometric enlargement of part of the framing which is shown complete in Fig. 15, Pl. xx., and illustrates very clearly how the string is connected to the top riser, also the dove-tail housing of the bearers to the riser and the trimmer joist.

To describe fully the details of construction of this stair would only be repeating matter that has been given in connection with previous examples, to which the reader is referred, but it may be useful here to give an outline of the procedure of **Fixing** after summarising the chief details.

First, having set out and prepared the various strings and flyer steps, the latter of course is glued-and-blocked together on the cradle, but not including the winders. Next cut the outside strings to shape, and mitre up each riser; this should be done throughout before cutting off to length and fitting in the wall strings. Each straight flight would then be put together and the wreathed string, previously built up on a cylinder, would be fitted to the strings of the two flights and connected up by counter-wedges, as shown in Fig. 9, Pl. XVIII. If the stair had not to travel far, the two flights might be connected together, glued and well braced; but generally, the connection would be made on the job, at time of fixing. If the two flights are fixed together, they would be offered up, after carefully testing for width overall, upon a rod and fixing the firring piece, or grounds to the staircase, so that the width rod just goes in neatly between them.

The mortises or apertures should be cut through the wall strings to receive the bearers (usually by boring holes at the four corners, then cutting the piece out with a table saw) and, when the stair is offered up and the top string is scribed over the landing, these apertures should be scratched on the walls with a scriber, or bradawl; the stair is then taken down and the holes cut in the wall with a " cold " chisel to receive the bearers. These holes should be made a little deeper than actually required for the length of bearers so that the latter may be moved back when fitting the outer end to the wreathed string.

Having arrived at this stage, the rough timbers are now fixed, viz. the pitching pieces, and, if not already done by the carpenters, the trimmers, rough strings, etc. The winder bearers are next marked and cut to length from the drawing, or by means of a length rod.

The stair should now be finally tried, and if made correctly will slip easily into its place on the timbering. Note, the winder treads, though fitted and the outer end returned on the bench, should not be fixed, until the stair is actually in position, for it is then easier to get the bearers in, there being always a chance of some adjustment being required at top or bottom of the flights, which their absence facilitates.

The stair being up, we next insert the bearers, wedging if necessary and filling-in with cement around their ends after screwing or nailing them to the outer string; the winder treads can now be blocked-in and the rough brackets nailed to the rough strings; be sure to cut these brackets with the grain vertical, that is to say, end grain must butt under the steps as shown. This seems so obvious that I would not mention it, but for the fact I have seen them placed the other way, when of course they quickly become useless through shrinkage. The next job is the fitting and fixing of the balusters and handrails, which however is dealt with in Vol. II, " Handrailing."

CHAPTER XIII.

SPIRAL STAIRS.[1]

(PLATE XXI.)

An Independent Circular Newel Stair with an Open or "Cut-and-Mitred" String, is Illustrated with
Full Details in Figs. 1 to 15, Pl. XXI.—Description of the Modern Type and Method of Con-
struction—Differences from Earlier Forms—Construction of the Solid Newel—Construction of the
"Straight" Radiating Steps—Construction of a Built-up Newel—Method of Glue-blocking the
Sections—Tenoning the Bearers—Marking for Length—Notching for the Rough Strings—Pro-
cedure in Fitting-up—Fox Wedging the Radial Bearers—Proper Direction for Grain in Cross-bearers
—How to Set Out the Newel—Method of Developing Outer Strings—Alternative Methods of Con-
structing Wreathed Strings—The Shaped-stave and Veneered-string, a Cheap Method—How
Glued up, Advantages and Drawbacks of the Method—The Laminated String (Best Method)—
Requirements in the Shop or Factory for Successful Work—Practical Operations—A Danger to
Guard against with Cut Strings—Further Details in Elliptic Stairs—The Solid String Method—
Practical Value of Veneered Work—Drawbacks of Solid Strings—Why Joints cannot be Per-
manently Tight—Obtaining Edge Mould for Solid Strings—Obtaining the Joint Bevels—Apply-
ing the Bevels—Method of Attaching Circular Nosings for Polished Work, also References to
Painted Work.

An Independent Circular Newel Stair, with open string (Pl. XXI.). These stairs are
termed "independent" or self-supporting, because they derive no support from any sur-
rounding walls, a characteristic which differentiates them from the earliest form of spiral
stairs. These earlier forms were invariably built within a well-like chamber, into the sides
of which the outer ends of the steps were inserted, or alternatively built-in during the construction of the building, the inner ends being reduced to small cylinders resting one upon the
other, and in some instances these were cemented together, so forming a solid circular
"newel" or column throughout the entire height of the stairway. The present example,
which illustrates the modern method of construction, consists of a series of straight, radiating
steps built up in the usual way, with relatively thin treads and risers, glued and blocked
together, the inner ends framed or notched into the separately built-up newel post, the outer
ends being mitred to a cut string. The string and handrail in this instance are "continuous,"
in the fullest sense of that term, for at least one complete revolution on the plan. Within
the depth of the steps, that is to say, between the treads and the winding soffit, there is constructed a complete framework of rough timbering, or carriages, the term "rough" merely
implying that such planing and shaping as it receives is for the purpose of construction solely,
and not for appearance sake. All the visible portions of the construction are of course
"wrought" to a superior finish.

A separate plan and elevation is made of this timbering (see Figs. 3 and 4, Pl. XXI.), to
avoid confusion with the constructive lines of the outside, or visible parts of the stair, which
are shown in the plan and elevation, Figs. 1 and 2, Pl. XXI. Several enlarged details of the

---

[1] The term "spiral" is used in deference to common usage, but of course the geometrical figure
produced by stairs of this type is rightly a helix, not a spiral.

construction are also shown on the plate, that will be referred to as occasions arise during the description. Referring again to the plan and elevation, Figs. 1 and 2, Pl. xxi., the balusters drawn are of course merely indicative of position; no useful purpose would be served by providing designs in this connection: these will be found in another chapter. The handrail provides an example of a true helical, or " screw," falling line, and is dealt with fully elsewhere in the book.

The newel post may be a solid cylinder, but to afford as much instruction as possible, the construction of a built-up newel is shown, which if carefully constructed will be equally strong and less than two-thirds the weight of a solid newel. The construction of the newel is clearly shown in Fig. 5, it should be first glued up in the square, in two halves and the joint in each part well blocked throughout; when these two sections are dry, the other joint, which is in effect a double-tongued " single " joint, should be well rubbed, screwed together under the steps, and blocked in the angles as far down as it is possible to reach, either by hand or with a jointed " long arm." The newel when fixed is shouldered over the joists as shown in Fig. 2, Pl. xxi., and fixed in like manner to the ceiling joists, or roof of the apartment at the top end (see Fig. 4, Pl. xxi.). This of course provides the main support, but the stresses occasioned by the weight of the stair, and the live load to be carried, resolve themselves eventually into a direct thrust upon the bottom step, which should be solid, as shown, to avoid the crushing that would probably occur if a skeleton step were used. One complete revolution of the stair is shown in the elevation, when it is assumed a landing is reached. From there, the stair ascends again in a " spiral." Above this landing the newel post is reduced in diameter, and a moulding to match the handrail is turned upon it. The nosing of the solid step is continued around the newel to form a finish, as indicated by the dotted line in Fig. 1, Pl. xxi.; those of the remaining treads are made tangent to the surface of the newel, into which these ends are sunk, in the manner shown at A, Fig. 5, Pl. xxi. Referring to the plan of the timbering (Fig. 3, Pl. xxi.), on one-half, the risers are shown cut-and-mitred to the string, with the angle blocks at back, the dotted lines parallel with the risers indicate the bearers beneath. In the other half-plan, assumed to be immediately below the risers, the outer string is seen plain, the rough string grained, as also are the bearers. These bearers are tenoned into the newel post, in the manner shown at No. 15b, Fig. 5, Pl. xxi.; each should be carefully fitted to a straight shoulder, and the tenon driven in very tightly; when finally fixed, they should be fox-wedged as shown in Figs. 6 and 7, Pl. xxi., but at first fitting, when all are driven up to the shoulders, they must be marked off to length with a radius rod from the newel, both for the cross-bearers and for length, then cut off plumb and half-notched at top, to receive the rough strings, as shown in Fig. 4, Pl. xxi. The latter are cut between them, glue-blocked, and, when dry, accurately rounded off, to fit the cut string which is offered up in sections.

Next the cross-bearers are cut tightly between the radial bearers, with their grain running up the stair as shown, so that there will be no yielding through shrinkage. The newel would be set out for mortising by developing its surface upon a long strip of lining paper on which the steps would be drawn as they occur in the development; a portion of which is shown in Fig. 9, Pl. xxi. The bearers would be drawn under their respective risers, and the mortise marked as shown at b, Fig. 9, Pl. xxi., which indicates the bearer under step 21. The corresponding development of the outside string is shown in Fig. 8, Pl. xxi. The method of obtaining these developments is fully explained in the next example (see p. 53).

Having obtained the development, the strip must be carefully pasted around the post, and its accuracy tested by comparing it with the story-rod shown in Fig. 1, Pl. xxi. When adjusted, the mortises can be made to the rake shown in the plans, Figs. 1 and 5, Pl. xxi.

The wreathed strings can be constructed in three different ways, each having its

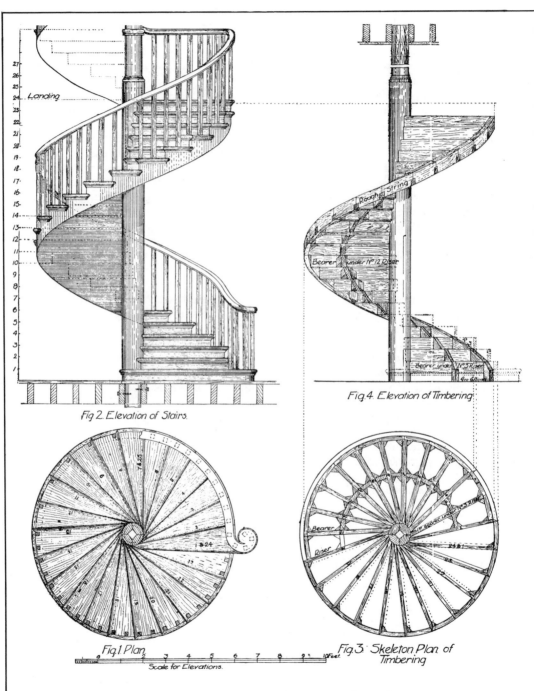

Fig 2. Elevation of Stairs.

Landing

Fig.4. Elevation of Timbering.

Roughts String

Bearer under N°12 Riser

Bearer under N°3 Riser

Fig.1 Plan

Scale for Elevations.

Fig.3. Skeleton Plan of Timbering

Bearer

Riser

AN INDEPENDENT CIRCULAR NEWEL STAIR WITH OPEN STRING.

PLATE XXI.

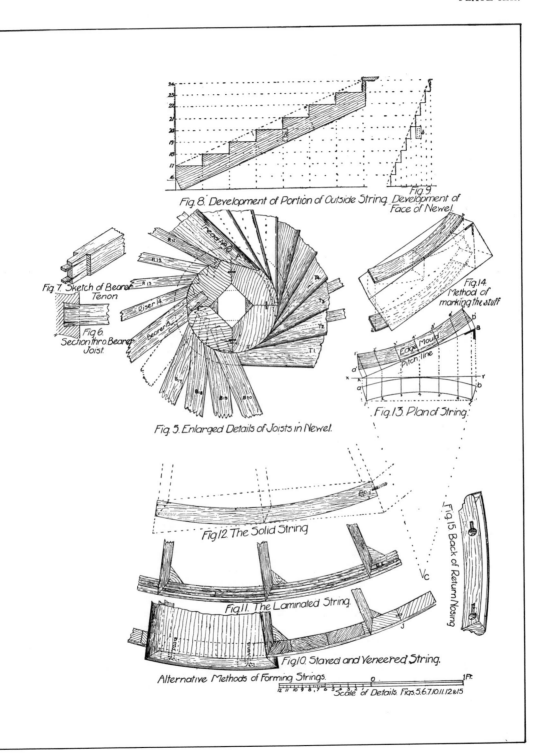

Fig. 8. Development of Portion of Outside String.

Fig. 9. Development of Face of Newel.

Fig. 7. Sketch of Bearer Tenon.

Fig. 6. Section thro' Bearer Joist.

Fig. 5. Enlarged Details of Joists in Newel.

Fig. 14. Method of marking the stuff.

Fig. 13. Plan of String.

Fig. 12. The Solid String.

Fig. 11. The Laminated String.

Fig. 10. Stayed and Veneered String.

Fig. 15. Back of Return Nosing.

Alternative Methods of Forming Strings.

Scale of Details. Figs. 5.6.7.10.11.12 & 15.

advantages and its drawbacks. The choice would be determined by the class of work and the appliances at hand.

The **Shaped Stave and Veneered String** shown in plan at Fig. 10, Pl. xxi., is perhaps the commonest method of construction, and as might be expected, it is also the least satisfactory. In this method, deal or pine battens, from 4 ins. to 7 ins. wide, according to the quickness of the sweep, are rounded on the face side to a templet, the edges shot radial, then cut into short lengths equal to the depth of the string required. These pieces are then glued together upon ribs, which are cut polygonal to fit the backs of the staves, similar to the rib shown in connection with the geometrical stair (Pl. xviii., Fig. 7). This backing is glued-up in sections about 2 ft. wide and tested with a radius rod for correctness. Two sections are then jointed with cross tongues as shown at J, Fig. 10, carefully braced at back, then veneered as seen in the drawing with the desired hardwood or other facing. These 4-ft. wide sections are successively fitted and fixed to the rough string. The advantages of this method are, first, its relative cheapness—most of the shaping can be done at the machine ; second, the few joints visible (in the stair we are considering probably four only would be necessary). The disadvantages are the numerous cross-joints at back—any one of these breaking will seriously weaken the stair ; (2) danger of the veneer splitting in consequence of unequal shrinkage, or expansion, owing to the grain of the backing and of the veneer traversing ; (3) the large sections of backing are fragile until veneered, and may be easily broken.

The **Laminated String** (Fig. 11, Pl. xxi.) is undoubtedly the best and strongest method, given good workmanship, but it can only be satisfactorily accomplished in a shop fitted with veneering requirements and appliances. It consists in bending, successively upon a drum or cylinder, a number of thin boards, the thickness of the laminæ depending on the kind and quality of the wood and quickness of the curve. The inner and outer surface boards should be continuous for the whole length of the string, but the interior layers may be in shorter lengths and break joint as shown. The drum needs only to be a portion of the cylinder in plan, as the work can be shifted around it during the operation. Each board must be wetted or steamed, bent to its place until set, then thoroughly glued down to the one beneath and allowed to dry before the next board is bent and glued to it. Apart from cost, there is only one objection to this method : the laminæ are always in a state of tension, and when cut to receive the risers, if there is any faulty glueing, they will fly at the cut part. For " close " strings this method is perfect. Further details of the method are given in connection with Elliptic Stairs (p. 54).

The **Solid String** (Fig. 12, Pl. xxi.).—This method is favoured by persons to whom all veneer processes are anathema ; as to the æsthetic view, I offer no remark, but to statements that veneered work is weaker than solid work I emphatically state that experience proves that the contrary is the truth, in so far as it relates to curved work. It is impracticable to get these solid strings out in longer pieces than about 3 ft., owing to the great thickness that would be required ; therefore numerous joints are inevitable, and, apart from thus marring the design, such joints cannot be kept absolutely tight for a lengthened period, owing to shrinkage, and the fact that end-grain wood will not hold glue permanently. Also the method is costly, if hardwood is employed ; also if the inside is not cut to a concentric curve—which by the way it seldom is—the dead weight is greatly increased by the superfluous thickness necessitating a stronger floor or foundation.

The **Method of Obtaining the Edge Mould** to mark the stuff for a solid string is shown to smaller scale in Fig. 13, Pl. xxi. Draw the plan of a section of the string, and a straight line X-Y, touching the outside face ; project the ends of the piece a and b perpendicular to this line. From the intersection A draw a line to B, at the given pitch obtained either from the pitch-board or the development (Fig. 8, Pl. xxi.). Divide the plan curve into a number of equal parts, as at 1, 2, 3, 4, 5, 6, 7, then draw ordinates from these points perpendicular to X-Y. Project these points to the pitch line, as shown by dotted lines, and from the intersections therewith draw other ordinates perpendicular to the pitch line. Number these to correspond with their originals in plan, as 1', 2', 3', etc., and make them equal in length thereto, measuring from X-Y. Also mark off points where the other curve line passes through them, and having thus obtained a series of points, draw the curved edges of the mould through these.

To Obtain the Joints of the mould, draw lines in the plan from the extremities *a* and *b*, to C, the centre of the curve, and project the points 1 and 7, the inner ends of the joints in plan to the pitch line; from the intersection erect perpendiculars, locating points 1', and 7', on the elevation curve. Join 1'-*a'* and 7'-*b'*, and the edge cut for the joint is obtained. The side cut will be simply square to the top edge or pitch line. The method of applying the mould to the stuff is illustrated in Fig. 14, Pl. XXI., where the block is shown pitched up approximately to its correct position, the dotted lines indicating the position of the notching to be done after shaping the block. To line out the stuff for shaping, the mould must be applied at the top and bottom edges, as shown, with the points *a* and *b* vertically over the points *a'-b'*, when the block is pitched at its correct angle. To ensure this, we must use the plumb bevel shown at B, Fig. 13, and having first applied the mould as in Fig. 14, Pl. XXI., at the top of the stuff, square the end *b* to the front side then apply the bevel as drawn and square in the line to *b'* on the bottom edge. Do likewise at the other end, and place the mould to these points, when it will be in position for lining out that edge.

The best method of attaching the return nosings to the treads in circular stairs is shown in Figs. 10 and 15, Pl. XXI. Two wood screws are turned into the end of the tread with their heads projecting about ¾ in. Then two holes are bored to receive them in the back of the return piece, as shown in the view, Fig. 15, Pl. XXI. Slots for the stem of the screws are cut in the driving direction shown in dotted lines in Fig. 10, Pl. XXI., and in driving the piece home to its position the head of the screw cuts a dovetail chose for itself, and, if the joint is not drawn up tightly at the first attempt, a half turn-in of the screws will rectify matters. This method is known as slot screwing, also as secret fixing; it is used in all polished work. Other methods suitable for painted work are shown on Pls. XVIII. and XXVIII.

CHAPTER XIV.

AN INDEPENDENT, OR CIRCULAR GEOMETRICAL STAIR.

(PLATES XXII. AND XXIII.)

Including Cut-and-Mitred String—Description of the Drawings—Reasons for Great Care and Strength required in the Construction of this Type of Stair—Method of Forming the String to Obtain Necessary Strength—Constructing the Outer String—Dowelled and Bolted Sections—Types of Steppings—Method of Marking for Dowelling—Method of Developing and Setting Out of Veneers, for both Strings—Obtaining Thickness of Blocks—Reinforcement of String by a Steel Band.

An Independent, Circular, Geometrical Stair with Open Well and Open Strings is shown on Pl. XXII., and details of its construction on Pl. XXIII. The plan, Fig. 1, Pl. XXII., shows in the first quarter the treads and handrails, starting with scrolls, over a double-ended commode step. In the next quarter the naked risers, strings and carriage pieces are shown. The remaining portion of the plan exhibits the tops of the steps with balusters and return nosings ; the handrails are indicated in dotted lines. The stair, after making a complete revolution, finishes at a landing directly above the second step, this landing running off to the right and left in curves following the lines of the handrails below. The elevation (Fig. 2, Pl. XXII.) gives a view of the stair with the soffit removed, that the general construction underneath may be observed. Stairs of this description require to be very strongly constructed ; the whole of the weight is carried by the strings, for although the balustrade adds considerably to the stiffness, and to the weight, it affords but little strength to the structure. The author recommends that the inside string should be made on the veneer-staved principle, the veneer bent around a cylinder made to the exact size of the well, as shown in Fig. 1, Pl. XXIII., then backed up with narrow staves as indicated on the enlarged portion of the drum (Figs. 2 and 3, Pl. XXIII.). One-half of this illustration shows the interior of the drum, the other half the exterior, with the string bent upon it. Fig. 1, Pl. XXIII., indicates how the veneer is secured to the drum before the backing is commenced. The outside string is constructed by a method that may be termed the solid back-veneered string (see Fig. 4, Pl. XXIII.). It is necessary, for a reason to be referred to presently, that this string should be shaped inside, and it must have solid wood there. Therefore the backing is got out solid, in pine or deal, in the manner shown in Fig. 5, Pl. XXIII., and fully described in connection with the circular newel stair (Pl. XXI.). The several lengths are dowelled and bolted together, as in the illustration, Fig. 4, Pl. XXIII., the joint being " butt," i.e. square to the pitch. Subsequently this backing must be cleaned off and veneered with hardwood. This method of construction has none of the defects of the staved-veneer method, because the grain of the backing and of the veneer run in the same direction. The steppings are cut and fitted by one of the three methods shown in Fig. 4, Pl. XXIII. At A the riser is mitre-dovetailed to the string, probably the best but most difficult method. At B the backing is cut back square to the thickness of the riser, and after the latter is mitred to the facing, both are dowelled together. The templet for marking the dowel holes is shown at T. This should be a piece of zinc, cut to the exact size

PLATE XXII.

AN INDEPENDENT OR CIRCULAR GEOMETRICAL STAIR.

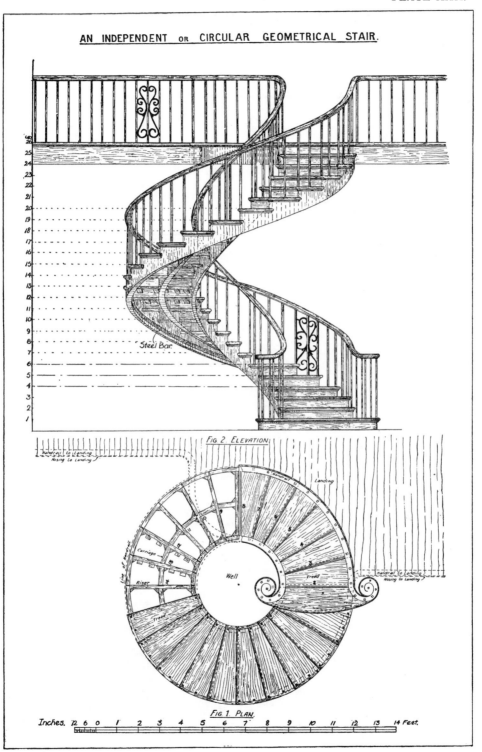

Steel Bar.

FIG 2. ELEVATION.

Handrail to Landing
Nosing to Landing

Landing

Line of Handrail

Carriage

Riser

Well

Tread

Tread

Handrail to Landing
Nosing to Landing

FIG. 1. PLAN.

Inches. 12 6 0 1 2 3 4 5 6 7 8 9 10 11 12 13 14 Feet.

PLATE XXIII.

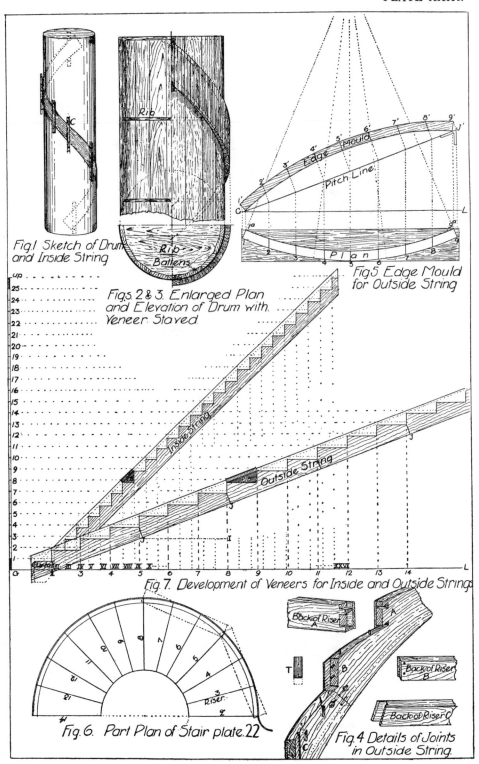

Fig.1 Sketch of Drum and Inside String

Figs. 2 & 3. Enlarged Plan and Elevation of Drum with Veneer Stayed

Fig.5 Edge Mould for Outside String

Fig.7. Development of Veneers for Inside and Outside Strings

Fig.6. Part Plan of Stair plate.22

Fig.4 Details of Joints in Outside String

DETAILS OF INDEPENDENT CIRCULAR STAIR.

of the joint and applied to the string with the tread in position, and to the riser with its bottom end flush with the lower edge. The centres can then be pricked through with a needle-point. The riser is drawn turned over at B, to show the marking at back. The method shown at C provides a strong joint, and the lip can be bradded. The treads may be either dowelled on, as shown at B, or screwed in thumb notches as at C.

The Method of Developing the Veneers for the inside and outside strings is shown in Fig. 7, Pl. XXIII., with their setting out. The two strings are arranged in their relative position, and set off from the same height rod; the two pitch-boards are shown on the eighth step. Owing to limitations of the plate only about one-half the outer string can be shown. The joint lines of the back string are also shown.

Half the plan has been redrawn at Fig. 6, Pl. XXIII., for the purpose of the development. Make a stretch-out of the face of each string on the line G-L, by stepping along the compasses as previously described, also transfer the riser distances, numbering them as shown; projectors drawn from these points to intersect horizontal projectors from the corresponding rises on the height-rod will furnish the outline of the steps and, as will be seen, the resulting nosing lines are straight lines, which is always the case when a true helical line is developed on the flat. Draw lines parallel with the nosing lines, shown dotted-in, to give working margins for the veneer, with sufficient also to cover the carriage timbers. The dotted rectangles on the plan, Fig. 6, Pl. XXIII., show the thickness of the blocks required to cut a section of back string to carry three steps. The edge mould (Fig. 5, Pl. XXIII.) shows its length. It is usual with stairs of this description to strengthen the outside string by the insertion of a steel band, screwed inside and under the steps, as indicated by the shaded lines in Fig. 2, Pl. XXII. This band is inserted after the stair is fixed. The method of setting out and constructing framed soffits for spiral stairs is described at page 96.

CHAPTER XV.

VARIETIES OF ELLIPTIC STAIRS.

(Plates XXIV. AND XXV.)

No. 1. An Elliptic Geometrical Stair, with cut-and-bracketed outside string, is shown in plan and elevation, Figs. 1 and 2, Pl. XXIV. Undoubtedly these are the most elegant of the geometrical stairs. The long sweeping curves of the strings and handrails have a very graceful appearance.

They are of course suitable for large apartments only. A considerable difference of opinion exists as to the best method of setting out the plans of elliptic stairs, and three principal methods are herein described, with their developments on Pl. xxv., to make clear their effect upon the falling lines. In the plan, Fig. 1, Pl. XXIV, the Walking Line has been made the guiding ellipse ; this has been set out at 18 ins. within the proposed line of handrail, as shown in dotted line, then the faces of the strings made parallel, or rather, equi-distant from it, throughout each curve. Neither of these curves, however, are true ellipses, from a geometrical point of view. Next, a suitable width of step being decided on, this is spaced out along the walking line to ascertain the number required to complete the going of the stair—the " going " in a curved stair being the distance between the faces of the first and last risers—then each string is divided up equally into the number of parts so found and the faces of the risers drawn between the corresponding points. With the exception of the first four steps, all the full lines show risers, the strings are drawn in full lines, the handrail in dotted lines, excepting the scroll and part over first five steps. The naked flooring of the landing is shown, with part of the rough curb lining the well. The position of the carriages, C, are indicated in full lines in the plan and in dotted lines in the elevation.

The double lines marked S are the herring-bone strutting between the joists ; F indicates the furrings for the apron lining to the well.

The Development of the Strings is shown in Fig. 1, Pl. xxv. The method of producing these has already been fully explained (see p. 48), and will be easily followed in the drawings. The wall string is formed by the laminated method, illustrated and described in connection with circular newel stairs. The shape of the drum required in this instance is

PLATE XXIV

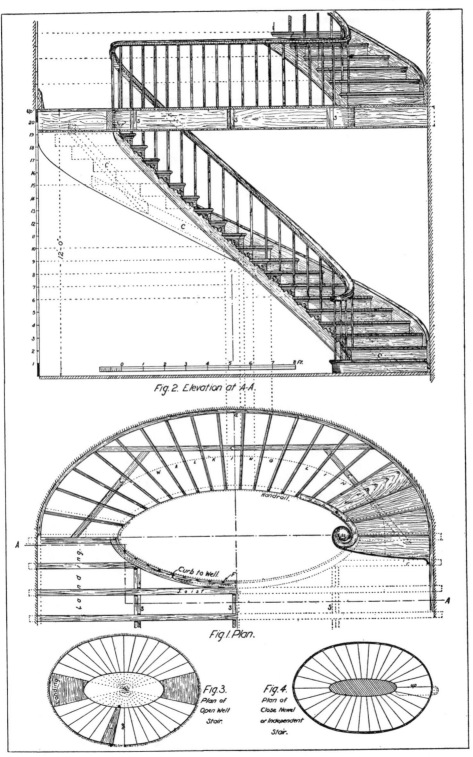

Fig. 2. Elevation at A-A.

Fig. 1. Plan.

Fig. 3.
Plan of
Open Well
Stair.

Fig. 4.
Plan of
Close Newel
or Independent
Stair.

VARIETIES OF ELLIPTIC STAIRS.

PLATE XXV.

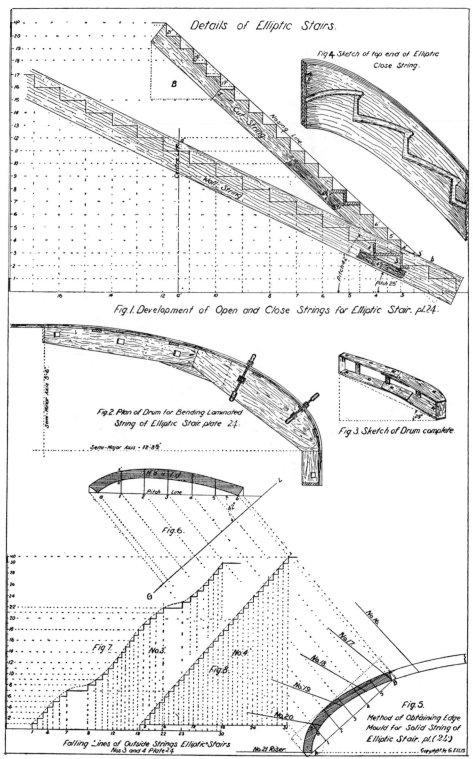

Details of Elliptic Stairs.

Fig 4. Sketch of top end of Elliptic Close String.

Fig. I. Development of Open and Close Strings for Elliptic Stair. pl.24.

Fig.2. Plan of Drum for Bending Laminated String of Elliptic Stair. plate 24.

Semi-Minor Axis 31·6"

Semi-Major Axis - 12·8½

Fig 3. Sketch of Drum complete.

Fig.6.

Pitch Line

Fig 7.

Fig 8.

No.3.

No.4.

No.16

No.17

No.18

No.19

No.20

No.21 Riser.

Fig.5. Method of Obtaining Edge Mould for Solid String of Elliptic Stair. pl.(24)

Falling Lines of Outside Strings Elliptic Stairs Nos 3 and 4 Plate 24

Copyright by G. Ellis.

CONSTRUCTIVE DETAILS OF ELLIPTIC STAIRS.

shown in the isometric sketch (Fig. 3, Pl. xxv.), as if standing at the correct pitch of the stair, drawn thus to indicate that the ribs must stand plumb over each other. A plan of the drum to larger scale is drawn in Fig. 2, Pl. xxv., to indicate the method of using it, two laminæ are there shown bent around the drum and held in position with handscrews, these laminæ are steamed in a steam chest until pliable, then gradually bent around and screwed as shown and left on the drum until they acquire a permanent set and are then glued together one at a time, starting at the lower end and working towards the middle ; one-half only should be glued up and allowed to dry before glueing the other half. The drum can then be reversed and used for the top half. A few headless wire nails should be driven in the waste parts of the first board, to keep it in position on the drum. Three half-inch boards are generally used for wall strings, and a sketch of the top end of the finished string constructed thus is shown in Fig. 4, Pl. xxv.

The open string is cut out of the solid, and joined up in sections, as described at page 50. The method of obtaining the edge mould for the top section, covering four steps, is shown in Figs. 5 and 6, Pl. xxv., the former being a part of the plan reproduced, showing the risers in their relative position, and the latter the elevation. This section of the string is also shown at B in Fig. 1, Pl. xxv., which is the falling mould, and Fig. 6, Pl. xxv., the edge mould. The method of obtaining both has been explained in connection with circular stairs, and does not need repetition.

No. 2. An Elliptic Spiral Open Well Stair, with two quarter landings, is shown in the plan, Fig. 3, Pl. xxiv. This type of stair is built within an elliptic apartment or well, and more usually they are constructed of stone or marble than of wood. The plan of the handrail is an ellipse, and the wall line is made parallel or equi-distant to it. The steps are set out equally around the wall line, to the maximum width desired, and the riser lines drawn therefrom, to the centre of the well, as indicated by the dotted projectors. The resultant falling line is shown in Fig. 7, No. 3, Pl. xxv., and produces over the landings what is known as a ramped wreath.

No. 3. An Elliptic Close Newel or Independent Stair is shown in plan, Fig. 4, Pl. xxiv., and its development in No. 4, Fig. 8, Pl. xxv. The " newel " in this instance, is a brick wall, elliptic in plan, and the stair winds around it in a complete spiral. The handrail is drawn " parallel " with the newel ellipse, and the steps are divided equally along the wall lines ; the maximum width, as in the last case, deciding how many steps are to be used.

CHAPTER XVI.

THREE–WAY BRIDGE STAIRS FOR RAILWAY PLATFORMS.

(PLATES XXVI. AND XXVII.)

Description—Difference between a Footbridge and a Stair—Limitations of Design—How Headroom
is Obtained—Design for a Rural Station—Timber to Use—Need for Thick Treads to Steps—
Details of Constructing Steps—Solid Bracketing—Framing of the Carriages—Fixing the Angle
Braces--Construction of the Braced Girder Balustrade—A Framed and Panelled Arched Balustrade—Construction of Platforms—Method of Securing the Newel Posts.

Three-way Bridge Stairs for Railway Platforms are illustrated on Pl. XXVI. These
accommodations, provided at railway stations for the purpose of enabling passengers to cross
the track from one platform to another, without danger from the trains running between
them, display in their design and construction characteristics both of the footbridge and the
stair. The essential difference between a bridge and a stair lies chiefly in the method of its
ascent. In the former the traveller advances gradually either along a level, inclined, or arched
footway; whilst in the latter he moves upwards and forwards in a series of intermittent
steps. It is impossible without breaking a fundamental rule in stair construction, viz. the
continuity of " going " or width of step in a flight, to have an arched stair; therefore in utilising
the bridge or arched form, for the string and balustrade, the constructor is limited within
chord lines of the arch adopted for the actual depth of the stair. For the purpose in view,
however, this proves no drawback, as the flight obtained within the chord lines of the given
arch in Fig. 2, Pl. XXVI., comprises twelve steps, which is considered by many authorities
the maximum number for an uninterrupted flight that may be ascended without fatigue.

The central space is occupied by a level platform, or landing, as it would be termed in
house stairs, and the necessary headroom over the main platform is obtained by springing the
bridge from a mid-platform, raised to the necessary height upon four posts, which serve also
as newels for the stairs above. This mid-platform is reached by flights of thirteen steps on
either side, the second flight of course only being necessary when there are exits at each end
of the station platform. The plans and elevations being symmetrical need only one-half of
each to be shown, and as the principles of construction are alike in both cases the drawings
are utilised to furnish two designs; the one referred to in Figs. 1, 4 and 6, is a somewhat
lighter and simpler construction—suitable for rural stations—than is the one shown in elevations, Figs. 2, Pl. XXVI., and 5, Pl. XXVII., and in plan, Fig. 3, Pl. XXVII., which is more suitable
for a large town station. The more important details of construction are given in enlarged
sections in Figs. 7, 8 and 9, Pl. XXVI. The dimensions of the timbers are for execution in
English oak or in Indian teak, with the exception of the carriages, which are calculated for
heavy pine, American (pitch-pine) or Baltic (" Dantzic "). The construction of the stairs
being in many respects similar to that of newel stairs already explained, only those details
which differ from standard types need be mentioned. The treads are thicker than is usual,

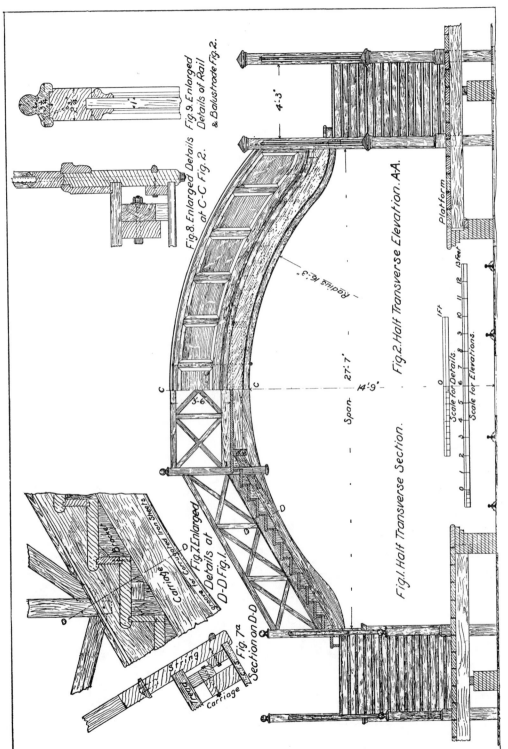

PLATE XXVI.

Fig.9.Enlarged Details of Rail & Balustrade Fig.2.

Fig.8.Enlarged Details at C-C Fig.2.

4'-3"

Platform

Radius 16'-3"

Fig.2.Half Transverse Elevation. A-A.

Span 27'-7'

14'-9'

3'-6'

C   C

Fig.1. Half Transverse Section.

1Ft

Scale for Details.

0 1 2 3 4 5 6 7 8 9 10 11 12 13Feet

Scale for Elevations.

Carriage

Groove for Corrugated Iron Sheets

Fig.7.Enlarged Details at D-D Fig.1.

Fig. 7ª Section on D-D

Carriage

D   D

A THREE-WAY RAILWAY BRIDGE STAIR.

PLATE XXVII.

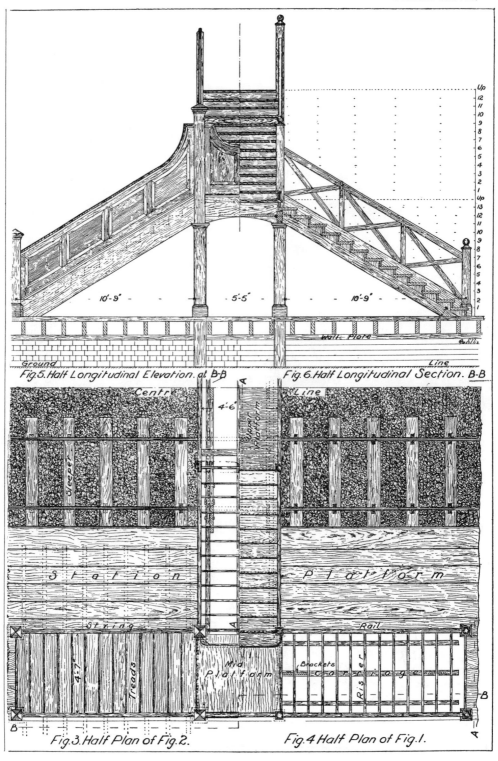

Fig.5. Half Longitudinal Elevation. at B-B   Fig.6. Half Longitudinal Section. B-B

Fig.3. Half Plan of Fig.2.   Fig.4 Half Plan of Fig.1.

A THREE-WAY RAILWAY BRIDGE STAIR.

finishing 2 ins. in consequence of the heavy traffic to which these are subjected. The risers finish 1 in. thick, and are tongued into the treads above and below, as shown in Fig. 7, Pl. XXVI.; the top tongue is glued but the bottom one left dry to accommodate shrinkage. The nosings overhang 1 in. only. Each step is housed into the strings ¾ in., and every third tread is stub-tenoned in addition. Each step is solid-bracketed along the middle carriage-piece, the brackets so cut that the treads rest on the end grain. Four of these brackets are shown in the plan, Fig. 4, Pl. XXVII., to indicate position of the remainder. The carriages are framed and bolted to cross-bearers, the angle-braces lapped and bolted together, as shown in the details, Figs. 7a and 8, Pl. XXVI., also in the transverse elevation, Fig. 1, Pl. XXVI. The open-braced balustrade in Fig. 1, Pl. XXVI., is framed into the strings and handrails as seen in the detail, Fig. 7, Pl. XXVI., and forms, with the arched string, a braced girder.

The braces are halved together at their crossings, and secured with screws. The framed balustrade in Fig. 2, Pl. XXVI., is made and fixed separately from the strings, to which it is secured by ½-in. bolts taken through the muntings, as shown in Fig. 8, Pl. XXVI. This framework acts also as a girder to support the stairs.

The method of fixing the handrail is indicated in the enlarged detail, Fig. 9, Pl. XXVI., which is drawn to double the scale of the remaining details.

The newel posts are taken through the platform down to the ground, where they are bedded upon a stone slab. It is most usual to cover the soffits of the bridge with corrugated sheet iron, bent to the required curve, to protect the woodwork against sparks from the engines, and the groove to receive the edges of the sheets is shown in the details, Figs. 7 and 8, Pl. XXVI. These are further secured by bolting them to cross-bearers that are not shown in the drawings.

Note.—Owing to the exigency of plate dimensions, the two sets of drawings have been crowded at the middle of the plate, but this was thought to be a lesser evil than to reduce the scale of the whole set, to obtain wider clearance between them.

CHAPTER XVII.

CONSTRUCTIONAL DETAILS OF STANDARD AND EXCEPTIONAL TYPES OF STAIRS, WITH METHODS OF EXECUTION.

(PLATES XXVIII, XXIX, AND XXX.)

Introductory Note—Types of Strings and Steps Illustrated—Close Strings—Connection to Newel—Proper Form of Tenon—Sunk Panels—Machine Recessing, Hand Processes—Moulded Strings—Open Strings, Varieties of—Why Brackets are Used—Step Construction, Good and Bad Methods Contrasted, Fixing the Backs—Cause of "Squeaking"—Shaped Steps—Straight Winders——Radiating Winders—Common Defects, how to avoid them—Raking Risers, their Advantage—Curved Risers—Construction of a Bullnose Step, forming Block, Bending Veneer—Thickness of Veneer for Various Woods—Method of Glueing-up—Round-End Steps—Construction of—Veneering—Commode Steps, Meaning of the Term, Two Varieties—Formation of Ribs—to Prevent Veneer Bulging—Attaching Round-end—Tower Steps—Cove Steps—Using the Caul—Curtail Steps, Construction of—Preparing Flyer Steps—Jointing—Use of Cradle, Construction of Same—Glueing-up—Building the Stair—Fitting the Nosings—Fitting the Risers—Wedging-up—Cut-and-Mitred Strings, Fitting up, Polished Work—Method of Securing the Mitres—Attaching Brackets—Method of Stiffening Balustrades—Iron Balustrades, Spacing, a Common Form, its Defects—The Kneed Baluster—Baluster with Three-way Flange—the Plug and Screwed Baluster—Method of Fixing Top Ends of Balusters—Wrought-iron Balustrades, how Fixed—Templet for the Core—Cappings, how Fixed—Balusters, Various Methods of Fixing—Dovetailing—Fixing to Solid Steps—Uncommon Forms of Stair—Open Soffit Stair with Wrought and Moulded Treads and Risers, Construction of—Stringless Stairs—Solid Steps—Framed Steps—Fixing Carved Ends.

In the several examples of various types of stairs described in preceding chapters their appropriate constructive details are included, but in addition to these standard methods, there are many variations of detail applicable both to these examples and to others under certain circumstances, that reference to, in those descriptions, would have tended to confuse the reader. Therefore it has been thought better to collect these minor variations—which, however, are in some instances themselves " types "—and constructive details to be dealt with in a separate chapter. The author believes this method will be found conducive to easy reference, even if, to some slight extent, it makes the treatment of the subject appear somewhat disjointed. Moreover, there are a few suggestions that the author has not yet seen in practice, which may be offered here for consideration.

Types of Strings and Steps (Pl. XXVIII.).—" **Close** " or **Housed Strings.** Figs. 1, 2, 3 are elevation, plan, and section respectively of an outside close string, framed into the lower newel, with a pair of tenons, drawbore pinned, showing various treatments of the steps, carriages and balusters. Referring first to the tenons on the string, no definite rule can be laid down for either their size or position, which will depend largely on circumstances, but the joiner must, whilst considering these, bear in mind that the main object of the tenon is to provide a means of bringing the newel up to the shoulder and retaining it there. Given sufficient strength for this purpose, any increase in size of the tenon merely weakens the newel. Wedging cannot be employed, because the newel must be tried on several times during the process of fitting the string, steps and handrail.

The post cannot conveniently be cramped up, thus we are constrained to use the draw-bore pin (No. 1, 2, Pl. xxvii.), and naturally this is kept as small as is consistent with strength, also it should not be driven through the face or outside of the newel for the sake of appearance. In setting out the mortises, great care must be taken not to make any undercut, or raking mortises, for obviously the newel could not then be got on, after the step is fixed in the string (which is the usual practice), if it had to move in two directions, that is to say, either upwards or downwards, whilst at the same time advancing to the shoulder. Illustrations in books frequently err in this item, at once stamping their writers as unpractical; a study of Fig. 1, Pl. xxviii., will make this point clear. The statement may be otherwise put, that the tenons must be so cut that the newel can be knocked on in a direction perpendicular to the shoulder, and that the portion of the tenon to be cut away in its width must leave the grain or fibre unsevered up to the shoulder. For painted and all common work bare-faced tenons are used, with the shoulder inside, as shown in Fig. 2, Pl. xxviii., but in a superior class of work, *double* shoulders would of course be used. It is not necessary to keep the tenon in the middle of the thickness.

The string shown in Fig. 3, Pl. xxviii., has a sunk panel worked in the solid, a method that would be adopted in machine shops, where the string would be placed upon the table of a recessing machine, and the sinking made with a vertical revolving cutter, the edges being afterwards moulded with spindle cutters, brought down in like manner from the top frame. If sham rails were to be shown, the moulder and recessor would finish at the rail line, with a circular end, to be squared out and mitred by hand. In a hand-shop, the lower rail would be ploughed-and-tongued on, as indicated in dotted lines, after the sinking for the panel had been made. This device is often adopted when the available stuff is not wide enough to make the string in one piece; the joint is hidden by the moulding (see also Fig. 9, Pl. xxviii.). It is common practice to stick an inch return bead on the lower edge of strings and to rebate the latter back to the quirk, for 1 in. deep, to receive the lath and plaster soffit, as shown in Fig. 3, Pl. xxviii. When the string is not sufficiently thick to provide a nail-hold for the laths, a fillet, or rough string, as shown in Fig. 12, Pl. xiv., and Fig. 5, Pl. xii., is fixed to the inside of the string.

Another form of moulded close string is shown in section and elevation (Figs. 9 and 10, Pl. xxviii.). This design is suitable for a hardwood string; the swelled central part is sometimes enriched with carving; the margin mouldings which are sunk into grooves may also be enriched. Further designs of close strings are given on Pl. xxxvii., Fig. 10, showing a sunk moulded and inlaid string, suitable for execution in mahogany or walnut; the inlays would be of darker coloured woods for the mahogany, and lighter coloured woods for the walnut string.

Open or Cut Strings are shown in Figs. 4, 5, 6, 7, Pl. xxviii. Methods of fitting cut strings in sundry ways have already been dealt with at pages 44-5 in connection with the geometrical stair, also with the circular stair, Pl. xxiii., and the views given on this plate may be considered supplementary thereto. The elevation (Fig. 4, Pl. xxviii.) shows, in the one view, two kinds of cut string. The lower two steps are called plain mitred or " cut-and-mitred; " the end of the riser is mitred to fit the notch in the string and finishes flush with its outside. The third step shows a " cut-and-bracketed " string, a thin ornamental fret or bracket is fixed to the face of the string under the tread, and eventually covered at its top edge by the return nosing and scotia, as indicated in dotted lines. The riser in this case runs over the string a distance equal to the thickness of the bracket, as shown in Figs. 6 and 7, Pl. xxviii. Brackets were first used to produce the effect of solid steps, in imitation of masonry; for the earlier forms of stair, both in stone and wood, has solid strings, either built into walls or supported on corbels, or brackets, projecting from the walls, and the purely ornamental brackets of the

Georgian period were made much thicker than in present practice. They were frequently richly carved. The modern bracket is simply a thin fret, glued to the string and utilised to hide the nails required in fixing the notched string to the steps, as indicated in Fig. 5, Pl. XXVIII.

Steps may be formed in numerous ways, but experience proves that generally the simplest methods are the best. The intricate groove and tongue joints between the risers and treads that are often shown in books would not, even if executed—and in many years' practice the author has not seen them used—produce stronger steps than the methods advocated in this book. Variations to meet special requirements are of course necessary, such as are shown in connection with circular stairs and curved steps at pages 47 and 48, but for all straight work there is no joint superior to the square, glued, rubbed and blocked joint shown at a and a', Fig. 1, Pl. XXVIII., and Fig. 22, Pl. XXIX. The necessary bench work in making these steps is described at page 69, etc. The best method of fixing the back of the tread to the riser above is by means of screws, passed through slots cut in the tread, as shown at d and d', Figs. 1 and 2, Pl. XXVIII.; a bevel chase is made in the tread, in which the head of the screw slides. Sometimes iron or zinc washers are used instead of this, see the sketch, Fig. $3a$; which makes it possible to use screws of a smaller size. In the commonest work wire nails take the place of screws, with the result very often that the treads split during shrinkage. The method of tonguing the bottom edge of the riser into the tread beneath, as at e, Fig. 1, Pl. XXVIII., is suitable for cut-string stairs, or in outside work, such as the railway stair shown on Fig. 7, Pl. XXVI., page 58, where much swelling and shrinkage may take place. Unless the middle of the steps are supported by blockings or rough brackets, shown at E and D, Fig. 1, Pl. XXVIII., this method of jointing is likely to produce objectional " squeaking." Carrying the riser below the tread, and tonguing the latter into it, as shown at f, is sometimes done when the tread is wide, to avoid the necessity of jointing, but there is nothing constructively to recommend it.

Shaped Steps.—Winders are the commonest form of shaped step and these may have either straight or curved risers, as will be seen on reference to the plans of newel stair on Pl. V. Straight winders are, apart from the shape of the tread, formed similarly to straight flyers, and the description of the process given at page 68 will refer equally to both. Curved winders are constructed similarly to bullnose and commode risers, to which reference is made further on. Some remarks upon the planning of winders have been made in Chapter I., page 3, and the appearance of a half-space of six winders, with their risers radiating from the centre of the newel, is sketched in Fig. 1, Pl. XXIX., to show that the crowded appearance produced in the plan by this arrangement is by no means so evident in the elevation, or in the actual stair. There is, however, one defect in steps so arranged that may be avoided by a slight alteration in the planning. This is the birdsmouthing over the angles of the newel made by the third and sixth winders. In the plan, Fig. 3, Pl. XXIX., it is shown how this may be avoided. Set out the first winder at such a distance from the front of the newel that the nosing of the tread will stand about $\frac{3}{16}$ in. back from its edge, then describe two concentric circles, as shown in dotted lines, one for the walking line at 15 ins. from the centre, the other just clear of the angles of the newel; divide up the risers equally around these two lines and draw them through the division points. It will be found in each instance to bring the nosing within the edge of the face of the newel upon which the riser impinges, as seen in the isometric projection of the newel in Fig. 4, Pl. XXVIII. This sketch is utilised also to show the method of obtaining more foot space near the newel by the device of raking risers. The method is seen more distinctly in the enlarged detail, Fig. 5, Pl. XXIX. The amount of inclination given to the risers is a matter of taste; here 1 in. is given, and provides 3 ins. of tread at the newel. These steps can be made as easily as the square variety, by using an appropriate cradle in which to rub them, but the face edge of the treads must be bevelled, as

PLATE XXVIII.

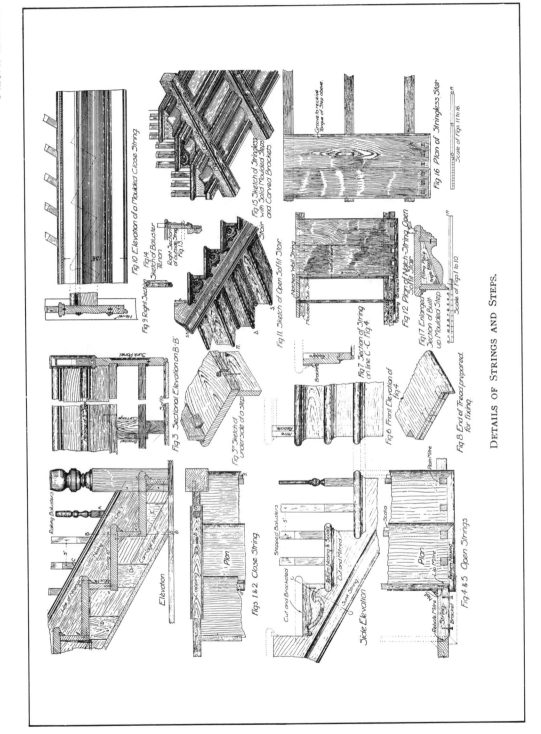

DETAILS OF STRINGS AND STEPS.

PLATE XXIX.

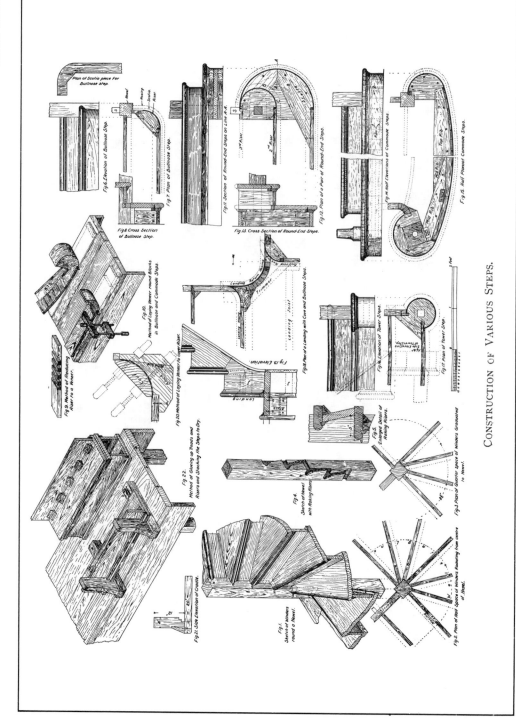

CONSTRUCTION OF VARIOUS STEPS.

indicated at *a*, before ploughing the scotia groove. Bevelling is not necessary when the ſtuff is to be machine grooved, but in this case either a tilting table muſt be used or the ſtuff run over a tilting piece fixed against the fence.

Curved Steps were formerly cut out of the solid wood to the required shape, but apart from the coſt of this extravagant consumption of material, such ſteps when polished do not show a pleasing regularity of grain ; moreover, we find these old ſteps generally much deformed through unequal shrinkage. The modern method, except in the case of cheap painted ſtairs, is to form such ſteps by bending the risers around shaped ribs, or solid blocks, as beſt suits the particular case. When the curved part is short, and is a continuation of a ſtraight part, the usual method is to reduce a portion of the riser, sufficient in length to cover the block, to a veneer, and to bend this portion around and secure it to the block, in the manner detailed below. When the entire length of the riser is curved, of course the whole face is a veneer, and alternative methods of forming the shaping ribs, or backing, are described subsequently.

The Bullnose or Quarter-round Step shown in the three views, Figs. 6, 7, 8, Pl. xxix., is conſtructed in the following manner. The riser is set out full size, similar to Fig. 7, Pl. xxix., the radius of the quadrant, of course, being a matter of choice, but there muſt always be at leaſt $1\frac{1}{2}$ in. of ſtraight wood beyond the springing, to serve as an abutment and fixing for the block. A turning piece or " block " is prepared, cut either from a solid piece of pine of the necessary thickness, or built up in two or more layers as necessary. It may be pointed out that nothing is gained by building such short thick blocks as this, in layers, and in faſt the facings are more likely to ſtand if the block is cut in the solid. As much side grain as possible should be placed at the front, because this holds glue better than the end grain. Shape the block as shown in the plan, making the end shoulder slightly undercut ; the other shoulder muſt be exaſtly on the springing line and be cut square to the front. The block should be firſt prepared, the ſtuff muſt be made bone-dry and well rubbed over with thin glue to fill the pores, and finally either toothed with a plane or well scratched with coarse glass paper. Prepare the riser by planing to a parallel thickness, then set off the diſtance of the end springing from the newel, making due allowance for the housing into the latter, then place the shoulder of the block on the springing line and roll the block carefully along the back of the riser until the opposite springing is reached. Mark this point, allow about $\frac{5}{8}$ in. extra for wedge room, then square across. Next, gauge the veneer from the face between these lines. The thickness of the veneer will depend upon the kind of wood used, also to some extent on the quickness of the sweep. Deal or soft pine, pitch-pine and English oak may be reduced to $\frac{1}{8}$ in. thick for curves of 5 ins. radius and upwards. For less radius than this, thinner veneer muſt be used. Mahogany, walnut, red cedar, teak or jarrah will not safely bend to above radius if above $\frac{1}{12}$ in. thick, unless ſteamed for some time, whilſt such woods as green ash, birch, crowsfoot, elm, cheſtnut, blackwood and Tasmanian red myrtle (all favourite ſtaircase woods) will bend freely up to $\frac{1}{4}$ in. thick. It may be added that, if sufficiently ſteamed, moſt of these woods would bend to a quarter circle even if 1 in. thick, but there are objeſtions to such high ſteaming, for the natural secretions in the pores often thus are dissolved and the wood quickly perishes. In a machine shop the recessed part of the risers would be cut out by the band saw, but if to be reduced by hand, the beſt way is to fix the riser firmly to the bench, cut in the shoulders and run several tenon-ſaw cuts across the core down to the gauge lines ; these cuts should not be more than 1 in. apart ; remove the core by chipping carefully between two adjacent cuts alternately, thus forming a series of trenches across the ſtuff, as shown at Fig. 9, Pl. xxix. ; finish each trench neatly with a router, taking care not to rout out too coarsely, and so ſtart a shake in the veneer. Having thus removed half the area of the core, next chip away one of the shaded portions at a time, and level its seat.   Leave the middle one until last, to serve as a bed for the router.   The method of gluing the block to the riser is illustrated in the sketch, Fig. 10, Pl. xxix., at the near side of the bench.   The riser, with its veneer part, well saturated on both sides with hot water, to render it pliable, is fixed firmly, as shown in dotted lines, near the tail of the bench, then the block, made as hot as possible over a gas jet, is glued at its undercut lip and screwed down to the riser.   Whilst an assistant spreads glue over the face of both block and veneer, the joiner must slowly roll the block along, pressing down as heavily as possible to squeeze out the glue, and listen intently for any sign of splitting ; should this unfortunately happen, the only thing to be done is to start afresh and use a caul outside, this will be described under " Cove Riser," but if all goes well, when the block reaches the back of the riser, as shown in full line in Fig. 10, Pl. xxix., the assistant should glue, and gently tap in, a pair of folding wedges.   The riser must be turned up and examined, the vaneer tapped with the knuckles to ascertain if it is everywhere solid, if not, the wedge on the slack edge must be further tapped, then the block laid back and the fixing screws turned in.   Some joiners prefer to soak the veneer end in hot water, then bend it " dry " (i.e. without glue) around the block, turning the screws in and allowing all the water to dry out before gluing up ; this is quite logical treatment, but the author has glued up dozens safely as described above.   The process has been rather fully treated in this simple case, because, with such obvious variations as the shapes determine, it will answer for all veneered steps, which are manipulated in a like manner. The sketch of a bench has been further utilised to show thereon the process of laying the veneer of a round-end commode step, presently to be described.   It would not of course be done at the end of the bench shown, except by a left-handed man, but space here is valuable. The process, up to the springing of the round end, will be exactly as described for the bull-nose step, but the veneer over the curved front must be laid with a caul ; a sheet of zinc is best for this purpose, if it can be obtained, because zinc retains heat longer than wood, but a piece of pine board ¼ in. thick will answer the purpose ; this is heated and applied to the face of the veneer after the latter is glued, and either cramped up to the back ribs shown in the sketch, with numerous handscrews, or rib cauls shaped to fit the face curve are made, with their back edges parallel to the shaping ribs, and these two are clamped together with the hot caul between.   The step shown is a single-ended one ; if it were double-ended the other end block would not be attached until the front veneer had set hard, because of the difficulty of dealing with such a long glued surface at once.

Also the wedging to bring the block veneer close would have to be done at the back end, and of course the undercut at that end would be omitted, being unnecessary, as the thick end can be bradded through the face, where it is hidden in the housing of the newel, or string, as the case may be.   Note that the grain of the backing pieces glued at the ends of the veneer must run in the same direction as that of the veneer, and not across.

Round End Steps, also known as semi-circular steps, but *not* as bullnose in the trade, are constructed as shown in Figs. 11, 12, 13, Pl. xxix.   Two round-end steps are here super-posed ; either variety may be used separately with practically no difference in the construction. Considering the bottom step first, the end of the riser is reduced to a veneer, which is bent around a built-up block in the manner previously described.   The top of the block is shown in the plan, Fig. 12, Pl. xxix., with the tread removed, the outer dotted line indicating its position, the inner that of the scotia-moulding beneath.   This block, being of large size, is built up in three thicknesses, the middle layer C running right across to stiffen the block. The proper direction of the grain of the several pieces is indicated in the drawings ; the pieces, are first glued and screwed, or nailed together ; when dry, cut to the shape and prepare for veneering.   The holes shown in the block in plan are for the passage of the screwdriver when turning in the screws used for fixing the scotia piece to the tread, because the scotia must be fixed in this case to the riser first. The scotia, or other bed mould, in shaped steps is always worked in the solid and must be sufficiently wide to overhang the back of the riser at back, as shown in the section Fig. 13, Pl. XXIX., that it may provide a means of fixing the tread to the riser. The newel post is housed into the tread, and tenoned right through the blocks (see etching on Fig. 12, Pl. XXIX.). The second step, being smaller, may have its block formed from a single piece of yellow pine; the side grain of the block should be at the crown of the curve, as this is the part that has to depend almost entirely on the glue to keep in position.

Commode Steps, a term borrowed from the French, who so describe any step with a swelling front, as in like manner it is applied to round front furniture. Commode steps are generally associated with either curtail or round ends, though occasionally they are intro-duced in close-string stairs, when of course they are housed, just as are the straight steps. Two varieties, with different round ends, are shown in plan, Fig. 15, Pl. XXIX. and elevation, Fig. 14, Pl. XXIX. For the sake of variety an iron newel post is introduced in the one case, in the other a square based wood newel; this of course has no special signification, as any form newel may be used. Dealing with the right-hand example first, to which some allusion has already been made in the paragraph on veneering, it will be seen that the round end has the ordinary solid block, which is attached to two 1-in. shaped ribs, which are lined with thin staves glued and nailed to the ribs, afterwards cleaned off accurately to the sweep as shown in the sketch, Fig. 10, Pl. XXIX., where the top rib is broken away that the backing may be seen more clearly. Around this backing, the veneer is bent; the chief objection to this method is that the backing and the veneer cross-grain, so are liable to shrink unequally and thus start shakes or bulges in the veneer. The risk is not very great if all the wood is thoroughly dry, but the method shown on the left hand of Fig. 15, Pl. XXIX., obviates this risk altogether. Here the backings are formed out of thick stuff placed on edge, first attached to a mid-rib which is crossed, screwed and blocked, then the front is cleaned off to the required shape and veneered as previously described. The round end being a large return, its block is built up sideways in like manner, tongued together for preference at the joints, though often only tush nailed. The central core in this instance is better set end grain up, as shown.

The Tower Step shown in front elevation, Fig. 16, Pl. XXIX., plan, Fig. 17, Pl. XXIX., and an end elevation in dotted line thereon, Fig. 16a, Pl. XXIX., is used to turn the corner of a project-ing square step. Its construction will be quite clear from the drawings: the veneer is generally laid with a caul, but may be bent and wedged as in the usual round-end step; the end backing and wedging pieces will, however, be cut away, as shown in Fig. 17, Pl. XXIX., when fixing the block to the string and riser, over the ends of which the block is slipped, and screwed as shown.

A Cove Step, used in association with a bullnose step on a landing, for the purpose of obtaining a better easing in the handrail, is shown in part plan, Fig. 18, Pl. XXIX., and sec-tional elevation, Fig. 19, Pl. XXIX. An extreme turn in the cove or hollow riser is shown, as being the most difficult to construct; usually less than a quadrant is formed, resulting in a blunt junction with the string; this, however, though easier to construct, does not look so well as a quadrant turn. The string is turned at the angle in the usual way upon a cylinder, as described in connection with the geometrical stair (p. 37).

The cove riser is reduced to a veneer at the end, which is steamed and bent into a hollow block, by means of a reverse mould or " caul." The latter is brought close up to the veneer by means of handscrews, as indicated in the enlarged drawing, Fig. 20, Pl. XXIX. The caul must be heated and a sheet of paper interposed between it and the veneer, in case any stray glue gets between. Four handscrews will be required, two upon each edge. When the block is dry, it is cut to the mitre line as shown. This portion of the landing must be set out full size on a rod to obtain the correct shape for the blocks and caul, also the mitre lines.

The other block has already been described; the end backing at C is cut away when fixing the riser to the string.

Scroll or Curtail Steps, so-called because, though the end of the tread is worked into a scroll concentric with that of the handrail, the curve of the riser is curtailed to avoid a narrow space that could not be kept clean. A description of the setting-out of these steps is given at page 75, and it need only be added to here that the veneer is bent around and attached similarly to that of the round-end step. That portion which lines the block on the hollow side, eventually to form part of the string, must be laid with a caul as described for the cove step preceding. If a joint in the string is not objected to, it is more convenient to lay this veneer before bending the face veneer around the curtail, but for polished work the usual requirement is to continue the string into the neck of the curtail step, as shown in Fig. 15, Pl. xxix., in which case the lower end must be reduced to a veneer and laid in the block when attaching the step to the string.

Preparing Straight Steps.—Ordinary closed-in steps are not wrought on the back or insides of the treads and risers, as obviously it would be waste of time, where they are not seen, and they also stand better if not planed, but as a glue joint must be made near the fore edge, also a groove sunk in, to receive the scotia or other bed moulding used, it is necessary to plane a portion of the tread underneath for about $3\frac{1}{2}$ ins. from the front edge to a true surface, which however will be bevelled or sloped towards the face edge; consequently the edge of the riser must also be bevelled to the complementary angle, to ensure its face being at right angles with the face of the tread. For the purpose of avoiding the trouble of setting a bevel for each tread, also to facilitate the rubbing of the joint, an apparatus called a **Cradle** is generally used. This appliance consists of a pair of frames having their interior faces square, that is to say, at right angles to each other, as shown in elevation, Fig. 21, Pl. xxix., with notches cut in the angle, to receive the projections of the tread and scotia slip; appropriate dimensions are figured thereon. These cradles are fixed, by a couple of screws in each, to the bench, near the tail end, as in the view given in Fig. 22, Pl. xxix. The treads, previously planed and grooved and squared off to neat lengths, with the scotia slips mulleted in, are placed on the cradle as shown, the button at the rear end turned to grip the back edge, then the riser is shot straight in the bench screw and tested; a couple of trials usually suffice to obtain a perfect joint, and the whole set of steps is thus gone through; the riser and treads folded together and piled in front as shown, ready for gluing. When all are ready, slips and risers duly squared off to length—by the way it will be found the best method to mark them all off to length by one length-slip, unless squared off to length in the machine, when this will be unnecessary—take a tread with its corresponding riser and slip, glue the latter in, push the tread tightly up to the notch, then glue both scotia-back and the edge of riser, and rub to a joint, finally rub in a few angle blocks at the back, keeping them $1\frac{1}{2}$ in. from each end, to clear the string wedges. The step may now be carefully removed from the cradle, and stacked in a pile either on the bench as shown in the drawing, or on the floor, according to their number, where they should remain twelve hours to dry, when they may be nosed and moulded either by hand or machine, and papered off. It is a mistake to mould them before gluing up, as is sometimes advised; very irregular work will result, if so done. The cradle, as described above, may be used also for winders, but with tongued risers, such as are required in the bridge stair (Fig. 7, Pl. xxvi.), a slight variation in the shape of the upright will be necessary. In this case the risers cannot be rubbed, therefore they must be wedged down into the tread. Consequently the upright leg of the cradle must be made about 6 ins. longer than the depth of the riser, and the thickness of the riser wider, so that it may be recessed sufficiently to receive the riser, and to provide an abutment for a pair of folding wedges above it. This is the only occasion on which wedges are used, as of course they are quite unnecessary for a rubbed joint, and are more likely to spoil than improve the joint if used, also their insertion and removal after each rubbing would be a waste of time. Cradles for special steps, such as Fig. 5, Pl. XXIX., require the leg to be set, or cut to the given angle, with the tread. Nailing or screwing risers at the back does more harm than good. A properly made, glued joint will never separate, except under the action of long-continued dampness.

Building the Stair.—These remarks on step construction may well be rounded off with a description of the process of assembling the steps and strings, generally termed " putting the stair together." It will be understood that only a general description of the process can be given, because in practice there are numberless variations in detail according to the particular circumstances, and to attempt a description of these would overload the book.

Each step should be tested for squareness at the ends before fitting. To do this, stand it up one end upon a true surface, such as a tryed-up panel board, and test it with a large set-square ; an ordinary try-square is of course useless for this purpose. Correct it if required by easing either riser or tread. We assume the string is a close one, and that the preliminary housings are made therein as described in previous chapters. Place the string on the bench and fit on the newel, if any, tightening up the shoulder with a drawbore pin (Ill. 1)—not the wood pin be it understood, that will be eventually fixed permanently, but the iron tool with a handle that is used for trying-up purposes. Offer up the first step, mark the positions of the newel thereon, and allow ¼ in. beyond for housing. Cut out to the housing line and again offer up, placing the step in its appropriate housing in the string, when the position of the housings round the newel faces may be marked, the newel removed and these duly cut in.

The next step is placed in its housing, brought up to the riser housing and the outline of nosing and scotia marked, trimmed out with gouges, then the step is fitted in, and dry-wedged. Being satisfied that it fits properly, remove and chisel-mark the end, for identification, and so continue

ILL. 1.—A DRAWBORE PIN.

throughout the string. Then treat the opposite string similarly, starting at the reverse end, as the steps are all piled now in reverse order ; mark these ends also, to avoid mistakes. During the fitting, the width of each riser must be marked by pressing into it a firmer chisel, with its face held tightly against the contiguous tread housing. Both ends being thus marked, shoot the superfluous stuff off, leaving it one shaving full, to make a tight joint. Do not remove any overhang of the tread, but chip off the corners to permit the passage of the next riser wedge. This, however, is generally done when the tread is in position, and the actual gluing-up process is going on. Having fitted all the steps and newels, including any winders that may come into the string, clean off the insides of the strings and prepare for gluing-up. This is managed according to circumstances ; the best arrangement, if possible, is to mount one string, usually the outside wall string, on the bench face up, enter all its steps, then place on their ends the outside string ; lay along this a stout piece of quartering the whole length of the string and strut it down from the joists above, with at least three struts. Observe that all the steps bed squarely and evenly, " look " the two strings out of winding, also the top and bottom nosings, carefully knock up all the treads into their nosings and commence wedging the string that is on the bench.

The wedges should fit exactly and be well glued, knocked home fairly tight, but not so hard as to spring the string, which is sometimes done by the inexperienced workman. Don't use a sledge-hammer ! Two men are required to wedge-up, one on each side of the stair, as the man wedging cannot see whether the treads or risers are home to their place or not, and he must tap them up as the observer advises. When the lower string is done, drive a nail at each end of the top one, into a step where it will not be seen, to prevent movement, unstrut and carefully turn the stair over. Re-strut, and proceed as before, then drive through the outside string three nails into each tread, and two into each riser; the holes for these should have been previously bored from the middle of the housings. Finally, trim off the wedges and block in the angles, then set aside to dry, when the face of the outside string can be cleaned off. Where a strutting bearing cannot be obtained the device shown in Ill. 2 the author has found to answer very well. (This is an invention by the author and first used by him in 1901.) Its construction will be apparent from the drawing. Also large box cleats may be made to slip over the strings. The stair must be mounted on two sawing stools for the purpose, but this method is suitable only for common work. The above described procedure will serve for ordinary cut-string stairs, with the exception that as there are no means of wedging the steps at the cut string, the cut ends must be fitted and fixed singly by either

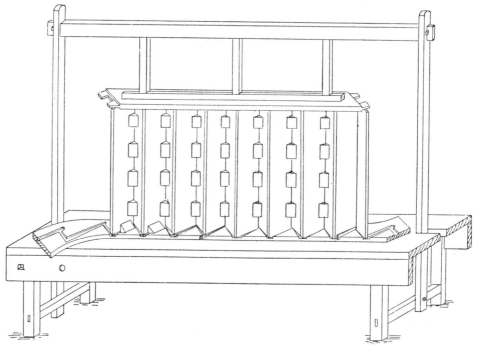

ILL. 2.—BENCH FITTED WITH SADDLE CRAMP FOR PUTTING STAIRS TOGETHER.

bradding them through the front or screwing and blocking at the back. This string must be allowed to dry before the stair can be turned over and the other string proceeded with. In the case of a high-class, cut-and-bracketed stair, the procedure will vary slightly with the form of joint adopted, but assuming the lip mitre shown at Fig. 5, Pl. XXVIII., which is no doubt the best form, then each riser would be mitred by aid of the apparatus shown in Fig. 1, Pl. XLIII., and fitted to the cut string before it was glued to the tread. The rebate or mitre, as the case may be, on the string, would be marked by a templet and gauged from the face, to ensure uniformity. The treads also must be mitred, dovetails run in and, if a tongue is used to fix the return nosing, as shown in Fig. 8, Pl. XXVIII., this groove must be made before the risers can be fixed to them. The scotia slip should be glued in the tread before cutting the mitre, and it is a good method to stop the shoulder cut about an inch from the mitre, and to run the saw only half way down the mitre, not finishing this piece off until after the nosing and scotia have been struck. It is perhaps unnecessary to say that the dovetail cuts are marked on the outside end, and run in, before cutting back the shoulder, whether they are done by hand or machine. When fitting-up, small blocks would be first glued, both to the string and the risers, and allowed to dry, when they would act as clamping pieces for handscrews or thumb-cramps. These temporary blocks would afterwards be chipped away with the chisel to within a shaving of the face of the work, and the remainder washed off with hot water to avoid damage to the surface. In cases where the ornamental bracket practically covers the face of the string, these cramping blocks will not be needed, because a sash cramp can be put on the end of the step to pull it up to the string, then brads driven in from the face as shown in Fig. 5, Pl. xxviii., to be afterwards covered by the bracket.

Another device the author has found useful in dealing with polished work is a method of fixing temporarily the return nosings, which of course cannot be permanently fixed until the balusters are in position. Hold them up with a cramp and drive wire nails on the rake through the core of the dovetails, leaving their heads projecting sufficiently to pull out with pincers.

Methods of Stiffening Balusters.—The balustrades of those stairs that have reverse flights with continuous rails and strings, especially when the wells are narrow, are, from the absence of newels or strengthening posts at the turns, liable to become somewhat insecure, or at least to appear so, as movement may be felt when the rail is pressed outwards. To obviate this defect, iron balusters, cast to the same pattern as the wood ones and provided with various shaped lugs at the bottom end for the purpose of fixing them to the strings in a more secure manner than is possible with the wood balusters, are interposed at intervals, according to requirements, but averaging one at every sixth step. A common form is shown at A, in Figs. 1, 2, 3 and 4, Pl. xxx. In the drawings the foot only of the balusters is shown. In this form the baluster is cast with a shallow sinking upon the outside, which should equal the thickness of the ornamental bracket to be fixed upon the string. The baluster is sunk into the face of the string as shown in Fig. 1, Pl. xxx., and is secured by four or more screws passing through holes drilled in it, and through the string, into a block fixed at the back, as shown in Fig. 3, Pl. xxx. The foot of the baluster is hidden by the return nosing and the bracket, as indicated in Fig. 2, Pl. xxx., where the covering bracket outside and the strengthening block inside the string is shown in dotted lines. The necessary cutting away of the face of the string is a serious defect which is by no means minimised by placing the baluster at the riser line, as is sometimes advocated, because this necessitates cutting away the back of the riser to receive the block at a part where it is already weak.

Obviously this form cannot be used in plain, cut strings, and the kneed baluster shown at B in the respective Figs. becomes necessary. In this form, the foot of the baluster passes down *inside* the string and the latter may, or may not, according to its thickness, be notched to receive the lug. If the stair is put together in the shop, without fitting the balustrade, a small pocket must be cut in the tread through which to pass the foot of the baluster, as shown at P in Fig. 3, Pl. xxx. After fixing, this opening is made good by gluing in a piece to match the tread.

Where this method is considered objectionable, one or other of the devices shown in Figs. 6 and 7, Pl. xxx., may be employed. In Fig. 6, Pl. xxx., the baluster is cast with a three-way flange at the foot, the longer one going under the tread, to which it is screwed, and the side wings fitted into notches on the string. These are drilled for screws, which must be passed through plug holes in the tread.

In Fig. 7, Pl. xxx., the end of the baluster is cast with a hole, in which a plug is sweated, or, in the case of a wrought-iron baluster, the hole is tapped and the plug threaded. In this form, all that is necessary is to bore a $\frac{5}{8}$-in. hole in the string and drive the plug down to the requisite depth, then to screw down the baluster until it is seated tightly on the tread.

PLATE XXX.

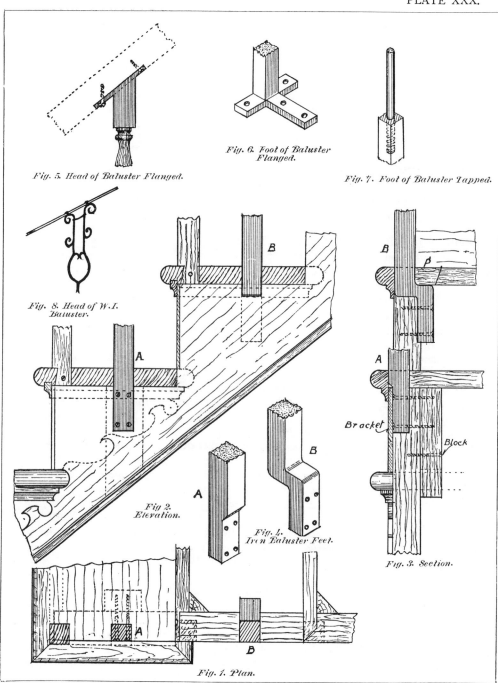

Fig. 5. Head of Baluster Flanged.

Fig. 6. Foot of Baluster Flanged.

Fig. 7. Foot of Baluster Tapped.

Fig. 8. Head of W.I. Baluster.

Fig 2. Elevation.

Fig. 4. Iron Baluster Feet.

Fig. 3. Section.

Bracket

Block

Fig. 1. Plan.

METHODS OF STIFFENING BALUSTERS.

Fig. 5, Pl. xxx., shows the method used to fix the top end of the baluster to the handrail. The lug or flange on the lower side should be longer than that at the top, and the screw-hole drilled vertically, otherwise the screw cannot be turned in. The upper screw should be square to the pitch of rail.

Wrought-iron balustrades are riveted at intervals to a flat iron bar called the " core," in the manner shown in Fig. 8, Pl. xxx., and this core is sunk into a groove on the underside of the rail. For a wreathed rail this core must also be wreathed or twisted, to fit the wreath. Usually a thin wood templet is prepared from the drawings, which is screwed on the ends of short pieces of stuff to represent the balusters. These keep the templet in shape and position. This templet is used both by the handrailer and the 'smith, the former fitting his wreath to it, and the latter his core. Sometimes the wreath itself when squared up and jointed is sent to the 'smith as a pattern for his bar, which he marks upon the underside, when the wreath is returned to the joiner's shop for grooving and moulding.

It is a wise precaution, where this latter method is adopted, to " pack " the joints, that is to say, to fix pieces of pine temporarily on the joint with brass sprigs, or if the bolt is left in, to turn the live nut hard down on the packing piece.

Capping is employed either as ornament or by necessity where the thickness of the baluster exceeds that of the string; instances of the latter are given on Pls. xxxvii. and xlii. Stair cappings are usually grooved to receive the strings, about $\frac{1}{4}$ in. deep, and housed into the newels at the ends, as shown in Fig. 1, Pl. xxi., and Fig. 3, Pl. xv., but sometimes they are simply ploughed and tongued, as in Fig. 9, Pl. xxviii., or in very common work, square jointed and nailed, as in Figs. 19 and 21, Pl. xlii.

Balusters are fixed in a variety of ways according to their size or the quality of the work. The commonest method is shown at C, Fig. 1, Pl. xxviii., where the baluster is cut square through to the pitch, and bradded to the capping. The method shown at B, Fig. 1, and at Figs. 6, 10, 13, and 14, Pl. xxviii., is adopted only in a superior class of work. For what may be termed good ordinary work, the method shown at A, Fig. 1 and *a*, Fig. 2, Pl. xxviii., is generally adopted. This is known as square-housed-

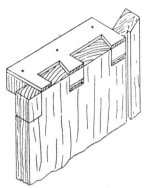

ILL. 3. METHOD OF MARKING DOVETAILS FOR BALUSTERS.

seating, and is managed by marking round the seat of each baluster, after its lower end is squared off to the longest point at A, then sinking in a housing with horizontal seat to receive the baluster, which is driven in tightly and secured by fine nails, punched and stopped. The method commonly followed in open strings is shown at Figs. 4, 5, and 8, Pl. xxviii., and in Figs. 12 and 13, Pl. xviii. The ends of the balusters are single or double-dovetailed into the treads, to which they are further secured by a nail or screw; the joint is then covered by the return nosing-piece, as shown in the several illustrations. The method of marking or setting out varies, but usually a templet is employed equal in width to the baluster, and this is applied at the *inside*, keeping the shoulder accurately to the shoulder line, previously struck over on the balusters. The object of marking on the inside is that a slight " drift " may be given to the saw in cutting them, and they will tighten as they go in. The sockets are marked by a corresponding templet, shown in Ill. 3, these templets, of course, being first fitted together. It is not usual to fit the balustrade together until after the stair is fixed, therefore, although the saw-cuts for the sockets must be run into the treads before they leave the shop (the author personally prefers to cut them before gluing up the steps), the core of the sockets should not be removed until the actual fitting in of the balusters take place, so that the edges may not receive damage, but it is wise to stub in the chisel to the shoulder line underneath, to facilitate the subsequent mortising.   There are special cases in which other methods of fixing are more suitable, for instance in the solid steps shown in Fig. 15, Pl. XXVIII., cross mortise and tenon joint is used, and in the open soffit stair, Figs. 11 and 12, Pl. XXVIII., the balusters are housed ¼ in., then bare-faced tenoned through the tread into the string, as this description of stair is built up differently from the ordinary closed-in stair, for obviously no angle blocking can be used, and the fixing of the treads must be accomplished in other ways.   The method of fixing the top ends of balusters is dealt with under " Handrailing."

The Open Soffit Stair (Figs. 11 and 12, Pl. XXVIII.) might more congruously be called an " open stair," but this term is already in use in two senses among stairbuilders, and to add a third use would lead to confusion, so the above title is adopted, although there is actually no soffit at all in this description of stair.

There are of course other details used than those shown, but all the constructive parts are here given.   The sketch, Fig. 11, is self-explanatory, and we may refer more particularly to the plan, Fig. 12, and details, Figs. 13 and 14, Pl. XXVIII.   The treads in this case are wrought on both sides and moulded on both edges, the under or soffit moulding varying from a simple nosing, as at *n*, to elaborate carving of the strapwork, or ball-and-billet type (*b*), etc.   The risers are also wrought on both sides, the backs being usually polished.   As no angle blocks at back are permissible, the risers are tongued and grooved into each tread, and to facilitate the insertion they are erected in situ upon the notched and moulded substrings, shown in the plan.   The cut or outside string is fixed after all the steps are up, as is sometimes the visible wall string, which is cut and notched down over the steps.   This form is not illustrated. The stair shown has a rough notched string beneath, which is afterwards covered with the moulded sub-string.   In lieu of angle blocks, a bed mould, as shown under the two first steps, is sometimes used.   The risers are grooved to the string and mitred to the brackets, which are of substantial thickness to receive carving, as seen in Fig. 13, Pl. XXVIII.   The balusters are housed solid into the tread and a bare-faced tenon cut on the inside (see Fig. 14, Pl. XXVIII.) goes through them into the string.   The mortise is indicated in dotted line in Fig. 11.

A Stringless Stair, with solid moulded steps, bracketed ends, and moulded carriages, is shown in the sketch elevation, Fig. 15, and part plan, Fig. 16, Pl. XXVIII.   These stairs are a modern adaptation of the old English solid stair.   The steps are either cut and moulded out of solid baulk, or more frequently built up as indicated in the section, Fig. 17, into roughly triangular shape, then moulded.   They are supported upon three or more substantial carriages, according to their width.   The carriages are recessed to the outline of the steps, and a chase is cut through each step, which saddles over the carriage, taking the dead weight of the step.   Each step is tongued into the one below it, and has stout filling pieces fixed inside, directly over each carriage.   The cavetto in this case is glued into the angle under the nosing after the step is made up.   The balusters are tenoned through the treads, the mortise for them running with the grain of the tread.   The return of the nosing across the ends is worked in the solid, but the return end of each step has to be inserted and must be mitred to the riser, and secured by blocking inside, before the tread is glued on.   This end piece is sometimes dropped slightly below the profile of the moulded soffit to form a stop or band, as shown at the second step in Fig. 15, Pl. XXVIII.

CHAPTER XVIII.

METHOD OF SETTING OUT AND CONSTRUCTING A CURTAIL STEP AND HANDRAIL SCROLL.

(PLATE XXXI.)

Method of Setting Out and Constructing a Curtail Step and the Handrail Scroll to a Cut String Stair —Reason for this Special Large Scale Drawing—Explanation of Method of Drawing— Reason for Drawing the Scroll first—Method of Setting Out the Scheme of Centres—Method of Building the Curtail Block—Method of Veneering the Block—Preliminary Shaping of the Veneer—Precautions to Prevent Breaking—Time for Setting—Working the Solid Scotia—Method of Fixing.

THIS subject has to some extent already been dealt with in several of the examples of stairs, but the numerous details in each of these cases requiring attention prevented that full description which will be found in this chapter with the special drawing made for the purpose. It may be added that the plate being intended as an example of practical setting-out was made full size by the author in the original, to show the exact relation of the parts, but necessarily the plate has had to be much reduced to bring it into conformity with the general dimensions of the book.

To facilitate reference, the handrail and its scroll are shown in broken dash lines ; the curtail riser and the string in full line ; the tread and nosing lines of the step in dot-and-dash line ; the scotia mould in chain lines ; the balusters and subsidiary projectors in dotted lines ; as the titles are printed near each line they should not be difficult to trace.

Procedure.—As the shape of the handrail scroll is in full view, whilst that of the curtail step is partly hidden, it is usual to design or describe the scroll first, then to make the step conform to this so far as is required, by striking its curves from the same centres.

To Draw the Scroll (Fig. 1, Pl. XXXI.).—Draw the springing line A-B-C at the first flyer nosing, set off on this line from A, three times the width of the rail, obtaining the centre C, for the first quadrant of the scroll B-C. The inside of the rail is struck similarly with point C as centre and A-C′ as radius ; draw the line C-2 at right angles to the springing line, and make it two-thirds of the width of the rail A-B in length, thus obtaining the second centre point 2. From this, describe the quadrants from C to III, and C to III′. Draw the line 2-3 at right angles to C-2 and make it three-quarters of C-2 ; with radius 3-III′, describe the third quadrant to point IV. The smaller quadrant is described from the same centre indefinitely, to be cut off later by the outside curve. To find the remaining centres, draw the line C-3 and a line from point 2 at right angles to it, then draw a perpendicular from 3, cutting the diagonal 2-4 in point 4, which gives that centre. Draw a line from this point at right angles to the previous line, which will cut the first diagonal in point 5, and so on, for any number of centres required. If the outer curve is continued in quadrants it will intersect the inner one from the 7th centre. The curtail is struck from the same centres, but, as will be seen, is not taken so far round as is the scroll. It is usually stopped just under the intersection of the tread, or nosing curves, as shown.

The next thing to do is to set out the balusters on the centre line of the handrail; this line is not shown, to avoid confusion.

I have indicated the balusters in dotted lines; their number and position depends upon their size, and the width apart of those on the flyers. In this instance one is drawn flush with face of second riser, and flush with face of string, the others are then spaced out towards the first riser as nearly equal apart as can be obtained and gradually diminishing their intervals towards the eye of the scroll. The face of the string can now be drawn to the springing line A-C and continued round the curtail as far as required, the curve being struck from the corresponding centres, as shown. The thickness of the veneers must next be drawn—in this case $\frac{1}{8}$ in. The width of the given baluster at C determines the thickness of the neck of the curtail, because the baluster must have its opposite faces flush with the opposite faces of the string as shown, and the face of the curtail riser is then drawn flush with the baluster, and the curve carried around until it cuts into end of block. The tread or nosing line is next drawn from the corresponding centres, and the back end of the curtail block drawn in will complete the setting-out.

The Curtail Block is built up in three thicknesses, with the grain crossing, to strengthen it at the neck, where it is very narrow, a templet being made to fit the back of the veneer, as drawn, for marking out the three pieces which, after cutting, are glued and screwed together. The end of the riser is reduced to a veneer as shown, the length of this being obtained by bending a strip of paper around the block. A recess for a pair of folding wedges is left at the springing; these are used for tightening up the veneer, on the face of the block. To get the veneer around, having " toothed " the back and face of block with either a coarse file or a piece of No. 3 glass paper and glued on a fillet as at f, Fig. 1, Pl. XXXI., cut a slot for this in the block and, standing it on its bottom, slide the end of the veneer into this slot, having first thoroughly wetted the veneer with boiling water, or better, by placing it in a steam chest for ten minutes; when ready, bring the veneer gradually around the block until it is at a part that can be laid on the bench as shown in Fig. 2, Pl. XXXI., then turn the block carefully on to the face of the veneer and, pressing as hard down as possible, slowly turn the block around until the riser is seated in the recess which is cut in the face of block, when the wedges may be slightly driven. The veneer should then be left several hours to dry, when, having acquired the proper shape, it may be released, and very hot glue applied both to the face of block and the back of the veneer, when the operation of rolling it around may be done again but more quickly. If the veneer shows signs of breaking, well wet the outside with hot water. Finally, wedge (not too hard) and screw the block as shown in Fig. 1, Pl. XXXI., to back of the riser.

A section of the top part of the step, tread and scotia, etc., is shown one-third full size at A, and a similar section at B, of the special scotia used for the curtail step. This is worked in the solid, about $3\frac{1}{2}$ ins. wide over the straight part, and squared out about the same width over the string, where it follows the curve of the string into the block; the remaining portion is cut to fit over the block, as shown by the chain lines; the scotia, after working, is glued and nailed, or screwed, as shown at B, to the riser, and then the tread screwed to it from underneath—this is the object of the overhanging portion; finally the riser is glue-blocked to the scotia.

PLATE XXXI.

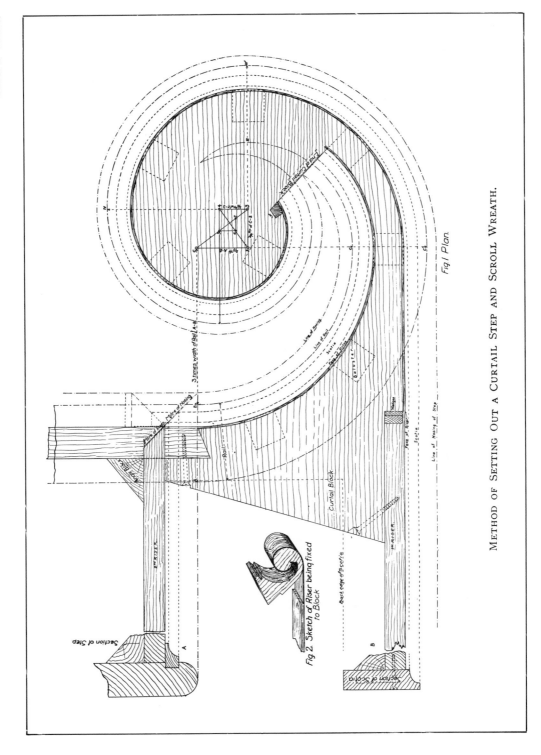

Fig 1 Plan.

Fig 2. Sketch of Riser being fixed to Block

Section of Step

Section of Scolio

METHOD OF SETTING OUT A CURTAIL STEP AND SCROLL WREATH.

CHAPTER XIX.

DESIGNS AND DETAILS OF NEWELS, BALUSTERS, BRACKETS AND HANDRAILS.

(PLATES XXXII.-XLII.)

Newels and Balusters of the Early and Late Renaissance Types (Pls. XXXII-XXXVII.)—Object of the Designs—An " Old English," or Gothic Style Newel—Suitable Material—Method of Construction —Pea Stopping—Working the Finial—Sections of Balusters—A Renaissance Type—Solid Newel —Alternative Treatments—Preparation for Electric Light Standard—Connection to Handrail, etc. —A Jacobean Type, Turned and Reeded Newel—Suitable Materials—Handrail with Curved Kneeling, Balusters en Suite—A Georgian Style Octagonal Newel—Method of Building-up—Inlaid Strings—Using the Scratch Stock—Method of Inlaying Newel—Fixing of Handrail—Varieties of Balusters—Methods of Working by Hand and Machine—Suitable Woods for Handrails.

Pl. XXXVIII—Designs for Balusters—Nine Typical Designs, including Double, Single, and Open Spirals, with Enrichments and Scale Sections at Various Points, also Tapered, Turned, and Fluted Specimens, with others of distinctly Modern Design.

Pl. XXXIX. contains Designs founded on Elizabethan and Georgian examples with further suggestions for novelties that can be economically reproduced—Suitable Woods for the several Designs ; nearly all of these are British Empire Woods—The Silhouette Baluster.

Designs for Brackets and Handrails (Pls. XL.-XLII.).

PLATE XXXII shows a representative selection of newels and balusters of the early Renaissance type, covering the Elizabethan and Jacobean periods, 1540-1640. Further contemporary examples are seen in Ills. 4 to 7. The tall newels, sometimes rising to the ceiling, but tapering downwards, have usually a dignified effectiveness, whether plain (Ill. 7) or highly ornate, as in Nos. D, B and A from the Charterhouse (Pl. XXXII) (also illustrated from a photograph on Pl. XLVIII.), and at Hatfield House (Pl. XXXIII.). The balusters are often turned as in C, E, G and L, but a flat type, often pierced, is also characteristic, as in F, H and K. The balustrade filling is sometimes in a continuous pattern, pierced with fretwork or strapwork, as at Castle Ashby (Pl. LIV. A), Aston Hall (see W. Niven's Monograph and Nash's " Mansions "), Cromwell House, Highgate (where the newels have vigorous soldier figures), and elsewhere. Further series of illustrations occur in W. H. Godfrey's " The English Staircase " (Batsford, 1911), and M. Jourdain's " English Decoration and Furniture of the Early Renaissance " (Batsford, 1924).

The illustration of the Hall i' th' Wood, Tonge, Lancashire (Ill. 8), is a perspective drawing showing a staircase built from designs of the types illustrated on Pl. XXXII.

Plate XXXIV. carries on the series on the last plate, and covers the later Renaissance period from 1640 to about 1760. At the start are plain square newels with straight or ramped strings, and large swelling balusters, sometimes carved (A–C). The staircase at Belton House, Grantham, *ca.* 1690 (Pl. VII., Chap. II.) is a stately one of this type, which recurs under Palladian influence about 1725, see Marble Hill, Twickenham ; it is also represented in Swan's " Designs " of 1750.

Contemporary are the florid but splendid series of " continuous scroll " staircases, dating from the period of the Restoration (Pls. I., LIV.-LVII.). Castle Ashby contrasts

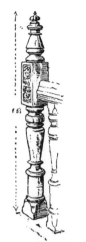

ILL. 4. AT SHELDON HALL.
(*Drawn by Sydney R. Jones.*)

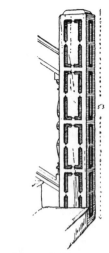

ILL. 5. A NEWEL AT
WHITTINGTON COURT.
(*Drawn by Sydney R. Jones.*)

ILL. 6. NEWEL AT CHASTLETON
HOUSE.

ILL. 7. AT SHOELANDS, SURREY.
(*Drawn by Ralph Nevill, F.S A.*)

EARLY RENAISSANCE NEWELS AND BALUSTERS.

effectively on the same plate the Early and Late Renaissance methods of continuous filling, the latter still immature; intermediate are the Trophy panels of Ham House.

Photographs of these scroll staircases are included from Dunster Castle (Pl. I, Frontispiece); Castle Ashby (Pl. LIV., LV.); and Eltham Lodge (Pl. LVI.), which is also illustrated from measured drawings, with Forde Abbey. The carved or plain newels of these staircases are of dwarf type, or are surmounted by a large vase of flowers. Example D (Pl. XXXIV.) is the next form, and the double spiral of E is also a transitional form. The eighteenth century saw the slight spirally-twisted, or sometimes fluted baluster, two or three to each tread, often of alternating designs, see G on this plate and Pl. XLI. The pulpit stair at St. Katherine Cree (Pl. XXXV.) has from two to five to each tread, according to the width given by the tread on the curve. The two London examples, Pls. XXVIII. and XXIX., in Vol. II. ("Handrailing") are good representative specimens, and Pl. XXXVI. shows a fine richly-carved twisted baluster applied to a curving pulpit stair, executed with the consummate craftsmanship of the workers in Wren's City churches. After the mid-eighteenth century the wooden baluster was usually replaced by iron work.

Further work of the Later Renaissance is illustrated in Godfrey's "Staircases" referred to earlier; Lenygon's "English Decoration, 1640-1760," 1928; Jourdain's "English Decoration of the Later Eighteenth Century" (1760-1820), 1926; Stratton's "The English Interior," 1920.

Pl. XXXVII. contains designs for newels of various types adapted to modern require-ments. As designs, they are merely suggestive, the object being to provide examples by which to describe the construction of the chief types of newels: framed, solid moulded, turned and built-up.

An Old English Newel (Figs. 1 and 2, Pl. XXXVII.). This design is suitable for execution in oak. It might of course be made in the solid throughout, but both on the score of expense and durability would be better framed-up in one or other of the methods shown in the enlarged section, Fig. 3, Pl. XXXVII. The left-hand half section is the better arrange-ment when the frame moulding is worked in the solid, and would require stuff $1\frac{1}{2}$ ins. thick. The method shown on the right hand is the more economical both in material and labour. It can be made equally strong by transverse screwing of the mitres as shown. The disadvantage of this method is that the mouldings have to be disfigured by bradding, but the holes can be to a great extent obliterated by filling in with "pea" stopping, which is made with Robinson's pea powder mixed with bleached glue and toned to match the wood with burnt umber. If the wood is to be fumed, the stopping should be made to the desired *finished*

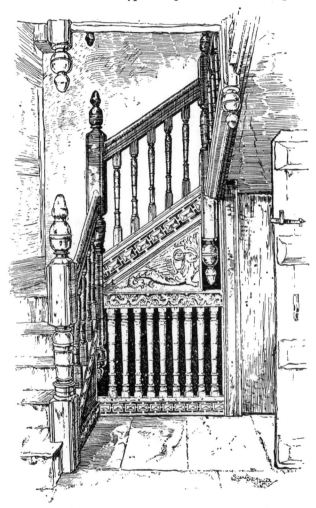

ILL. 8.—HALL I' TH' WOOD, TONGE, LANCASHIRE.
(*Drawn by Sydney R. Jones.*)

tone. Two square blocks, as shown in Fig. 2, Pl. XXXVII., are required, on which to build the frames; one should be placed at the level of the handrail to receive its fixing screws, seen in the elevation, the other between the top of the plinth and the first step. These should be glued and blocked to the back of one frame, and the other sides rubbed on successively.

PLATE XXXII.

EARLY RENAISSANCE NEWELS AND BALUSTERS, 1540-1640.

A. Charterhouse.	E. Ordsall Old Hall, Salford.	K. Cheetham's College, Manchester.
B. „	F. Cromhall, Glos.	L. Castle Ashby Church, Northants.
C. Talbot Inn, Oundle.	G. Merton College, Oxford.	
D. Aston Hall.	H. Cheetham's College, Manchester.	

PLATE XXXIII.

Varieties of the Newels.

DETAILS OF THE GREAT STAIRCASE, HATFIELD HOUSE (*drawn and engraved by Henry Shaw, F.S.A.*)

PLATE XXXIV.

LATE RENAISSANCE NEWELS AND BALUSTERS, 1640-1760, *ca.*

A. Coleshill House, Berks.
B.   „   „   „
C. Sunderland.
D. Prince's Tavern, John Dalton Street, Manchester.

E. Kersal Cell, nr. Higher Broughton, Manchester.
F. 12 Devonshire Square, London.
G. 15 Queen's Square, Bath.
H. Singlewell, near Gravesend.

PLATE XXXV.

PULPIT, ST. KATHERINE CREE, LONDON.

Georgian Type of Geometrical Handrail and Newels.

PLATE XXXVI.

A Pulpit Stair with Wreathed Strings and Handrails, and Spiral Turned and Carved Balusters.
St. Mary at Hill, London.

All but the laſt side can be angle-blocked throughout; the laſt, which should be the inside, facing the baluſters, can be blocked only from the two open ends. The joints on the left-hand frame can be brought up with handscrews and profile blocks, as indicated in dotted lines.

The finial is worked in the solid, and its pin carried down inside the newel about 3 ins. The plinth is sunk into the face of the newel, as indicated in dotted line, the capping scribing over it, the ſtring passing through the plinth and tenoning into the newel block inside. The **handrail** should be housed solid into the newel about ½ in. deep, and screwed thereto from underneath, before the baluſters are fixed. The heads of the baluſters are cut square across to the pitch, and secured with screws sunk into pelleted holes. The baluſters are square-turned. Two half seƈtions to enlarged scale are shown between Figs. 1 and 4, Pl. xxxvii., which may be used as alternatives, or both in the one baluſter, as shown in elevation.

A Solid Square Newel, with oƈtagonal head, the enrichments of Renaissance type, is shown in Figs. 4, 5 and 6, Pl. xxxvii. Slightly differing designs are given for the finish of the newel cap—a half plan of each is seen in Fig. 5, Pl. xxxvii. Alternative methods of dealing with the moulded panel is shown in Fig. 6, Pl. xxxvii. The newel is adapted to carry an electric, or gas, light ſtandard; the supply pipe is shown carried down the centre through a ¾-in. hole bored therein. Alternatively, this could be brought out under the rail to the back surface and be carried down a channel in the newel. The handrail is ramped into the newel with a level easing which is tenoned into the same in the manner indicated in Fig. 5, Pl. xxxvii.; the joint with the ramp would be made with a handrail screw and dowels. The baluſters, which have turned shafts and square ends, would preferably be housed up into the rail ⅜ in. and tenoned into the capping, as shown in Figs. 4 and 6, Pl. xxxvii.

A Solid, Turned and Reeded Newel with Carved Finial, for an open ſtring ſtair of modern Jacobean type, with a heavy ramped handrail and square moulded baluſters, is shown in Figs. 7, 8 and 9, Pl. xxxvii. Several of the details are supplied with alternative designs; for inſtance, the rose panel upon the square head may have inſtead a square sunk panel with a boleƈtion moulding, and the bellied and reeded shaft may be tapered and fluted, as shown at B. The baluſter also is shown fluted, but may be reeded if preferred, and, as in the previous designs, one baluſter is given in templet form for setting out purposes. The whole design is massive, adapted for a large building, and would be suitably executed in Spanish or African mahogany, which are rich toned woods. The handrail has a curved kneeling; the end of this is housed for a depth of half an inch, and secured with a bolt, the dead nut of which would be sunk into the newel under the panel moulding, and the live nut inserted in the rail above the firſt baluſter, which would cover the mortise.

A Built-up Newel of a substantial type, oƈtagonal in plan and pyramidal in seƈtion, ornamented with surface inlays, is illuſtrated in Figs. 10 to 13, Pl. xxxvii. The ſtring, which is of the Close type, is also inlaid with banding. The elevation in this inſtance is taken at the outside of the ſtring, etc. Half plans at various points, as indicated by the lettering, are given in Figs. 12 and 13, Pl. xxxvii.; Fig. 11, Pl. xxxvii., is a vertical seƈtion through one side of the newel. The moſt economical conſtruƈtion, consiſtent with good workmanship, in designs of this nature is to true up the inside of the ſtuff after it has been shaped to the given seƈtion (Fig. 11, Pl. xxxvii. would be the templet with which to mark the square edges), then mitre each panel according to the plan, set-out full size, to obtain correct bevel; plough the edges for cross tonguing, from the inside. Joint up firſt four pairs, and allow them to dry; they can be rubbed in the bench screw. Next, prepare two oƈtagonal rubbing blocks to fit the interior, as shown in the plan. These blocks will eventually be fixed inside the newel, one at the bottom, the other with its top surface in line with the middle of the handrail; but firſt they will be utilised as bearers upon which the remaining joints are rubbed. Fix them upon the bench at a suitable diſtance apart, also fix one pair of panels by means of dogs

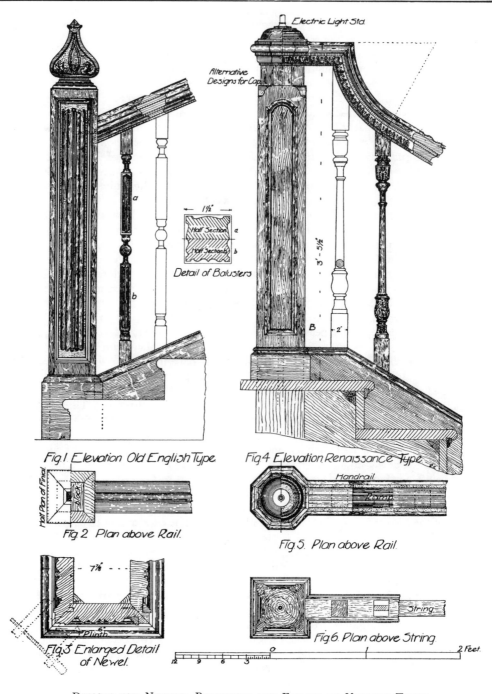

Electric Light Std.

Alternative
Designs for Cap.

3'-5½"

B

2"

1½"

Half Section a
Half Section b

Detail of Balusters

Fig 1. Elevation Old English Type.

Fig 4. Elevation Renaissance Type.

Half Plan of Final

Block

Fig 2. Plan above Rail.

Handrail

Ramp

Fig 5. Plan above Rail.

7⅞

Plinth

Fig 3. Enlarged Detail of Newel.

String

Fig 6. Plan above String.

0   1   2 Feet.
12   9   6   3

DESIGNS FOR NEWELS, BALUSTERS AND FINIALS OF VARIOUS TYPES.

PLATE XXXVII.

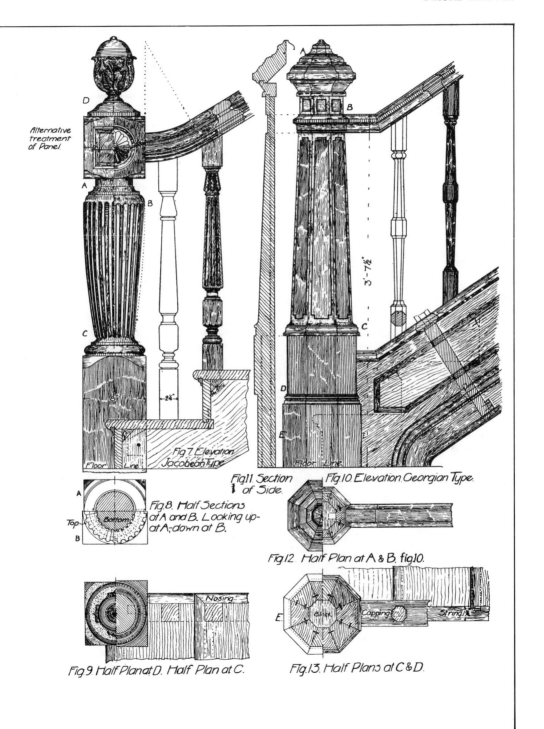

Alternative treatment of Panel.

Fig 7. Elevation Jacobean Type.

Floor Line

Fig 8. Half Sections at A and B. Looking up at A, down at B.

Fig 11. Section of Side.

Fig 10. Elevation Georgian Type.

Fig 12. Half Plan at A & B, fig 10.

Nosing

Fig 9. Half Plan at D. Half Plan at C.

Fig. 13. Half Plans at C & D.

3'-7½"

2½"

upon the blocks, bring the adjacent pair up to position, and rub the joint between them. Dog the two ends, and lift off to dry. Repeat the process with the other two pairs, thus leaving one joint to be made at each edge of the two halves of the newel. The blocks can now be removed and fixed in their place in one-half of the newel. When the final joint is rubbed, it may be cramped across from opposite sides. This joint is indicated in the plan, by double tongues, which are used because it will be almost impossible to rub the double joint unless the tongues are made very slack, therefore after the joint is set and cramped up, the additional tongues are driven in from the end ; the height to which the groove can be carried is indicated in dotted lines in Fig. 11, Pl. xxxvii. The stem of the newel can next be cleaned up and the sinkings made for the mouldings and plinth. The grooves for the inlay may be made in either of two ways : (*a*) a templet is made to fit the inside edge of the stringing inlay, and a " scratch," which may simply be a bradawl, should be held in a small " stock " or block of hard wood, with the cutter projecting from it the required depth of the groove, plus the thickness of the templet, as shown in Fig. 9, Pl. xliii. The cross-cut grooves should be knife-cut in first, to prevent fraying of the edges, a piece of the stringing held tightly to the templet will furnish the guide for the outside cut. (*b*) A scratch stock is made with its fence or guide shaped to fit the angle of the post, as shown in Fig. 9, Pl. xliii., with the bradawl set in the bar, at the proper distance from the edge, and projecting just sufficiently to take a shaving at each stroke. The stock must be kept hard down on the face of the work and run along the whole length of the post to be grooved, then brought back, and the bradawl knocked out another shaving, and so on, until the required depth is reached ; for if the bradawl projected the whole depth at first, the stock would move outwards as the sinking proceeded. The cross grooves and corners in this case must be cut in with chisels. The author prefers the first method. The cap of the newel is worked in one length, then cut into appropriate lengths, taking care to mark and to follow on, then the eight sides mitred around the neck. Each mitre should be cross-tongued, and the interior blocked before dropping upon the rebated neck. The kneeling-piece of the handrail is fixed with a tenon, as shown in the plan, running through the side of the newel and half notched over the top block, to which it can be screwed before the cap is attached.

Designs for Balusters.—Pl. xxxviii. contains examples of nine types of balusters of modern design, with numerous sections.

Any of these designs may be adapted to required lengths by means of proportional enlargement, as described on page 38, Pl. xviii., Fig. 5*a*.

Spiral turned and twisted balusters are shown in Nos. 1, 2, 3, Pl. xxxviii., with their principal sections arranged axially (see the adjacent reference letters). The carved enrichments shown upon these may if preferred be omitted without altering the profile. The fluted baluster, No. 4, Pl. xxxviii., has one-half shaded, to give the effect of roundness, the other half left plain, so that the profile may be seen clearly.

The reeded baluster No. 5, Pl. xxxviii., is intended to be " square turned " throughout, but could of course be turned circular if preferred. So-called " square turning " is accomplished by fixing the blanks to the periphery of two circular discs, or upon the surface of a cylinder mounted upon a revolving axis in a lathe, and the cutting tools are applied as in common turning, tangentially to the revolving surface. The larger the discs, or cylinder, the more nearly the resulting surfaces approach square in section ; such surfaces are, however, never really plane or flat ; but, except in large pieces, the curve is unobtrusive. The reeding in this example, like the fluting in No. 4, must be worked subsequently by an appropriate therming machine.

No. 6, Pl. xxxviii., design has its shaft, the reeded cap and the fillet at U, square ; the remaining members are turned circular.

No. 7, Pl. xxxviii., is a substantial design, suitable for a large open newelled stair; the upper part of the shaft might be curved similarly to the lower part to obtain a lighter effect. The carving on the vases is very simple gouge work.

No. 8, Pl. xxxviii., is suitable for a light baluster with three to the step.

No. 9, Pl. xxxviii., may be alternatively treated as circular or square-turning; each effect is shown at opposite ends.

The Open or Double Spiral No. 1, Pl. xxxix., is in the early eighteenth century style, and is especially suitable for large close string stairs with handrails of types 1, 2 and 3, Pl. xlii. The vase at bottom is frequently enriched with a conventional leaf ornament carved in relief. The sections B and C show the climbing spirals as elliptic; this is due to the horizontal section lying obliquely to the pitch. The true section of the spirals is shown at A-A. An Elizabethan type, with suggestion of rusticated masonry, a favourite subject with the early turners, is shown in No. 2, Pl. xxxix., which is again especially suitable for a close stair. An elegant early Georgian type of baluster is seen in Fig. 3, Pl. xxxix., with an appropriate handrail section. A general idea of the effect of this form of baluster may be gathered from the photograph of the fine open-well grand stair, with stepped strings and wood panelled soffits to be seen in the Treasurer's House at York. The shaft of the baluster, as shown by the sectional plan at F, is hexagonal.; the remainder, with exception of the block at G, is turned circular. This mid-block is a prevailing feature of the Georgian baluster, although seldom so elaborately shaped and moulded as in the present example, which has four hollow curved faces that are sunk into solid moulded panels, as shown more clearly in the enlarged section. More usually, the block is a plain square slab, about $\frac{1}{2}$ in. thick. To wear well, these balusters should be prepared in some firm, close-grained hardwood, such as Spanish mahogany, Australian salmon Jarrah, Tasmanian blackwood, or Queensland silky-oak. This latter wood has the valuable property of receiving a stain of any tint (excepting black) without obscuring its beautiful figure.

No. 4, Pl. xxxix., is a design for a light circular baluster, suitable for a cut string stair, in either oak, mahogany, or walnut. A lighter effect could be obtained by the use of Queensland " Crows Ash," or even the real Japanese ash (Tamo), both light yellow-brown woods.

No. 5, Pl. xxxix., is a design susceptable of either square or circular turning, as indicated in the sections J, J, and both in elevation and section, one-half is treated as square, the other half as circular. This design is suitable for soft woods.

No. 6, Pl. xxxix., is a somewhat conventional example of the modern turnery mill, although proportioned more suitably than the usual stock pattern.

No. 7, Pl. xxxix., is a suggestion for a " cheap " baluster that can be used with some approach to artistic effect. The idea is to stick lengths of square moulded stuff as indicated in the sections, or similar simple sinkings, then to cut these off to appropriate lengths, and either turn the ends down to form pins, as indicated in dotted lines, or to simply bore holes of suitable depth to receive beech dowels. The square blocks at each end are bored through in like manner to receive the pin or dowel, which may project if desired, as shown at No. 8, Pl. xxxix., to form a plug to enter the tread or handrail respectively. The block may be set either parallel to the face or diagonally, as shown in the section on No. 8, Pl. xxxix.; the latter arrangement increases the apparent thickness of the baluster without actually increasing the material, and by judicious grouping, as for example alternate double and treble balusters to a step, or alternate parallel and diagonal fixing, many attractive effects may be obtained, as suggested in the sketch, Fig. 11, Pl. xxxix. This method is peculiarly suitable for the prevailing fashion of enamelled balustrades, as any fairly strong soft wood may be used, such for instance as yellow deal, Carolina pine, Honduras cedar, or the " Philippine mahogany," otherwise Red Lauan—all cheap and plentiful woods.

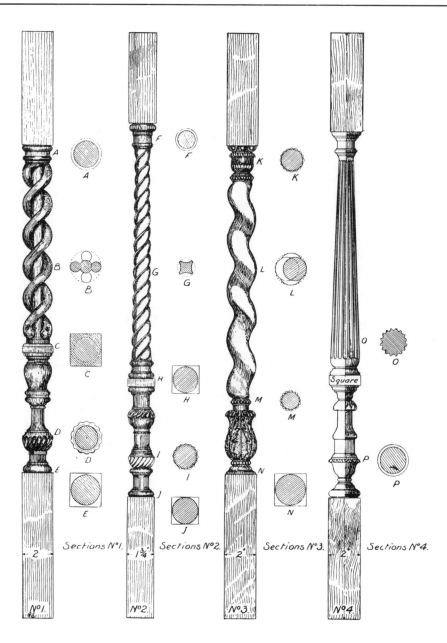

DESIGNS FOR BALUSTERS.

PLATE XXXVIII.

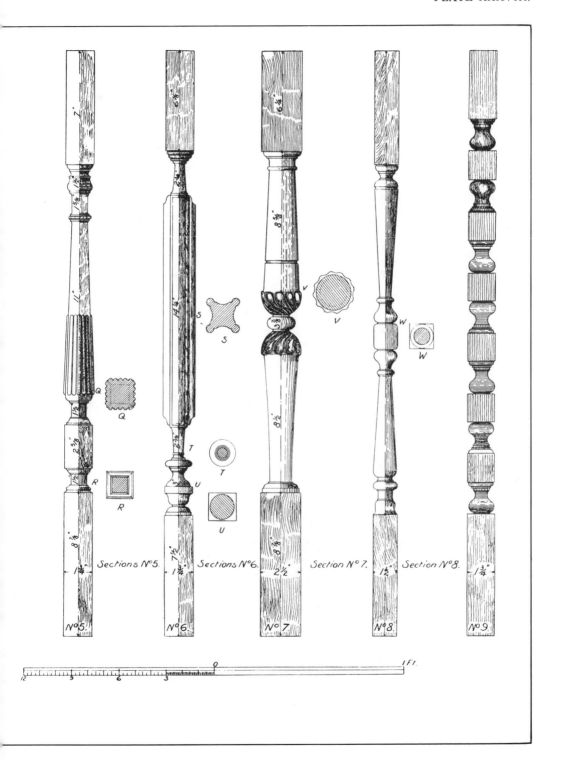

Sections Nº 5. Sections Nº 6. Section Nº 7. Section Nº 8.

Nº 5. Nº 6. Nº 7. Nº 8. Nº 9.

PLATE XXXIX.

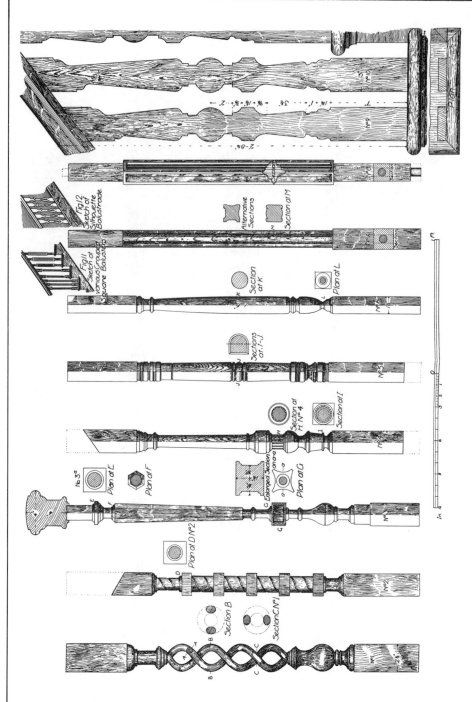

DESIGNS FOR BALUSTERS.

PLATE XL.

Fig. 1. Fig. 2. Fig. 3. Fig. 4. Fig. 5. Fig. 6. Fig. 7. Fig. 8. Fig. 9. Fig. 10. Fig. 11. Fig. 12. Fig. 13. Fig. 14. Fig. 15. Fig. 16. Fig. 17. Fig. 18.

STAIR BRACKETS.

Nos. 1–6. Abraham Swan.
7. Melton Constable, Norfolk.
8 House in the Close, Salisbury.
9. 15 Queen Square, Bath.

10. 15 Lincoln's Inn Fields, London.
11. 16 Cheyne Row, Chelsea.
*12. 2 Great Queen Street, London.
13. Manor Hall, Great Church Lane, Hammersmith.

*14. The Great House, Leyton.
15. Eagle House, Edmonton.
16. Greyfriars Lodge, Norwich.
17. Rivercourt House, Hammersmith.
18. St. Magnus the Martyr, London.

(Figs. 10, 11, 12, 13, and 17 are reproduced from the L.C.C. " Survey of London " Series.)
(Fig. 14 is reproduced from the fourth monograph of the Committee for the Survey of the Memorials of Greater London.
* Destroyed.

PLATE XLI.

B

Example of Early Georgian Carved Brackets.

A

Early Georgian Stepped Balusters and
Solid Brackets.

The Silhouette Baluster, Nos. 9 and 10, Pl. XXXIX., is a modern adaptation of a Jacobean century type used just previously to, or concurrently with, the first-turned balusters. These balusters are relatively much wider than thick, although their sectional area is about the same as that of the square balusters they might replace.

The effect aimed at in the design of these balusters is to cause the space between the two profiles to present a pattern more or less a reverse of that shown by either baluster. Obviously there must be two patterns on each step when used at a cut string, but these may repeat each time. Most usually, these balusters are either painted or stained, to contrast with the adjacent wall covering, which then throws them into relief, as indicated in the sketch, Fig. 12, Pl. XXXIX. Russian birch or Canadian elm are very suitable woods to use in making these balusters, and for staining purposes English beech or American cherry-birch may be utilised; whilst if polished in the " white " English sycamore or Canadian sugar maple, show a pretty and suitable figure, and are easily worked.

Brackets.—The accompanying plate (XL.) of historic carved brackets shows a number of varieties both of shape and decorative treatment; though laid out on the same general lines, this feature presents many little differences in detail. Nos. 1 to 6 are from designs by Abraham Swan, *ca.* 1750, and exhibit marked rococo influence; not many of these occur in actual examples, and cost and difficulties of carving no doubt led to much simplification in execution, as in No. 18.

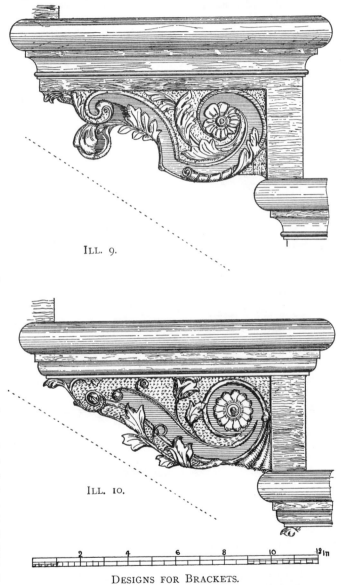

ILL. 9.

ILL. 10.

DESIGNS FOR BRACKETS.

Most carvers seem fond of a fairly naturalistic flower or two, and the photo (Pl. XLI., B) illustrates the deep undercutting of an able craftsman; the lower of the two brackets shows its frequent fate. The other part of the plate shows the earlier solid plain brackets, which became universal again in the early nineteenth century. No. 17 is a wooden bracket on the curve, fairly rare, but the most original is the shallow No. 7, with its peony-like flower. The bracket at St. Katherine Cree is also of unusual design, and Pl. xxxv. shows interestingly the adaptation of the proportions to the varying width of the tread dictated by the curve.

Several designs are given incidentally in the Examples of Stairs, and, in addition, a large-scale series of various types are shown on pages 86 and 87. Ills. 9 and 10 are designs of richly carved brackets, suitable for large, open-newelled stairs of oak, and may be from $\frac{3}{8}$ in. to $\frac{5}{8}$ in. thick. The recessed parts of the design shown pitted are to be surface-punched, and those parts shaded with ruled lines are to be finished smooth. The parts in relief are generally shown white.

The strapwork designs, Ills. 11 and 12, are of a simpler type, suitable for geometrical

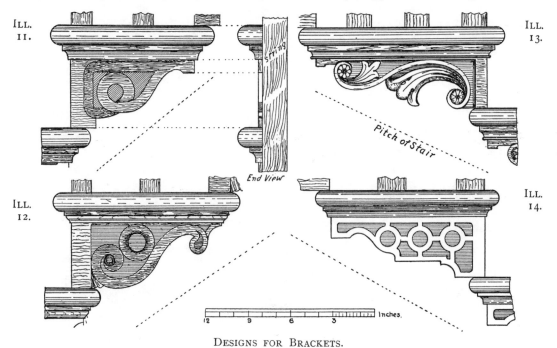

DESIGNS FOR BRACKETS.

stairs, and if made thin, as shown, would be in the nature of flat applied ornament. The ruled shading is merely added to emphasise the design. If preferred, these brackets could also be made thicker, and the shaded portions then sunk in the solid, which would give a panel effect to the design. The scroll design, Ill. 13, may be treated alternatively either as a thin applied ornament with incised lines to indicate the leaf and flower pattern, or, prepared in thicker stuff, cut to the outlines, then glued to the string, and afterwards recessed and carved with rounded surfaces.

The fret design, Ill. 14, is a variation of the strapwork treatment specially suitable for deal or painted strings. The parts that are shown shaded are really the surface of the string-board, and would be picked out in darker tint than the raised strapwork.

The fret designs afford an inexpensive, easy and perfectly legitimate means of ornamenting a stair.

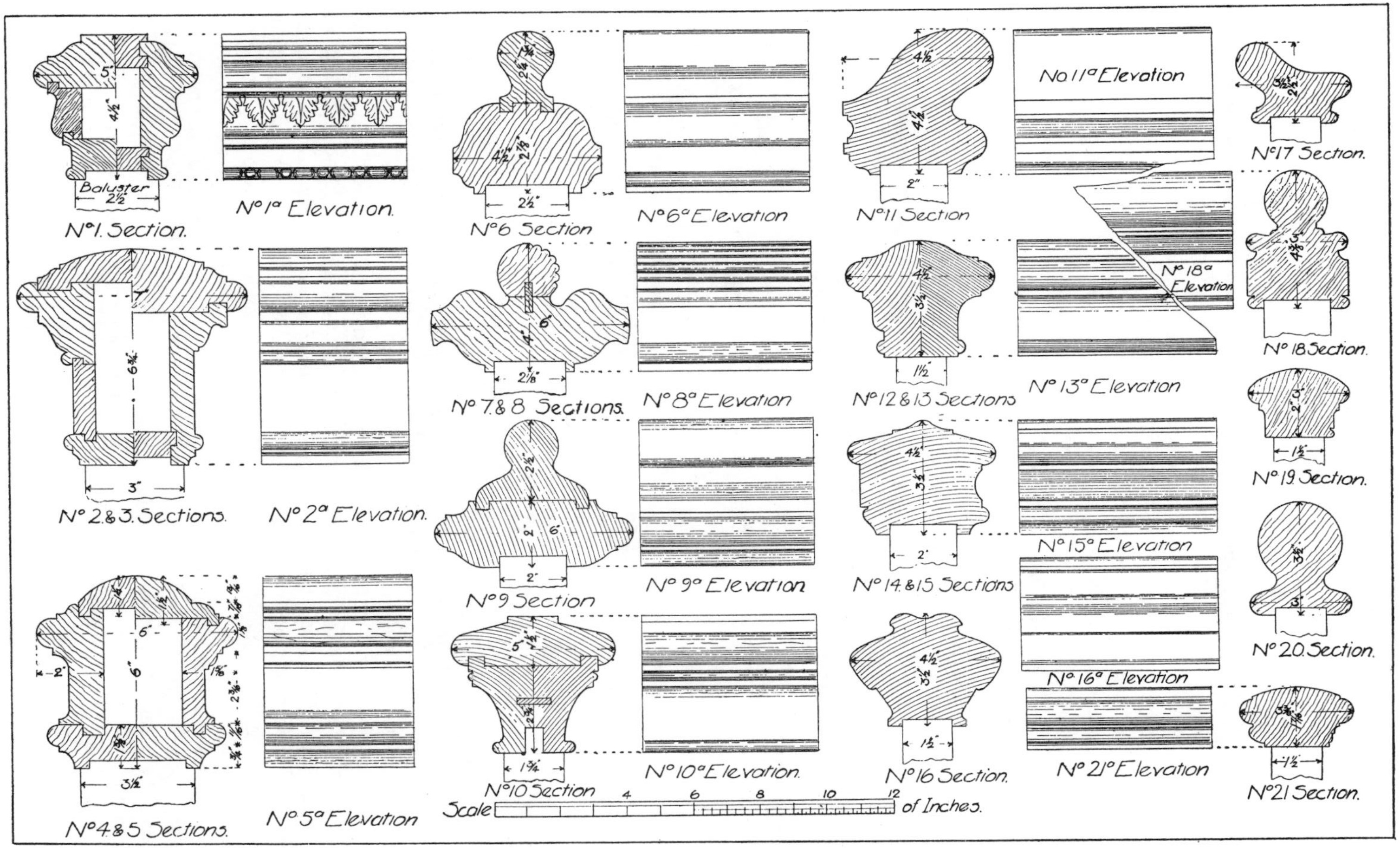

PLATE XLII.

Nº 17 Section.

Nº 18 Section.

Nº 19 Section.

Nº 20 Section.

Nº 21 Section.

Nº 11ª Elevation

Nº 18ª Elevation

Nº 13ª Elevation

Nº 15ª Elevation

Nº 16ª Elevation

Nº 21ª Elevation

Nº 11 Section

Nº 12 & 13 Sections

Nº 14 & 15 Sections

Nº 16 Section.

Nº 6ª Elevation

Nº 8ª Elevation

Nº 9ª Elevation

Nº 10ª Elevation

Nº 6 Section

Nº 7 & 8 Sections.

Nº 9 Section

Nº 10 Section

Scale of Inches.

Nº 1ª Elevation.

Nº 2ª Elevation.

Nº 5ª Elevation

Nº 1 Section.

Baluster 2½

Nº 2 & 3 Sections.

Nº 4 & 5 Sections.

PRACTICAL DESIGNS FOR HANDRAILS.

They can be cut in the solid by a jig-saw or machine fret-saw, and afterwards cut into laminæ of requisite thickness by a fine circulat saw ; they will then only require glass-papering up after glueing to the string.

Designs for Handrails.—No. 1, Pl. xlii., is a design of Renaissance type, suitable for a large close string stair of the open well newel class. Alternative methods of building up the section are shown, provided to meet varying thickness of stuff available ; either method may be adopted, but of course is to be used on the opposite side also.

If machine-wrought, it would be preferable to run through each piece separately, marking the grooves and tongues thereon accurately before sticking, and to put all together, afterwards glueing and cramping up with box cleats. About every 3 ft. or so 1 in. division or spacing pieces should be carefully fitted and glued in place, before the last side is attached. Large rails, except in the case of wreaths, are more conveniently made in the solid, though as a matter of fact many wreaths of large dimensions could also be built up similarly, but in all except a well-fitted machine shop, the cost would be prohibitive. The method of building up a boxed ramp is shown in Vol. II., page 10, Pl. v.

Rails built in the manner shown in Figs. 1 to 5, Pl. xlii., are, in all essential matters, as strong as if in the solid, whilst they are but little more than half the weight, and of one-third the cost in material. They are less likely to split or warp, and undercut mouldings can be worked upon them that would be impossible in the solid. For hand-moulding it would be better to glue up in the square, and to mould them afterwards, of course taking care to arrange the grooves in the right places, that is to say, so that the joints, when the rail is worked, will be invisible.

Two rails of very large section are shown in Figs. Nos. 2 and 3, Pl. xlii., and an elevation of one side in Fig. No. 2a, Pl. xlii. These are both Renaissance in type, and suited for a large open newel stair.

Nos. 4 and 5, Pl. xlii., are half sections of " square rails," as such sections are termed, when the greatest depth equals the greatest width. These are both Jacobean in type and suitable also for a large open newel stair with heavy balustrade or stout spiral balusters.

Nos. 6 to 10, Pl. xlii., are sections of medium size rails that are preferably made in the solid, as some of them are suitable for wreathing ; that is to say, for geometrical stairs. They may, however, be jointed, as shown, without any ill effect, should stuff of sufficient thickness to get them out in one piece be not available.

In cases where the section of a rail that is made in one piece requires it to be deeply cut into, as for instance, in Nos. 6 and 7, it is both economical and otherwise advisable to saw out rectangular pieces to the depth of the recessed parts, and to allow the interior to dry before running the piece through the moulding machine ; for dense woods such as island mahogany, teak, or black walnut, will invariably cast when so opened up, and due allowance must be made for this. Nos. 11 and 17, Pl. xlii., are sections known as " Rest " rails, or sometimes as railway rails, because they are a form much used for passenger stairs, the chief object being to afford an easy rest for the hand in descending the stair ; the ascending traffic, usually passing up the middle, does not use it, but when required the deeply undercut mould on the offside offers a secure grip. A minor advantage of these sections is, that there are but few sharp edges to damage. The sections from Nos. 12 to 21, Pl. xlii., though of various widths and thicknesses, may all be described as light or small rails ; most are suitable for geometrical stairs, as being capable of wreathing and scrolling, No. 18, Pl. xlii., being an excellent section for the latter purpose. The toads backs, Nos. 19 and 21, Pl. xlii., are chiefly used in cottage dogleg stairs. In several instances, alternative sections are shown on either side of the centre line, for the sake of economy in the one rail, the more elaborate section being upon the inside or stair side.

CHAPTER XX.

APPARATUS AND TOOLS USED IN STAIR CONSTRUCTION AND HANDRAILING.

(PLATE XLIII.)

The Riser Mitre Shoot—Construction and Uses— The Baluster Bevel, Construction and Method of Using—The Handrailer's Bench Screw: Varieties of—Construction—The Handrailer's Scratch Stock: Method of Use—Reversible Stocks—Thumb Scratches—The Adjustable Quirk Router—the Quirk Cutter, Special Shapes—Thumb Planes—Designs, Suitable Woods for—Blank Irons, Temporary Alteration of Sweep—References to Bent Gouges, Chisels and Files, Callipers, etc.—to Tool Dealers.

PLATE XLIII. contains numerous sketches of apparatus and tools specially adapted to the requirements of the stair and handrail joiner. Certain of these would be equally serviceable in other branches of joinery, but many are indispensable to the craftsman specialising in these two subjects. Most of the general tools and appliances used by the joiner are also used by the specialist, but as these have been exhaustively treated in the author's work on " Modern Joinery," it will be unnecessary to reproduce them here.

The Riser Mitre Shoot (Figs. 1 and 2, Pl. XLIII.), is used for the rapid and accurate production of mitres upon the ends of risers, for cut-string stairs. The apparatus is fixed to the bench by wood screws, inserted at back and front, as shown in the sketch, Fig. 1, Pl. XLIII.; the riser, previously rebated as described at page 70, is slipped down the bottom of the box until its shoulder rests against the fence-piece (which is shown in the enlarged detail, Fig. 2, Pl. XLIII.), where it is wedged at the rear end of the shoot in the manner shown. The projecting lip is then planed off to a true mitre with either a trying or a block plane, the latter of course being the more suitable. Probably little description of the apparatus is needed—the drawings are self-explanatory—but it may be mentioned that the dimensions figured on are merely suggestive, and probably no two " shoots " would be found exactly alike. The essentials are, first, that the bottom of the box shall be at an angle of 45° with the front, that is to say, the ends of the sides ; and that its upper surface is about $\frac{3}{8}$-in. above the plane bed. Next, that the space between the bottom and the underside of the triangular fence, marked a in Fig. 2, Pl. XLIII., exactly equals the lip of the mitre. The fence must be a right-angle triangle in section, and either side must equal the depth of the rebate made in the string—a reference to Fig. 12, Pl. XVIII., will make matters clear. This shoot will suit any size or form of mitre joint, if an appropriate fence-piece is prepared ; therefore, this part should be dry-screwed only for quick removal. A plain mitre may equally well be shot in this box by adjusting the fence to the thickness of the piece to be mitred ; also the brackets can be mitred in it by similar means.

The Baluster Bevel (Fig. 4, Pl. XLIII.) is a contrivance of my own which I have found very useful when fitting balusters under the wreathed portions of a handrail ; of course, under the straight portion, the bevel is readily obtained from the pitch-board, or by setting an ordinary sliding bevel to the pitch of the string, but at the circular portions the bevel on each side of

(91)

each baluster differs, and a winding surface is obtained on its end.   The apparatus consists of a piece of 1¼-in. deal, the width of a baluster and about 2 ft. 6 ins. long, in which is made either a dove-tail or a rebate groove—the former is shown in the drawing.   An appropriately shaped slider about 1 in. to 10 ins. long is made to work stiffly in this groove (see enlarged section, Fig. 5, Pl. XLIII.).   A set-screw is sometimes added as shown in Fig. 3, Pl. XLIII., for further security, but if properly made this is hardly necessary.   At the top of the slider, which is notched as shown in the edge view, Fig. 3, Pl. XLIII., to bring it in line with the inside face of the stock, is pivoted stiffly a small piece of hard wood or sheet zinc, with one of its ends square, the other end bevelled, as shown.   At the bottom end of the stock, which must be cut square in both directions, is fixed a cross-piece, called the shoe, that is afterwards bevelled off, as in Fig. 4, Pl. XLIII., to the inside bottom edge ; the object being to reveal the seat of the baluster, which is marked or cut, on the tread.   To use the apparatus, place the shoe, as shown in Fig. 4, Pl. XLIII., in line with one side of the baluster, which is marked on the tread, and the inner face of the stock in line with the other side ; place one foot on the shoe to keep it steady, plumb the edge of the bevel with a plumb line or a large square, and move the slider upwards until the blade adjusts itself under the rail ; carefully remove the bevel upwards and outwards, where it releases easily, and place the stock on the baluster, keeping the shoe in line with the shoulder, then mark the bevel at top.   Repeat the process on the other side. Thus the exact length and bevel is quickly set off.   The dotted lines in Fig. 4 indicate the position of the baluster.

The Handrailer's Bench Screw shown in Fig. 6, Pl. XLIII., in front and side views, differs considerably from the ordinary joiner's bench-screw.   The latter has its chocks invariably horizontal, but in the one under consideration these are placed vertically.   Usually the height of the screw is so arranged that the ordinary screw block can be utilised without alteration.   Whatever the height of the bench, the top of the chocks, which are double, should rise about 9 ins. above the top, to obtain freedom for working spokeshaves, etc., around the wreath pieces.   The runner is kept near the lower end, so that the tails of long wreaths may be passed between it and the screw.   A taper mortise is driven through the back chock immediately above the runner, and a long wedge is passed through, as shown, to fix the runner at any desired point.   Some workmen prefer the chocks set at an angle of about 60°, usually managed by placing the screw and the runner on opposite sides of the bench leg ; others keep the chocks short enough to revolve on the screw, so that they can be arranged at any angle ; with this method the runner is replaced by a pair of folding wedges driven between the ends of the chocks.   These, however, are more or less fads to which specialists are prone.   Shaped, pine pads are also used after the rail is moulded, to grip it between the chocks and so prevent bruising ; these blocks have projecting wire points that press into the face of the chock and so prevent slipping.

The Handrailer's Scratch Stock (Figs. 7 and 8, Pl. XLIII).   This is an indispensable tool which is not yet obtainable from the tool shops ; consequently it varies in form with the taste of the maker.   The design shown is that of the author's own tool.   It consists of a straight cylindrical stock, 1¾-in. in diameter, the off end rounded, the near end shaped to a ball handle ; any close straight-grained piece of hardwood will do ; my own is of black walnut. The stock is made in two halves which, after slotting for the knives or " scratches," are screwed together and shaped.   A ¾-in. hole is bored through at right angles, to receive the adjustable fence, which should be of some very hard close-grained wood, such as *Lignum vitæ* or box-wood—the former is the better, in consequence of its greasy nature.   It is advisable to have this stem turned in a lathe first, then to make the hole to fit it.   The scratches are really moulding cutters made of any required shape by filing or grinding pieces of thin steel, such as a broken table-knife blade, or piece of tenon saw blade, to the required contour and fixing

PLATE XLIII.

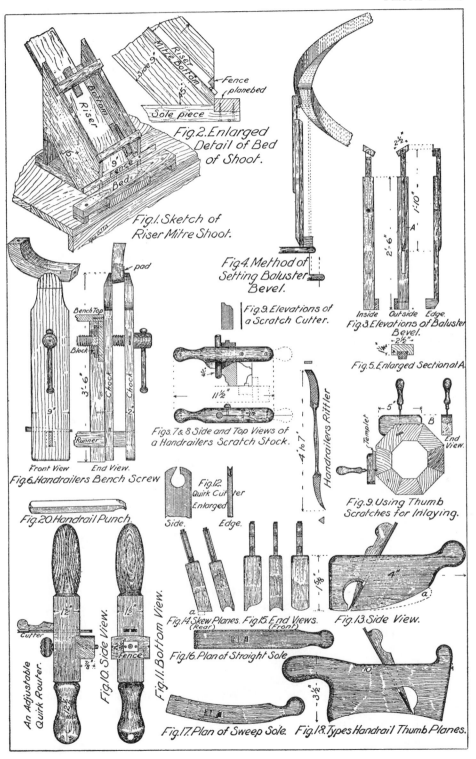

Fig. 2. Enlarged Detail of Bed of Shoot.

Fence planebed

Sole piece

Fig. 1. Sketch of Riser Mitre Shoot.

Fig. 4. Method of Setting Baluster Bevel.

Fig. 3. Elevations of Baluster Bevel.

Inside   Outside   Edge.

Fig. 5. Enlarged Sectional A.

Fig. 9. Elevations of a Scratch Cutter.

pad

Bench Top

Block

Chock

Chock

Runner

Front View.   End View.

Fig. 6. Handrailers Bench Screw.

Figs. 7 & 8. Side and Top Views of a Handrailers Scratch Stock.

Handrailers Rifiler

Fig. 9. Using Thumb Scratches for Inlaying.

Fig. 20. Handrail Punch.

Fig. 12. Quirk Cutter Enlarged.

Side.   Edge.

An Adjustable Quirk Router.

Cutter

Fig. 10. Side View.

Fig. 11. Bottom View.

Fence

Fig. 14. Skew Planes. Fig. 15. End Views.
(Rear)   (Front)

Fig. 16. Plan of Straight Sole.

Fig. 13. Side View.

Fig. 17. Plan of Sweep Sole.   Fig. 18. Types Handrail Thumb Planes.

APPLIANCES AND TOOLS USED IN STAIRBUILDING AND HANDRAILING.

them as shown, in the stock. They are worked around the wreath piece, to finish the mould-ing, after it has been roughed out with gouges or thumb planes. The scratches should be filed square across, and their edges turned with a bradawl similarly to a scraper's edge. The stock is worked rather slowly backwards and forwards, keeping the cutter quite upright, until an absolutely perfect surface is obtained, the operation being in the nature of scraping rather than planing; therefore the tool must be worked down gradually. The scratches are frequently made double-ended, so that they can be reversed, as shown in dotted lines in Fig. 7, Pl. XLIII., also the stock can be double-ended, as indicated in dotted lines, with an extra hole for the stem. This is useful when more than one wreath of similar section is to be moulded, as their successive sections can be worked without disturbing the setting of the other scratch.

The Thumb Scratches shown in Fig. 9, Pl. XLIII., are improvised tools used in connection with the inlaying of the newel post shown on Pl. xxxv., and the method of using them is referred to on page 84.

The Adjustable Quirk Router (Figs. 10 and 11, Pl. XLIII.) is, in its specialised form, a home-made tool. There are varieties, both in wood and iron, to be met with in the tool shops, but the former are intended for ordinary woodworkers' use, and do not exactly meet handrailers' requirements, whilst the latter, though stronger than wood, do not, at least in the author's opinion, work so sweetly as the home-made article.

The form shown is somewhat elaborate; many workmen are satisfied with simply a square stick with the rough edges filed off and a wood screw driven through the fence. Cer-tainly a good workman will accomplish wonders with makeshift tools, but, other things being equal, the better the tool the better the work, and the author always had a penchant for making his own tools, so he offers his own design for those who care to follow it. The quirk cutter, which is a piece of tempered steel about 3 ins. long and ¾ in. wide, of various thicknesses, is shown in the two views, Fig. 12. The ordinary shop-made article is always flat or straight across the face, but cutters work much easier if slightly curved in section, which can be done by softening the cutter in a gas jet, then bending it in a steel vice between two hardwood blocks to the required curvature, afterwards re-tempering it—a little job that any black-smith will do. The author did his own, but the description of the process would be rather lengthy. The stock is 1½ in. square, about 12 ins. long, with small handles turned at the ends; the cutter fits tightly in the mortise, which must be quite upright and is wedged as shown. The sliding fence, lips over the stock, is reversible; one side is rounded slightly, the other straight. It is fixed in any desired position with a thumb-screw. An ordinary "plough-stop" screw answers the purpose. A small slotted plate is sunk in the top side, in which the screw works; the amount of adjustment is about an inch, as shown by the dotted lines. The underside of the stock should be slightly rounded, because the tool must have a rocking motion when worked, because the V part of the cutter, which is in advance of the chisel edge, has to be scored-in before the cut is made.

Thumb Planes.—A few typical designs of these tools are shown in Figs. 13 to 18, Pl. XLIII., but these by no means exhaust the varieties used by handrailers. Almost every workman has his own special fancies, and chiefly they are home-made, though a few tool-makers, like Buck's of Tottenham Court Road, stock the commoner shapes, in boxwood. Those shown are from the author's own kit, and vary in size from 1½-in. long to 10 ins. Thumb planes of course are used only on wreaths, or similar curved work, and generally they accumulate as one or more are made to suit the job in hand.

When one is in a hurry they are "knocked up" in mahogany, or any odd bit of hard wood that comes to hand; but for permanent use, nothing is better than boxwood; ebony works equally well, but its colour prevents the edge of the iron showing. Blank "irons" can be obtained from the tool shops and ground to shape required. The design of " stock " shown in Fig. 13, Pl. XLIII., is best for round-soled planes, and in Fig. 18, Pl. XLIII., for hollow-soled. In the former, you need to " feel " the shape as you work, and the plane must tilt as required, but in the latter case the plane must bed firmly on the work throughout. For temporary purposes, either kind can have the sweep altered, by gluing loose slips (as at *a*, Fig. 13, Pl. XLIII.) to the sole, and shaping them as the work requires. Any of the shapes shown in end views, Figs. 14-15, Pl. XLIII., can be made in plan, as either Figs. 16 or 17, Pl. XLIII.

Note that the throat, as shown in Fig. 13, Pl. XLIII., should be bevelled from nothing at the bottom of the mouth, and on the near side, to nearly ⅛ of an inch on the off-side and the top, for the purpose of throwing the shavings out. Mr. George Buck, toolmaker, of 242 Tottenham Court Road, London, W.1., makes and stocks various sizes and shapes of handrailer's thumb planes, as shown here.

Among other special tools required by the handrailer are : curved and front-bent gouges and chisels, egg callipers (these will be found illustrated in " Modern Practical Joinery " or any large tool dealers' catalogues, notably Melhuish & Sons, of Holborn Bars, London); rifflers (bent files and rasps, see Fig. 19, Pl. XLIII.), handrail punch (Fig. 20, Pl. XLIII.), etc.

CHAPTER XXI.

THE CONSTRUCTION OF WREATHED AND TWISTED SOFFIT LININGS AND FRAMINGS TO STAIRS.

(PLATES XLIV.–XLVI.)

Wood Soffits, Former Practice—Plaster Makeshifts, Defects—A Twisted Soffit Lining—Treatment of the Plan, its Objects, taking the Dimensions—Necessary Drawing, Rule of Thumb Methods—Setting Out the Linings, Fitting and Fixing—Obtaining Shape of the Pitching Piece, Working the Twisted Edge—A Framed Panelled Twisted Soffit—Method of Reading the Drawings, how to Set Out—Ellipse with Circular Axis—Method of Construction, Projecting the Elevation—Obtaining the Moulds—Face Moulds, Edge Moulds, Moulds for Wall Rails—Fitting the Panels—A Wreathed Soffit to a Spiral Stair—Moulds Obtained by Tangent System—To Set Out the Rod—Considerations in Arranging Joints—Obtaining the Developments—Face Moulds, how to Set Out—Panel Moulds—Radial Rails—Method of Working—Fitting-up in Sections, Fixing, etc.

THE ceiling or lining of the soffits of stairs, with wood panelling, was a much more common practice in former times than it is at present; the speed and relative cheapness of the slap-dash plastered soffit doubtless appeals strongly to the economical builder and his clients; but many artistic possibilities are sacrificed to the whitewashed ceiling.

A plaster soffit at best is but a makeshift; the inelastic and fragile material is quite unsuited for positions in which there is intermittent movement and constant liability to damage. Occasionally, however, an architect will specify for a panelled or lined soffit, and the concluding chapters of this volume are devoted to an explanation of the ways and means of overcoming the difficulties incidental to the construction of these attractive finishings.

A Twisted Soffit Lining to a return flight of stairs, with five winders in the quarter turn, is shown on Pl. XLIV. As, of course, no difficulty will be experienced in lining the straight portions, the drawings, etc., are confined to the wreathed portions. Fig. 1, Pl. XLIV., is the plan of the angle containing the winders, with a couple of flyers above and below the springings. As the essential things in these drawings are the component parts of the soffit, everything else is treated as subordinate, and mostly indicated in dotted lines. It may be explained that the plan is drawn in its proper position, that is to say, the dotted lines marked " riser " indicate the right position of the steps, and although the soffit is drawn in full lines, these must be understood to lie *underneath* the stair, and represent the face side as it would be seen looking up. The object of this method of setting out is to prevent mistakes in the hand of the stair, which might occur if it were upside down, though of course this would be the natural way to view the soffit. The double line drawn at the outside string represents the lip of the rebate into which the lining is sunk flush. This lip may be moulded or return-beaded as taste indicates. The return nosings over the cut string are not shown in plan, though they are in the elevation. It may be added that although these three drawings are necessary for explanation it does not follow that they must be all made for the purpose of obtaining the linings. In practice, the necessary dimensions would be taken on thin laths, bent around the strings, after the stair was erected. The author has, however, seen them fitted that way tentatively, a board at a time, without preliminary drawings, and the result

(96)

was neither happy nor economical in cost. The method here explained will obviate both these defects.

Fig. 2, Pl. XLIV., is the elevation of the stair, as seen from point A at bottom edge of plate, or from behind the wall string. In this view most of the soffit is visible, and although the linings as projected from the plan look irregular and out of level, they have not this appearance when actually seen from beneath, the normal view.

Fig. 3, Pl. XLIV., is an elevation taken again at the back of the stair, as seen from point B. In this view none of the soffit is visible, but the face of the upper flight is seen. The dotted lines in both drawings indicate the shaped pitching-piece, shown on the plan. It is only necessary to draw one view to obtain its shape, and frequently in practice this is also dispensed with, the pitching piece being shaped out to fit the soffit, as the boards are fixed. Fig. 4, Pl. XLIV., is a stretch-out of the well or " cylinder," and is necessary to obtain the true widths of the boards at their narrow ends for the purpose of setting out the widths on the string. It has not been thought necessary to make a development of the soffit, partly because a very complicated and intricate process is required, quite unsuitable for workshop practice, and partly because if it were shown it would be unnecessary, as the true dimensions can quickly be obtained from the stair itself, as we shall see. Fig. 5, Pl. XLIV., is the mould for the pitching-piece, and is referred to subsequently. The object to be aimed at in setting out the plan is to so arrange the linings that they shall all appear of one width, or radiate symmetrically, when viewed from beneath. This cannot be obtained by spacing out equal widths along the wall strings, the usual rule-of-thumb method. Describe a quadrant from the centre of the well touching the face lines of the strings. Space out the boards on this line as nearly equal to the general width of the linings as possible, bearing in mind that it is not desirable to have the boards in such number that the outer ends are very narrow, for the narrower they are, the more difficult are they to fix. From the points on the quadrant draw lines to the centre, and continue them to intersect the backs of the strings. These points, numbered 1 to 10, on each string in the plan, are projected to the respective strings in elevation, where they are indicated by the dotted projectors at points 1' to 10'.

These points are transferred to the strings themselves by taking them off the rod upon a pliable strip which is to be bent closely around the edge of the string and marked thereon. In like manner, the narrow ends are taken off the stretch-out (Fig. 4, Pl. XLIV.) and the strip carefully adjusted to the springings, when the points can be transferred to the edge of the wreathed string. If the reader is not familiar with the making of the stretch-out, let him refer to page 36, where the method is detailed. The linings can now be fitted, one at a time, starting at the bottom springing and working to the joint lines marked on the strings. The length is first marked by accurately pencilling against the strings, then the widths can be measured off at each end, and the joint shot. The boards should not exceed $\frac{3}{8}$ in. in thickness, and are best secured by cups and screws. But if they are to be nailed and painted, it will be advisable to steam each board before bending, as there will be considerable twist as the central board is approached. These plain soffits are frequently made in mahogany, and they not only enhance the appearance of the stair, but add considerably to its strength.

To obtain the shape of the pitching piece, which may be placed in any convenient position, but is best situated as near the middle of the width as possible, it is necessary to draw in the elevation of the joints as shown in Fig. 2, Pl. XLIV. This is done by projecting each end of the joint into the elevation, as in the case of joint No. 7, which is completely projected to indicate the method, and joining the two points as at 7'-7'', Fig. 2, Pl. XLIV., the double line represents the bead or chamfer on the joint, and is not necessary for the purpose now discussed. Next, taking either side of the pitching piece in plan as a working face, project the joint intersections as at a, b, c, d, e, etc., Fig. 1, Pl. XLIV., into the elevation, cutting the corresponding joints at a', b', c', d', e', etc., Fig. 2, Pl. XLIV., and draw a regular curve through the points so found. These of course will be points in the face of the soffit, and the pitching piece will be at the back, but the difference is so slight that it may be disregarded, as it is easy to correct any slight discrepancy when the piece is fixed and a straight edge is swept around the edges of the strings. The perpendicular heights of the several points have now to be arranged approximately on the plan, at least that is how it would be done in the workshop, but here, to avoid confusion of lines, this projection is made separately in Fig. 5, the base line C-D representing the face of the pitching piece C-D, Fig. 1. The various points a', b', c' to k are transferred thereto and perpendiculars erected. These are marked at the same heights, as the correspondingly lettered points in Fig. 2 are, above the level line L-L, as measured on each projector. Thus a series of points are obtained through which the curved surface can be drawn. The point at e is shown in the plan to indicate how it could be drawn thereon. The edge surface will be twisted, but this is readily obtained by applying a straight edge as described above, after fixing and working the edge off to fit with a spokeshave.

A Framed and Panelled Twisted Soffit to a rectangular stair, with a quarter space of winders in a right angle, is shown on Pl. XLV.

This is a more difficult piece of work than the previous example, although in principle the construction is similar. These explanatory drawings have the disadvantage of containing a confusion of lines which make them apparently more complex than they really are, or will be found in practice, for, in setting out upon the rod, each series of construction lines may be obliterated, as the particular part they are designed to obtain is reached, but of course upon these drawings *all* must be retained for reference, and the readiest way to follow the construction is to attend only to those lines and figures mentioned at the time, ignoring the others until they are reached in due order.

The general plan of the soffit framing is shown in Fig. 1, Pl. XLV., and consists of a $1\frac{1}{4}$ in. sunk, shaped and moulded, panelled framing, the inside rails following the walls, the outside rail wreathing around the well. The wall rails are interrupted by a great arch rail running concentrically with the outer rail. Between these two the panel is broken up by spur rails in alternative designs, supporting an elliptic centre piece (the construction of this will be referred to later). A portion of the moulding is omitted for the sake of clearness, and the positions of steps and strings are indicated by dotted lines, this drawing being made, like the previous examples, as if the stair were transparent and the underside visible through it ; the reason for this has already been stated (see previous example). It will of course be readily seen that the face of the stuff will be placed downwards when setting out on the rod, then the lines placed thereon will all be in their appropriate positions. The method of making the several projections will not be detailed here, as it is assumed the student will have gained sufficient information from preceding examples ; but it may be stated that, except for explanation, the details shown in the elevations, Figs. 2 and 3, Pl. XLV., are not necessary for the purpose of setting out. Fig. 10, Pl. XLV., is the kind of drawing required on the rod for setting out purposes, this being a reproduction of the constructive parts of Fig. 2, Pl. XLV. Of course, the exact shape of the ornamental panelling would have to be blocked in to obtain the shoulder lines.

Fig. 4, Pl. XLV., is the stretch-out of the cut string, and is required to obtain the shape of the lower edge in Figs. 2 and 3, Pl. XLV.

The central elliptic frame in Fig. 1, Pl. XLV., is trammelled in its outer half upon a circular axis, as shown thereon, the object being to flatten the outside of the ellipse and so obtain greater space for the margin panels. The design is a matter of taste, and a true ellipse may be used if preferred, the method of obtaining the moulds would be the same.

Construction.—The twisted surface of work of this description does not admit of

PLATE XLIV.

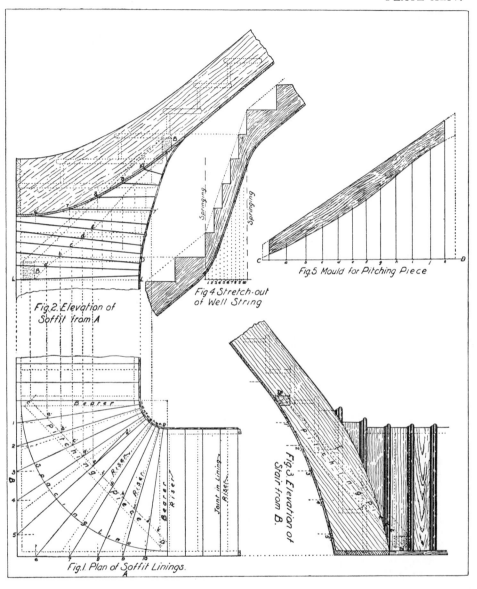

Fig.2. Elevation of Soffit from A

Fig 4 Stretch-out of Well String

Fig.5 Mould for Pitching Piece

Fig.3 Elevation of Stair from B.

Fig.1. Plan of Soffit Linings.

A TWISTED SOFFIT LINING UNDER A QUARTER TURN OF WINDERS.

geometrical development as a whole, that is to say, it cannot be resolved into a true plane; therefore, to obtain its shape, it is necessary to break the surface up into a number of parts that are sufficiently small to contain plane surfaces within their boundaries, and having obtained sections of these, placed in their appropriate positions, the moulds to reproduce those surfaces on the material are deduced.

These constructive "planes" are represented on the plan by the triangles formed by drawing straight lines from the series of points, numbered 1 to 9, on the edges of the strings, to the centre of the plan curves. A comparatively few lines are drawn in the figure to avoid confusion. Drawn at full size, more would be needed; moreover, they need not be equal or symmetrical, but may be placed just as the exigencies of the mould suggest. Two such "afterthoughts" are indicated in chain-line at O and M, the first to obtain an intermediate point at the end of the ellipse, the second to locate the position of the joint D on the mould.

Having drawn these radial lines on the plan, project their ends to the appropriate strings in the elevations, as shown at points 1a, 2a, etc., and 1b, 2b, etc. Join these corresponding points, and so obtain the elevation of the lines as shown by the line marked Line No. 1 in Fig. 2, Pl. XLV.

At first sight it may not be clear how the heights of points 1a, 2a, 3a and 4a, Fig. 2, Pl. XLV., are located. A reference to the elevation of this wall string (Fig. 3, Pl. XLV.), will, however, make it clear. Hereupon, the points are shown projected from the plan, Fig. 1, Pl. XLV., and their "height," or relation to the bottom of the string, is indicated. It will be found more convenient to work all heights from a common level line, one of which is shown taken through the lowest point in the soffit at the springing in Figs. 2 and 3, Pl. XLV. Having now produced the constructive lines passing through the surface of the required solid, we proceed to utilise them in obtaining points on the mould that will coincide with like points in the required surface; obviously, the more numerous these points are, the truer the subsequent surface is likely to be. As the principle and its application is the same throughout all the moulds required, it will only be necessary to describe the procedure in full details in one instance, and for this purpose the larger section of the ellipse frame (Fig. 1, Pl. XLV.), between the joints D-E, is selected. Draw the chord line marked "chord to great arc," joining the inner ends of the joints (these latter are made "normal" or perpendicular to a tangent to the curve at the outside of the joints) and a parallel with it X-X', touching the crown of the ellipse. The distance between these lines indicates the width of stuff required for this piece of the framing. Usually the last drawn line is utilised as a base line for the required section, but for the convenience of having the lines clear of the circular rail this base line is moved on this drawing a few inches further back. Proceed to draw perpendiculars (dotted) to the base line through points D, 3', 4', 5', 6', E, obtained at the intersections of the like numbered radial lines, with the convex curve of the ellipse, also at the joints. To obtain points or "heights" on these lines, project the points of intersection into the elevation, where they are numbered similarly, cutting the corresponding lines in points M°, 3°, 4°, 5°, 6°. Incidentally it may be noted, these are also location points, through which the elevation curves of the frame may be drawn, but with this we are not now concerned. Measure the height of each point perpendicularly above the "level line," and transfer these heights to the perpendiculars in plan, as M", 3", 4", 5", 6", e", measuring from the "Base Line," and draw a regular curve through them. Add the required thickness and draw a parallel curve, when a section of the rail is obtained upon a curved line, representing its convex edge; this is shown hatched. Enclose this section by a rectangle, as shown, thus obtaining the requisite thickness. From this section is deduced the edge mould, Fig. 5, Pl. XLV. Upon a straight line d-e, equal in length to the curve line D3', 4', 5', 6', E, Fig. 1, erect perpendiculars at these points and make them equal in height to the corresponding perpendiculars in the section just found. The

PLATE XLV.

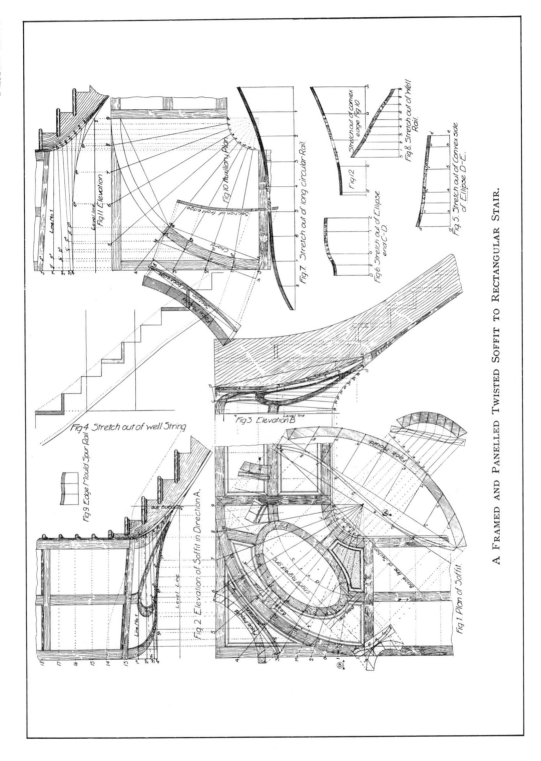

Fig 1 Plan of Soffit

Fig 2 Elevation of Soffit in Direction A.

Fig 3 Elevation B

Fig 4 Stretch out of well String

Fig 9 Edge Mould Spur Rail

Fig 11 Elevation

Fig 10 Auxiliary Plan

Fig 7 Stretch out of long circular Rail

Fig 8 Stretch out of Well Rail

Fig 5 Stretch out of Convex side of Ellipse D-E.

Fig 6 Stretch out of Ellipse end C-D.

Fig 12

Section of front edge

A FRAMED AND PANELLED TWISTED SOFFIT TO RECTANGULAR STAIR.

PLATE XLVI.

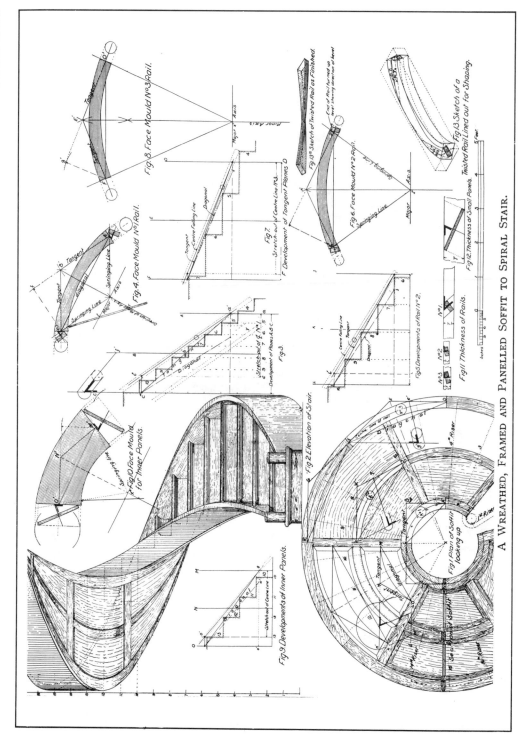

Fig.8. Face Mould No.3 Rail.

Fig. 13a Sketch of Twisted Rail as Finished.

Fig.13 Sketch of a Twisted Rail Lined out for Shaving.

Fig. 4. Face Mould No.1 Rail.

Fig.7.
Stretch out of Centre Line No.3.
F Development of Tangent Planes D

Fig.6. Face Mould No.2 Rail.

Fig.3.
Stretch out of C No.1
D Development of Planes A.B.C.

Fig.5 Developments of Rail No.2.

Fig.12. Thickness of Small Panels.

Fig.11 Thickness of Rails.

Fig.10 Face Mould for Inner Panels.

Fig.2. Elevation of Stair.

Fig.9. Developments of Inner Panels.

Fig.1 Plan of Soffit looking up

A WREATHED, FRAMED AND PANELLED SOFFIT TO SPIRAL STAIR.

curve drawn through these points will produce the correct edge mould, as shown hatched. The joints may be marked by the mould, or if preferred may be made square to the surface at the point, but in this case the *length* of the piece must be marked through the middle of its thickness. If desired, a corresponding mould can be obtained for the inside edge, in like manner, but generally in practice the outer edge mould is considered sufficient, for when the various parts are cut out and jointed together, the surface is finally trued by sweeping a straight edge radially across the framing, and easing down the face where required, then the rebates, thickness, etc., is gauged therefrom.

The Face Mould is obtained by producing the perpendiculars across the face of the frame in plan, as shown by the full line ordinates at 3′, 4′, 5′, 6′, Fig. 1, Pl. XLV., also across the section to the back edge, and squaring out corresponding ordinates therefrom. Upon each of these ordinates set off from the edge a like distance to that of the corresponding ordinate in plan, measured from the face line X-X′, and draw the curves through these points; for instance, the height D-X equals d-x on face mould. It will be observed that the above construction is carried out by first determining the section placed at its proper altitude and inclination to the horizontal, then turning the face up at right angles to the edge, and making the two moulds coincide at the various points selected. In like manner, the sections and moulds with their stretch-outs, for the end piece of the elliptic frame, two of the spur rails, the outside wreathed rail and the long circular rail in one piece are shown in the hatched portions of the plan, and in Figs. 6, 7, 8, 9, Pl. XLV. It is not thought necessary to detail the construction of these, the main projectors are drawn and lettered, and they are all produced in the manner just described, but in Figs. 10 and 11, Pl. XLV., redrawn to indicate the minimum number of lines required to obtain any one section of moulds, opportunity is taken of showing the necessary variation and construction when the joints are arranged differently from Fig. 1, Pl. XLV. Referring to the long circular rail therein, if made in one piece, a thickness of over 6 ins. and a width of nearly 20 ins. would be required, whilst if made in two lengths, as shown in Fig. 10, Pl. XLV., $3\frac{1}{4}$ ins. thickness and 7 ins. width will be sufficient; or if made in three pieces, 2 ins. by $5\frac{1}{2}$ ins. would suffice. The projection of the construction lines 1, 2, 3-9 can be more readily seen in this drawing.

Draw the chord X-d^x, connecting the ends of the joints and its parallel y-z; upon this line erect perpendiculars drawn through points j, a, b, c, d, make these equal in length to the projectors $a′$, $b′$, $c′$, $d′$, above the level line in Fig. 11, measured from the line y-z. These give the points through which to draw the curve of section; and the corresponding stretch-out, to produce the edge-mould, is shown in Fig. 12, Pl. XLV. The face mould is drawn turned up on the edge of the section rectangle by the process previously described.

The method of finding the section at the concave edge is also shown, and the stretch-out of this edge in like manner will produce a mould for the edge X-d.

The moulds for the wall rails are obtained from the lower edges of the strings, as shown in Fig. 3, Pl. XLV., the enclosing rectangle a-b-c-d showing the size of piece required. In all cases no allowance has been made for tenons, as the details of framing up are not dealt with, but in setting out these must be allowed for, as the method of construction adopted determines.

No moulds for the panels are shown, because these can more readily be obtained from the respective edges of the rails after the latter are framed together, or, if the panels are to be sunk into rebates, which is the easier way, the stuff after cutting to shape in plan can be quickly scribed to fit the rebates by placing each panel over its respective opening. Sometimes for an inferior class of work the panelling is formed by sheet lining, as described in the preceding example, and the " framing " cut to shape as a thin mounting which is fixed to the face of the panelling by screws sunk in pelleted holes. This method, though cheaper than the solid method, is of course false construction.

A Wreathed, Framed and Panelled Soffit to a Spiral Stair, Pl. XLVI.—The soffit of this stair forms a true helical surface, therefore its setting out can readily be carried out by the tangent system described in the subsequent chapters of this book, under the head of "Handrailing of Double Curvature." As the theory and principles of this method are fully explained, and the several manipulative details dealt with therein, it would be superfluous to repeat them here, and these explanations are confined to the special application needed in this instance. For a complete understanding of the methods described, the reader is advised to refer to Chap. III., Vol. II. The plan, Fig. 1, Pl. XLVI., shows a portion of one revolution of the soffit as it would be seen looking up from below or as it would appear if it were possible to see through the stairs above; these latter are indicated by dotted lines and are twenty-one in number. The soffit consists of a $1\frac{1}{2}$-in. solid framework, containing three circular rails, described respectively as No. 1, No. 2 and No. 3 rail, divided into bays, by six straight radial rails, which are filled in with flush, sunk and chamfered panels.

The elevation, Fig. 2, Pl. XLVI., is projected upon a plane parallel to the diameter X-D; thus, as the first step lies at an acute angle with this plane, the two newels appear much nearer together than they really are, the true width of the stair is shown above the fourth riser. The apparent diminish in the raking rails of the soffit is of course due to their projection at an inclined plane, and it may be added, that this drawing is in no way necessary for the purpose of making either the soffit or the stair, but is here given to facilitate the understanding of the procedure now to be described.

Assuming the plan set out full size, or rather one bay is sufficient, as all are alike, although two are used in this drawing to avoid confusion, the first step is to decide the position of the joints in the rails; to a great extent this will depend upon the thickness of stuff available, but also the convenience of fitting up the framework must be considered, thus the joints of the inner and outer rails should range in line at not too great a distance apart; as arranged in the drawing, the inner rail is divided into four equal sections or lengths, and the joints in the outer rail are made to range with these, each section of the outer rail having an intermediate joint, also of course the middle rail must join at the centres of the radials. We will now consider each rail in turn. No. 1 rail. Describe the circular line from A to C, passing through the middle of the rail, and draw the lines A-B and B-C tangent to this circle at the joints.

Draw also the diagonal line A-C, produce the riser lines to cut the central line in points 5, 6, 7, 8, 9. This completes the work on the plan, and we proceed to make the developments, Fig. 3, Pl. XLVI. First draw the horizontal line a-c equal in length to the stretch-out of the curved line A-C, Fig, 1, Pl. XLVI., and set off thereon the points of intersection of the risers 1 to 9, as they occur in the plan. Erect perpendiculars at a and c, which become the "springings" of this rail. Upon one of these set up eight risers and by cross projections from these points and those upon a-c, obtain the development of the steps, as shown in section. The nosing line touching the top angles should be a straight line if the projection is correct, because, as explained in a previous example, a helical curve develops on a plane as a straight line. Upon this line we draw a parallel at a distance apart equal to the thickness of the required framing. This is shown in dotted line in Fig. 3, Pl. XLVI. Of course the ultimate position of the soffit is *under* the steps, but as the shape is the same whether drawn above or below these, and for other reasons, it is more convenient to have the drawing on the nosing line; it is thus placed, but a portion of the rail is shown in true position at Y to obtain the depth of string required to make the elevation, Fig. 2, Pl. XLVI. Next draw the full line a'-c'', at the middle of the thickness. At the intersections with the springing lines, defined by small circles, are the joint points, from which the heights of the tangents upon the development are obtained. Proceed to make the **Development of the Tangent Planes** which are shown in plan at A-B-C in Fig. 1, Pl. XLVI. Draw the vertical lines A, B, C at a distance apart equal to that of the same points in plan.

To obtain the heights of the tangents thereon, draw horizontal projectors, as shown, from the points on the two springings on the stretch-out. The lower one at a' coincides with that already found, as this springing of the two developments is made to agree. The upper one is projected to point C^2. Draw a straight line from C^2 to a', and the inclination and length of the tangents A-B and B-C is shown. Next, we require the length of the diagonal A-C. Through a' draw a level line to cut the perpendicular C, Fig. 3, Pl. XLVI. From C on this line set off the length of A-C in Fig. 1, Pl. XLVI. Join the point to C''', and the real length of the diagonal is seen. With these data the face mould, Fig. 4, Pl. XLVI., is produced. Make the line A'-C' equal in length to the diagonal in Fig. 3, Pl. XLVI. From A' and C', as centres, the radius equal to length of either tangent a'-b' or b'-c', describe arcs intersecting at B' and X'. Draw lines from these two points to A' and C', thus locating the position of the tangents and springing lines on the face mould, as shown. Draw a line through B'-X', and a line at right angles through X'. These two lines give the directions of the minor and major axis respectively of the elliptic curves required in the mould. To obtain the *lengths* of these axes proceed as follows. Take the perpendicular length C'-f, Fig. 4, Pl. XLVI., and lay it off on the development at C-f'. The angle at C is the slide bevel for the mould. Describe a circle on this line, as at O, equal in diameter to the width of the rail in plan, draw two lines touching this circle and parallel the bevel line, to cut line C. The semi-circle drawn on these points indicates the width of the mould at the springings. Produce the tangents in Fig. 4, Pl. XLVI., and describe this circle upon them; draw parallels to the tangents, touching the circles, to cut the springings as shown in dotted lines. These are the points required to draw the elliptic curves. Take a light rod as t-r in Fig. 4, Pl. XLVI., place the pointed end at the inside of the rail joint on the plan, Fig. 1, Pl. XLVI., laying the end across the diameter, and mark on the edge the centre X, place the end of the rod at the point just found on the inside of the springing, Fig. 4, Pl. XLVI., with its length lying across the axes. Make point X coincide with the major axis at t, and mark the point r upon it where it crosses the minor axis. These two points kept upon the corresponding axes will guide the end of the rod in the right position all round for marking points in the elliptic curve; proceed in like manner for the outside edge. Draw the joints square to the tangents through their intersection with the springing lines, and mark off from the *outside* of the joint the full width of the rail, as shown by the circles. Continue the inside ellipse to these points, and the mould is complete. The size and relative positions of the two ends of the wreath piece are shown in section, as if turned up on the joint lines of the mould in Fig. 4, Pl. XLVI., also the direction in which the bevel is applied thereon. The dotted rectangle shows the necessary width of the wreath piece; all these points are fully detailed in Chapter XXVII., " Practical Work in Wreath Making," Vol. II., to which the reader is referred for further information.

The procedure for obtaining the face moulds for rails Nos. 2 and 3 shown in Figs. 6 and 8 is the same as that just described, up to the point of obtaining the slide bevel. For reasons that will be found fully detailed in Plate IX. and page 34, Vol. II., the perpendicular distance between the tangent and the springing, as shown at F'-g, Fig. 8, Pl. XLVI., must be laid off between parallels in the plan, as at g'-e', Fig. 1, Pl. XLVI. The angle formed between the parallel and the line g'-e', contains the bevel, and the width of the mould is found thereon, as in the preceding case. The centre of the elliptic axes in face mould No. 3, situated at point X'', is found by bisecting the diagonal F'-D', drawing a line from E' through the bisection, and marking off a length thereon equal to that of the line E-X in the plan, Fig. 1, Pl. XLVI., and similarly in case No. 2.

The Panel Mould (Fig. 10, Pl. XLVI.) is found in precisely the same way as are the rail moulds: the tangents are drawn in the plan to a concentric line lying in the middle of the width, which must include the edges sunk in the rails, as indicated by dotted lines. The developments of these lines in reference to the inner panel is shown in Fig. 9, Pl. xlvi., and should be clear to the reader following the first instructions. The construction of the face mould presents no fresh difficulty, its only difference from the rail moulds is in its greater width. The construction lines to obtain this are shown at the side of the tangents O-N, N-M, and the necessary thickness of stuff is shown in Fig. 12, Pl. xlvi. Edge moulds may be obtained if desired by the method described under " Falling Moulds " at page 53, Vol. II.

The radial rails will wind slightly in their length, though each lies level on its centre line. It is hardly worth the trouble of setting out the cross-sections and obtaining moulds for these, as the work can be accomplished quite as accurately and much quicker by gauging the tenons slightly further back from the face than are the mortises, thus causing the face of the radials to project an equal amount when framed up, and the necessary " cleaning off " is readily accomplished, as each bay must be framed up (temporarily) and cleaned off before the whole can be assembled. The soffit cannot be put together and handled as a whole, it must be fitted together in sections, then each section fixed under the stair in succession and secured with " wood screws," either sunk in pelleted holes or bedded into brass cups. The joints of the sections may be brought up by wedging from temporary stops fixed to the inside of the strings.

Fig. 13, Pl. xlvi., is a sketch illustrating the method of lining out the curved rails with the necessary alteration of the tangents to obtain the sliding of the mould, as fully described in Chapter V., Part II. The references on the plate are : O.T. = original tangent, N.T. = new tangent.

CHAPTER XXII.

A GEOMETRICAL STONE STAIRCASE WITH DETAILS OF CONSTRUCTION.

(PLATE XLVII.)

Detailed Description of the Drawings and Method of Construction—Reason for Unusual Drawing—
How to Set Out and Construct the Curtail Step—Method of Fixing the Newel Post into Step
and Handrail—Development of the Tangent Planes to Obtain Joint Bevels – Enlarged Plan and
Details of Balustrade—Construction of the Corridor Landing—How to Set Out and Cut a Spandrel
Step—The Making and Placing of Templets.

DESCRIPTION OF DRAWINGS.—The example shown on the accompanying plate is described, so
far as the ſtair itself is concerned, as an open well, rectangular ſtone ſtair with short return
flight, quarter-space of winders, a quarter-pace landing, with three ſteps in the well, and a
curtail ſtep at ſtart of the ſtair. The return landing at the top end of the well leads to a room
on the left hand, and on the right hand at the same level is a long corridor landing, leading
to similar flights on successive floors. So far as the plan of the handrail is concerned the
description would be that of a rectangular geometrical ſtair with quarter of winders and a
quarter-landing, rising three ſteps to return and reverse landings, with scroll cap, to an iron
newel post.

Fig. 2, Pl. XLVII., is a vertical sectional elevation, on the line A-B in the plan, showing
the ſtairs and the landing baluſtrade in elevation, the upper landing being in section, with view
of underside of the three ſteps and the quarter-landing; the dotted lines indicate the tailing
of the ſteps into the walls, which also is shown similarly in the plan.

Fig. 1, Pl. XLVII., is a general plan of the ſtairs, landings, and the enclosing walls. The
seats of the baluſters are indicated by short dash lines.

An enlarged detail of the joints in the landing ſtones is shown in Fig. 7, Pl. XLVII., at
L-M, the particular joint being termed a taper joggle. These are usually made dry, the landing
of course being laid when the walls are carried up to the level; the " well " ends are supported
temporarily by ſtrutting from the floor below until all are fixed by the super-incumbent walls,
when the whole becomes self-supporting.

As indicated in Fig. 13, Pl. XLVII., a cantilever bracket may be introduced at V-W, if
thought necessary, this depending upon the probable traffic, the said bracket being oſtensibly
a support for a gas or electric light. The method of projecting the ſteps from the ſtory
rod is also shown : this has been fully explained in a previous example.

Fig. 3, Pl. XLVII., is a transverse of the ſtair enclosure taken on line C-D in the plan,
this cuts the two landings and the well ſteps. Although not actually in the line of section the
seats of these ſteps are shown in full line ; this will be clear on inspection of the enlarged detail,
Fig. 8.

Fig. 4, Pl. XLVII., is a sectional elevation on line E-F on plan given to show the variation
in the landing. An enlarged detail through the same parts is given in Fig. 7, Pl. XLVII.

Fig. 5, Pl. XLVII., is a sectional elevation on the line G-H in the plan, and is somewhat
unorthodox in treatment, inasmuch that, owing to the necessity of keeping all the drawings
upon one sheet of somewhat limited size, it has been attempted to show two views or projections upon one drawing. Thus all that portion of the ſtair that occurs to the right hand

of the line of section is drawn in full lines, whilst all to the left of the line G-H is shown in dotted lines, so that the reader must imagine these portions are behind him when he faces towards the parts shown in full lines.   This arrangement permits the omission of another section, and so saves space.

Fig. 6, Pl. xlvii., is an enlargement of the end of the curtail step which is shown complete in Fig. 18, Pl. xlvii.   This drawing indicates position of the balusters and the handrail in dotted lines.

Figs. 7 and 8, Pl. xlvii., are enlarged sections through the steps and landings at the points marked and lettered in the plan, showing the " check " joint to prevent sliding of the upper step ; the bevel is set at right angles to the soffit, the seat lining with top of the step.   The corresponding sinking in the next step is a birdsmouth.   The tailing in the wall is indicated in dotted lines, but is shown more clearly in the isometric sketch, Fig. 14, Pl. xlvii.

Figs. 9 and 10, Pl. xlvii., are similar sections through the upper landing.

Fig. 11, Pl. xlvii., is an enlarged detail at the top of the flight adjacent, the quarter landing particularly showing the setting out for the baluster.

Fig. 12, Pl. xlvii., is a similarly enlarged detail of the balustrade, showing the fixing of the balusters to the iron core in the handrail, also their feet into the stone steps by means of jagged notches cut in the baluster end, sunk into a dovetail hole in the step, which is afterwards filled with molten lead, or sometimes neat portland cement.

Fig. 13, Pl. xlvii., has already been alluded to.

Figs. 14 and 15, Pl. xlvii., show to larger scale one flyer step and one winder step.

Fig. 15, Pl. xlvii., shows the wood templet, which is made the exact size and shape of each winder as shown in the plan, Fig. 1, Pl. xlvii., a separate one of course being required for each step, as the corresponding step on each side of the winder space must be made opposite hands, whilst the angle, or kite winder, No. 7, obviously differs at each side of the re-entrant angle. The templet is made to the sight line or visible parts of the step, as shown on the rod, and the outline lightly marked with a scriber, then the amount of tailing (the portion of the step that is built into the wall) is measured off and marked on the stone.   The outer end at M, Fig. 1, Pl. xlvii., is marked to shape with a slip-templet, made to fit the curve and having a fence piece as shown at T, Fig. 16, to keep it in the right position whilst scribing the stone.   This templet is made the exact width between the splay and the face of the riser.   Fig. 17 shows the templet on the rod when marking it to shape, the length to the back is immaterial.   This Fig., drawn to enlarged scale to make the method clear, shows how the winders are set out on the rod, which is a large planed and battened board, large enough to take the winders from 5 to 10 at full size.

Fig. 18, Pl. xlvii., is an enlarged plan and elevation of the end of the curtail step, newel post, and terminal of the handrail, which has been sketched in the general plan and sections.

This drawing is not actually necessary for the setting out of the practical work of the stair, but is useful as showing the method of projecting the wreathed rail, curtail step and balusters. As this has been fully explained in connection with previous examples the reader is referred to similar details in connection with wood stairs.

Figs. 19 and 20, Pl. xlvii, are the necessary drawings for the moulds and bevels for the handrail, which are placed here to complete the set of drawings for this stair, but it would be simply wasting space to attempt the explanation to one unacquainted with the details of the tangent system of handrailing, which is fully treated in that section of this work which deals with handrailing comprehensively, and to which the reader is referred.   See Vol. II. " Handrailing."

PLATE XLVII.

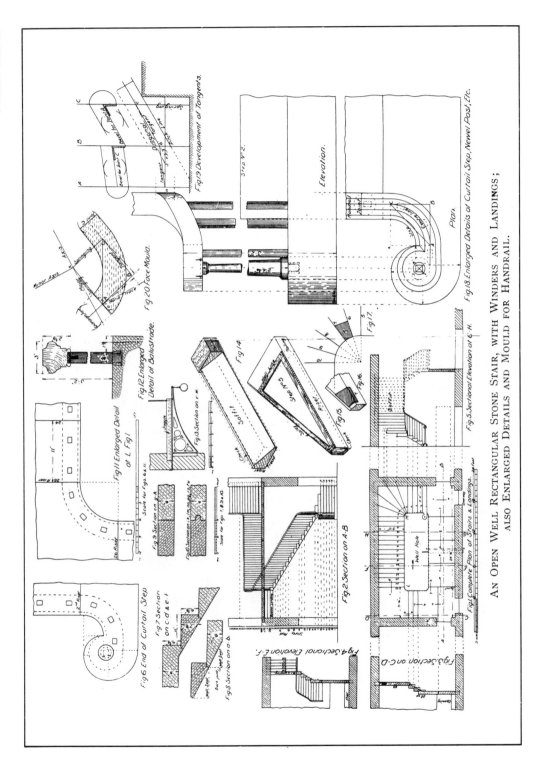

AN OPEN WELL RECTANGULAR STONE STAIR, WITH WINDERS AND LANDINGS;
ALSO ENLARGED DETAILS AND MOULD FOR HANDRAIL.

PLATE XLVIII.

THE CHARTERHOUSE, LONDON, 1564-8 : AN ELIZABETHAN DOGLEG STAIR.
With a Wall Open Balustrade, and Strapwork Apron.

CHAPTER XXIII.

REPRESENTATIVE EXAMPLES OF STAIRCASES, HISTORICAL AND MODERN.

(PLATES XLVIII.–LXXVI.)

Standard Types to Present-day Requirements—Early Renaissance Examples—Jacobean—Charter-house—Elaborate Strapwork—The Guildford Example of 1619—Moor Park—Deddington—Later Renaissance Examples from Coleshill and Belton—Ramsbury—Balusters of 1699—Carved Scrollwork—Castle Ashby—Eltham—Forde Abbey—The Work of the Brothers Adam—Stratford House—Iron Bulastrade at Chesterfield House—Modern Examples—Steyning—Cadogan Square, London — Headley and Surrey—Leweston Manor, Dorset— Messrs. Harrods, London — Marble Staircasing and Panelling—Australia House—Science Museum, London.

THE following series of illustrations of stair construction does not aim at being complete, but it is felt that there can be no craftsman or student who will not fail to appreciate and learn something from a comparative range of typical specimens, showing how the builders of the past three centuries treated in arrangement, shape and ornament, the standard types of construction which have already been differentiated and exemplified. The series of modern staircases shows the adaptation of standard types of arrangement to present-day requirements, especially the methods of design applicable to large commercial and public buildings, with the uses of a wide range of costly and varied materials. Further examples of historical staircases will be found in W. H. Godfrey's " The English Staircase " (Batsford, 1911); A. Stratton's " The English Interior " (Batsford, 1920), and the four volumes of " The Library of Decorative Art," Lenygon and Jourdain (Batsford, 1922-29). The Early Renaissance is represented by three examples, two doglegged, and one open newel. The Jacobean solidity of the Stranger's Hall, Norwich (Pl. XLIX.), is joined to the Georgian rails along the front of the Minstrel's Gallery, and it is interesting to compare some characteristic Yorkshire stairs in which a narrow flight leads up to an imposing gallery running round two or three sides of the room. The Charterhouse example dates from 1564-68 (Pls. XLVIII. & XXXII., A, B). Newels and balusters richly ornamented with strapwork are typically elaborate ; the greyhound is the crest of Sir Thomas Sutton, the founder. No contrast can be sharper than that shown on Pl. L. ; while both stairs are of the open newel type, the Guildford example, 1619, is own cousin to the Charterhouse, with the same Jacobean emphasis on tall tapering newels ; at Moor Park the newel is replaced by ramped handrails. The house was built by Leoni, but it is possible that this staircase is a later insertion not very late in the nineteenth century.

Turning now to the Later Renaissance to which Pl. II., from Deddington, forms a transition, the pedestal stairs at Coleshill (Pl. LI.), by Sir Roger Pratt, produce a fine monumental effect ; the comparison with Belton (Pl. VII.) is instructive. The Ramsbury stair from a house designed by John Webb (Pl. LII.) is plain and solid, and chiefly of interest for its curious planning. Plate LIII. comes from a very pleasant tile-hung house dated 1699 ; the balusters are simple, but well proportioned and refined.

In a remarkable type of English staircase the repeated baluster is replaced by panels of floridly carved continuous scrolls, giving an effect of rich elaboration ; a fine example forms the frontispiece. Most of these staircases date from 1670-90, but a variant of the type is also found in the Early Renaissance, where the panels are of strapwork. Pl. LIV. illustrates the Early and Late Renaissance staircase of this type from the same house, and Pl. LV. gives general views of the later stair, where, however, the design is still tentative, indeed fumbling. The Eltham example (Pl. LVI.) is very fine, with the allied example from Forde Abbey, and Pl. LVII. shows a measured drawing of part, also Ill. 15. And now, with a century's jump, we illustrate Stratford House (Pl. X.), a fine example of the Brothers Adam's work, though the very delicate ironwork balustrade is a possible later insertion. Other examples of ironwork stairs are also shown in Chapters I. and II.: the magnificent balustrade of Tijou type, originally at Canons and now at Chesterfield House (Pl. VIII.), and the curved Adam type stair from Sheen House, which has now disappeared (Pl. III.).

It has been thought advantageous to present also a series of typical examples of modern practice in stair-building from the designs of a number of well-known architects. Several of the examples are from town and country houses, and these are usually of wood, and follow traditional lines in the design, with a certain amount of adaptation to modern requirements. This domestic type of wooden staircase can be used for moderate sized shops and offices, as in the example from Brighton (Pl. LXI.). In addition, a selection has been obtained of large staircases showing how the traditional types of plan are adapted to the needs of large modern buildings, chiefly to provide for the accommodation of large numbers of people. One of the chief

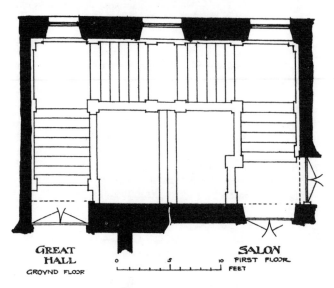

GREAT HALL
GROUND FLOOR

SALON
FIRST FLOOR

0   5   10
FEET

PLAN OF STAIRS

ILL. 15.—FORDE ABBEY, DORSET—(For Drawing v. Pl. LVII.).

developments of recent times is the big multiple store. In addition, provision has to be made, and designs and craftsmen have to be ready, to carry out large and imposing staircases for large blocks of offices and important public buildings. These great structures are frequently carried out in an elaborate fashion, and lavish use is made of very varied materials in order to get texture and fine colour effects. Coloured marbles from a number of sources, tropical woods, stone, brass or bronze, are constantly pressed into the craftsman's service. The requirements of modern Bye-laws, particularly the London Building Acts, have also to be complied with, and these examples show how this has been carried out.

It is interesting to note, for instance, that the walnut stair at Messrs. Harrods, with its inlaid panels, is of the open string and well type, with a very narrow well, but the grand stair erected by the same firm at Brompton Road has the double central flight which continues upwards at the sides.

PLATE XLIX.

THE STRANGER'S HALL, NORWICH.
Elizabethan Dogleg Stairs.

PLATE L.

CONTRASTING EXAMPLES OF OPEN WELL STAIRS.

ABBOT'S HOSPITAL, GUILDFORD, 1619.
Jacobean Style, Large Pillar Newels, Arched Balustrade,
Raking Handrail.

MOOR PARK, HERTFORDSHIRE.
Newel-less, late eighteenth or early nineteenth century.

PLATE LI.

COLESHILL, BERKSHIRE: PEDESTAL STAIRS, *ca.* 1640.

Sir Roger Pratt, Architect.

PLATE LII.

RAMSBURY, WILTSHIRE, *ca.* 1660.
Close Well Stair of Newels Type.

John Webb, Architect.

PLATE LIII.

RAMPYNDENE, BURWASH, 1699 : DWARF NEWELS AND TURNED BALUSTERS.

PLATE LIV.

B

A

CASTLE ASHBY, NORTHAMPTONSHIRE.

FLIGHTS OF SCROLL STAIRCASES, EARLY AND LATE RENAISSANCE TYPES.

Raking Pierced Strapwork Panels.   Solid Dwarf Newels, Solid Carved Frieze and Handrail.

Note Small Running Carved Hunting Frieze.

PLATE LV.

Castle Ashby, Northamptonshire.
A Charles II. Continuous Scroll Staircase, Rather Immature Design.
Open Well, Solid Dwarf, Carved Newels, Balustrade of Pierced Panels, Carved String, Solid Carved Handrail.

PLATE LVI.

Eltham Lodge, Kent: Open Newel Continuous Scroll Staircase, *ca.* 1680.
Carved Newels, with Flower Vase Finials.

PLATE LVII.

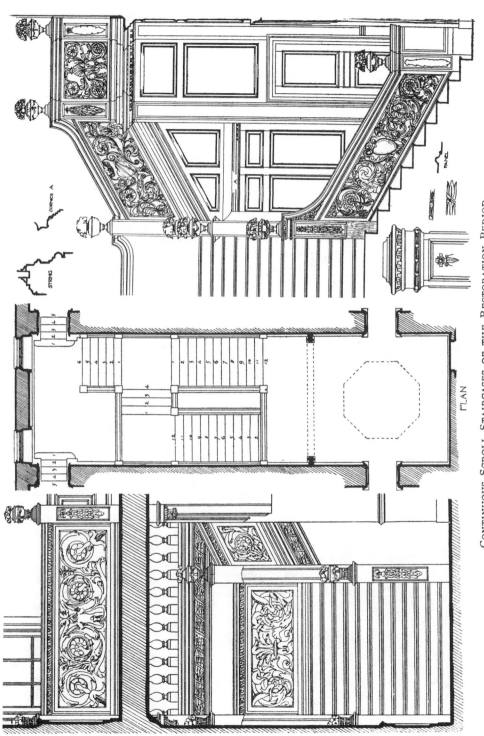

CONTINUOUS SCROLL STAIRCASES, OF THE RESTORATION PERIOD.

1 and 2 Eltham Lodge, with Plan.
(For view *v.* Plate LVI.) (*H. M. Fletcher.*)

3. Forde Abbey, Dorset.
(For Plan *v.* Ill. 15.) (*H. Inigo Triggs.*)

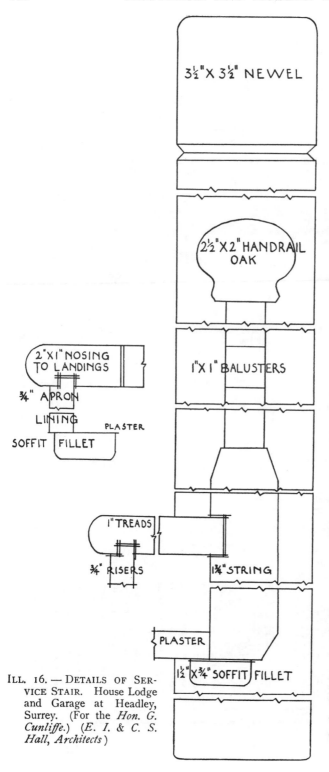

ILL. 16. — DETAILS OF SERVICE STAIR. House Lodge and Garage at Headley, Surrey. (For the *Hon. G. Cunliffe*.) (*E. I. & C. S. Hall, Architects*)

Detail of a Service Stair erected at Headley, Surrey, for the Hon. G. Cunliffe. — The beauty of this stair (Ill. 16) is its simplicity.

The construction is sound and all unnecessary embellishment has been eliminated; the rounded and chamfered edges, and the quirk at the top of the square newel, provide all the " finish " required for such a stair.

Tudor Staircase: Wappingthorn, Steyning, Sussex (Pl. LVIII.).—This charming modern stair, executed in sixteenth-century style, was designed by Maxwell Ayrton, F.R.I.B.A., and made by Charles Kerridge, jun., of the firm of Kerridge & Shaw, Cambridge. It is built entirely of old oak, selected from timber which had been previously used in some old farm buildings, now demolished. It will be noticed that none of the timber is covered; all beams, strings, and the soffit of the stairs are clearly visible. A notable feature of this staircase is that it is stringless (see Plate XXVIII); the treads are constructed of solid blocks of oak; there are no risers; these are supported by the strings which are framed into the newels, the tops of which are carved to an unique design; at the other end they have carved finials, as seen in the photograph. The steps are shaped or moulded in front, that is at the " riser," the moulding being returned at the end so as to form a bracket; the arcading in the balustrading and the modern and comfortable shaped handrail are well in keeping with the general design. The whole of the work is left in its natural

PLATE LVIII.

WAPPINGTHORN, STEYNING, SUSSEX : THE STAIRCASE.

Maxwell Ayrton, F.R.I.B.A., Architect.

PLATE LIX.

TYPE OF TWIN NEWEL STAIRS, WITH ARCHED COLONNADED SCREEN
73 CADOGAN SQUARE, LONDON.

Hall Walls and Ceiling Glazed Blues and Greens.
Walnut Stairs, Green Marble Columns.

state, that is to say it has been left clean from the tools, without stain or varnish of any kind, and the colour is of a rich warm brown.

Stair at Cadogan Square, London.—The stair shown on Pl. LIX. is somewhat remarkable on account of its setting and unusual type of twin-newel. It is constructed of walnut wood, and is placed between the green marble columns of an arched colonnaded screen, the arch giving headway for the stairs.

The hall, walls and ceiling are decorated and glazed with blue and green so as to harmonize with the columns. The base blocks under the two end balusters or newels are somewhat crude in appearance, and a little out of keeping with the adjacent classic design.

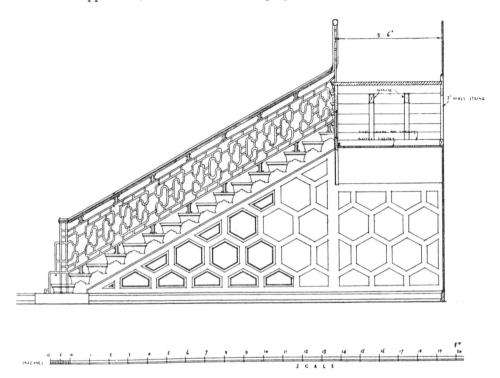

ILL. 17.—LEWESTON MANOR, DORSET. DETAILS OF HANDRAIL ON MAIN STAIRCASE.
(*Maxwell Ayrton, F.R.I.B.A., Architect.*)

"Charters," Ascot, Surrey.—This is another stair with a somewhat peculiar feature and is shown on Pl. LXI. It is depicted in the illustration in course of construction, and the ramp and horizontal portion adjoining the scroll wreath appear to be unnecessary except to warn the person descending that the flight is approaching its termination. Another and a more pleasing feature of this stair is the variety of design in the balusters (Pl. LX.); these have been considered of sufficient interest to warrant a separate page illustrating them in detail. The stair was built by Messrs. Higgs & Hill, Ltd., for "Charters," Ascot, Surrey.

The adjacent illustration (Pl. LXI.) is of a flight and landing with a continuous handrail, which was made and fixed at Brighton by a former pupil of the author, Frederick W. Pratt, of Chichester. It may be noted how carefully the "regulation" height of the rail over nosings and landings has been adhered to. It was designed by Messrs. Clayton & Black, AA.R.I.B.A.

PLATE LX.

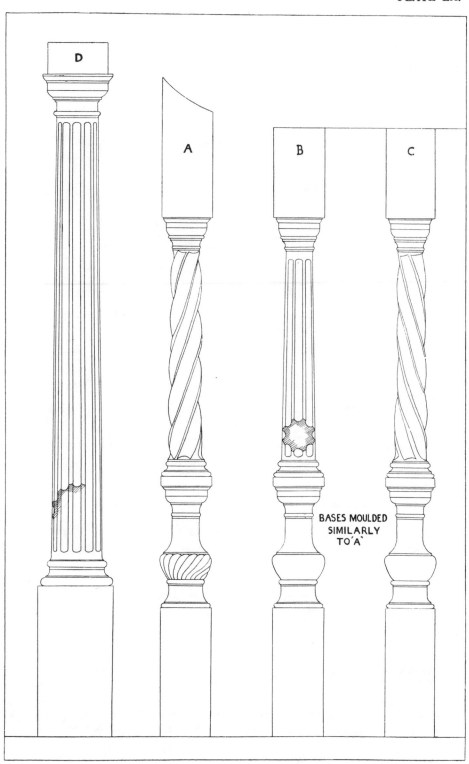

FORMS OF BALUSTRADES, "CHARTERS," ASCOT
(v. also Pl. LXI.)

PLATE LXI.

"CHARTERS," ASCOT, SURREY.
A Modern Country House Stair, Georgian Type, during Construction.
For Drawing of Balusters *v.* Pl. LX.
E. Stanley Hall, F.R.I.B.A., Architect.
Messrs. Higgs & Hill Ltd., South Lambeth, London, Builders.

MESSRS. HANNINGTONS' PREMISES, BRIGHTON.
Stair made and fixed by the Author's Pupil, Frederick W. Pratt, Tower Street, Chichester.
Designed by Clayton & Black, AA.R.I.B.A,

PLATE LXII.

"St. Edwards," Murrayfield, Edinburgh.

Type: Open Newel Modern Stair with Geometrical Handrails and Twisted Balusters.

Henry & Maclennan, Architects.

PLATE LXIII.

LEWESTON MANOR, DORSET: THE STAIRCASE.

Maxwell Ayrton, F.R.I.B.A., Architect.

PLATE LXIV.

LEWESTON MANOR, DORSET: THE STAIRCASE.

Maxwell Ayrton, F.R.I.B.A., Architect.

PLATE LXV.

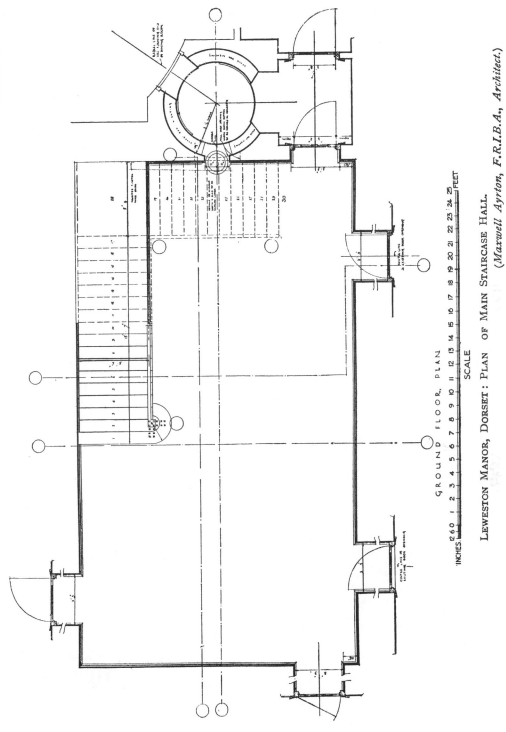

GROUND FLOOR PLAN

SCALE

INCHES. 12 6 0   1 2 3 4 5 6 7 8 9 10 11 12 13 14 15 16 17 18 19 20 21 22 23 24 25   FEET

LEWESTON MANOR, DORSET : PLAN OF MAIN STAIRCASE HALL.

(Maxwell Ayrton, F.R.I.B.A., Architect.)

PLATE LXVI.

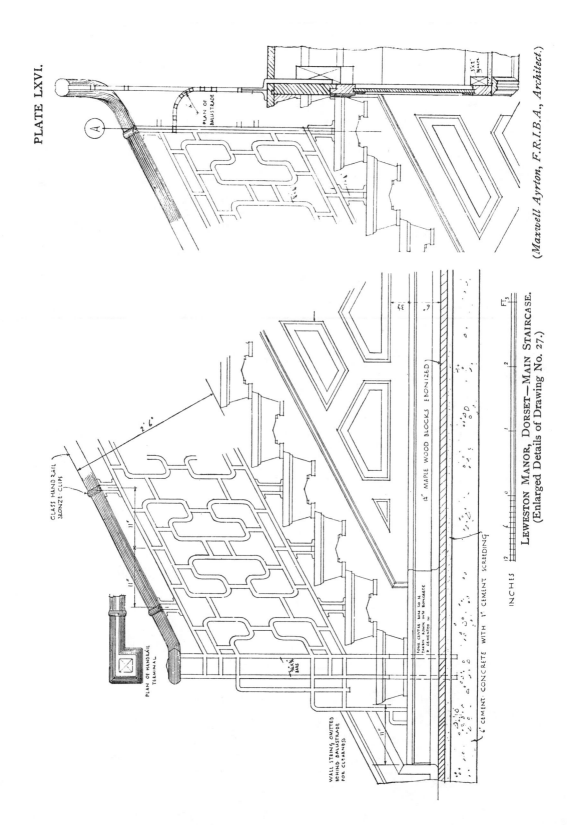

(Maxwell Ayrton, F.R.I.B.A., Architect.)

LEWESTON MANOR, DORSET—MAIN STAIRCASE.
(Enlarged Details of Drawing No. 27.)

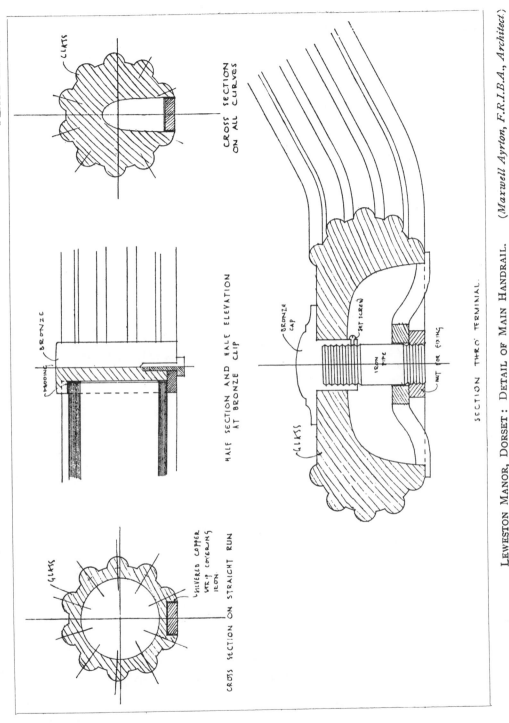

PLATE LXVII.

GLASS

CROSS SECTION
ON ALL CURVES

BRONZE

PADDING

HALF SECTION AND HALF ELEVATION
AT BRONZE CLIP

BRONZE
CAP

SET SCREW

IRON
PIPE

GLASS

NUT FOR FIXING

SECTION THRO' TERMINAL.

GLASS

SILVERED COPPER
STRIP COVERING
IRON

CROSS SECTION ON STRAIGHT RUN

LEWESTON MANOR, DORSET: DETAIL OF MAIN HANDRAIL.   (*Maxwell Ayrton, F.R.I.B.A., Architect.*)

St. Edwards, Murrayfield, Edinburgh.—A delightful modern stair, designed by Henry D. McLennan, Esq., illustrated on Pl. LXII., shows how the monotony of a long straight flight may be avoided by a quarter-space turn. The decorative treatment of the newels and the twisted balusters, together with the arched colonnade and panelled soffit and finishings, are particularly pleasing. It will be noted that the upper portion of this stair is fitted with a geometrical handrail.

The Staircase and Stairs at Leweston Manor, Dorset, possess so many unusual features that it has been deemed advisable to include, in addition to the two full-page photographs, a number of the working details of this structure, which have kindly been supplied by

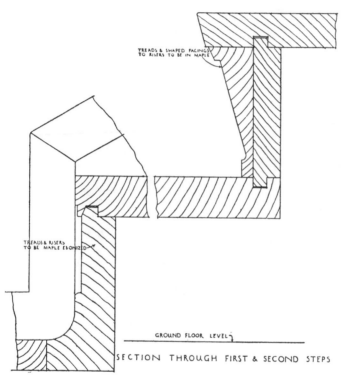

the architect, Mr. Maxwell Ayrton, F.R.I.B.A. A study of these will clearly convey to the reader how the stair has been built up. The treads and risers (Ill. 18) are of maple wood and ebonised, together with the shaped facings and bracketing, which are of an unusual and original design. The hexagonal panelling and the walls have been decorated by Mr. Geo. Sheringham, the well-known artist, in a peculiar and pleasing shade of yellowish Chinese lacquer.

Some idea of the effectiveness of this combination with the black treads and brackets can be gathered from the two full-page photographs (Pls. LXIII. and LXIV.).

The balustrade and handrail are of particular interest; the former is constructed of finely wrought iron, blacked and slightly

ILL. 18.—LEWESTON MANOR, DORSET: DETAILS OF STAIRCASE. (*Maxwell Ayrton, F.R.I.B.A., Architect*).

bronzed; the handrail (Pl. LXVII., and Ill. 17), consists of jade-coloured glass especially made by the famous firm of Messrs. Osler & Faraday; it is made in lengths and the joints are covered and secured by handsome bronze clips; the details of these can clearly be seen in the illustrations.

Illumination is obtained from numerous invisible lamps; the reflected light can be discerned in the photograph (Pl. LXIII.).

New Grand Stair, Harrods, Brompton Road, London.—Pl. LXXI. is a photograph, and Pl. LXVIII. is a working drawing indicating the type of staircase required by the London Bye-laws in large modern business buildings. It is designed to provide the safe and easy movement of a large number of people, should fire or panic cause a sudden crowding of the staircase. It is entirely closed in by brick walls, and can only be entered at each floor through fire-resisting doors, and at the ground floor it opens directly on to the street.

The going of the stairs is easy—11¼-in. treads, and 6¼-in. risers.

The staircase rises from each floor level, with a flight 9 ft. wide, and divides at the half landing into two flights each 4 ft. 6 ins. wide. The central handrail on the 9-ft. flight enables four persons to walk abreast, each with one hand on a rail. This is an important safeguard in any case of panic, as nearly all the accidents are caused by persons falling and causing others to fall over them through want of a hand hold.

The landings are of ample width, and all doors are arranged to swing clear of the steps, so that there is no obstruction to persons using the stairway.

The construction is entirely fire resisting.

The steps and landings are formed of ballast concrete supported on steel stringers and girders. The steelwork is entirely cased in concrete in no part less than 2 ins. thick. The treads, risers and landings are laid with Travertine and Italian limestone, which is durable and non-slipping.

Plate LXX. is a working drawing of a modern staircase in the same fire-resisting building. The wooden steps and risers are set up on a steel and concrete foundation. The details are similar to ordinary wooden construction, the concrete and steel taking the place of the strings and carriages. The treads and risers are fastened to fixing fillets which in turn are nailed to plugs let into the concrete.

The handrailing and balusters are fixed as for an ordinary wooden stair.

The type of wood panelling indicated on Pls. LXX. and LXXII. is used in many modern buildings, and the large panels are made possible by the use of ply-wood.

The warping, which usually takes place when large panels are formed with ordinary timber, has been overcome by the use of this modern material. Ply-wood can be obtained in sheets up to 8 ft. by 4 ft., and there are now on the market sheets of other compositions 12 ft. by 6 ft.

These ply-wood sheets are covered with selected veneers, and are fastened to grounds fixed on the walls. The joints between the sheets are covered with a fillet arranged to form part of the general design.

Pls. LXX. and LXXII. show the use of Ancona walnut veneers, laid on 8 in. by 4 in. sheets of 6-ply wood. The veneers are inlaid with an ebony line to form a border and an ebony strip to cover the joints. The capping and base are of walnut worked in the ordinary way out of solid timber.

The fine circular staircase at Australia House, Kingsway, London, was designed by A. G. R. Mackenzie, F.R.I.B.A., and is built into the commanding premises situated in the Strand, London, representing the Australian Dominions Chief Offices in the Metropolis. The adjacent photograph (Pl. LXXIII.), kindly lent by the architect, so clearly conveys the appearance of this staircase that but little need be added save the undermentioned particulars.

The stair passes from the basement continuously to the seventh floor.

The strings are of Granolithic, representing Australian marble.

The treads and risers of the steps are in Australian marble.

The handrail is of polished brass.

And the very handsome balustrading is of wrought iron carried out by the well-known architectural smiths, Messrs. Starkie Gardner of London.

Science Museum (Pls. LXXIV. and LXXV.). — This is the south-east staircase with wrought-iron balustrade.—The staircase of this important public building has been selected in order to illustrate the method adopted by the architects to prevent accidents through falling over the balustrades, as well as to show the type of stair suitable for such institutions.

PLATE LXVIII.

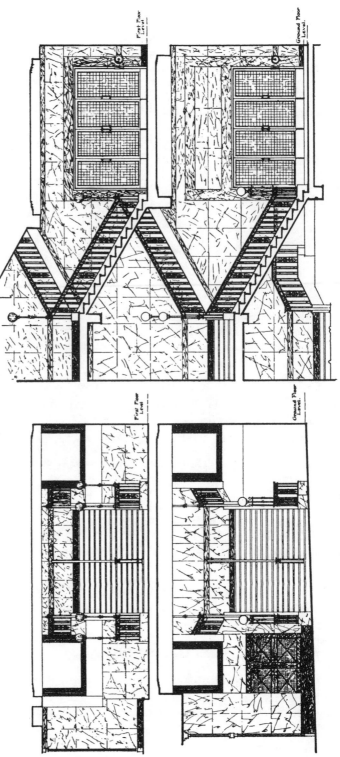

MESSRS. HARRODS LTD., BROMPTON ROAD, LONDON.
PLANS & ELEVATIONS OF NEW MARBLE STAIRCASE.
GROUND TO FIRST FLOOR.

ELEVATION ON LINE · D·B·

ELEVATION ON LINE ~ A·A·

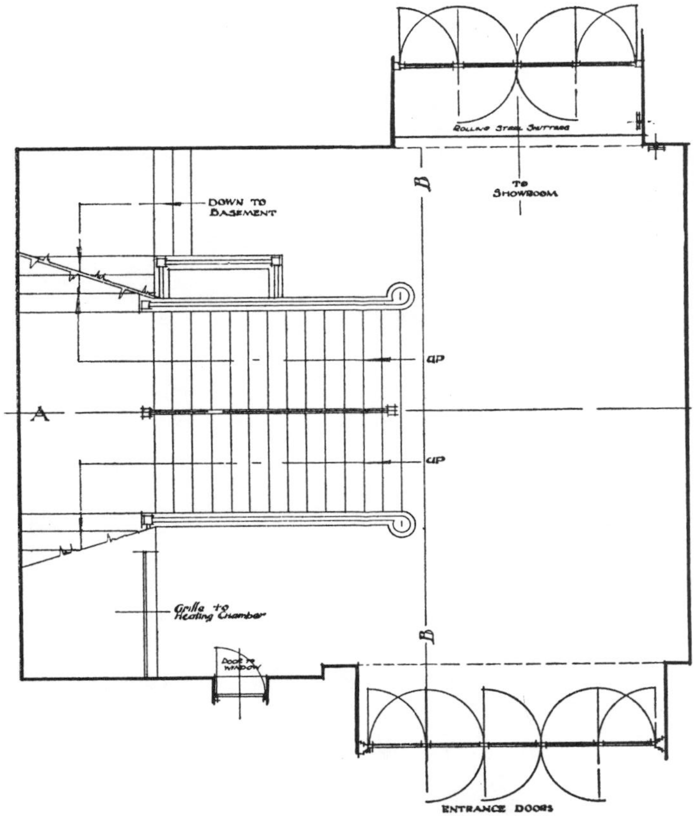

PLATE LXIX.

FIRST FLOOR PLAN

GROUND. FLOOR PLAN

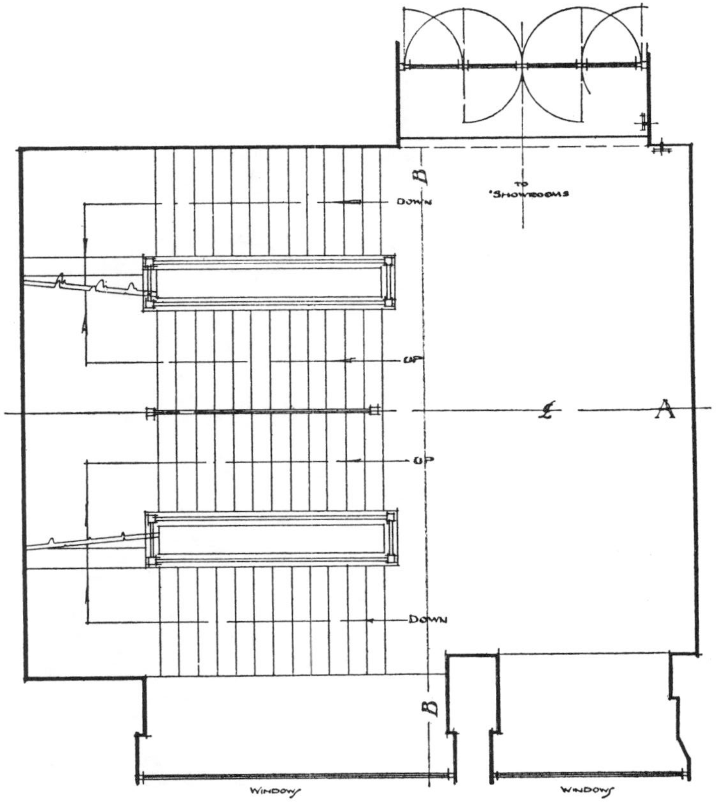

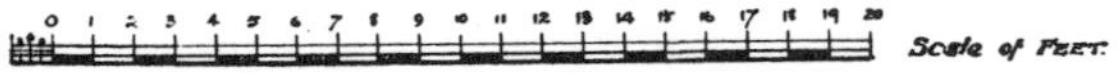

LOUIS BLANC
ARCHITECT

PLANS OF THE STAIRCASE.
Shown on Plates LXVIII. and LXXI.

Scale of Feet

Messrs. Harrods Ltd., Brompton Road, London.

Plans & Elevations of Walnut Staircase.

First to Third Floor.

2nd Floor Level.

1st Floor Level.

Elevations on Line ·A·A·

Elevations on Line · B·B

PLATE LXX.

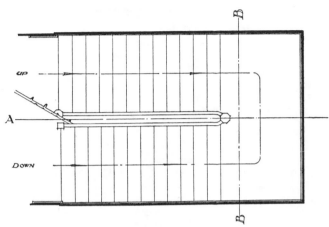

FIRST TO SECOND FLOOR PLAN

Scale of Feet.

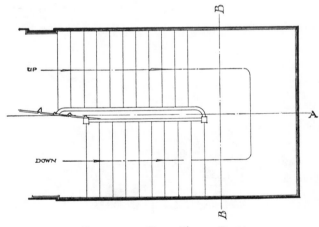

SECOND TO THIRD FLOOR PLAN

LOUIS BLANC
ARCHITECT

PLATE LXXI.

NEWEL GRAND STAIR, HARROD'S STORES, BROMPTON, LONDON.
A Modern Grand Stair of Steel, Concrete and Marble, with Wrought-iron Handrailing.

Louis Blanc, Lic.R.I.B.A., Architect.

PLATE LXXII.

INTERNAL STAIRCASE, MESSRS. HARRODS, BROMPTON ROAD, LONDON, S.W.

Louis Blanc, Lic.R.I.B.A., Architect.

PLATE LXXIII.

AUSTRALIA HOUSE, STRAND, LONDON.

A. G. R. Mackenzie, F.R.I.B.A., Architect.

PLATE LXXIV.

MAIN ENTRANCE TO THE SCIENCE MUSEUM, SOUTH KENSINGTON.

With Terraced Steps to Ground Floor.

Sir Richard Allison, C.B.E., F.R.I.B.A., Architect.

PLATE LXXV.

SCIENCE MUSEUM STAIRWAY.

Note.—"Stairway" is incorrect.   See Glossary.

Sir Richard Allison, C.B.E., F.R.I.B.A., Architect.

PLATE LXXVI.

BUSH HOUSE, ALDWYCH, LONDON.

Helmle, Corbett & Harrison, Architects.

It is constructed in reinforced concrete, and the width of the stair is 8 ft. ; the somewhat heavy appearance of the stringer beams as seen in the photograph is due to the long span of 36 ft. between the bearings.

The soffits and spandril ends are finished with " Keene's " cement on Portland up to the hard York facings.

The balustrade is constructed of wrought iron with fine cast-iron rosettes in the panels. The handrail is of 4 in. by 3 in. moulded section in polished oak.

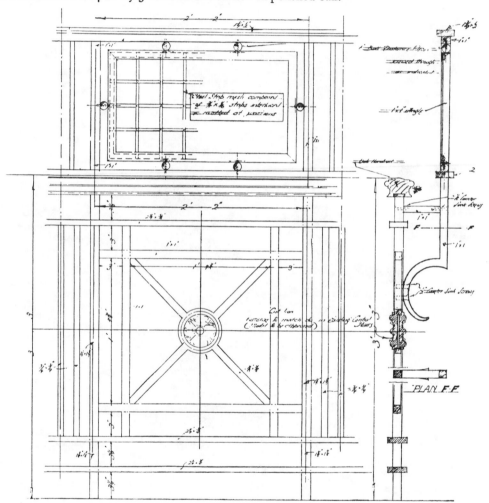

ILL. 19.—SCREEN OF THE SCIENCE MUSEUM STAIRCASE.

The screen work above the balustrade is kept clear of the handrail to give hand room, and is intended primarily for the protection of children. It is constructed of wrought-iron framing with flat strip mesh panels. The balustrade railings to both main staircases in the building are similar in character, as also is that to the large open well, except that in the latter case the screen is omitted, as the railings are flanked by museum cases for their whole extent.

A detailed working drawing of the screen (Ill. 19), showing the section and the method of fixing to the balustrade, has been kindly supplied by Sir Richard Allison and is illustrated herewith.

GLOSSARY OF PHRASES AND TERMS USED IN STAIRBUILDING.

(For those special to Handrailing see Vol. II.)

A.

APRON LINING.—A thin wrought and beaded vertical covering board to the rough trimmer in a stairway or opening in the floor. *See* Fig. 2, Pl. IV., and Pl. XI., Fig. 7, Pl. XIV., and Pl. XLVIII.

B.

BALANCED STEPS.—Winders that do not radiate from a common centre (*see* dancing step; and details Pl. VI., Fig. 4, and Pl. XVII.). The application of the term is that the extended space for winders enables the user to keep his balance in descending the stair.

BALUSTER.—A turned, carved, or otherwise ornamented vertical column, or division between the handrail and string or the steps of a flight of stairs. Collectively a complete series of balusters together with the connecting string and handrail is termed a balustrade or balustrading, *which see*. When, as in common stairs, the balusters are plain thin rods or rectangular strips they are known as banisters. In both cases the object of the balusters and balustrade is to prevent users falling off, or over the side of the stairs.

BALUSTRADE.—(1) The combination of balusters, posts, handrails, and strings forming the fence or outside boundary to a flight of stairs, to prevent the users falling over the side into the well of the stairs. (2) In the case of stone stairs the balustrade is chiefly an ornamental feature, comprising a series of dwarf columns or heavy turned balusters, a continuous plinth and a moulded cap, or back rail. (3) In the case of iron stairs the balustrade is frequently formed of a series of open, wrought, square, or flat bars and rails following the general contour of the stairs. Sometimes the bottom bar is omitted and vertical parts of the design are continued down to the face of the step into which they are sunk and cemented like lugs, as in the case of the King's staircase at Hampton Court Palace. *See also* Pl. LXXIII., Spiral Stair, Australia House.

BEVEL CUT.—A system of preparing handrail wreaths in which the "blank" has its sides cut vertical, or as they would stand when the rail is in its true position over its plan; now nearly obsolete, superseded by the square-cut system, *which see; also* Vol. II.

BLOCK PLANE.—A comparatively short and heavy plane of either wood or metal used with the block mitre-shoot apparatus (Pl. XLIII.), chiefly for preparing hardwood joints in handrails, etc.

BOXED STEP.—The ordinary step in stairs, formed by gluing a relatively thin riser and tread together at right angles; as distinguished from the solid step, which is formed of one block of wood or stone. *See* Pls. XXVIII. and XXIX.

BLOCKINGS OR ANGLE BLOCKS.—Short piece of wood glued to the under-surface or angles of boxed steps to strengthen the joints. *See* Pls. XXII., XXIII., XXIX. and XXXI.

BRACKET BALUSTERS.—Those rising from the ends of, or outside the step, chiefly in stone or marble stairs, and necessarily of metal, as they are cranked over the moulding.

BRACKETS.—Carved, shaped or otherwise ornamented imitation ends to boxed steps, which are planted upon the face of the string in open, or cut string stairs. These roughly triangular-shaped brackets are, in modern practice, made thin, less than $\frac{1}{4}$-in. thick, but in the old examples are often an inch or more thick. *See* Pls. XL. and XLI.

BULLNOSED STEP.—One with a quarter round end, returning upon a newel post. *See* Pls. IV. and XXIX.

BULLNOSE WINDER.—One in an interior angle. *See* Fig. 5, Pl. IV.

C.

CAPPING.—A moulded member planted on the top edge of a close string to provide a fixing for balusters thicker than the string. *See* Fig. 2, Pl. XXVIII., and Fig. 13, Pl. XXXVII.

CARRIAGES.—Rough timbers fixed under a wide flight of stairs to stiffen them. *See* Pls. XI. and XVIII.

CAUL.—A piece of wood, or metal, shaped to fit a curved surface that is to be veneered, so that it can be cramped up and the glue squeezed out when pressure is applied. Generally, cauls are heated when applied either by wet, or dry heat as the job requires. *See* Fig. 20, Pl. XXIX.

CIRCULAR STAIR.—One circular in plan, that is to say, with its steps radiating from a common centre or a newel post. *See* Pls. XXI. and XXII.

CLOSE NEWEL STAIRS.—An alternative term for a dogleg stair, *which see;* term also used in contra-distinction to open newel stair (*which see*, Pls. V. and XV., *also* Pl. LVI.).

CLOSE STRING.—One in which the ends of the steps are sunk or housed so that they are not visible outside the stair. *See* "Open Strings." *See* Pl. LVI.

COMMODE STEPS.—One or more steps at the bottom of a flight having curved, usually segmental or elliptic risers, with wider treads than the average, hence derivation of the term ; they are more commodious. *See* Pl. XXIX.

CONTINUOUS STAIR.—A circular or other curved flight of stairs composed entirely of winders unin-terrupted by landings.

CROSS FLIGHTS.—*See* return flight.

CURB.—The rough timbers around a circular, or an elliptic stairway. *See* Pl. XXIV.

CURTAIL STEP.—The bottom step of a stair having a curved end corresponding with the curves of the handrail scroll above it, but cut short or curtailed at the front where it intersects the string. *See* Pl. XX.

CUT STRING.—*See* "Open String."

D.

DANCING STEPS (*see* "Balanced Steps").—Term implying that the winders, in virtue of the extended space allotted them, are so easy of descent that the user might dance down them. *See* Pl. XVII.

DIMINISHED FLYER.—The top step of a flight adjacent to winders which, although tapered in length, is not radial from the common centre of the winders. *See* Fig. 5, Pl. VI.

DOGLEG STAIR.—One in which the outer strings of the successive reverse flights are directly over, or in same plane as each other, without any space between them. *See* Pl. XI., *also* Pls. XLVIII. and XLIX.

DOUBLE NEWEL.—Two large newel posts of similar size and design placed close to each other on a landing. A historic device to avoid the cutting away of the lower handrail where it crosses the string of the upper flight in narrow stairs of the dogleg type, a precursor of the open newel type. *See* Pl. II.

DROP.—An ornamental end to a newel post which projects below the soffit. *See* Pls. L. and LIX.

DUBBED-OFF.—A short or abrupt easing to any part of a construction to permit its easy entry into an aperture, e.g. the end of a tread into its housing. Also a clumsy or careless easing at the joint of a moulding, etc.

F.

FINIAL.—The ornamental top end of a newel post carved, shaped, or turned. *See* Pls. XI., XXXVII., XLVIII. and LVI.

FIRRING-OUT.—The process of fitting and fixing firrings or firring-pieces (*which see*) at the backs of stair strings to correct irregularities, either in the wall or in the stair itself, also to the lower edges of wall strings to carry the latter into same plane as the outside string.

FIRRINGS OR FIRRING PIECES.—Light strips of fir nailed across the back, or to the edges of stair strings, either to make up their width and apparent thickness or to provide solid fixings for nails, screws or plugs as the case requires. *See* Fig. 5, Pl. XX.

FLIGHT OF STAIRS.—Is an uninterrupted series of steps and strings reaching from one landing to the next. It may be straight, curved, or polygonal in plan but commonly is straight, and winders are considered an interruption, and in this case the " flight " terminates at the springings.

FLYERS, OR FLIERS.—The paralled steps in a flight of stairs as distinguished from the winders, or non-parallel steps.

G.

GEOMETRICAL STAIRS.—The class of stair in which the string and handrail is continuous from end to end, the straight portion being connected at the turns, or ends of the well by wreaths of double curvature (*see* Pls. III., VI., and XXII.), so called, because some acquaintance with the science of solid geometry is necessary to their setting-out.

GOING.—The amount of horizontal advance in a flight, or the same between the surfaces of two successive risers. The first gives the length of the flight, the second the clear width of a step. *See* Fig. 1, Pl. IV., and Fig. 1, Pl. XXVIII.

GRAND STAIRS.—The main stairs in mansions, public buildings, large shops and stores, etc., usually very elaborately designed and ornamented. *See* Pls. V., VIII., and LXXI.–LXXV.

H.

HALF LANDING.—A landing at about half the height of the staircase irrespective of the size in plan : not to be confused with half-pace landing, *which see*, and Fig. 3, Pl. V.

HALF-PACE LANDING.—One going right across the stairway to receive two reverse flights. *See* Fig. 2, Pl. VI.

HALF-SPACE OF WINDERS.—Triangular steps that occupy the same dimensions in plan as a half-pace landing. *See* Fig. 2, Pl. XVII.

HALF TURN STAIRS.—Those forming a half circle in plan or those with advancing and reversed flights starting and finishing at a common landing.

HAND OF STAIRS (THE) is determined by the hand applied to the handrail when ascending the stairs, i.e. if the right hand is used the flight is called a " right-hand " stair, and *vice versa*.

HANDRAIL.—A moulded rail following the inclination of a stair and landings, and forming the top or connecting member of the balustrade which protects the outside of the stair. In geometrical stairs the handrail is wreathed at the change of direction. *See* " Wreaths and Wreathing " in Vol. II.

HANGING STAIRS.—Stairs in which the steps are not visibly supported at the well end, but are built-in, or otherwise supported at the inner, or wall end ; chiefly constructed in stone, marble, or concrete.

HEADROOM is the provision made for passengers on a stair to avoid striking the head against the soffit of the opening in the stairway. *See* Fig. 2, Pl. XI.

HELICAL STAIRS are those which rise regularly around a cylinder, real or imaginary ; alternative names are, circular, geometrical, spiral, wheeling and winding ; *which see, also* Pls. XXI. and XXII.

HOLLOW NEWEL.—A term sometimes used by non-technical writers for an independent circular stair in contradistinction to a solid circular newel stair. There is, of course, *no* actual newel, but a circular well in these stairs. *See* Pl. XXII.

I.

INDEPENDENT STAIR.—One rising from floor to floor without intermediate support from walls or staircase. Term is usually applied to circular geometrical stairs. *See* Pl. XXII.

INCLINED PLANES.—In primitive times these, formed in rammed earth, then later with slabs of stone, were used to reach considerable heights, before the advent of steps constructed similarly in the sides of cliffs, etc., which were followed by portable ledged planes, from whence stairs were evolved.

K.

KITE WINDERS.—A triangular step in the angle between transverse wall strings. *See* Fig. 1, Pl. IV.

KNEED BALUSTER.—A metal baluster which is bent, or cranked, at right angles to the face of the string, then turned down behind the latter, where it is hidden by the tread. *See* Fig. 5, Pl. XXX.

L.

LANDING.—(Any platform.)   A resting place, or wide step at the top of a flight or at the junction of two flights. *See* Pl. V., Figs. 1, 5 and 8.

N.

NEWEL STAIRS.—Those in which the strings and handrails are framed, or connected to substantial posts called "newels" at each end of the flights. There are two types, "open" newel and "close" newel ; the latter are known as dogleg stairs, *which see ;* Pls. IV., X., and XLIX. The derivation of the term newel is from a "nave," the hub or centre from which the spokes of a wheel radiate ; so the steps radiate from the newel in these stairs.

TYPES OF NEWEL STAIRS may be classified and defined as follows :—

1. A close newel stair is a newel stair with an uncut or housed string (*which see*).
2. An open newel stair is a newel stair with a cut or notched string (*which see*).
3. A newelless, or non-newel stair, is a geometrical stair without a newel post and finishing at a group of balusters.
4. An open string, close newel stair is a newel stair with a cut string but without a well.
5. A close string open well stair is a newel stair with close, or housed strings, and having a well.
6. A close string, close newel stair is a newel stair with an uncut string, without a well, or in other words is a dogleg stair with housed strings.
7. An open newel, open string stair is a newel stair with a well and cut strings.

NEWEL OR NEWEL POST.—A solid rectangular, circular, or elliptic section vertical post at the centre and at angular turns and junctions, in various forms of stairs, forming the main support of the strings, handrails, and under-carriages at the outside. *See* Pls. IV. and LVI.

NOSING.—The moulding worked on the salient edge of stair steps usually consisting of a round or semi-circle equal to the thickness of the tread, and under this a narrow fillet separating it from the scotia or elliptic cavetto moulding. *See* Pl. XXXI., Fig. 1.

NOSING PIECE.—A narrow strip with one edge moulded similar to the step nosing, the other edge bevelled and fixed on a trimmer at a landing or other opening to cover the cross grain of the transverse floor. *See* Fig. 2, Pl. XVII.

O.

TO OFFER UP, OR OFFERED-UP.—A preliminary trial of the complete stair to ascertain whether it fits the position correctly.

OPEN NEWEL STAIR.—*See* under "Newel Stairs."

OPEN STRING.—One cut, or notched at the top edge, to fit the profile of the steps. *See* Pls. XI. and XVI.

P.

PEDESTAL STAIRS.—Those in which the outer string is framed into a dwarf square pillar at the start, and the handrail, usually of a heavy description, is mitred around the pillar in from 2 or 4 breaks, the head of which forms a flat or pyramidal cap. The pedestal is usually sunk-panelled and moulded in the solid, but is sometimes enriched with floral carving. A Renaissance type (*see* Pl. LI.).

PITCH.—The inclination of a stair with, or to, the horizontal.

PITCHING PIECE.—A rough timber under the head of a flight or junction with winders into which the carriages are fixed. *See* Pl XI., and Fig. 3, Pl. XIII.

PLINTH.—A skirting or flat moulded piece at the base of a newel, column, pedestal, or wall. *See* Fig. 3, Pl. XXXVII.

Q.

QUARTER LANDING is a square or nearly so, landing at the junction of two flights.

QUARTER-PACE LANDING.—One reaching half across the stairway. *See* Fig. 1, Pl. VI.

QUARTER-SPACE OF WINDERS.—Two to four triangular steps in a stair, forming in plan a right-angle turn, in a flight or at the junction of two flights. The term is also applied when the turn is slightly more, or less, than a right angle. *See* Pl. XV., Fig. 1, and Pl. IV., Fig. 5.

QUARTER-TURN STAIRS.—A stair of two flights at right angles to each other, as Pl. V., Fig. 5.

R.

RADIAL STEP.—A winder whose nosing edge radiates from a point outside the string. *See* Fig. 4, Pl. VI.

RAKING BALUSTERS.—Those in which the ends of the head and foot blocks are made to follow the inclination of the stair, instead of being horizontal, as in the more usual practice ; *see* Pls. XXXVI. and L. *Also* the term is applied to metal balusters that are arranged other than vertical.

RAKING BALUSTRADES are those in which either the main constructional lines or the general features of the panelling follow the rake or inclination of the stair. *See* Pl. LIV.

RAKING RISERS.—A method of increasing the foot space of winders at the newel. *See* Fig. 5, Pl. XXIX.

RAMP.—A vertical curved easing in a string or a handrail. *See* Figs. 4 and 5, Pl. XXXVII., and Fig. 2, Pl. XVI.

RESPOND NEWEL.—A pilaster or half newel in a staircase dado corresponding with the newel opposite. *See* Fig. 1, Pl. XVI., *also* Pl. LII.

RETURN FLIGHT.—One crossing the direction of the main flight, usually at right angles. *See* Fig. 1, Pl. XVI.

REVERSE FLIGHT.—One in which the user travels in opposite direction to that taken in the preceding flight. *See* Figs. 1 and 2, Pl. XIII.

RISE.—The distance between the surfaces of adjacent steps, and the perpendicular height of the top step in a flight above the floor, or top of the lowest step in same. *See* Fig. 1, Pl. XXVIII.

RISERS.—The vertical face pieces of boxed or hollow steps which are glued and blocked to the under, sides of treads to form the steps in a flight. *See* Pl. XXIX, Fig. 22.

ROUGH BRACKETS.—Pieces of unwrought fir nailed to the sides of the carriages to support the middle of the treads and to prevent creaking due to shrinkage. *See* Pl. XXVIII, Fig. 3, D.

ROUGH STRING.—The term "rough" signifies that the string board in question is not wrought or planed and presumes that it is hidden. The term is sometimes used instead of "carriage rough," *which see*. Rough strings are sometimes used where considerable strength is required in a stair of the open string class, where the visible string is weakened by cutting, also where expensive woods are used for the outer string, which in some cases are brittle, therefore not to be relied upon to carry the load. *See* Fig. 1, Pl. XV.

S.

SAFETY RAIL.—An additional handrail to a stair, lower than the ordinary rail, to accommodate children ; generally confined to geometrical stairs, or when in public buildings placed above the ordinary rail. *See* Pl. LXXV.

SCROLL STEP.—A common misnomer for curtail step (*which see*), because no *steps* are scrolled.

SKRIM OR SCRIM.—Thin, or coarse mesh canvas, used for lining walls, backs of dados, wainscotting, etc. In stairbuilding, specially, for the purpose of strengthening backs of wreathed strings and other built-up circular parts ; for details *see* Index.

SOFFIT OF A STAIR.—The visible sloping under-surface between the opposite strings or the enclosing wall. *See* Fig. 8, Pl. XIV. The level portion under landings is called the ceiling. *See* Pl. XV., Fig. 4. Open soffit (*see* Pl. XXVIII., Fig. 12, *also* Pl. LII.). A plane moulded soffit (*see* Pl. LXXI.). A wreathed plain soffit (*see* Pl. LXXIII.).

SPANDREL is the more or less triangular space between the lower edge of a stair string and the floor surface below the stair, which is enclosed usually by a panelled or plain framing. *See* Fig. 2, Pl. XIII., Fig. 2, Pl. XXIV., and Fig. 2, Pl. XX., *also* Pl. XXXV.

SPANDREL FRAMING.—A triangular, panelled framework closing the space between a stairs and the floors beneath. *See* Fig. 4, Pl. IV., Fig. 3, Pl. XVI.

SPANDREL LINING.—A matchboarded partition under a common dogleg stairs. *See* Fig. 2, Pl. XII.

SPANDREL STEP.—A solid step of wood, or stone, triangular in section. *See* Pl. XLVII.

SPIRAL STAIR.—One consisting entirely of winders turning around a central newel or similar well and making at least one complete revolution in plan. An actual "spiral" stair is, of course, an impossibility as there could be no exit from the top. A true spiral is a continuously diminishing curve finishing in a point, the "eye."

SPIRAL STAIRCASES.—The linings to the walls of the apartments in which a so-called spiral (or circular) stair is enclosed and usually conforming generally to the shape of the stair, which may be circular, elliptic, or polygonal in plan.

SQUARE STEP.—One rectangular in cross-section, without a nosing ; alternatives, solid steps, block steps.

STAIRCASE.—The framed panelling to the walls of the apartment in which a stair is placed. In modern work this usually takes the form of a sunk panelled and moulded dwarf wainscot following the lines of the stair strings. Frequently termed a dado framing.

STAIRS are a combination of steps, framed into strings and newels, which support the balustrade and handrails ; numerous variants and details are given in the preceding chapters. *See* Newel Stair, Geometrical Stair.

STAIRWAY.—A workshop term for the openings formed in and through the floors, roof, partitions, and other constructive timbering of a building, to provide a passage for the stairs, now generally completed in the stairbuilder or joiner's shop and brought to the building ready for fixing. The term is also used in similar circumstances, in stone, concrete and steel structures.

STEP is the unit of a gradient. A stair is a series of steps. Steps are of two types, solid and built-up, or boxed ; the former is chiefly confined to stone and brick stairs and consists of rectangular or triangular blocks of material built into the staircase at one end, and either resting on a parallel wall at the other, or, is unsupported at the outer end but resting in a check or rebate in the surface of the step beneath. *See* Pl. XLVII. The steps, triangular in section, are termed spandrels, in masonry. Boxed, built-up or hollow steps consist of a substantial "tread," the horizontal surface, and a thinner vertical "riser," which are glued and screwed together as shown in the several examples given in this book.

STEPPED BALUSTERS are those in which the plinths, or squares below the moulded portion, are kept of uniform height above the steps, resulting in a differing length to each pair in the moulded part. *See* Figs. 2 and 3, Pl. XVI., and Georgian staircase, Queen Square, Bath, in Stratton, "The English Interior."

STEPPED STRING.—One notched out on its upper edge to the profile of the steps. *See* Fig. 2, Pl. XVIII.

STEPPINGS.—The rectangular notchings in a cut string, forming the seats for the treads and mitre angles for the risers. *See* Fig. 12, Pl. XVIII.

STORY ROD.—A square staff on which is set out the number and height of the steps in a stair. *See* Fig. 2, Pls. XIII. and XIX.

STRING OF A STAIR is the inclined board at the ends of the steps in a flight, into which the steps are fixed in various ways, as described in detail in preceding pages.

STRINGLESS STAIRS.—Wood stairs constructed without strings. *See* Pl. XXVIII.

SQUARE CUT.—A system of handrailing in which the joints are all square to the surface of the plank ; fully detailed in Vol. II. *See* Bevel Cut.

T.

TOADS BACK.—A flatly curved moulding to a handrail. *See* Pl. XIX., Fig. 5.

TOOTHED.—Veneers and the like, also their "grounds" or backings, scored, or scratched on the surfaces intended to be glued (either by means of a special toothing plane or by rubbing with the teeth of a hand saw) for the purpose of providing a key for the glue, to increase its adherence.

TOWER STEP.—One at the foot of a flight, approaching a complete circle in plan and projecting, like a turret, or tower, from the angle corner of a building. *See* Pl. XXIX., Fig. 16.

TREAD.—The horizontal part of a step upon which the foot rests.

TUSH NAILED.—A workshop term for so driving two nails at opposite angles, that they act as dovetails and increase the holding power of the nails.

TWIN NEWELS.—A newel or pair of newels wrought out of a solid block with turned balusters supporting a return horizontal handrail at the foot of a semi-grand stair. *See* Pl. LIX., 73 Cadogan Sq., S.W. ; also a pair of dwarf newels framed together with a narrow space between. *See* Pl. LII.

V.

VICE OR VISÉ STAIR.—A French term for a twisted or spiral newel stair.

W.

WALKING LINE.—An arbitrary line drawn on the plan of the curved part of a stair on which the width of the treads are spaced out equally. Commonly this line is drawn at 18 inches from centre line of handrail. *See* Pl. XXIV., Fig. 1, and Pl. XXIX., Fig. 2.

WEATHERED STEPS.—Those with treads slightly inclined towards the front edge for the purpose of discharging rain water quickly. Used only for outside steps and stairs.

WELL OR WELL-HOLE.—The enclosure or space between the opposite strings of a stair. The latter term is usually confined to the aperture provided between the upper floor timbers for the passage of the complete stair to the floor below. *See* Pls. V. and XLVII.

WHEELING STAIRS.—An obsolete name for spiral or winding stairs.

WINDERS.—Radiating steps in the angle of two flights of stairs. *See* Pl. VI. The treads of these are wider at one end than at the other, to accommodate the differing radii of the inside and outside strings. In circular stairs all the steps are winders. *See* Pl. XXII.

WREATH.—Part of a handrail or of a string which is curved both in plan and elevation. To distinguish between the two ; the first is called a handrail wreath and the second a wreathed string. The term wreathed or writhed signifying twisted, concave curves in strings and handrails which are not regular, or geometrical curves, but are graduated to satisfy the eye. *See* Fig. 2 (H), Pl. XIX. ; *also* Vol. II.

INDEX TO ILLUSTRATIONS.

(For Index to Subjects in Text, see page 130.)

The references in *Roman* numerals are to *Plate* numbers ; text illustrations are indexed under the numbers of the pages on which they occur.

INDEX TO TEXT.

(For Index to Illustrations, see page 128.)

MODERN PRACTICAL STAIRBUILDING AND HANDRAILING

* *

HANDRAILING AND WREATH MAKING

MAHOGANY MODEL OF A TWO-STAGE STAIRCASE, EARLY NINETEENTH CENTURY.
2 FT. 3 INS. HIGH.   VICTORIA AND ALBERT MUSEUM.

An interesting little *tour de force*, remarkable for its curious plan and fine workmanship.
The whole is reminiscent of Stairwork on Shipboard.

Given by H.M. Queen Mary.

Part Two

**

HANDRAILING AND WREATH MAKING

COMPRISING MODERN METHODS OF PRODUCING SOLID AND BUILT-UP HANDRAILS, RAMPS, KNEES, BREAKS AND EASINGS OF SINGLE AND DOUBLE CURVATURE; ALSO METHODS OF SETTING OUT FACE AND FALLING MOULDS; LARGE SCALE WORKING DRAWINGS OF TYPICAL WREATHS, INCLUDING THE FORMATION OF RAMPS, KNEELINGS AND SOLID EASINGS, AND A FULL DESCRIPTION OF SETTING OUT SCROLLS, SPIRALS, MITRE CAPS, AND OTHER TERMINALS

PREFACE.

MR. GEORGE ELLIS long had the intention of expanding the chapters on Stair-building and Handrailing which appeared in the earlier editions of "Modern Practical Joinery" into a comprehensive treatise, by the inclusion of his lessons on these subjects, and the incorporation of his wide additional knowledge.

It was the author's purpose that the work should be primarily a practical treatise on the art of Modern Stair Construction and Handrailing as it had been evolved during his long practical acquaintance with the subject, when he had opportunities of taking part in, or directing, the construction of stairs of almost every class to be found in the country.

The execution of this important project was steadily proceeded with, although its final completion was hindered by the frequent attacks of severe ill-health to which the author was long subject.

It is a matter for deep regret that Mr. Ellis was not spared to see in book form the result of his long and arduous task, having died suddenly while the work was still in an advanced stage of preparation.

The author has included types of handrailing according to a system which he worked out which combines the "Square Cut," "Tangent," and "Falling-Line" methods. As in the case of the Volume I. on Stairbuilding, a series of large scale working drawings with full practical constructional text covers the problems presented for the chief current types, and these include solid and built-up handrails, ramps, knees, etc., of single, and where applicable, double curvature, and wreaths for quarter, half, and three-quarter paces in rectangular, circular, elliptic and oblique plans, including the formation of ramps, kneelings, and solid easings in wreaths. The work also deals with the setting out of face and falling moulds for all types in stair plans in stone and wood, and the setting out of a variety of terminals to handrails.

The work of giving the book its final overhaul and seeing it through the press was, with the approval of the executors, entrusted to Mr. Ellis's old friend and colleague, Mr. William Cox, Vice-President, Incorporated British Institute of Certified Carpenters, Lecturer and Head Instructor at The Polytechnic, Regent Street, London, who has spared neither time nor trouble in completing the work in conformity with the author's views.   The grateful thanks of everyone must be accorded to Mr. Cox for his invaluable co-operation.

Acknowledgment is due to the following who have generously placed at the publisher's disposal a full selection of drawings and photographs of certain examples illustrated :—

Oliver Hill, Esq., F.R.I.B.A., Plate II.; The Authorities of the Victoria and Albert Museum for the frontispiece, Plate I.

THE PUBLISHERS.

January, 1932.

CONTENTS.

CHAPTER I.

HANDRAILING OF SINGLE CURVATURE.

Reasons for Including this Chapter—Method of Moulding a Straight Handrail—Precautions with Joints: The Profile Box, a Stock Section, Preliminaries to Moulding, Order of Moulding, Finishing, Jointing, Position of Bolts and Dowels—Easings—Knees and Kneelings, the Curved Knee, Level Turn—The Curved Kneeling, How to Draw—The Ramp, where Used—Working a Solid Mitre on Ramp—Construction of a Built-up Ramp—Swans Necks, Where Used, How to Draw—What Constitutes an Easing—The Easing Board, its Construction—Lining Bands where Obtainable—Mitre Caps—Obtaining the Section—Cutting the Mitres—The Mitreing Block—Enlarging or Reducing Rail Sections.

BEFORE dealing with the more difficult double curvature, or wreathed handrailing, it has been thought proper in this work to follow the traditional usage of the workshop in respect to the order in which a young joiner is entrusted with handrail work. Naturally his skill is first tested in the moulding of a straight rail, next in the preparation of the joints, bends, curves, etc., which for convenience is termed handrailing of single curvature, because all the hand-rails dealt with in this chapter are straight in one direction. Successful with these—and many of them need skill fully equal to that necessary for the simpler kinds of wreathed railing—he will in due time make his first essay in " geometrical " handrailing, and success in this will largely depend upon the experience gained on work of single curvature.

Method of Moulding a Straight Handrail.—These instructions are of course for handwork; machine struck rails are managed differently, but their production does not much concern the joiner. Where possible, it is better to set the handrail out for shouldering, jointing and mortising, to receive the balusters, as described on page 5, before moulding, and the author personally prefers to run in a dovetail-saw cut around the shoulders or joints just sufficiently to get below the profile of the moulding before commencing the sinkings, as, of course, after the moulding is done all pencilled joint lines will be lost. Where this is not practicable, as in the case of machine-struck stuff, the best way to mark joints and shoulders is to make a profile box of 1 in. stuff in two sections that can be screwed together around the rail, each end being perfectly square; when this box is slipped to the required position the shoulder, etc., can be scribed in by its aid. Assuming this preliminary work done and the rail in the square, as indicated upon the right side of the section (Ill. 1), the example chosen is a favourite one in the workshop, because all the mouldings can be worked with stock planes. On the left side the finished section is shown, with the necessary centres for striking the curves. Proceed to plough grooves or sinkings in the order numbered on the section, working from the bottom of the rail. The last sinking, No. 7, Ill. 1, is a chamfer. All of these sinkings should finish just a shaving outside the profile, that the surface may be cleaned up accurately with the shoulder and moulding planes. Remove as much of the " core " as possible with the plough and rebate plane, as these can be sharpened quicker and easier than can the moulding planes. Before making the chamfers at the back, line them in from the

edges on both sides, as shown at C-C, Ill. 2, and plane off to the lines.   This also is impera-
tively necessary in shaped work, to which we shall refer presently.

The back of the rail is moulded from each side with a 1¼-in. handrail lambs-tongue plane,
which is a reverse of the lambs-tongue sash plane; the rounds ſtuck with a ¾-in. nosing
plane or a No. 8 or No. 10 Hollow, according to make; the cavetto, with a small round,
and the cock beads with a slipped ¼-in. bead plane having its quirk ground slack.   The only
general inſtruction that can be given for all cases is that the grooves and sinkings should be
finished before removing any core between, and that the moſt remote from the outside should
be worked firſt.   The moulding being finished, glass-paper up, avoiding too near approach
to joints and shoulders, which should be finished and fitted to the adjacent part before papering
across them.   The templet used for marking the profile is generally of zinc or ſtiff cartridge
paper, and should have fine pinholes pierced in the appropriate position to mark the centres
of the bolt and the dowel holes.

The handrail bolt should always be in the centre of the section, and the direction at right
angles to the joint.   The dowels one-quarter the width from the outside at the widest part

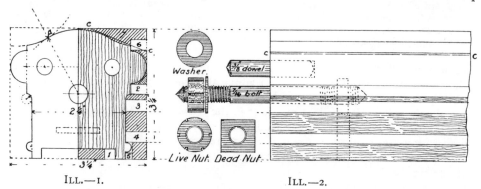

ILL.—1.   ILL.—2.

METHOD OF MOULDING STRAIGHT RAILS AND MAKING JOINTS.

of the rail, and in the case of a section much deeper than its width, a third dowel, or a small
tongue, as indicated in dotted lines at a similar diſtance from the bottom.   Dowels should
be $\frac{5}{16}$ in. or $\frac{3}{8}$ in. diameter and 2 ins. long, half on each side of the joint; they should be cleft,
not sawn, out of tough wood such as beech or oak, driven through a dowel plate, and a score
made up one side with the tenon saw to provide an escape for the glue.   The nuts for the
handrail bolt are sunk in from the underside, that for the dead nut pelleted carefully to keep
the nut in right position, because the bolts are generally removed after fitting together, and
the joints packed with a piece of deal bradded on the ends.   Always place the live nut c n that
side of the joint that will be moſt accessible when the rail is being fixed, and not merely so
when it is on the bench.

Knees and Kneelings.—The handrails of newel ſtairs are usually brought into the level
at or near the newel poſt, by means of a mitred joint, as shown in Figs. 1 and 3, Pl. IV., for
the purpose of interſecting any return mouldings with a right mitre, and to raise or lower,
as the case may be, the raking rail to the same level as the return rail.   When this change of
direction in a rail is at the top end of a flight the angle piece is called a knee (see Figs. 1 and 2,
Pl. IV.)   When at the bottom end of the rail, as in Figs. 3, 4 and 11, Pl. IV., the angle is termed
a kneeling, or kneeling-piece.   A curved knee in a modern ſtair is shown on Pl. II.; rather
awkwardly it is followed closely by a ramp.   When these angles are eased off into circular
curves and the mitre-joint thereby dispensed with, as in Figs. 5 and 7, Pl. IV., the correspond-

PLATE II.

GAYFERE HOUSE, SMITH SQUARE, WESTMINSTER, LONDON: OPEN WELL SOLID NEWEL
KNEED AND RAMPED HANDRAIL.

Pine Staircase: colouring of Soft Green and Shell Pink.

Oliver Hill, F.R.I.B.A., Architect.

PLATE III.

A RAMP IN A GEORGIAN STAIR: TOP FLIGHT, 15 QUEEN SQUARE, BATH.

Transition-type Balustrade.

John Wood, Sen., Architect.

ing portions of the rail are known respectively as curved knees and curved kneelings. The earlier types are distinguished as straight knees and straight kneelings ; thus we may define shortly a knee as a convex bend at the upper end of a rail, and a kneeling as a concave bend at the lower end. Similar " bends " in the rails of geometrical stairs are known as " Wreaths," because they are curved both in plan and elevation, whilst those we are considering are curved only in the vertical plane.

In modern work straight knees are invariably mitre-jointed, as shown in Fig. 1, Pl. iv. ; the pitch of the joint is found by bisecting the angle ; the hole for the handrail bolt must be bored perpendicular to the joint in both directions ; the joint at the newel end is usually secured with a tenon, as shown, but of course much depends on the shape of the newel. The length of the knee depends chiefly upon the height of the newel, but an endeavour should be made to arrange the length so that an equal space on each side of a baluster is obtained, as at Fig. 11, Pl. iv.

The Curved Knee (Figs. 5 and 6, Pl. iv.), which is connected to a level turn on a landing, is struck from a centre found by drawing perpendiculars to the pitched and level rails, the intersection of these lines locating the centre. The distance the easing is taken down the rail depends upon the amount we desire to lower the rail from the level. Moulds or templets are required, cut to the shapes shown, with which to mark the stuff for cutting. Level turns are usually worked in the solid on the long rail, as shown in Fig. 6, Pl. iv., but if the sweep were a large one it might be more economical to joint it at the springing. Sometimes the knee is also worked separately from the rail, in which case the joint should be made about 3 or 4 ins. beyond the springing, to provide a shank for the handrail bolt, also because the curves can be eased into the straight shank more sweetly than they can be when starting at the joint.

The Curved Kneeling (Figs. 7 and 8, Pl. iv.) is shown attached to a mitre cap for the sake of variety, though of course it might, with equal propriety, butt into a newel post, similar to Fig. 3, Pl. iv., or mitre with a ramp above the newel as in the photograph to be found of a Georgian stair., Pl. iii. and Ill. 3.

To Draw the Kneeling (Fig. 7, Pl. iv.), commence by marking the centre line of the cap or newel, set off to the left, the line of mitre with the rail M-E in Fig. 8, Pl. iv. Draw the level line C equal to the height it is desired to raise the newel : in the example this is half a rise, as shown by the pitch-board. Produce the pitch line of the underside of rail B-C and make C-D equal to C-E. At points D and E raise perpendiculars to the respective lines, and their intersection (which is outside this drawing) will be the centre for the curve lines of the rail. When cutting the templet for this easing, take care to carry it to point *m*, the extreme end of the mitre. If the piece is to be jointed, make the joint 3 ins. above the springing line and bolt, similar to the cap. Note, in all cases where a curved easing is to be jointed to a straight rail it is advisable to mould the straight portion first, make the joint, dowel it, and bolt up ; then scribe the outline upon the shank of the easing ; gauge around from the bottom all the guide lines and take around the sinkings as described for the straight rail in a former paragraph : by this method the continuity of the lines will be ensured.

A Ramp (see Figs. 9 and 10, Pl. iv.) was perhaps the commonest form of easing to be met with in handrailing before the introduction of the wreathed rail for turning corners. It is chiefly confined to newel stairs, although sometimes employed in that type of stair which is a cross between the open newel and the geometrical, wherein the return flights join the advancing flight at right angles, neither strings or newels being used, but the handrails turned on iron balusters at the corners. Pl. iii. shows a ramp in the beautiful refined stair at 15 Queen Square, Bath, dating probably from about 1730. Ill. 3 shows the treatment of the turn at a landing, and Ill. 4 a different version from Mompesson House, of about the same date. The example in Pl. IV. is of an open newelled stair, and the ramp is used in connection with a knee, which mitres at the angle with a kneeling upon the upper rail, as shown in the plan, Fig. 10, Pl. IV. To describe the ramp—whose length depends upon the going of the stair—draw sufficient of the flyers to obtain the pitch, as in Fig. 9, Pl. IV. Draw the rail resting on the nosing, produce the back of the rail to meet a perpendicular dropped from the end of the knee in point D. The length of the knee and its height above the landing are arbitrary. The data in the example are : height above the landing 3 ft. 5½ ins., which would be a lift of 9 ins.,

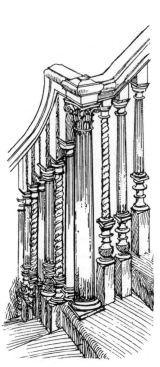

ILL. 3.—ANGLE OF BALUSTRADE
(No. 15 Queen Square, Bath).
(*A. Stratton.*)

ILL. 4.—THE TURN AT A LANDING (Mompesson
House, Salisbury). (*G. C. Horsley.*)

with the back of the rail at 2 ft. 8½ ins. above the flyers. The length of the knee equals that of the kneeling on the other side, and, as before explained, the length of the latter depends upon the position of the baluster (see Fig. 11, Pl. IV.). The ramp finishes at the second riser. From point D as centre, with radius D-B, describe the arc A-B. Draw the line A-C perpendicular to D-A, and B-C perpendicular to the pitch of the rail. C is the centre of the curves. The knee and the ramp are usually got out in one piece, with the mitres of the mouldings worked in the solid, a job that will test the capabilities of a skilled wreath-hand-railer. The author's method of working was to stop the grooving and shaping about ½ in. on each side of the mitre, until the moulding was worked down satisfactorily to these points, then to make a saddle mitre templet in two halves, to be screwed together on the rail, then carefully to scribe down the mitre with a sharp paring chisel, gradually continuing the sinkings until the mitre line was reached, when the moulding was finished off. The butt joint at the other end is made the length of a handrail bolt beyond the springing as usual. In the case before us, the end of the knee is mitred to the level rail, and secured with a double tenon, as indicated at T, Fig. 10, Pl. IV. Here again a box mitre will be required with which to mark and shoot the mitre.

Construction of a Built-up Ramp.—In the preceding paragraph the construction of solid ramps is dealt with, but as indicated in a subsequent chapter on the design and construction of handrails, it is sometimes found advisable to build up the larger rails, in four or more sections, according to their design. Consequently when ramps occur in these, the construction of the ramped portion must follow that of the remainder of the railing. Figs. 1 and 2, Pl. V., are the elevation and plan of a typical ramp, mitred to a level return rail.

Fig. 3, Pl. V., is an enlarged section of the ramp, taken on the plane of the joint. The general methods of building up rails and the chief points to consider are fully dealt with in the paragraph referred to above; they need not be repeated here, although they apply equally to ramps and other easings.

The detail drawings, Figs. 4 to 9, Pl. V., show in plan and elevation the several pieces forming the ramp; the elevation in each instance giving the mould with which to mark out the block that is indicated in fine lines. The plans, projected on a plane parallel with the bottom of the block, show the required width and length correctly. The elevations, Figs. 4 and 6, Pl. V., are placed at their proper pitch, as indicated in Fig. 1, Pl. V.; through exigency of space, Fig. 8, Pl. V., is drawn as if laid horizontally; little difficulty will be met in setting out in this way if a perpendicular to the top of the block is drawn through its middle, and the centre of the particular sweep, as shown at Fig. 1, Pl. V., located thereon. It will be noticed that the curves of the moulds are carried a little beyond the springing line at the mitre end, and the bottom piece C is arranged to come up square with these.

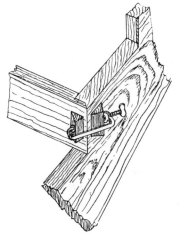

ILL. 5.—METHOD OF GLUEING-UP MITRES IN CUT STRINGS.

A little stuff might be saved if it were cut shorter by the depth of the level rail, but it is an advantage in fitting up to have a little extra to play with.

The templets, shown section-lined at the end of each piece, should be applied to the temporary joints at each end, after the pieces are dressed to size and shape in the square, and the grooves and tongues—previously tested for correctness—are carefully marked thereon. The pinholes for locating the centres of the dowels or bolts, whichever are used, may be made in the templets, but should not be used until the joints are finally made.

The various pieces are next grooved and moulded, as described at page 1, "Moulding straight rails," put together, and the joints tested with the straight rail. In this method of construction the top section is fitted on last, after the sides are glued and blocked to the bottom. It will not be possible to bolt the top piece, but if so desired, the two sides and the bottom can be bolted up, as indicated on the left side of Fig. 3, Pl. V.; more often, however, the joint is drawn up by counter-wedging, as indicated at B, Fig. 3, also in dotted lines on Fig. 1, and, so arranged, dowels only will be required, as shown in Fig. 3 at B.

After the mitre joint is made and fitted to the level piece, a solid deal block, about 2 ins. thick, should be fitted tightly in the opening and glued in, projecting half its thickness beyond the joint, and allowed to dry to one piece, then the other, well glued and cramped up to this, will make a sound joint. The cramping should be done by means of handscrews (Ill. 5), biting on two temporary blocks glued at either side of the joint, with their pressure faces parallel with the joint.

Swan Necks are a combination of ramp and curved knee. Like the ramps, they are invariably used at the upper end of the handrail and may mitre together over a landing, as in Figs. 12 and 13, Pl. IV., or mitre into a newel cap, as in Figs. 14 and 15, Pl. IV. The curves in Fig. 12, Pl. IV., are circular on the ramp, and elliptic on the knee portion. The striking lines are found as follows : the points d and B are first decided. B is usually in line with a riser, d varies according to the balusters or in case of an iron balustrade must follow the core rail. The lines d-c and B-C are drawn perpendicular to the pitches, and the circular curves struck from C, as centre. Produce C-d to A. Draw A-D vertical, in line with the outside of the landing rail. Then A-D is the semi-major, and A-d the semi-minor, axes of the elliptic curves, which may be trammelled through them or if preferred the curves may be described by aid of the easing-board described at page 7.

The commoner form of swans neck (Fig. 14, Pl. IV.), is struck from the centres located on reverse sides of the rail. The construction will be readily followed from the drawing. The enclosing rectangle marked 1-2-3-4 indicates the dimensions of the stuff required to cut the easing, and the plan, Fig. 15, Pl. IV., shows the thickness.

Any change in the direction of a handrail or stair string which is accomplished by connecting the two different lines of direction by means of a curved line, is called an Easing ; therefore all the curves previously described in this chapter are " easings," but these being regular curves described from known centres or axes as the case may be, are identified by the specific names given, but there are other curves more subtle in their direction, which cannot be produced geometrically—are in fact frequently produced either partly or entirely by freehand drawing—that are known in the workshop as easings, and it is to these we now refer.

It is required to ease off the angle of a handrail A-C-B, Fig. 16, Pl. IV., to an agreeable curve. It will be observed that A is a greater distance from C than is B. This is a common requirement, but were they equal the procedure to be described would be the same, though the resulting curve would be different. Assuming the drawing to be a templet which is required full size : divide the line A-C into any convenient number of equal parts, the points should not exceed 1 in. apart ; number them consecutively from A ; next divide C-B into a like number of equal parts and number these from C. Then draw straight lines between the similarly numbered points, i.e. 1 to 1, 2 to 2, etc. The points of intersection of these lines indicated by dots in the Fig. are points in the required curve, and pins driven in at these points, with a thin lath bent up against them, will enable one to draw the curve correctly. Having worked the edge to the curved line gauge the opposite edge from it. This method, though common enough, has a drawback : it needs two persons for its execution, one to hold the lath, the other to pencil the curve. The author devised an apparatus to dispense with this helper, shown in the four Figs., Ills. 6, 7, 8, 9.

The Easing Board consists of a piece of deal about 2 ft. 6 ins. long, 6 ins. wide, and $1\frac{1}{4}$ in. thick. One edge is rounded to a flat curve. At one end is a projection which is undercut, at the other end a dovetail groove is formed about 9 ins. long ; in this groove slides the stop, shown enlarged in Ill. 8. A steel band, or straight-edge, $1\frac{1}{4}$ in. wide, is inserted between the undercut end and the sliding stop. When this is pushed inwards the steel band bends outwards as shown, and any desired curvature can be obtained. If the stop is fitted stiffly it will not move back with the pressure of the band, but as a precaution a wood screw can be turned in, as shown. The above procedure gives circular curves. To obtain elliptic, or irregular curves, an additional slider is required, as shown in the middle, also in the section, Ill. 6. A dovetail groove runs across the middle of the board, in which moves a short sliding piece; to this, by means of a thumb screw, a radial slotted arm is pivoted, having a rounded fence at its outer end,

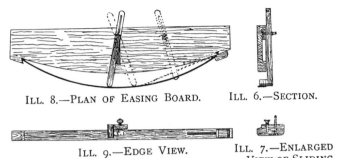

ILL. 8.—PLAN OF EASING BOARD.   ILL. 6.—SECTION.

ILL. 9.—EDGE VIEW.   ILL. 7.—ENLARGED VIEW OF SLIDING STOP.

HANDRAILING OF SINGLE CURVATURE.

which works against the steel band. By this means the arm can be placed in any desired position and in conjunction with the stop a curve of any flexure can be obtained. By the addition of a second arm, similar to the first, attached with a screw in an appropriate position, as indicated by the dotted lines, curves of contrary flexure can be produced. The author has found this board of considerable assistance in lining out strings, as any sort of easing is quickly obtained. A piece of thin ash or lancewood will answer the purpose, but has not the range that a steel band has. These steel bands can be obtained from engineers' tool dealers, such as Buck's of 39 Goodge Street, or Buck and Hickman, Whitechapel Road, London.

Mitre Caps are frequently used as terminals to handrails above a newel post. They are always turned circular in plan, with a similar moulding to the rail, which is mitred at each intersection, hence the term mitre cap to distinguish them from those newel caps which stand above the rails as in Figs. 1 and 10, Pl. IV. The method of securing the cap to the rail and to the newel is shown in Figs. 7 and 8, Pl. IV. The method of obtaining the section of the cap from that of the rail is shown in Ill. 10. The section varies according to the angle decided upon for the mitre joint. The more usual method is shown on the left-hand side of the figure, which will be first described. Lay down the plan of the rail and cap as in Ill. 10. Set out thereon a section of the rail, draw lines parallel to the sides of the rail from the point in the moulding at the greatest distance from its edge. Set off on the diameter of the cap A–B a

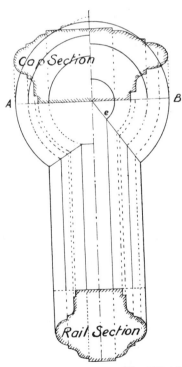

ILL. 10.—OBTAINING MITRES AND SECTIONS OF MITRE CAPS.

like distance from the edge, and describe a circle thereon from the centre. At the intersection of this line with the line on the rail draw the mitre to the intersections of the outside lines. It is a matter of taste whether the mitre is continued to the centre line of the rail, as shown in Figs. 8 and 15, Pl. IV., or stopped at the flat disc on the cap, as drawn in Ill. 10 ; whichever is adopted, the remaining procedure will be the same. Draw parallel lines from the various members of the moulding on the given section to the mitre line. Describe arcs from the points of intersection to cut the diameter A-B ; upon these points raise perpendiculars. Make each equal in height to the corresponding height, or ordinate, upon the rail section, and draw the contour of the cap mould through the points so found. The cap turned to this section, which differs but slightly from that of the rail, will intersect correctly with the rail at a straight mitre. If absolutely the same section is desired to the cap and the rail, then a circular mitre will be required which, besides being more expensive to make, does not look so well as a straight mitre. Sometimes it is required to carry the mitre right to the centre of the cap, as shown on the right-hand side. The same procedure is necessary to obtain the section of the cap, which will however differ from that of the rail considerably, as can be seen. In some cases a button or pateræ is affixed to the top of the cap, as indicated in dotted lines. When this is done, it is usual to fix the cap with a long screw through the top into the newel, instead of by means of a turned pin or dowel underneath, as shown in Fig. 8, Pl. IV.

The Cap Mitring Block illustrated (Ills. 11 and 12) will be found useful for cutting the mitres on moulded caps, which are difficult to mark with exactness. It is quickly and easily made with a foot length of deal 2 ins. thick and an inch wider than the cap to be mitred. Gauge down a centre line C, and square the end. Bore a dowel hole, $4\frac{1}{2}$ ins. from the end, on the centre line, to fit the hole in the cap. If the latter is not to be dowelled, pass a stout screw through the block from the back, to form a pivot for the cap to turn upon. Next refer to the drawing, Ill. 13, which is

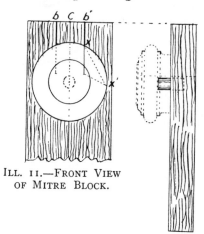

ILL. 11.—FRONT VIEW OF MITRE BLOCK.

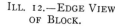

ILL. 12.—EDGE VIEW OF BLOCK.

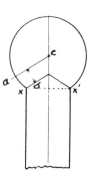

ILL. 13.—PLAN OF CAP AND RAIL.

METHOD OF CUTTING MITRES IN CAPS.

a plan of the joint required. Draw the line *a-c* parallel to the mitre *b*, through the centre of the cap. Set off the square distance between the lines *a-b* at each side of the centre line C upon the block, and gauge them down 4 ins. Run a fine saw down the lines, noting that the thickness of the saw-cut must be on the outsides of the lines, i.e. away from the centre line. Bring the square end of the rail up to the cap, and scribe its greatest width upon the side as at X-X′, Ill. 13. Now mount the cap upon the pin or screw, as in Ill. 12, when the first saw-cut *b′* can be run in, then the cap twisted to the left until point X′ lies under *b*, when the second cut can be run in to meet the first. In the case of a mitre taken to the centre of the cap, as on the right-hand of Ill. 10, the saw-cut will be made down the centre line C, twisting the block round as before to bring the two marks X and X′ successively to the cut.

Method of Enlarging or Reducing a Rail Section, as desired, in either dimension (Ill. 14).—Let G be the given section, which, full size, is 3 ins. wide and $2\frac{1}{2}$ ins. thick. The

PLATE IV.

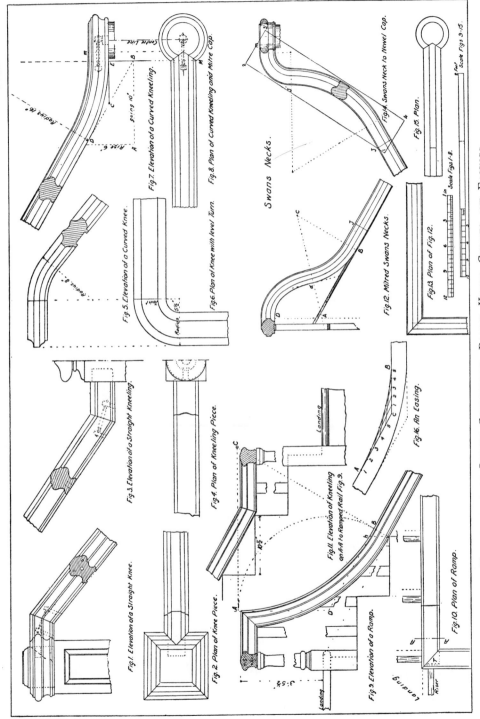

Fig. 7. Elevation of a Curved Kneeling.

Fig. 8. Plan of Curved Kneeling and Mitre Cap.

Fig. 14. Swans Neck to Newel Cap.

Fig. 15. Plan.

Fig. 5. Elevation of a Curved Knee.

Fig. 6. Plan of Knee with level Turn.

Swans Necks.

Fig. 12. Mitred Swans Necks.

Fig. 13. Plan of Fig. 12.

Scale Figs. 3–15.

Scale Figs. 1–8.

Fig. 3. Elevation of a Straight Kneeling.

Fig. 4. Plan of Kneeling Piece.

Fig. 16. An Easing.

Fig. 11. Elevation of Kneeling on A-A to Ramped Rail Fig. 9.

Fig. 1. Elevation of a Straight Knee.

Fig. 2. Plan of Knee Piece.

Fig. 9. Elevation of a Ramp.

Fig. 10. Plan of Ramp.

HANDRAILING OF SINGLE CURVATURE—RAMPS, KNEES, CURVES AND EASINGS.

PLATE V.

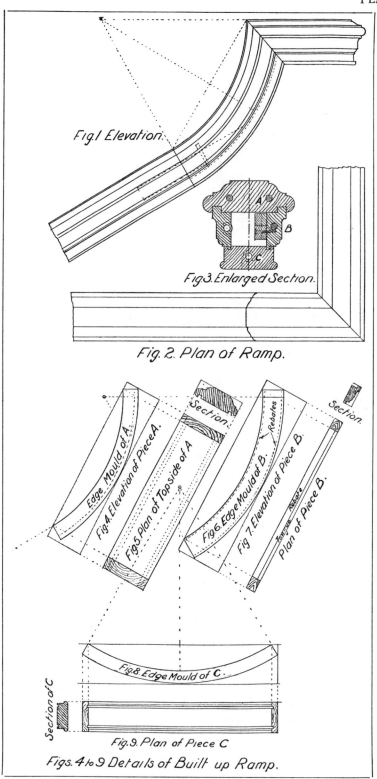

Fig.1 Elevation.

Fig.3 Enlarged Section.

Fig. 2. Plan of Ramp.

Edge Mould of A.

Fig.4.Elevation of Piece A.

Section.

Fig.5 Plan of Topside of A.

Rebates.

Fig.6.Edge Mould of B.

Fig.7.Elevation of Piece B.

Section.

Tongue. Rebate.

Plan of Piece B.

Fig.8. Edge Mould of C.

Section of C.

Fig.9. Plan of Piece C

Figs. 4 to 9 Details of Built up Ramp.

METHOD OF BUILDING UP A RAMP.

required section is to be 3¾ ins. wide and 3 ins. thick. Draw the right angle BEC coincident with the bottom and side of the given section, and make the lines equal its width and height. Upon C-E construct a right-angled triangle ECD equal in height to the required thickness of rail. Upon B-E construct the right-angled triangle ABE equal in height to the required width of rail. Draw parallel projectors to the lines C-D and A-B from the various members of the moulding, to intersect the hypotenuse E-D and E-A in points 1'-2'-3'-4', etc.

Draw other projectors from these points parallel to the sides A-B and C-D as shown, which will indicate at their intersections the proportionate widths and thicknesses of the new

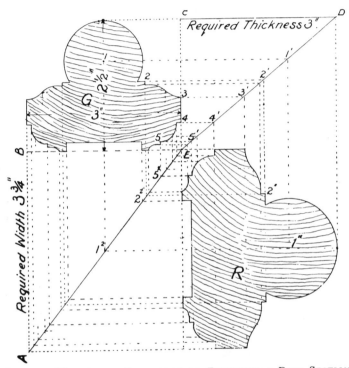

ILL. 14.—METHOD OF ENLARGING OR REDUCING A RAIL SECTION.

members. This method of enlargement affords a ready means of copying any of the sections given in this book to suit any specified rail. By reversing the process of drawing the projectors any given section may be reduced as required. Thus the section R, Ill. 14, would be reduced to G by first setting off the lines B-E and C-E to the required dimensions, and constructing the triangles upon them as before. The principle involved is that the subdivisions made upon the base line are increased or decreased as the case may be in the same proportion upon the hypotenuse that the latter bears to the base line of the triangle; and we control this proportion by determining the height of the triangle.

CHAPTER II.

HANDRAILING OF DOUBLE CURVATURE OR GEOMETRICAL HANDRAILING.

INTRODUCTION AND REVIEW OF VARIOUS "SYSTEMS."

Explanation of Terms—Description of the Author's System—The "Square Cut"—The "Bevel Cut"
—The "Tangent" System—The "Falling Line" System—What the Author's System Will Do
—Necessary Knowledge.

HANDRAILING of double curvature is a description of the means and methods of applying the science of geometry to the practical requirements of the joiner in the production of those portions of stairs that are commonly termed wreathed handrails, or more shortly "wreaths." This branch of the subject of stair construction has probably received more attention from writers—both theoretical and practical—than has all other branches of joinery put together; and, in reviewing a large number of these writers, one is compelled to admit that they seem to make the subject much more difficult and involved than the author of this book has found it to be in his own experience. Many of the "systems" devised are redolent of the drawing-class rather than of the workshop, with its rough-and-ready requirements and appliances. Doubtless some of the methods described are correct, but in the author's opinion they are eminently unsuited for workshop use. In some cases the wreath would have been made and forgotten by the usual "crude" methods, whilst the student of these ultra-scientific systems was setting out its intricate maze of lines. In the following descriptions and examples the author explains methods founded on geometrical principles which he has proved to give entirely satisfactory results. Moreover, he has taught the methods to a large number of workmen both personally and by correspondence, who have tested them in the workshops with unfailing success. Briefly, the methods may be described as a combination of the square-cut and tangent systems, also of the falling-line system. It will be necessary, to avoid mis-understandings, that some explanation of what these terms signify shall be given.

"**Square Cut**" refers to the method of cutting out the rough wreath-piece, or "blank" as it is frequently termed, square to the surface of the plank, in contradistinction to the earlier "Bevel-Cut" system, now obsolete, in which the wreath-piece was cut in such a manner that its sides were vertical when placed in position on the nosings of the steps, but, relatively to the surface of the plank, the sides were bevelled. Incidentally it may be mentioned that the bevel-cut system of the seventies followed in sequence the still earlier method of fitting wreaths directly to a cylinder, as practised when the author first came into the trade some sixty years ago, which will be found briefly described at page 95, Chap. XXVIII., Pl. XXXII.

The "**Tangent**" System refers to the method of enclosing the plan curves of the rail within straight lines that are made to touch the curves at certain points, thereby becoming "tangent to the curve" at these points, and by projection (a simple geometrical process) obtaining the heights of the aforesaid points upon the "tangent planes," a process which will be fully explained in subsequent chapters when we come to deal with practical examples.

The " Falling Line " System refers to a method of producing an imaginary central longitudinal section of the wreathed rail and utilising this section as a basis for obtaining moulds with which to line out the surfaces of the plank.   Each of these methods have been previously published by their inventors, and the author lays no claim to their origin, but each system in itself has been proved by experience to have defects, or at least limitations, to its utility.   What the author then lays claim to is a system combining the good points of each of the above methods, and the elimination of their bad points.   The methods herein described will give the handrailer absolute control over the shape and position of the wreath ; that is to say, for instance, if he decides to make his rail cling closely to the nosing line of the stairs, or to depart from it at certain points, and thereby conform to certain prearranged curves or ramps, he may feel quite confident that if the directions herein given are carried out his wreath when finished will fall absolutely into the position desired, and will be of the shape that he has determined ; also he need be under no apprehension that any eccentricity in the planning of a stair or the disposition of its risers will produce a " case " which this system is unable to deal with satisfactorily.

No previous knowledge of geometry is presupposed in these explanations, but it is assumed the reader will have sufficient experience in drawing to make a necessary transcription of the lines to a setting-out rod ; and it may be added, that as he gains experience, many of the lines given on the drawings can be dispensed with.   It will be readily understood that much more has to be placed on a drawing to make it clear to a beginner than would be necessary for the requirements of an experienced man in carrying out the job.

CHAPTER III.

THEORY AND PRINCIPLES OF HANDRAIL CONSTRUCTION.

Why Face Moulds are Used—Practical Limitations of Wreaths Produced by Tangent Systems—Sections of a Cylinder and their Properties—The Ellipse and its Properties—Purpose of Tangent Planes—The Oblique Plane, Pitch of the Plank, its Limitations—Classification of Tangents—The Standard Arrangements of Tangents, Properties of Each Type—The Handrail Prisms, Why Used—Springing Lines, Uses Of—Methods of Drawing Elliptic Curves—Determining Direction of Elliptic Axes—The Adjustable Axis Finder—The Falling Compasses, Use in Drawing Ellipses, Instruction for Making—The Characteristics of Tangents—Properties of Standard Types—Handrail Joints of Various Types, their Non-effect on Shape or Appearance of the Wreath—Ignorant Criticism—Cause of Ill-shaped Wreaths.

Preliminary Geometry.—It has been stated that no previous knowledge of geometry is assumed, but it will be necessary for a complete understanding of the subject that the reader should make himself familiar with the principles involved in the processes to be described in connection with the examples; and a few remarks are offered to make these clear, in so far as they bear upon the subject of handrailing.

A **Wreathed Handrail** may be considered, apart from its ornamentation by mouldings, as a rectilineal solid, winding regularly around a cylinder, also it can be conceived as forming a part of the surfaces of a hollow cylinder, and in this conception the plan of the cylinder would represent also the plan of the rail, as shown in Ill. 15, where the plan of a semi-cylinder may represent a " half-turn " handrail, and the shaded projection represents the outside surface of the cylinder, the unshaded portion representing the side of a wreath,[1] over a half-space of winders lying in that surface. The interior surface of the cylinder and the other side of the handrail are indicated by dotted lines that will be easily followed.

It will now be clear that the two *sides* of a handrail, whatever the inclination of the wreath may be, must be vertical, consequently parallel, that is to say, the wreath, like the remainder of the handrail, must be of equal width throughout. Next we have to consider that the straight portions of the rail are level across their top and bottom surfaces; therefore, the corresponding surfaces of the wreath must also be level, or in other words, square with the sides. How this is obtained will be described later; it will suffice here to point out that this squaring of the wreath produces twisted

ILL. 15.—PLAN AND PROJECTION OF CYLINDER CONTAINING WREATHED HANDRAIL.

[1] For explanation of technical terms see glossary at the end.

(14)

surfaces above and below.   It is not practicable to prepare moulds or templets that will lie on twisted surfaces, hence, as the wreath must be cut from a plane plank of parallel thickness, a mould is required that will lie upon a *plane*, surface and its edges then indicate the true shape of the wreath in plan.   This templet, called the face mould, is a plane section of the appropriate cylinder, and of course produces (after certain operations) the two sides of the wreath.   When these have been obtained it is, if not an easy matter, at least a mechanical process soon learned, to square the top and bottom surfaces from them.   The dotted lines C-C and *d-d*, Ill. 15, indicate the thickness of plank that would be required to cut the wreath shown, in one piece ; but there are practical objections to so doing, especially when using the tangent system, by which to procure the moulds, although the author has seen such wreaths got out by the old cylinder method.   In the tangent system a wreath is never made to cover more than one-third of a circle, and rarely more than a quadrant in one piece.

The thick lines *a-a* and *b-b* represent the surfaces of the plank, from which one half of the wreath would be cut, to be jointed at the centre to the other half, as shown, thus indicating the reduced thickness of plank required as compared with that necessary to make the wreath in one piece.

Having now seen that the sides of the wreath form part of a right cylinder, and that its shape can be determined by a section of that cylinder, we will consider how that section can be obtained.

Any section of a cylinder that is inclined to the axis or central line will be an ellipse. This is demonstrated in Ill. 16, which is the plan and projection of a cylinder, having three sections made upon it at varying inclinations.   These sections are all elliptic in shape, approximating nearer to a circular outline as they approach the horizontal, or position at right angles to the axis, a section which yields a circular outline, as shown by the plan.   The method of obtaining these sections may be detailed.

ILL. 16.—PLAN, ELE-VATION AND SEC-TION OF A RIGHT VERTICAL HOLLOW CYLINDER.

ILL. 17. — PLAN AND SKETCH ELEVATION OF A HOLLOW CYL-INDER SHOWING EL-LIPTIC SECTION.

It will be noticed that one-half of the plan shows the section of a solid cylinder, the other half that of a hollow or annular cylinder.   The method of obtaining the sections is the same for either.   Take the former one first.   Divide the outline or semi-circumference of the half-plan into any number of equal parts, as 1 to 9.   Project these points to the line of section *a-a*, that is, draw lines through the points, perpendicular to the diameter 1-9, and at their in-tersections 2', 3', 4', 5', 6', 7', 8', draw perpendiculars to the line of section, which are dis-tinguished as ordinates.

Make each of these ordinates equal in length to the corresponding ordinate in plan, shown in full lines, as for example 4'-4" is made equal to 4-4*a* in plan, and draw the outline of the section through the points so found ; the opposite side is obtained similarly.   The other two sections may be obtained in like manner, as also the curve of the inside cylinder, shown in dotted line on the upper section, which is assumed to be revolved into the vertical plane, upon the line *a-a*, as a hinge.   Ill. 17 is a plan and a sketch elevation of the same cylinder, turned so that the section on *a-a* faces the reader, where its shape may be better realised.   It will be observed that although the plan of the cylinder shows that its sides are of equal thickness throughout, the edges of the elliptic section are not parallel; the section is much wider at the ends than at the sides.   This reveals a property of the ellipse that we shall have to take note of later.   The diameters of an ellipse are distinguished as axes, the longer is called the major axis, the shorter the minor axis, and these are always perpendicular, or at right angles to each other.   The minor axis *equals the diameter of the cylinder*, and is always horizontal, when the section is in its true position on the cylinder.   These are all special properties we shall make use of when drawing moulds.   Having seen from Ill. 16 that each and every section of a cylinder differs in shape if taken at a differing inclination, we may deduce the contrary truth, that every section of the same cylinder, wherever taken, will be of the same shape if the inclination remains the same; or, put into other words, it is the inclination of the section, not its position on the cylinder, which determines its shape.   This being understood, revert to Ill. 15.   The line *a-a* represents a section of that semi-cylinder, and the shape of that section can be produced as shown in Ill. 16.   The line *b-b*, Ill. 15, is parallel with *a-a*, therefore its inclination is the same; consequently, the shape of the section on *b-b* is identical with that of *a-a*.   Now if we consider the lines *a-a* and *b-b* as representing also the top and bottom surfaces of a plank, it will not be difficult to see that if these surfaces are lined out by the face mould, which is the section *a-a*, and cut straight through to the curved lines on each surface, then we shall have a wreath-piece whose sides will exactly cover the plan of the cylinder (between its springings) when placed at the inclination shown in the drawing.   All then that remains to be done so far as the shape of the wreath in plan is concerned, is to determine what is the exact section of the cylinder required, and where to place it upon the plank.   Now as the cylinder exists only in the imagination, we cannot place any dimensions upon it, therefore resort is made to the device of enclosing the cylinder within plane surfaces, upon which the dimensions to determine the inclination can be placed, and in effect transferred to the cylinder.   These enclosing planes are known as tangent planes, and in the constructive drawings made for the purpose of obtaining the moulds to simplify the operation, a line representing the centre line of the rail in plan and elevation is used, instead of the inside and outside faces of the rail that we have hitherto been considering, and the tangent planes are made to enclose this central imaginary cylinder.

The upper edges of these tangent planes in elevation represent the edges of the section to be made, which, when brought into position, is called the oblique plane.   There are cases in which the plane of section is not oblique, as we shall see shortly, but that does not affect the principle.   Also, the tangent in elevation represents the pitch of the plank out of which the wreath has to be cut, and if the reader will consider that it is only possible to pitch or incline a plank in two directions he will see not only the necessary limitation of the relative positions of any pair of tangents, but also the reason why it is not practicable to obtain much more than a quarter circle in any one wreath-piece, as indicated by the dotted joint lines on Ill. 17.

Classification of Tangents.—Throughout this book, the term " tangent " is used to indicate the imaginary plane referred to above and, although it may occur in three distinct places on the drawings—(*a*) in the plan, (*b*) in elevation, (*c*) on the plane of section, in all cases the reference will be to one and the same line, although it is in different positions.   The inclinations at which tangents can be placed is practically unlimited, and one of the chief problems of handrailing is to ascertain the best position in each case; but although the number of positions in which individual tangents can be placed is unlimited, the relative positions in which two sets of tangents can be placed is reducible to three, or at most, four types, as shown in Nos. 1, 2, 3, 4, Ill. 18, p. 17, and these are known as the standard arrangements of tangents.

There are certain properties connected with each arrangement which, if committed to memory, considerably facilitates their use. These are referred to under the head " Characteristics of Tangents."

The **Four Standard Arrangements of Tangents** are shown in Ill. 18. In No. 1, one tangent is inclined, the other tangent is level; or, in other words, the plank in this case is inclined in the direction of its length, and horizontal in the direction of its width.

In case No. 2 both tangents are inclined alike, that is to say, if revolved into the same plane they would produce a straight line, as shown in the elevation.

Case No. 3. Both tangents are inclined, but unequally. These three positions comprise all possible variations in principle, but the combination shown in case 4 occurs perhaps more frequently than any of the others, and as in combination the arrangement possesses some characteristics not possessed by the others, it is treated as a special case. Each of these cases has the tangent at right angles in plan. There are other two cases in which they are not at right angles, but this makes no difference in principle, although it causes different construction in detail, which will be dealt with subsequently.

To clearly understand the relation of the tangents to the imaginary cylinder, to which reference has been made, it will be well to consider the lines shown in the elevations, Ill. 18, as

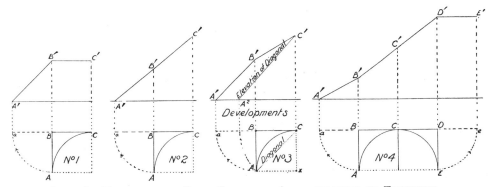

ILL. 18.—TYPES OF THE FOUR STANDARD ARRANGEMENTS OF TANGENTS.

the edges of solid prisms, of which the respective plans are the bases. Thus in Ill. 19, p. 18, are shown four rectangular prisms, cut upon their upper surfaces to the angles of inclination indicated at the corresponding numbers in Ill. 18. These are drawn in isometric projection, therefore the *angles* cannot be shown correctly as they recede into the picture, but the dimensions are exactly as in Ill. 18. The curve line on the base represents a quadrant in Nos. 1, 2, 3, and a semi-circle in No. 4, and is the base of the imaginary cylinder. Upon the plane of section, which contains in its edges the tangents of No. 1, Ill. 18, is drawn the elliptic curve, which would be produced by the penetration of the plane by the cylinder. The reader is not expected to draw these prisms, which are merely furnished as illustrations of the remarks, but he would learn much by actually producing them, say in a piece of pine planed to 1½ ins. square, on this, setting out the lines shown in Ill. 18 upon the respective sides, then cutting them to the section, describing a quadrant on the base, and, by means of level ordinates obtained as described at page 15, and as indicated by the dotted lines in No. 3, Ill. 19, drawn from one side to the quadrant, then squared up to the oblique plane, and repeated thereon, making these equal in length to the base ordinates, and tracing the elliptic curve through the points. The essential principle of this construction is that level lines upon an inclined plane are always shown in true length.

In the plan of tangents Nos. 1 to 4, Ill. 18, dotted lines are drawn from the centre of the curve to the points of contact with the tangents. These lines are known as springing lines, and are always parallel with the tangents, both on the plan and on the plane of section; they are required to locate upon this plane the centre of the elliptic curves, which lies in the axis of the cylinder, and the plan of which is the point X, see No. 3. In constructing this plane, on which to set out the elliptic curves, the elevation as in No. 3, Ill. 18, supplies the length of two sides of the section, viz., A'-B' and B'-C', but it is necessary to obtain a third dimension by which to determine the true angle between these sides, as shown at A, B, C, No. 3, Ill. 19.

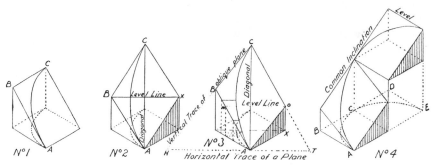

ILL. 19.—THE FOUR STANDARD PRISMATIC SOLIDS.

This is supplied by the diagonal line connecting the two ends, A and C, shown on the surface of the prism.

To obtain the true length of this line, which rises from A to C, its plan A-C must be revolved into the vertical plane on point C, as indicated on the plan No. 3, Ill. 18; then the end A, projected to the ground line at A², is joined to its highest point C by a straight line which is the true length of the diagonal. To set out the section, Ill. 20, draw the line A''-C'' equal in length to A²-C', No. 3, then with C' as centre and B'-C', No. 3, as radius, describe an arc; intersect this arc by another, struck from A'' as centre and A'-B' as radius, join this point to

ILL. 20.—CONSTRUCTION OF PLANE OF SECTION OF PRISM No. 3, ILL. 19.

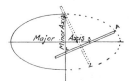

ILL. 21.—METHOD OF DESCRIBING AN ELLIPSE BY TRAMMELLING.

the ends of the diagonal, when the true shape of the triangle seen on the section No. 3, Ill. 19, will be obtained, and lines parallel to the sides A''-B'' and B''-C'', drawn from their ends, will complete the section of the prism and locate at X'' the position of the axis of the cylinder, which is also the centre of the axes of the elliptic curve.

Methods of Drawing Elliptic Curves.—One method, by means of ordinates, has already been shown in No. 3, Ill. 19, but more frequently in the workshop the process known as trammelling is adopted; this method is illustrated in Ill. 21. The two axes are drawn at right angles, and the length of each axis marked off equally on each side of the centre, then any light rod, or in the case of a small drawing a strip of paper, has marked off from one end half the length of the major axis, point L, also from the same end A, half the length of the minor axis, point S, and keeping these two points upon the transverse axes as shown, points are marked off at the end of the rod A, which will be points in the ellipse. The rod is shown in two positions; as many points as desired may be obtained in like manner and the curve drawn through them, either by freehand or by bending a lath successively over as many groups of points as can be managed, with an assistant to pencil in the line against it. Several other ways of drawing ellipses are given in the author's " Modern Technical Drawing " (Batsford, 10s. 6d. net). When drawing face moulds in cases of tangents of type No. 3, Ill. 18, the problem arises of determining the *direction* of the elliptic axes. The geometrical method of ascertaining this is by a process known as " finding the traces " of the oblique plane ; and determining thereby the direction of a level line, which will be parallel to the minor axis of the ellipse. This method is shown in dotted line on No. 3 prism, Ill. 19, and will be explained in connection with the example, page 30. It is, however, only suitable for small scale work on the drawing board, where angles may be plotted with extreme accuracy ; it is eminently unsuitable for use in the workshop, where things must be set out full size by means of relatively coarse and oft-times extemporised instruments. For the latter purpose the following method, used by the author for many years, which was first published about 1880 by G. Collings, in Messrs. Crosby Lockwood's " Weale's Series of Practical Handbooks," will be found a very quick and accurate way of ascertaining the direction of the axes. Prepare a piece of thin board about 8 ins. long with one end square to the sides, gauge a line down the middle. Then this line can take the place of the minor axis of the proposed ellipse, and the end of the board that of the major axis. Keep the point of intersection of the two axes at the centre of the required curve and, using the trammel rod as described in the preceding paragraph, so arrange the two axes by moving around the piece of board, that the lengths on the rod will " fit," that is to say, lie upon the two axes on the board, when the outer end A is held to any two points in the curve. In the case of a handrail face mould, these two points are always at the springings, as will be seen in the example given on Pl. IX. Several adjustments of the square may need to be made before the exact direction is found, and it facilitates the operation to drive a sprig into the centre or axis of the ellipse and make a slight V notch in the end of the square, which will allow the latter to work round the point without losing the central position. It will be understood that it is not required that the two marks on the trammel rod shall fall at the same points on each side of the axes, but merely that they shall fall somewhere upon the axes. It may be added that the above method may be utilised at the drawing board, by substituting a sheet of paper for the wood square and placing a fine pin at the centre for a pivot.

Another method of drawing ellipses, very useful in the workshop, especially for handrail moulds, where the direction of the axes is unknown, is by means of the " falling compasses " as suggested by Peter Nicholson in 1842. The one made for my own use, containing slight improvements on Nicholson's idea, is illustrated in the sketch, Ill. 22, p. 20. A hollow brass rod, $\frac{3}{8}$ in. diameter, about 3 ft. long, is set up perpendicularly on the plan rod, at the centre of the well, either by boring a hole to receive it or by driving in a wire nail and setting the end of the tube over this, as shown in the detail of foot. The top end is stayed upright in any way convenient, sometimes by a wood stay, hooked over the end and sprigged to the bench, at others by guying it as shown in the sketch by means of a length of chalk line ; all that is needful is that it shall be firmly fixed upright. Sliding freely but not loosely on this rod is a short square sleeve of hard wood A, which has a $\frac{3}{8}$-in. hole bored through one side (see enlarged detail A). A $\frac{3}{8}$-in. beechwood rod (B), of suitable length, slides easily through this hole, carrying at its end the pencil guide C.

The guide should be of light wood and about 3 ins. long, with a hollow groove on the face to keep the pencil steady. In my instrument all the parts take to pieces and occupy but little space when closed up. Next, cut two pieces of inch board to the bevel of the pair of tangents and nail them together at the angle to form two sides of the imaginary prism ; secure these in position on the plan rod, as shown, then lay the piece of stuff from which the mould is to be cut upon it, as shown by the dotted lines—a couple of brads will keep the piece in position ; slip the sliding bar into the sleeve A, and move the sleeve down to the plan, where the length of the slider may be adjusted, so that the pencil point stands exactly on the curve of the wreath.   Next, move the sleeve up as high as required to allow the pencil to just touch the top end of the mould.   Then, by gently moving the arm forward, at the same time allowing the sleeve to slip down the rod, the elliptic line required will be traced on the templet in the manner shown.   Repeat the process for the other curve.   Nicholson advised this method to be used on the plank itself, as an economy of time, but although it can be so done, I have found the difficulty of adjusting a 2-ft. length of Spanish mahogany, 4 ins. thick by 10 ins. wide, make it more economical to get out a mould as described above.   Of course, the principle

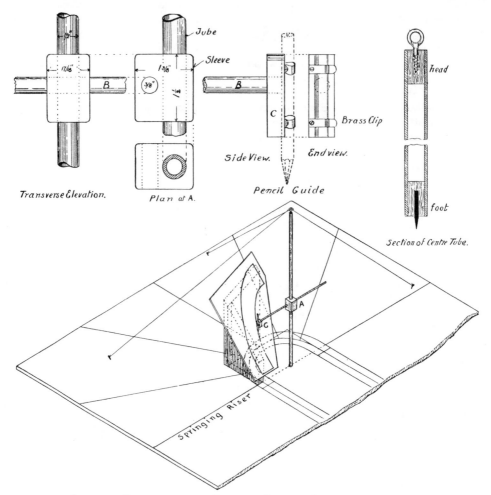

ILL. 22.—SKETCH OF THE FALLING COMPASS DESCRIBING ELLIPSE.

is the same in either case.   Incidentally, this method of striking moulds confutes those shallow reasoners who argue that a plane ellipse cannot yield a spiral wreath, because, obviously, the revolving pencil describes an ellipse whilst travelling in a spiral path.

The Characteristics of Tangents.—These are properties constant to the several types of tangents mentioned in the preceding paragraphs, and reference to them will sometimes clear up an uncertainty :—

Type 1 : *When one Tangent is Level and the Other Inclined.*—The major and minor axes of the elliptic curves coincide with the springing lines on the face mould section, also they agree in length with the springings. One end of the face mould will be of the same width as is the rail in plan. One bevel only is required to locate the position of the mould for bevelling the sides of the wreath; one tangent on the mould will not be altered.

Type II. *When the Tangents are Inclined Alike.*—The major axis of the ellipse will be parallel with the " diagonal " on the face mould. The mould is wider at both ends than the rail in plan, but these widths are equal. Two bevels are required for sliding the mould, but as their inclination is alike one bevel answers the purpose.

Type III. *When Both Tangents are Inclined, but Differently.*—The direction of the axes of the elliptic curves must be found, either by construction or by trial, as described in a preceding paragraph. The face mould will be wider at each end than the rail in plan, and the widths will be unequal. Two bevels are required, and they differ.

Type IV. Either half-wreath will have the characteristics of its special tangents as given previously. There will be three bevels to obtain, one will be common to both half-wreaths. In the example No. 4, the widths of the ends of the mould at the centre joint will be alike, but this will not occur when the central pair of tangents are of different inclinations. When the top and bottom tangents are alike in inclination, one mould will answer for both wreaths, by reversing it on the plank.

A Type V. might be formed of tangents not at right angles in plan, as such cases have one special attribute, the springings are not parallel to the tangents, therefore not only has the *direction* of the elliptic axes to be found by construction, but also their centre. Apart from this, obtuse and acute angle tangents conform to the rules of cases I., II., III., whichever type they agree with in elevation.

Before commencing the description of the typical examples of wreaths it may be advisable to offer a few remarks on joints, as much discussion has raged around this matter in the technical press, and a great deal of misconception exists as to their bearing or influence upon the wreath. I may perhaps be misunderstood if I state that the joints have absolutely no effect or control upon the wreath, although such a statement would be right in principle. The point may be stated in another way that may be clearer.

I, or any one following the methods advised in this book, could make wreaths by them with joints either butt or square or bevel or splice, or even the old mortise and tenon joint, used before handrail bolts were invented, and when finished they would be exactly the same as if made with the joints herein advised. Personally I use the butt joint known as " square to the tangent " and square to the plank, wherever I can, simply because it is the easiest, most rational and most economical to make, but on occasions there are certain inclinations of the rail in which the joint, known as " square to the falling line," would be preferable, and instructions for this kind of joint are included, but it is a troublesome and expensive joint to make, as it requires three bevels and special manipulation of the moulding-templet at each joint; but to assert, as one book writer has, that a wreath will be "lumpy" unless this joint is employed, is absurd, and the writer, if not ignorant of the subject himself, is certainly trading on the ignorance of his readers. One might as well say that if a plank were square jointed, say, in the middle of its length and then inclined, that its surfaces would suddenly become irregular because it was inclined !

It is not to be denied that wreaths and rails *are* made " lumpy," but this is not owing to the joints but to the incapacity of the workmen, which may be either in the manipulation of their tools or in faulty draughtsmanship when setting out. The original or crude " tangent system " of the sixties, in which developments of the tangents were used without clear knowledge of their disposition on the plan, also led to the construction of many faulty rails, but these errors are generally eliminated in modern practice.

CHAPTER IV.

A PAIR OF WREATHS OVER A HALF-PACE LANDING.

(PLATE VI.)

Wreath brought to the Level—How to Set Out the Plan—Position of Risers Relative to the Springing
—Influence on the Tangents and the Appearance of Wreath—Drawing the Developments—
Locating "Heights" of the Tangents, Why this is Important—Obtaining the Face Mould—
Properties of a Level Line—Obtaining Bevels, What the Bevel Is—To Ascertain Thickness of
Plank—How to Project a Wreath, its Value.

A Pair of Wreaths over a Half-pace Landing (Pl. VI.).—Wreath brought to level. Pl. VI.
contains the working drawings for the above-mentioned wreath, and in addition a projection
of the squared wreath jointed and ready for moulding, set up in its appropriate position on
the stair, the better to indicate to the beginner the requirements of this system. A key plan
and section of the stair complete, to smaller scale, is also shown that the reader may understand the relation of the wreath to the stair.

In this and some subsequent drawings, the plan of the rail and its elevation are shown
in geometrical connection, that is to say, they are so placed that one can be projected from the
other. It is rarely possible to do so when setting out full size in the workshop, unless the
work is set out upon the floor, a most awkward position. However, the reader will see later
that this conjunction of the drawings is no necessity of this system, as it is with most others.
Each of these drawings, including face moulds, can be drawn upon separate boards or positions
as circumstances dictate, but it facilitates the necessary explanations to place this one in the
position shown.

The Plan.—Fig. 1, Pl. VI., is first drawn, showing part of the landing risers, one step
above, and one step below the same, a portion of the well, and the wreathed handrail. The
centre line of the handrail is enclosed by the tangent lines A-B, B-C, C-D and D-E. In this
wreath, for reasons presently to be seen, the tangents A-B-C are all that would be used in the
workshop, but the others are included here for the sake of clearness. Next, the springing line
A-E is drawn at right angles to the tangents and through the centre of the curves X, also the
diagonal A-C. All of the data for drawing the plan is figured thereon, with the exception
of the position of the landing risers, relative to the springing. The position of these makes
considerable difference both to the appearance of the wreath and to the inclination of the
plank or tangents. Three other positions are given in subsequent examples; the present
arrangement is selected because it results in the simplest case of tangents, viz., Type I. Place
the landing risers half a going from the crown tangents B-C-D, which in this case is $4\frac{1}{2}$ ins.
We are now ready to draw the development of the tangent planes to ascertain the inclination
of the tangents, at least this would be the procedure under the simple " tangent system," but
that method has drawbacks, not so patent in this case as it will be in some more difficult
ones to follow. However, as the author wishes the reader to adopt a more scientific system,
he is requested to carry it out in this simple case also, where perhaps it is not so necessary,
but will at once give him an insight to the new method. This being agreed, we will next
make the development of the central plane (a quite imaginary one) and produce the approved

"falling line" of the wreath. For the moment the reader is requested to ignore all letters and lines on the drawing that are not referred to; these others will receive attention later.

Fig. 3, Pl. VI., is the development of the centre line of the handrail in plan, with the steps and landing as they cut this line. Commence this by drawing the landing line as shown, and, perpendicular to it, the centre line C. Set off on a line parallel to the landing, as A-E, the length of the curved centre line A, C, E, Fig. 1, on each side of C, Fig. 3. This is best done by running the dividers along the curve in a series of steppings of about ½ in. each. Of course their length will depend on the quickness of the curve, the shorter they are the more nearly will they approximate to a curve. Transfer the same number of steppings to the development, thus obtaining the positions of the springings A and E. Draw lines at these points parallel to C. Set off the steps as they occur in the plan. These are indicated by section lines in Fig. 3. We have now a view of this stair, as it would be if it were possible to turn the two adjacent flights into one plane, that is, out flat before us. For our purpose we need not draw the handrail at its proper altitude, as shown in the small elevation, Fig. 9. To save space, the rail is drawn resting on the nosings, or, to be strictly accurate, on the "nosing line" (refer to stair construction to ascertain the difference). Draw the nosing line of the upper and lower steps, Nos. 13-14 and 11-12. We have discussed in an earlier chapter the height of handrails over landings, winders, etc., and need not repeat it here. Suffice to say the under side of the wreath is to be raised 4 ins. over the landing at the centre; mark this point, also the centre, and top surface of the rail. The easing curves are a matter of taste; those shown are circular arcs, and their centres are indicated on the drawing.

Complete this drawing by marking shank joints 4 ins. from the springings and square to the pitch, as shown. Three small circles are shown on the centre line of the wreath, where it crosses the springings and the centre joint line C. These are the three necessary points to locate the heights of the tangents upon the development of tangent planes.

A little reflection will make it clear that, given the requisite thickness of plank (to be ascertained presently), if its centre is kept at the points indicated, it will not only ensure our getting out the right wreath, but also that its heights will be correct over the nosings; that is to say, all the balusters will be of one length over the flyers, and up to the landing risers 12 and 13, whilst the landing baluster will be the same length as the second balusters on the flyers. This latter arrangement is however arbitrary, and not essential, to the system. Now, having ascertained definitely *all* the data required to make the development of tangents (Fig. 2), which was a matter of guess-work by the old tangent system, we can proceed.

Referring to Fig. 1. Turn the tangent points A and E into the same plane as B-C, D; that is, revolve them on points B and D, as indicated by dotted arcs, and project the points *a*, B, C, D, *e* into the elevation. Mark these lines A, B, C, D, E for identification. We may or may not set out the steps as they occur on the tangent planes, for they serve no useful purpose, but as the old system worked on these lines and therefore was wrong, they are shown on some of the drawings in this book to emphasise the fact of their uselessness to the setter-out.

Proceed to locate the tangent heights by drawing level lines from points *a*, *c*, *e* in Fig. 3 to intersect the corresponding tangent lines A, C, E which are theoretically the three joint points, the shanks at the upper and lower ends of the wreath being merely constructional devices to make the working of the wreath easier; the effect of our construction is precisely the same as if these joints were actually at the springings. Having obtained the heights of the tangents, draw the inclined tangents through these points on A and E to the pitch of the stair, obtained in the workshop from the pitch board, and on the drawing board by setting the edge of a set square to the pitch line on Fig. 3, and then sliding its other edge along the T-square until the proper points are reached. Produce the inclined tangents to the lines B and D, drawing the level tangent over the landing to connect them. The tangents as they

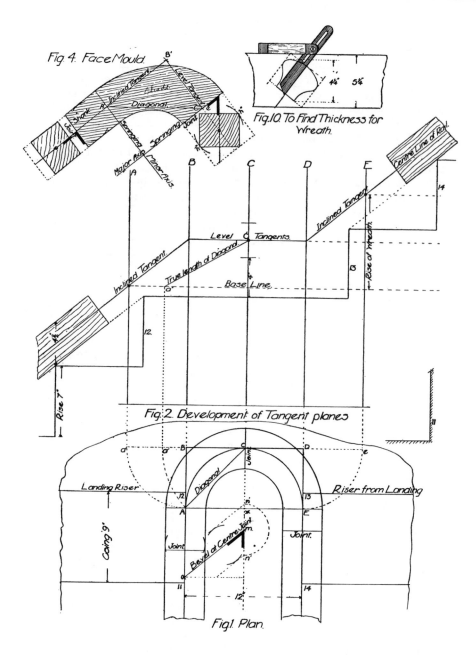

Fig. 4. Face Mould.

Fig. 10. To Find Thickness for Wreath.

Fig. 2. Development of Tangent planes

Fig. 1. Plan.

A PAIR OF WREATHS OVER HALF-PACE LANDING (Tangents: Type I).

PLATE VI.

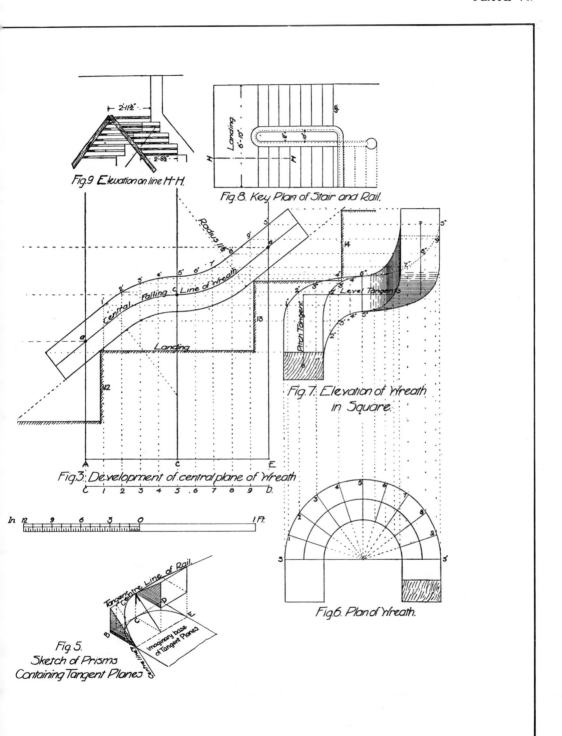

Fig.9 Elevation on line H-H.

Fig.8. Key Plan of Stair and Rail.

Fig.7. Elevation of Wreath in Square.

Fig.3. Development of central plane of Wreath

Fig.6. Plan of Wreath.

Fig.5.
Sketch of Prisms
Containing Tangent Planes

now appear represent the two inclinations of the plank out of which the wreath is to be cut, and the next step is to obtain the face mould. In a former article, page 15, it has been explained that the face mould is contained in a given section of the cylinder, also that the most convenient way of obtaining that section is to produce the section of the enclosing prism, which we will now proceed to do, the prism in this case being represented by its base line A, B, C, X, A, Fig. 1, and the edges of its section by the tangents A-B and B-C, Fig. 2. For the better understanding of this matter, a sketch of the imaginary compound prism is shown in Fig. 5, with the centre line of the wreath winding over the inclined planes.

The Face Mould (Fig. 4, Pl. VI.).—To draw the section containing the required ellipse, we must have the length of the diagonal A-C, Fig. 1. As this line rises from A to C, it is obviously longer than is shown by its plan, so we construct the plan into the elevation by turning the end A into the same plane as point C, its upper end, as indicated by its dotted path to *a'*. Project this point to a level line drawn through the lowest point of the tangent A. This line is distinguished as the " base line "; it happens to coincide with the horizontal projector from *a*, Fig. 3; but that is immaterial. Join point *a''* to C', the highest point of the diagonal, and its true length *a''-c'* is obtained. Reproduce this line at A'-C' in Fig. 4, then, with the compasses set to the length of the inclined tangent A-B, describe an arc from point A' as centre; also from C' as a centre, and the length of the level tangent B-C as a radius, describe another arc, intersecting the first at point B'. Join these points by straight lines and the triangle A'-B'-C' is the required section. To complete the section of the prism and to ascertain the centre of the elliptic curves, draw lines from A' and C' parallel to the opposite tangents. These will be springing lines, and, according to the list of characteristics, page 20, will define the *direction* of the major and minor axes. Before, however, we can use these, the width of the mould at each end will need to be ascertained. As one of the tangents is level, the joint opposite to it will also be level, and in this case it is the shank joint. Now a level line upon an inclined plane is always of the same length as its plan, therefore to obtain the width of the mould at the shank end mark off on each side of the tangent line half the width of the rail in plan, as seen in Fig. 1. This is most accurately done by describing a circle on the tangent equal in diameter to the width of the rail; complete the shank by drawing lines touching the circle, parallel to the tangent, and draw the joint square to the tangent at the distance beyond the springing A, shown on the inclined tangent, Fig. 2. Before the width at the other end can be found, the bevel at the centre joint must be obtained. This bevel is really a plumb line, when the wreath is in its proper position, and is represented by the angle between the surface of the plan and the surface of the cylinder. There is more than one way to ascertain this angle, as will be shown in a succeeding example, but here the method adopted is to take the perpendicular distance between the level tangent on the face mould and the opposite springing A', and lay it off in the plan between the centre line of rail and a parallel line thereto, drawn through the centre joint C, as at *o-m*. The " bevel " is the acute angle seen at M. Next, describe on this line as centre a circle equal in diameter to the width of the rail in plan. Draw two lines touching this circle and parallel to the bevel line, intersecting the centre line at N-N'. The width shown between these points is the required width of the mould at the centre joint. Set the compasses at M, with radius M-N, and describe the circle N''-N''', upon the extension of the tangent B'-C', Fig. 4, then draw lines parallel to the tangent and touching this circle to the springing line. Now we have on the two springings the necessary points for determining the elliptic edges of the mould, which may be trammelled upon the two axes (extensions of the springing lines), as described on page 18 *ante*.

The dotted rectangles shown at the ends of the face mould (Fig. 4) represent the ends of the wreath, turned up into the same plane as the mould, to indicate the position and application of the bevels for the purpose of squaring the wreath; also they indicate the necessary size of the wreath-piece at the joints, to obtain the twist. The application of the mould and the working of the wreath in this and other cases is described in Chapter XXVII., where the subject is considered in all its bearings.

To Ascertain the Thickness of the Wreath, see Fig. 10, Pl. vi.—Set a bevel to the angle shown at *o-m* in the plan, and apply it to the edge of a plank or board as shown, then either lay the section templet with its centre on this line and outline the same, or set off on each side of the bevel line half the width of the rail in plan, drawing parallels as shown, to intersect the edges. At one or other intersection, square out a line from the side and, parallel to this, another line, at a distance equal to the thickness of the straight rail, obtaining the rectangle indicated in dotted lines. The perpendicular distance between the top and bottom angles indicates the thickness of the plank necessary to cut out the wreath " in the square," which is a method that should be pursued by beginners for the reasons given in Chapter XXVII. The expert railer may cut the wreath out of thinner plank, as indicated by the dotted parallels, touching the extreme moulded edges of the rail, which will effect a saving in this case of 1 in. of stuff.

The Projection of the Wreath (Fig. 7, Pl. vi.) is a supplementary drawing that is sometimes useful to make, so that the appearance of the proposed wreath may be observed before finally settling the approved falling section, Fig. 3. This, of course, can be done upon the original plan, but to do so here would confuse the beginner, so a separate plan is reproduced in Fig. 6, and the manner of projecting the elevation is described. Divide the inner curve in plan into any number of equal parts, as 1 to 9. Draw radials from these points to the centre. Make a stretch-out of this line at C-D, Fig. 3, with the points as they occur thereon. Draw vertical projectors from the points to the back of the rail in Fig. 3. At the intersections 1', 2', 3', etc., draw horizontal projectors to meet the correspondingly-numbered vertical projectors from the plan, Fig. 6. These intersections will give a series of points through which the curved inside or convex edge of the rail can be drawn, as shown. A similar series of projectors from the outside circle in plan, with its corresponding stretch-out, will supply points for drawing the outside top edge of the wreath. A few of these projectors are drawn on the right hand. It will be readily seen how the bottom edges are projected from the same points.

CHAPTER V.

A WREATH FOR A QUARTER TURN TO A LANDING.

From Rake to Level—Example of Simple Tangent System—Length of Shanks—Producing the Face Mould—Projection of the Wreath—Knee Easing to Mitre Cap.

A Wreath for a Quarter Turn to a Landing.—From Rake to Level (Pl. VII.).—This wreath forms part of the handrail to the stair shown in Fig. 8, Pl. VI., and is the wreath for the top landing. It is a very simple case of double-curvature work, and would rightly precede the example given on Pl. VI., to which it now forms a complement, but for the fact of its affording no opportunity of explaining the system advocated in this book. Fig. 1, Pl. VII., is the plan, showing one step, and sufficient of the landing for setting-out purposes. The wreath has a shank at each end, and its central line is enclosed by two tangents, A-B and B-C. It will be observed that in this case the elevation, Fig. 2, is not projected from the plan, although it is made to agree with it exactly. The problem here is so simple that there is no need to make a stretch-out to ascertain the position of the tangents, these can be determined off-hand by the pitch-board. This, in fact, is a typical example of the simple tangent system, and we proceed to make the development of the tangent planes by drawing the floor line and setting up the tangent lines A, B, C perpendicular to the floor line, and as they occur in the plan. The term " tangent lines " is herein used for these projections in elevation, because it is the familiar term in the workshop. The use of the same term for the vertical edges of the planes, to which they are the boundaries, is slightly confusing in writing, though it becomes quite clear when one is setting out. Rightly, the lines A, B, C in Fig. 2 should be described as the " edges of the prism," but this description would be cumbrous. Draw one step with its nosing line, and rest the rail thereon. Draw its centre line, and produce it to the second tangent line B. From this point draw the other tangent level and mark the joints thereon as shown. The length of shanks is purely an arbitrary matter. It is probably more often decided by the stuff available than anything else, but two points influencing them may be noted, the longer the shank the more difficult the wreath is to mould ; secondly, a short shank may bring the handrail-bolt hole dangerously near the surface when moulding. No rule can be laid down : common sense must be exercised. The observant reader may notice that the rail on this landing is one inch higher than the one on the landing in the previous case. This is due to the position of riser, which in this case lies in the springing. We could lower it by introducing a ramp in the wreath, and this is done in a subsequent chapter. Here we decide to use the simpler method and allow the position of the riser to decide the height over the landing.

 The Face Mould (Fig. 3, Pl. VII.) is produced by first making a section of the prism A-B-C-A, Fig. 1, obtaining the length of its sides from the development, Fig. 2. Thus, the length of the diagonal A-C is found by setting off on the base line *a-c*, Fig. 2, the length A-C, Fig. 1, and joining point *a'* to C. Make A'-C', Fig. 3, equal *a'-c*, Fig. 2. Make A'-B' equal the length of the inclined tangent *a-b*, Fig. 2, and B-C equal that of the level tangent *b-c*. Draw the springing lines parallel to A'-B' and B'-C, thus completing the section of the

PLATE VII.

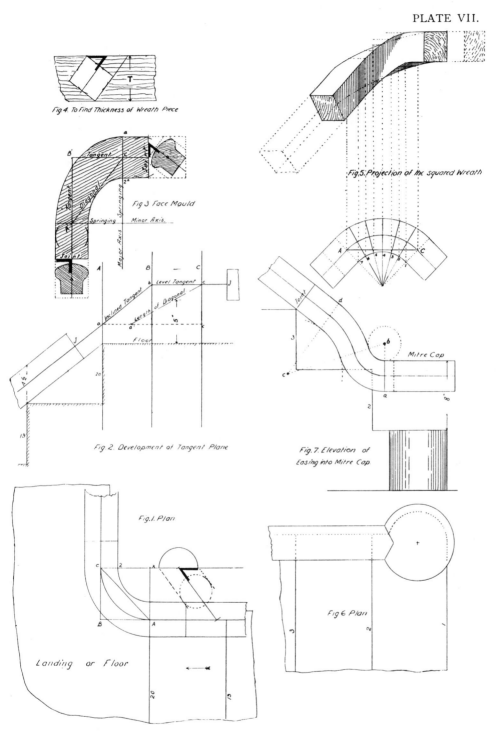

Fig 4. To Find Thickness of Wreath Piece

Fig.5. Projection of the squared Wreath

Fig 3 Face Mould

Tangent

Diagonal

Springing

Minor Axis.

Major Axis

Joint

Fig. 2. Development of Tangent Plane

A   B   C

Level Tangent

Inclined Tangent

Length of Diagonal

5"

Floor

J

20

19

Joint

d

Mitre Cap

Fig. 7. Elevation of
Easing into Mitre Cap

Fig. 1. Plan

c   2   A

B   A

Landing   or   Floor

20   13

Fig 6 Plan

3   2   1

WREATH FOR A QUARTER TURN TO LANDING, FROM RAKE TO LEVEL (Tangents Type 1)
ALSO A KNEE-PIECE TO A MITRE CAP.

prism. The widths of the mould at each end are ascertained as in the previous chapter. Extend the tangents and make these equal in length beyond the springings to the length of the shanks shown in the elevation, Fig. 2. Draw them square to the tangents and trammel in the elliptic curves, thus completing the face mould. The sections at the ends indicate the direction in which the bevels lie for the purpose of sliding the mould, the " bevel " at the joint A being a square or right angle, in consequence of the opposite tangent (which, of course, represents the pitch of the plank) being level. The manipulation of the bevels and mould is dealt with in the chapter on " Working the Wreath," page 90, Chap. XXVII., Pl. XXXI.

Fig. 5 is a projection of this wreath in the square, made on a plane parallel to the diagonal A-C, as described in the previous chapter.

A Knee Easing to a Mitre Cap (Figs. 6 and 7, Pl. VII.) completes the curved work for the handrail shown in Fig. 8, Pl. VI., and is merely introduced here to finish off this stair. All the work is of single curvature, and has been fully dealt with in Chapter I., to which the reader is referred for further particulars.

CHAPTER VI.

A PAIR OF WREATHS FOR A HALF-PACE LANDING WITH JOINTS SQUARE TO TANGENTS.

(PLATE VIII.)

Effect of Riser Position on Balusters—Production of a Helical Curve—Developing the Tangent
Planes—To Obtain True Length of an Inclined Line—Comparison of Joints—Obtaining Bevels
—Finding the Horizontal Trace—Description of a Trace—Testing Accuracy of Bevels—To Find
Width of Wreath-piece—Theory of Bevels.

**A Pair of Wreaths for a Half-Pace Landing, with Continuous Falling Line, Butt
Joints Square to the Tangents** (Pl. VIII.) contains the working drawings of the landing
wreaths for a stair with a small well, 8½ ins. between the strings. The landing risers are so
placed that the balusters are nearly equally spaced throughout stairs and landing. This is
accomplished by setting the risers half a going from the centre of the well C, measuring along
the centre line of the rail in plan. Fig. 1, Pl. VIII., is the plan, showing positions of all necessary parts.

The elevation, Fig. 2, placed for convenience of demonstration in geometrical connection
—i.e. resting on the ground line G-L, which is common to both planes—contains the developments of both the tangent planes and the central falling line sections, superposed, the usual
workshop method. In this instance, the two developments are made to coincide at the
centre line C. It is immaterial to the result whether this is done or the two developments
are made to coincide at one or other of the springings, as in some subsequent chapters; this
is simply a matter of convenience. Proceed to make the stretch-out of the centre line in plan,
with its risers as they occur in the manner described in Chapter IV., page 25—this drawing
is shown in dotted lines, A' and E' being the springings. Draw the rail resting on the
nosings and it will be seen that the central section of the rail falls across the well in a straight
line, producing, when folded around the cylinder, a true helical curve. The points a, c, e,
where the centre falling line of the rail intersects the springings and centre lines A', C', E',
shown by small circles, are the points governing the height of the tangents, which if made to
pass through these points on the corresponding tangent planes, will ensure the wreaths being
pitched at the right inclination, also at the required heights in the centre and at the springings,
to produce the rail shown on the development.

The Development of the Tangent Planes, A, B, C, D, E, is next required, produced
as described in the first example, page 23. The full lines show the sections of the landing
risers and the two adjacent steps, with the straight rails resting upon their salient angles;
produce the centre lines to intersect B and D, and it will be found that these will pass through
the springings A and E, at the required heights, as indicated by the short level lines drawn
from a and e. Obviously this would not have happened unless the position of the landing
risers had been prearranged, that is to say, if a continuous falling line is required, they *must*
be so arranged, and the reader will now see how the plan can be arranged by first drawing the
development.

Draw the middle tangents, connecting the ends of the inclined tangents, and it will be
noticed that the angle between each pair of tangents is alike, although inverted, therefore it

(29)

will be necessary only to draw one face mould, as this can be inverted for the other half wreath. The next thing required is the true length of the diagonal A-C, Fig. 1. Turn point A into the same plane upon point C as at *a*°, project this to the base line drawn through the lowest point of the tangents at *a'*, and the line drawn from this point to C, the highest point on that wreath, shows the true length of the diagonal.

Before proceeding to draw the face mould, we will discuss the joint at C. The full line shows a joint square to the pitch of the tangent, and is the one we shall use. The dotted line shows a joint square to the developed falling line. In the next example the methods of making this latter joint are shown, the two are placed here in juxtaposition, that the reader may see the slight difference they exhibit, and consider whether it is worth while for the sake of satisfying the geometrical purist to adopt a joint that will take twice as long to set out, and three times as long to produce, with the added risk, which even the most expert sometimes incur, of confusing the numerous bevels required in the construction of the so-called "true butt" joint. As a matter of fact, both are butt joints, and both equally "true," the only difference is, that one is easier to make than the other. As to the question of appearance, when a rail is moulded, if the wood is matched as it should be, the joint is practically invisible, it is only in ramps where the grain has to be cut across in two directions that the joint becomes obtrusive.

The Face Mould (Fig. 3, Pl. VIII.) next demands attention. First construct the section of the prism represented by its base A-B-C-A, Fig. 1, forming the triangle A''-B''-C'' with the two tangents and the diagonal shown on Fig. 2, and draw the springings parallel to the tangents, thus completing the section of the prism, as fully described at page 19.

To Obtain the Bevels and ascertain the widths of the mould at each end, take the perpendicular distance from each tangent (on the face mould) to its opposite springing, and lay these distances off in the plan, at points 1-1' and 2-2'', upon the centre line of rail and its parallel, when the bevel is disclosed. The theory of this construction is explained further on. On the bevel line as centre, describe a circle, equal in diameter to the width of rail in plan. Draw lines parallel to the bevel line and tangent to the circles, cutting the centre line at *m* and *n*. These points give the radii of circles to be described on the respective tangents, and parallels to the tangents, drawn touching their sides, will give at the springings the necessary points for describing the elliptic curves. If the reader will learn the following rule there will be no need to specify each time to which tangent the bevels apply, the reason of it will be made clear presently. Rule: The bevel with its corresponding width at the springing is to be applied at the joint end of that tangent from which the length was taken, to ascertain the bevel; thus, the acute bevel for joint C'' is obtained by the length A''-*i* between the opposite springing, and the tangent in question.

We now have two points on the elliptic curves and their common centre X'. We need the direction of the two axes. If one of these is known the other can readily be obtained because they are always perpendicular to each other. As this is a case of Type 3 of tangents, i.e. they are inclined unequally, the direction of both axes is unknown. Elsewhere the method of finding the direction by means of a "square" is described. Here is explained the method of obtaining it geometrically by means of traces. The problem is to find the direction of a horizontal, or level line, that will pass through the centre of the ellipse. The "centre" is already upon the section, so that all that remains to be found is the direction of a level line on the plane of section. Now, level lines on any particular plane are all parallel, therefore, if the direction of one can be found it follows the direction of any other can easily be ascertained by drawing it parallel to the known one.

The line called a "trace" is the line of junction or penetration of any two planes, where one passes through or impinges on the other; the line of junction is its trace upon the other plane, also the trace is common to both planes, that is to say, if one of the planes penetrated is vertical, the line of junction on that plane is a vertical trace; if the plane penetrated is horizontal, then the junction on that plane is a horizontal trace. All lines drawn on the horizontal plane are necessarily level or horizontal; it would be impossible for them to be otherwise, hence it follows that the trace of an oblique plane upon the ground is a horizontal line, see Ill. 19, sketch of a prism, No. 2, page 18. Imagine the side of the block, No. 3, whose upper edge is B-C, to be close up to a vertical surface and its base resting on the ground. If the oblique plane (upper surface) is extended to touch the vertical plane, it will make a junction as shown, by the dotted line C-H, and this is its vertical trace. A similar vertical trace would be made upon the other side, if a vertical plane were there. Where the oblique plane reaches the ground, it forms the horizontal trace, as shown by the dotted line H-T. This line intersects the vertical traces at their junction with the ground or horizontal plane; also it will be observed that it passes through the point A, where the oblique plane reaches the ground. These facts being realised, the reader will doubtless understand the following construction.

The tangent lines a''-b and b-c, Fig. 2, Pl. VIII., form the upper edges of the prism, also two edges of the oblique plane unfolded into the vertical plane; if therefore the upper tangent b-c is produced, as indicated by the dotted line, until it meets the ground plane of the prism at point V, the vertical trace of the oblique plane is obtained, also a point on the horizontal plane that, joined to any other point upon that plane, will be a horizontal line. Now revert to the face mould section, Fig. 3, produce the tangent B''-e'', and make it equal in length to c-b-v, Fig. 2, join points V and A'', which are both points in the horizontal plane, and we have the horizontal trace. Draw the minor axis of the ellipse parallel with this line through the centre X', and the major axis at right angles to the same. To trammel the curves, take the length of the minor axis of the outside curve from the plan, i.e. from X, the centre, to the outside of the rail, because, as stated in paragraph 7, page 16, the minor axis of any ellipse is the same as the diameter of the generating cylinder. Lay the trammel rod on the face mould with its end to one or other of the points already marked at the springings, keep the semi-minor axis, mark length on the rod, upon the *major* axis, and tick off the point on the rod where it crosses the minor axis; this point gives the *length* of the semi-major axis and, keeping these two points on the rod accurately upon the axial lines, the end of the rod will pass through the curve of the required ellipse, as described at page 20. Finish the mould by drawing the shank sides parallel to the tangent A-B, mark thereon an equal length from the springing to that shown in the elevation, and draw the joint square to the tangent. Do likewise at the other end, drawing the joint through the point where the springing line is intersected by the tangent.

Two dotted lines parallel with the diagonal are shown on the face mould. These are to be used as tests of the accuracy of the widths obtained by the bevels; proceed, after the points are marked at the springings, to draw lines parallel to the diagonal from each point; if they do not intersect, then one or other of the bevels is wrong, and the work must be searched for the error.

The method of ascertaining the thickness of plank required is shown in Fig. 4, Pl. VIII., and has already been described at page 25. Both bevels are here shown, not because they are required, but to prove the necessity of using the more acute bevel with which to ascertain thickness. Obviously, the bevel A would yield a plank too thin to carry the twist necessary for bevel C. As before, the minimum thickness with missing corners is also shown, but is not advised to the beginner.

The end sections of the wreath at the joints are drawn as if turned up, in Fig. 3, to indicate direction of applying the bevels, also to show that in this case a blank, lined out as usually advised by the face mould, would be insufficiently wide to obtain the corners of the wreath.

PLATE VIII.

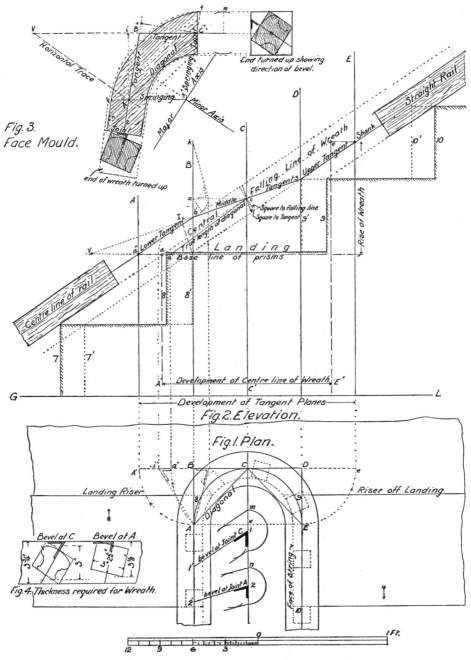

Fig. 3.
Face Mould.

End turned up showing
direction of bevel.

Horizontal Trace

Tangent

Diagonal

Springing

Major

Minor Axis

Springing Joint

Joint

end of wreath turned up

Falling Line of Wreath

Tangents Upper Tangent

Straight Rail

Shank

Rise of Wreath

Square to falling line
Square to Tangent

Central Middle

Lower Tangent

run length of diagonal

Landing

Base line of prisms

Centre line of rail

Development of Centre line of Wreath

Development of Tangent Planes

Fig. 2. Elevation.

Fig. 1. Plan.

Landing Riser

Riser off Landing

Diagonal

bevel at Joint C

bevel at Joint A

Face of String

Bevel at C   Bevel at A

Fig. 4. Thickness required for Wreath.

1 Ft.

12   9   6   3

PAIR OF WREATHS FOR A HALF-PACE LANDING. BUTT JOINT SQUARE TO TANGENT ON FACE.

The enclosing rectangle at each end indicates the required width of the blank, and the dotted outline around the face mould indicates its shape. This matter is fully explained in Chapter XXVI.

The Theory of "Bevels" may now be explained. It has already been stated that the "bevel" referred to in the tangent system is really a plumb-line, and its use is to so bevel the sides of the wreath in relation to the face of the plank that, when placed in its true position over the plan, the aforesaid sides shall be vertical or plumb. This object is accomplished, as will be seen later when explaining the practical work, by sliding the mould so that its edges coincide with the bevel required. This need not be further discussed now, and these remarks are confined to showing why the construction used in the foregoing plates yields the required bevels. On reference, Fig. 3, Pl. VIII., it will be seen that the joint at C″ does not coincide with the springing line, but that it is parallel with the line A″-*i*, which must consequently be square to the joint tangent. A plumb-line is required at joint C, so if an angle is made with the line A″-C that will stand plumb when the oblique plane is

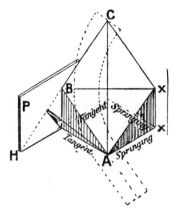

ILL. 23.—THE THEORY OF BEVELS
IN HANDRAILING.

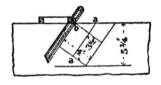

ILL 24.—METHOD OF FINDING THICK-
NESS OF WREATH-PIECE.

raised to its position, it follows that angle or "bevel" will apply at the joint. This will be clear upon inspection of Ill. 23, which is a sketch of the prism with the mould lying on the oblique plane, and the line A-C shown lying perpendicular to the vertical trace of the upper tangent, with the bevel in the upper angle. Now the two parallel lines B and C in the plan, Fig. 1, Pl. VIII., represent the width of the prism, and the length 1′-1 laid off between them is a reconstruction geometrically of the line A-C in the sketch, Ill. 24. To make this clear the line has been constructed in the vertical plane at I, Fig. 2, by drawing a perpendicular to the vertical trace of the oblique plane from the base angle B, rebatting or turning it into the horizontal plane and projecting the upper end into the plan at point *i′*; on joining this point to A on the ground plane, the same bevel is disclosed, and the construction is seen to be the same as in the sketch. The bevel for the other joint may be found by a similar process, as shown on the other side of tangent A-B, or if preferred may be constructed on the elevation thus. Draw a horizontal from point *c* to *x*; from the latter point draw a line perpendicular to the lower tangent produced, and join it to point *k*, which is distant from *x*, equal to the width of the prism at B-C.

CHAPTER VII.

WREATHS FOR A HALF-PACE LANDING WITH JOINTS SQUARE TO THE FALLING LINE.

(PLATE IX.)

Number of Bevels Required in this System—The Joint Pyramid—The Bevel Diagram—Obtaining the Vertical Trace—Construction to Obtain Bevels—Alternative Method of Producing Face Mould—To Obtain the Slide Bevel.

THE plan, Fig. 1, and elevation, Fig. 2, are those of Pl. VIII. redrawn, that the reader may the more readily judge the difference in setting out required between this class of joint and that of the square-to-the-tangent class, as shown in the previous and succeeding chapters. As the only difference in the drawings is as to the methods of obtaining bevels, nothing need be repeated up to the point where it is necessary to procure the bevel.

Three bevels are required for each joint by this system, in place of one by the square-to-the-tangent system. These are (1) The slide bevel or plumb-line on the joint. (2) Joint bevel on face mould. (3) Edge bevel for side of plank. This latter is usually termed the dihedral bevel. The necessary construction to obtain these, which is somewhat abstruse, will be better understood if we first conceive the joint as forming one surface of a solid triangular pyramid, of which the oblique plane, containing the face mould section, forms another surface, and the vertical plane, containing the developed tangent planes, forms a third surface. The base of this pyramid would be a triangle formed by the traces of the above three planes upon the horizontal plane. Such a solid is shown in the isometric sketch, Fig. 5, Pl. IX., containing the usual prism shown in plan and elevation, Figs. 1 and 2, plus the triangular piece added, to contain the joint plane as at F, Fig. 2. The base triangle formed by the traces is indicated by the letters V-F-f. The oblique plane and joint plane are clearly indicated thereon, and the tangent plane is at the back. The several bevels required are first shown in skeleton form in position at the angles, then in full black line at the same angles unfolded into the horizontal plane. These angles, of course, are not geometrically correct, but they graphically indicate the procedure now to be described in obtaining them geometrically.

The Bevel Diagram (Fig. 3, Pl. IX.) is a reproduction of the essential lines of Figs. 1 and 2, drawn separately for sake of clearness; the construction could, of course, be made on Fig. 2, but would be confusing. The production of the plan, *a-b-c-x*, and the elevation of the tangent planes A-B-C will doubtless be clearly understood, and we can proceed to consider the remaining lines. The line C-F is the vertical trace of the joint plane, obtained from Fig. 2, either by measuring the degrees in the angle between the tangent B-C and the joint line C-F, or by measuring the lineal distance between V and F on the base line—either way will be correct. Join the point so found to C, in Fig. 3. Draw the line F-*f* perpendicular to the ground line X-Y, produce the upper tangent to intersect the ground line in point V. Draw the horizontal trace from this point, through the angle at *a*, to intersect the perpendicular from F, in point *f*. Join point C²-*f*—this line is the plan of the arris or junction between the

(34)

PLATE IX.

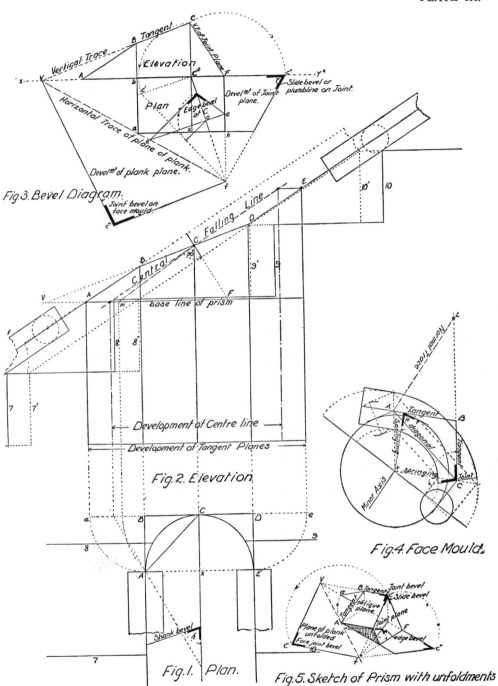

Fig.3. Bevel Diagram.

Fig.2. Elevation.

Fig.4. Face Mould.

Fig.1. Plan.

Fig.5. Sketch of Prism with unfoldments

WREATHS OVER HALF-PACE LANDING WITH JOINTS SQUARE TO FALLING LINE.

oblique plane and the joint plane, see the correspondingly lettered line in sketch, Fig. 5. The springing line a-x, produced to intersect F-f in point h, completes the projections of the solid, and we can now unfold the inclined planes into the horizontal, to ascertain the true shape of their angles. We will develop the joint plane first, as it is necessary to ascertain the length of its arris line, before the other side can be drawn. With F as centre, and radius F-C, describe an arc, cutting the ground line at point C″, join this point to f, and the true length of the side C²-f is seen, and in the angle at C″ is the slide or plumb bevel to be drawn on the joint. Next, to find the true shape of the oblique plane.

With f as centre and f-c as radius, describe an arc. With point V as centre and V-C as radius, describe an arc, intersecting the first one in C‴. Join up these points, and in the angle we have the bevel to apply on the face of the mould, with which to mark the joint, as shown at C, upon the face mould, Fig. 4. Next we have to obtain the edge bevel, with which to mark the down cut at the joint; as before stated, this is a dihedral angle, and is ascertained similarly to the angle-cut of a hip rafter in a roof. Commence by drawing an elevation of the line C²-f, Fig. 3, upon its plan; erect a perpendicular at C² equal in height to C²-C. Join this point to f, as shown in dotted lines. Anywhere on the plan line as at o, draw a line at right angles to the plan line C²-f, cutting the horizontal traces in points e and e′. From point o erect a perpendicular to c′-f, revolve this line in the direction of the arrow head upon the plan, and join the intersection to points e and e′, revealing the required bevel at C. Take note that this edge bevel must be applied with the stock of the bevel square to the plane of plank.

The Face Mould (Fig. 4, Pl. IX.) is, of course, the same shape, save at joint c, as the one in the previous plate, and all its details of construction are the same, but with a view to giving the reader a choice of construction sometimes useful, an alternative method of ascertaining the width at each end of the mould, and consequently the starting points of the elliptic curves, is here shown. Assuming the rhombus A-B-C-X forming the section of the prism to be constructed, describe on X as centre a circle equal in diameter to the semicircle in plan, Fig. 1. From the ends of the diagonal A and C, draw lines tangent to this circle, as shown. At the point of contact describe a circle equal in diameter to the width of the rail, and tangent to these circles, draw lines parallel to the first drawn line; their intersection with the springings supply the starting points of the elliptic edges of the mould. The slide bevel for the shank joint is shown at H, and is obtained by drawing a perpendicular to the tangent, connected with that joint to the centre X′. At the point of intersection with the tangent, draw a line touching the well circle, and the angle between the two lines is the bevel sought, and is exactly the same as the bevel at h in Fig. 1 found in the usual manner.

CHAPTER VIII.

PAIR OF WREATHS FOR A HALF-PACE LANDING WITH RISERS IN THE SPRINGINGS AND A NARROW WELL.

(PLATE X.)

A Rail for Stone Stairs—Working Drawings—The Face Mould—How to Obtain Lengths of Elliptic Axes—Lining Out the Blank—Requirements in a Blank.

THE previous examples of landing wreaths have been for wood stairs; the arrangement indicated in this case is the usual one for stone stairs. The appearance of the squared wreath jointed-up to the flying rails is shown by the two views, Figs. 5 and 6. A key plan is given in Fig. 4 from which the views are projected as described in connection with the first example. Fig. 7 shows the method of obtaining the thickness of wreath piece. For details see Chapter IV.

Working Drawings.—Lay down the plan of the rail and its centre line to the given dimensions, produce it on both sides to meet the cross tangent B-D. Draw the landing risers at the springing, also one step on each side. Unfold the tangents A and E and project the five tangent lines into the elevation. Draw the steps as they occur thereon. Rest the rails on the nosing lines and draw the centre lines parallel to meet the projectors B and D. Join up with an inclined tangent across the landing. No other arrangement of the tangents is possible in this case, and it would be considered unnecessary to make a stretch-out to ascertain their heights, but this central section has been dotted in that the beginner may see the resulting falling line. The slight easings that occur over risers 9 and 10 would be made automatically when obtaining a fair line on the arrises of the wreaths.

The Face Mould (Fig. 3, Pl. x.) is common to both wreaths, and is produced as fully described in previous examples. The three constructive lines A-B, B-C and A-C are indicated by similar lettering in the elevation, the springings are drawn parallel to the tangents, locating the centre of the elliptic axes. The direction of these in this type of tangent must be found, either by obtaining the horizontal trace, and so discovering the direction of the minor axis, or by means of the trammel square described at page 18, the *length* of the minor axis being taken, as before, from X in the plan to the inside and outside of the rail respectively, and the length of the major axis discovered thereby, upon the minor axis line. Note that the centre joint is made square to the tangent and does not lie on the springing line. The perpendicular distance of each tangent from its opposite springing is laid off in this instance between the parallels A-B and B-C on the elevation, instead of on the plan, for the purpose of obtaining the width at each end of the mould. This obviously makes no difference in the length of the line.

The sections of the wreath ends are shown at Fig. 5 to indicate the direction of the bevels, which in the drawing are intended for the lower wreaths, and would be reversed in direction

(37)

PLATE X.

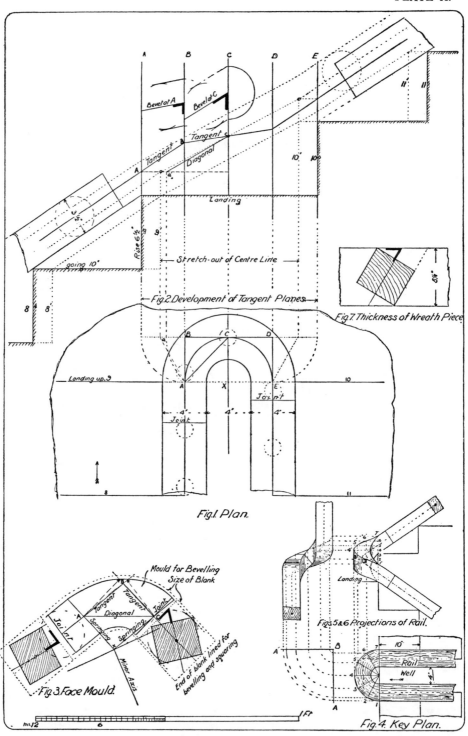

Fig.2. Development of Tangent Planes

Fig.7. Thickness of Wreath Piece

Fig.1. Plan.

Fig.3. Face Mould.

Figs 5 & 6. Projections of Rail.

Fig.4. Key Plan.

WREATHS OVER A HALF-PACE LANDING WITH NARROW WELL, AND RISERS
IN THE SPRINGINGS. (Tangents, Type 3.)

for the upper wreath. The dotted lines parallel to the mould indicate the width of the blank. This is usually lined out by pushing the mould inwards and outwards sufficiently to touch the lines indicated on the springings as the required width, and drawing in the shape by the mould. There are cases, as we shall see later, where a special mould or lining-out direct on the stuff is required for the blank, but for such cases as this, lining-out by the face mould is near enough, as the only requirement is to have sufficient stuff to hold the sides of the wreath when the moulds are slid into position, as described in Chapter XXVII.

CHAPTER IX.

A WREATH FOR A QUARTER-SPACE OF RADIAL WINDERS BETWEEN RETURN FLIGHTS, WITH AN EASING IN THE WREATH.

(PLATE XI.)

Description of Drawings—Determining the Height of Wreath over Winders—Drawing the Face Mould—Effect of Steep Pitch on Width of Mould—Obtaining the Blank Mould.

The Plan (Fig. 1, Pl. XI.) shows a portion of the return flights, with three winders in the quarter-space, one riser being in each springing. The central curve of the wreath is enclosed by tangents A, B, C, produced by continuing the centre lines of the rail until they meet.

The Elevation, Fig. 2, Pl. XI., is the stretch-out of the centre curve A-C, with the steps as they fall upon it, also one above and one below the springings to obtain the common pitches. Upon these, the longitudinal section of the handrail is placed, and it is assumed the requirement is that the rail shall be 4 ins. higher over the winders than it is over the flyers. The method of determining the height is thus : measuring the depth of the rail perpendicularly over a riser, as at No. 5 step, it is found to be 3 ins. to the back. Assuming the height over the flyers to be 2 ft. 8 ins.—a common height—3 ins. is deducted, leaving 2 ft. 5 ins. as the " lift " of the rail over the flyers. Now the requirement is 4 ins. more than the flyer height, i.e. the rail is to be 3 ft. high to its back over the winders ; 2 ft. 5 ins. from 3 ft. leaves 7 ins., this is the height at which the back of the rail must be drawn above the winders, as shown, to bring about these conditions. Having drawn the rail at this height parallel to the nosing line, it is seen that these balusters will need to be 1 in. longer than those over the flyer risers ; produce the pitch lines until they intersect, then ease the angles off to a gentle curve. In the example, 3 ins. is measured on each side of the intersection, the centres are found as described at page 3, and the curves struck therefrom. It is a matter of taste, or circumstances, whether one or both easings are included in the wreath—it would be possible to include neither, but an extra joint would then become necessary. As elsewhere is given an example of a wreath with easings at both ends, this one is formed with the top easing only, in the wreath, and the joints are marked accordingly square to the tangents. The heights of these are indicated by dots at *a* and *c* on the springings.

The Development of Tangent Planes (Fig. 3, Pl. XI.) is probably now becoming familiar to the reader, and only the chief points will need recapitulating. The edges of the planes A', B', C' are made equal in distance apart to the tangents in the plan. The steps, as they occur thereon, may or may not be drawn as the reader chooses ; personally the author omits these in setting out, if a pitch-board is available, to obtain the common pitch. Locate the tangent points on the springings by either drawing horizontals from the same points on the stretch-out, or by measuring their height above the respective risers. Produce the upper tangent to B, and so obtain the missing point of the lower tangent. Draw the joint lines

PLATE XI.

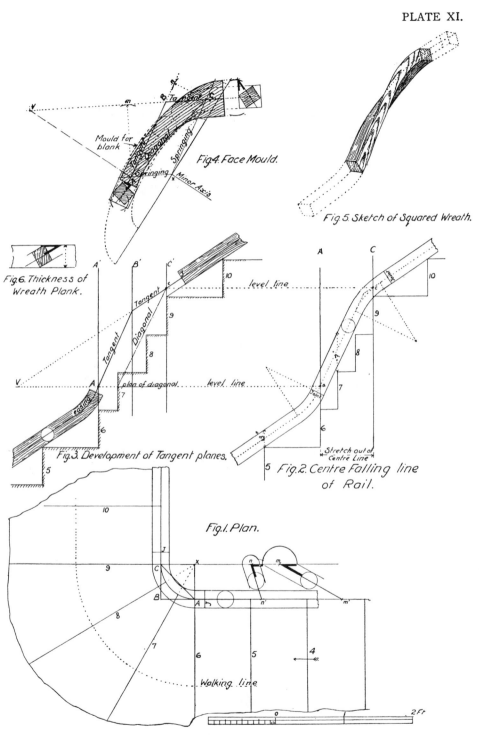

Fig.4. Face Mould.

Fig.5. Sketch of Squared Wreath.

Fig.6. Thickness of Wreath Plank.

Fig.3. Development of Tangent planes.

Fig.2. Centre Falling line of Rail.

Fig.1. Plan.

Walking line

2 Ft

WREATH FOR A QUARTER-SPACE OF RADIAL WINDERS, WITH AN EASING IN WREATH.
(Tangents, Type 3.)

square to the tangents.   The easings need not be re-drawn, for the side moulds can be obtained from the stretch-out.

The Face Mould (Fig. 4, Pl. XI.) is drawn as in previous examples by constructing a triangle, with the tangents and diagonal lines found in Fig. 3, then drawing the springing lines parallel with the tangents.   The bevel and width at the wide end of the mould are found by laying off the perpendicular distance A-*m* between the parallels in the plan at *m-m'*, which discloses the bevel for that end ; then, describing a circle on the line, equal in width to the rail in plan, and drawing tangents thereto parallel to *m-m'*, to intersect the centre line from X, a semicircle drawn on these points from *m* gives the width of the mould at springing C, as shown.   In like manner, the perpendicular distance C-*n*, Fig. 4, laid off at *n-n'*, Fig. 1, yields the bevel and width at the springing A.   The elliptic curves are trammelled upon the conjugate axes, drawn through the centre X', as shown.   The direction of the minor axis is found by obtaining the horizontal trace of the oblique plane, as previously described.

The steep pitch of the lower tangent in this case is the cause of the great width of the mould at joint C, but it does not follow that the wreath-piece or blank needs to be so wide. The rectangles projected at the ends of the face mould indicate the necessary width of the piece at the two ends, and it may be as well to show on this drawing how a blank templet may be obtained.   They are not really often used, but the saving in material and time in working in this case is considerable, and one would pay for the making.

With the same pair of axes that the edges of the mould were trammelled upon, trammel a central ellipse, as shown in dotted line from A to C.   Produce the sides of the wider rectangle, containing the joint section, up to the springing, taking half the width of this as radius, describe a number of circles upon the central ellipse, then draw with a pliant rod curves tangent to these circles, as shown in the dotted lines, which represent the edges of the blank.

A projection of the squared wreath on the plane of the diagonal A-C is shown in Fig. 5.

Fig. 6 shows the method of finding the thickness of the wreath.   For details see Chapter IV.

CHAPTER X.

A PAIR OF WREATHS FOR A QUARTER OF BALANCED WINDERS AND A QUARTER-PACE LANDING BETWEEN REVERSE FLIGHTS.

(PLATE XII.)

Arranging the Plan to Obtain a Straight Falling Line—Method of Setting Out, Plan, and Developments
—Method of Avoiding Trials to " Obtain the best Pitch of Tangents to suit Thickness of Stuff "—
How to avoid " Lifts " in the Wreath—Characteristics of the Moulds.

THIS plan has three balanced winders in the quarter-space, the landing is set back 4 ins. from the centre of the well and the springing riser moved forward 2 ins. below the springing. This arrangement gives a straight falling line over the winders and landing, also improves the appearance of the stair.

To Set Out the Plan, Fig. 1, Pl. XII.—Draw the two flights of stairs to the springings, lay down the straight rails and draw their centre lines, connect these at the springings with the semicircular centre line of the wreath. At 15 ins. from this line, describe a semicircle for the walking line. Set off the landing riser 4 ins. out of the centre of the well ; produce the springing line to cut the semicircle. Divide the portion between the springing and the landing risers into three equal parts. Set off 2 ins. from the springing on the centre line of rail and divide the arc to the landing also into three parts. Join the division points, and so determine the position of the winder risers, produce the centre lines of rails to B and C, and join these points by a line at right angles, so obtaining the plans of the tangent planes.

To Set Out the Developments, Figs. 2 and 3, Pl. XII.—First set off upon a horizontal line the length of the curve line A-C-E, Fig. 1, either by stepping or by the angle of 60° method, described at page 36, Vol. I. Set off the risers as they occur thereon, and draw the springings and centre line perpendicular. Set off on one springing eight risers and complete the section of the steps by projections from these points, and the points on the horizontal line. Draw the nosing line, and the section of rail resting upon this. The parallel line through the middle of the depth gives the central falling line, which controls the tangents. The easing in this case falls outside the springing and is formed upon the straight rails, by aid of a side templet. The easing seen at the top end is formed naturally by the alteration in pitches, brought about by the straight line winding around the cylinder. Mark the three centre points at the joint and springings, a, c, e', which completes the stretch-out.

Development of the Tangent Planes, Fig. 3, Pl. XII.—Draw the perpendiculars A, B, C, D, E at distances apart equal to the width of the tangent planes in the plan. Project one step above the landing, and two below the springing, to obtain the common pitches, making them correspond with those on the stretch-out. Project the three heights, a, c, e to the corresponding tangent lines, and draw the tangents through them, as shown, thus obtaining their pitches. It will be observed throughout these examples that we do not worry about the " best pitch of the tangents to suit the thickness of the rail " or make a series of empirical trials to find this out, but straight away determine what sort of a falling line we desire, then

(43)

at once project the tangent points that will produce this.   The upper and lower tangent must always proceed to the second tangent line, for the all-sufficient reason that the tangent represents to all intents and purposes the surface of the plank, and it is obviously impossible to have, as we have already remarked, more than two pitches in one plank, i.e. lengthwise and breadth-wise, and always the lengthway of the wreath will run as far as the cross tangents in the plan, these latter representing the width pitch.   It will be observed that for the centre of the plank in this case to coincide with the centres shown on the falling line causes the middle pair of tangents to fall out of a straight line, a matter which gives some concern to those who slavishly adhere to " square to pitch " joints.

Certainly if this wreath were made with square-to-pitch joints in the centre the rail would lift over riser No. 11 and be crippled in appearance, but there need be no difficulty, either in theory or in practice, in circumventing this.   All that is needful in such cases is to bisect the angle, and set a bevel to the bisector, as shown.   This bevel is to be used in place of a square in making the joint, and the geometrical purist need not be alarmed, as no principle is sacri-ficed, because a " square " joint is also a bisector of the angle of 180°, which forms a straight line.   This bevel of course, like a square, will apply equally on either side of the joint.   The method of bisecting is indicated by the dotted lines.

The Drawing of the Face Moulds should now be familiar; if not, for details refer to pages 19, 24, 30, and Plates VI.-VIII.   The bottom mould, Fig. 4, Pl. XII., having tangents of Type 2, has the major axis of its elliptic curves parallel with the diagonal, therefore is readily drawn.   For the same reason the bevels are alike at each end, conse-quently the mould is of equal width at each end, and the bevels lie in contrary directions, as shown by the end sections.   The upper wreath requires two bevels, consequently one end is wider than the other, and, owing to the amount of twist, the wreath-piece requires to be wider than the mould, as indicated by the dotted lines.   This mould is of Type 3, and the direction of the minor axis must be ascertained in one or other of the ways previously described for this type of tangent.

Fig. 6 indicates the necessary thickness of plank for each wreath.   The formation of this pair of wreaths is detailed in Chapter XXVII.

PLATE XII.

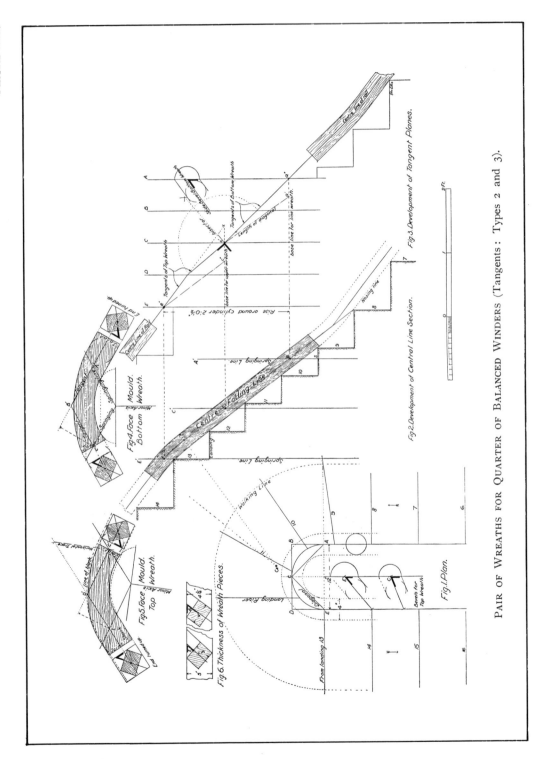

PAIR OF WREATHS FOR QUARTER OF BALANCED WINDERS (Tangents : Types 2 and 3).

PLATE XIII.

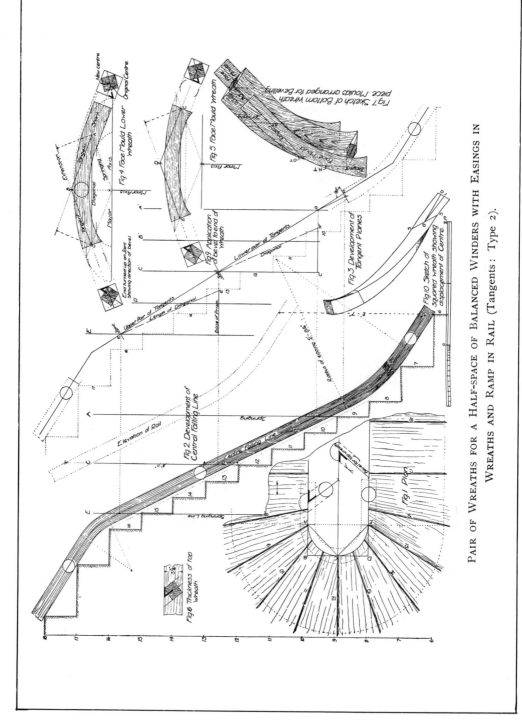

PAIR OF WREATHS FOR A HALF-SPACE OF BALANCED WINDERS WITH EASINGS IN
WREATHS AND RAMP IN RAIL (Tangents: Type 2).

CHAPTER XI

A PAIR OF WREATHS FOR A HALF-SPACE OF BALANCED WINDERS WITH AN EASING ANDRAMP TO THE RAIL.

(PLATE XIII.)

Where Joints are Inadvisable at the Springings—Effect of a Joint in the Springing—The Falling Line Section, How Decided—Method of Calculating Height of Wreath over Winders—Alternative Treatment when not tied to given Data—Displacement of Centres in Wreath, How to Set Out—Note for Beginners, on Irregular Centre at Joint.

IT is assumed that the reader will have now become familiar with all the preliminary construction necessary to the setting out of the developments and obtaining face moulds. As each of these examples is selected to illustrate a type, consequently has differences from those preceding, to avoid monotonous repetitions only these new features will be dealt with in this and succeeding examples. The reader desiring information in the more elementary matters must refer back.

It will be seen that the planning of this stair results in a continuous or true helical falling line over the winders, the rail falling at a steep pitch, consequently the change of inclination to the common pitch over the flyers is considerable. The abruptness of the change at each end of the wreath is overcome by forming an easing in the straight rail at the top, and a long ramp at the bottom. It is advisable, where an arrangement of the risers brings the straight rail direct to the springings, to avoid making a joint *in* the springing, because the inclination of the tangents may cause considerable twist at the springing, and in such an event that portion of the straight rail that fell inside the springing owing to the joint being made square to the pitch would require an extra width with which to form the curved part; this is one reason why shanks are made to wreaths so that the straight rail shall be kept away from the springing. In the present case this rule is violated, because it is intended that the knee easing at the top end shall be worked as a separate piece and be jointed over the second riser from the springing, the extra width required on such a short piece becomes inconsiderable. The joint at the lower end is taken outside the springing, because the falling line naturally carries on for some little distance beyond the latter, and the result of placing this joint in the springing would be that extra width and depth would be required for the ramp piece.

The Falling Line Section of this wreath (Fig. 2, Pl. XIII.) is assumed to be arbitrarily decided so as to lift the back of the rail 4 ins. higher over the winders than over the flyers, and the requisite height to draw the wreath over the winders is found thus. Assuming the common height to back of rail to be 2 ft. 7 ins., the height of the back over the winders will be 2 ft. 11 ins., as indicated in the dotted elevation of the handrail, so the calculation to be made before the height of the centre line can be fixed is 2 ft. 7 ins. minus 3 ins., the perpendicular thickness of the rail over a riser leaves 2 ft. 4 ins., which, subtracted from 2 ft. 11 ins., the required height, gives 7 ins. as the height of the back of rail over the winders.

(45)

The resulting pitch of the tangents, as shown on their development at Fig. 3, is a straight line, consequently, as all the pitches are alike, the same slide-bevel will do for both wreaths, and, apart from the shank at the end of the bottom wreath, both moulds are alike.   However, as it would be troublesome to adjust the one mould to suit the differing conditions, one for each wreath is drawn and the two bevels are shown in position, as they would be if dissimilar, more for the purpose of assuring the reader of the correctness of the method than for any utility in the second bevel.   The requirement of the approved section, Fig. 2, that the bottom of the ramp shall bend closely down to riser No. 7, ties the handrailer to tangents that will bring about that position, otherwise, by extending the length and flattening the curves of the ramp, the displacement of the centre of the bottom wreath could have been avoided and an " easier " job attained.   As, however, the object of the system herein described is to provide solutions for all and any disposition of the rail, the given conditions are adhered to.

Referring to Fig. 3, the lower tangent is produced until it intersects the centre line of the flyer rail ; perpendiculars drawn from the two pitches locate the centre of the ramp curve, as shown in dotted lines on Fig. 2.   Next draw the joint square to the tangent at the proper distance beyond the springing.   It will now be seen that the centre of the ramp does not coincide with the centre of the wreath shank.   Draw a line from the ramp centre to the centre of the wreath at the springing, this line, a-L, should agree in pitch with the centre falling line, Fig. 2 ; if it does not, the ramp curve needs readjustment.

The distance O-L, Fig. 3, is called the displacement, and to mark the wreath a triangular templet of the exact size and shape of a, L, O, must be made.   This is applied at the side of the wreath-piece *after* it has been bevelled, as shown in the sketch of the wreath, Fig. 10 ; the edge marked O is kept upon a line square out from the original centre of the joint.   The wreath requires to be thicker by an amount equal to O-L, as shown at the end section, Fig. 4, where the ordinary depth is indicated by the dotted line.   The centre of the joint is first marked at the middle of the depth required for the wreath in the ordinary way, that is to say, as shown at Fig. 6.   The slide bevel is taken through this centre, and the new tangents drawn as the bevel indicates.   Then the moulds are applied, as shown in the sketch, Fig. 7. After the sides are bevelled, the new centre is placed on the bevel line of the joint, as shown on the joint section, Fig. 4, the amount of displacement being, as previously stated, equal to the distance of L below O, at Fig. 3.   The new centre thus being located is squared across the joint to the outside, and the templet applied as in Fig. 10.   The wreath is squared to the lowered centre, as seen in section at Fig. 4, and eased off from the springing line into the ramp, as seen in Fig. 10.   The reader is scarcely expected fully to understand these instructions until he has read the description of " squaring a wreath " in Chapter XXVII., when he will readily see the necessity of the above special variation.   One other point may be noticed that may possibly not be clear to the beginner.   The centre of the joint at C, Fig. 4, is out of the middle thickness of the stuff so far as the shape of the wreath is concerned, it is immaterial whether the excess wood is equalised, or all kept at the bottom, but there is less likelihood of a mistake if both ends are gauged for centres at the same time and by the same gauge, as shown.

The top wreath will be wide enough if cut out full to the face mould, but the bottom wreath will require some excess stuff, as indicated by the dotted lines, on the convex side.

PLATE XIV.

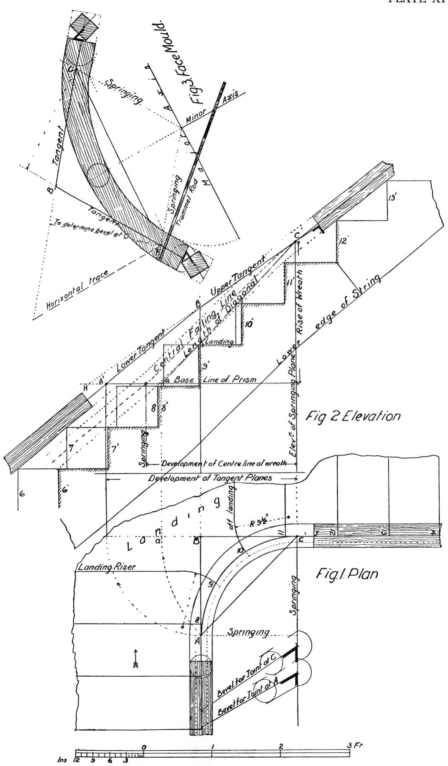

Fig 3. Face Mould.

Springing.

Minor Axis

Tangent

Springing

Trammel Rod a

To determine bevel at C

Horizontal trace

Upper Tangent

Lower Tangent

B

Central Falling Line

Length of Diagonal

Landing

Base Line of Prism

Fig 2 Elevation

Springing

Lower Rise of Wreath

Eleva of Springing Plane

edge of String

Development of Centre line of wreath

Development of Tangent Planes

Landing

off landing

R 9½"

Springing

Fig. I. Plan

Landing Riser

Bevel for Joint at C

Springing

Bevel for Joint at A

0   1   2   3 Ft

Ins 12 9 6 3

A LARGE QUARTER-TURN WREATH OVER TWO BULLNOSE STEPS ON HALF LANDING.
(Tangents, Type 2.)

CHAPTER XII.

A LARGE QUARTER-TURN WREATH OVER A LANDING BETWEEN RETURN FLIGHTS WITH TWO BULLNOSE STEPS ON THE LANDING.

(PLATE XIV.)

Slight Easings made during Squaring—Superposed Developments—Control Points in Quarter-turn Wreaths—To Avoid Displaced Centres.

THE object of bringing four steps within the springing, and curving the two landing risers is to obtain an approximately continuous falling line, as indicated by the dotted central section of the rail. Two slight easings are made in the wreath, with not sufficiently pronounced departure from a straight line to need a falling mould, such easing can be managed when squaring up the wreath.

In this example, the two developments are shown superposed, as they generally would be upon working drawings in the shop. The central falling section, or development of the centre line in plan, is distinguished by the sectioning of the steps, and the rail will easily be followed resting on the angles. There are only two controlling points in quarter-turn wreaths, and these occur on the springing lines, where they are marked by small circles, see Fig. 2. These points are projected to the corresponding springing lines on the tangent plane development, locating the heights of the tangents, through which points the latter are drawn. In effect, the lower tangent is produced at the common pitch, to point B, and the upper tangent taken from this point to the required height at C, which causes a displacement of the centre upon the joint at this end, and if, as is most convenient, the joint on the straight rail is made square to the pitch, then the joint on the wreath must be made to the bevel shown thereon ; also, as in the last example, the wreath-piece will need to be thicker by the amount of displacement. Should it be desired to avoid doing this, a ramp can be worked upon the straight rail instead. This blank may be marked out by the face mould shown in Fig. 3, but it should be lined out full on both edges, especially so at the minor axis, indicated by a circle on the mould, the said circle being equal to the width of the rail.

PLATE XV.

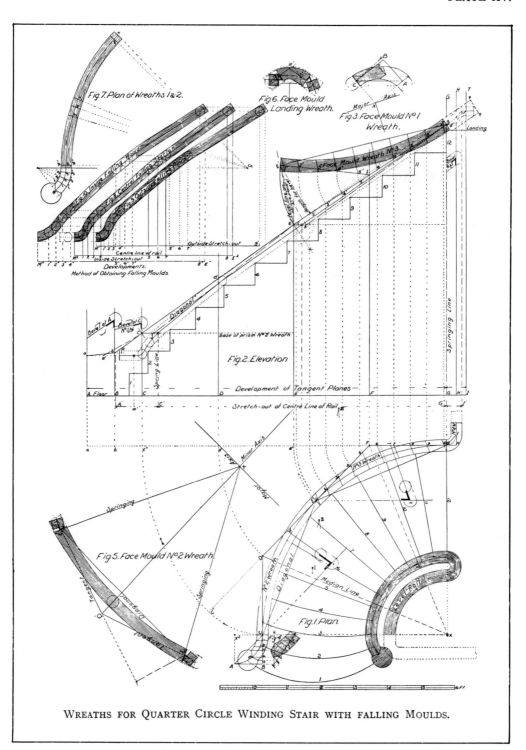

Fig.7. Plan of Wreaths 1 & 2.

Fig.6. Face Mould Landing Wreath.

Fig.3. Face Mould No 1 Wreath.

Major Axis

Fig. 10. Inside Falling Mould

Fig.8. Central Falling Mould

Fig.9. Outside Falling Mould

Face Mould Wreath No 3

Landing

Springing Line

Centre line of rail
Outside Stretch-out
Inside Stretch-out
Developments.
Method of Obtaining Falling Moulds.

Diagonal

Base of prism No 2 Wreath

Bevel at A Bevel at C No 1 Wreath

Spring Line

Fig.2. Elevation

Development of Tangent Planes

A Floor

Stretch-out of Centre Line of Rail

Minor Axis

Major Axis

Springing

No 3 Wreath

Fig.5. Face Mould No 2 Wreath.

Tangent

Torsion

Torsion

Springing

No 2 Wreath

Diagonal

Median Line

Level Rail

Fig.1. Plan.

WREATHS FOR QUARTER CIRCLE WINDING STAIR WITH FALLING MOULDS.

CHAPTER XIII.

A SET OF WREATHS FOR THE OUTSIDE RAIL OF A QUARTER-CIRCLE WINDING GEOMETRICAL STAIRS WITH COMMODE STEPS AND MITRE CAP TO NEWEL, SHOWING TWO METHODS OF OBTAINING FACE MOULDS AND THE METHOD OF PRODUCING FALLING MOULDS.

(PLATE XV.)

Type of Shop Stairs—Description of the Plan—Rail with Reverse Turn—Deciding Position of Joints—Planning the Tangents—The Developments—Bad Effect in Rail of Adhering to Rule-of-Thumb Methods—Face Moulds—-How Position of Centre is Found in Obtuse Angles—Finding the Bevels —Face Moulds by Level Ordinates—The "Director" of Level Lines—Variations on Wreath for a Mitre Cap—Mould by Perpendicular Ordinates—Variation in Method of Finding Thickness of Plank—Falling Moulds, Where Used, How to Produce—Application to the Wreath.

THE stair shown in the plan, Fig. 1, Pl. xv., is a typical shop or store stair, having commode steps to facilitate quick entry and exit, the circular sweep affording easy passage in opposite directions. The drawings are utilised to illustrate two distinct methods of obtaining face moulds, but both based on the tangent system, and though differing widely in detail, as will be seen, they produce moulds of similar character. The first, or trammelling method, is the one described in previous examples, therefore details of moulds for Nos. 1 and 2 wreaths need not be repeated. The second method used to obtain moulds for Nos. 1 and 4 wreath is known as the **Level Ordinate** method, and is described in due order. The outside rail only is dealt with in this article, the inside rail drawing will be found on Pl. xvi.

The plan, Fig. 1, Pl. xv., is set out to the given dimensions, the centre lines of the hand-rails drawn first to coincide with the central line of the balustrade, which will vary slightly in position according to the finish of the string. On this centre line of the outside rail, the risers, from Nos. 5 to 12, are spaced equally, and radiate from point X, the centre of the curve. The four commode steps are made of equal width on the central walking line, also at the centre line of the inner rail; their width at the outer end increases by geometrical progression determined by the curves, which are arbitrary. The centres of those drawn are indicated at points I., II., III., IV.

At the bottom end the rail makes a reverse turn into the mitre cap, and its centre is at X². At the landing the rail turns at right angles into the level. The disposition of the tangents next claim attention, and, as these are largely controlled by the joints, the position of the latter must be decided. The number and position of the joints in rails of this type will depend upon several circumstances, such as the thickness of stuff available, amount of twist, shape of the section, etc., so that no invariable rule can be laid down, each case must be decided upon its merits. Obviously the less number of joints the better, other things being equal.

In this example it is decided to make the rail covering the quadrant in two pieces, thus there will be joints at C, E and G. Draw these radial from the centre. The mitre-cap joint and landing joint will be discussed later. We can now proceed to draw the tangent square to the joints, resulting in this instance, with tangents of equal length, which simplifies the setting out. Mark the five main tangent points, C, D, E, F, G. The remaining tangents A-B and H-I, may be drawn in at right angles to the main tangents, as shown, to complete the plan, and the diagonals A-C, C-E, E-G and G-I drawn, also the median line of each wreath, D-X and F-X, which completes the plan.

The Elevation (Fig. 2, Pl. xv.) contains the two developments superposed, the top springing line G is common to both developments and the section of the steps is made only upon the stretch-out of the centre line. The method of producing these developments has been fully stated in connection with previous examples, and need not be repeated, but it may possibly be necessary to explain the slight variation in projection of these planes that are not at right angles. Taking C-D, point C is first brought into the same plane as D by turning it upon point D, until C', D, E, F lie in a straight line. Then F becomes the pivot, and the aforesaid points are revolved into the plane of F, G, as indicated by the dotted arcs. Thence they are projected perpendicularly to the floor line A-I, and the tangent heights located at the joints by level projectors from the points of intersection of the centre falling line, and the several springing lines of the stretch-out. These points are indicated by small circles. It will be observed that each pair of tangents in the main wreath forms a straight line, thus being of Type 2, the characteristics of which are specified at pages 17 and 18, but the contiguous tangents on each side of the central joint E do not run in a straight line. The followers of the ordinary tangent system would consider this a departure from principle, and would probably " rectify " it by lowering the tangents at E until they fell into line, with the result that when jointed up the rail would " dip " at this point, thus spoiling the falling line. The handrailer who adopts the method advocated in this book will not be fettered by hard and fast rules, but will just place his tangents where they will best suit the object in view, that is to say, will so tilt his plank that it will conform to any falling line he desires. In a previous case it has been fully explained what to do in such cases as this, and we need only repeat that when the tangents are not straight the joint is made on a line which bisects the angle formed between them, as shown at e.

Face Mould, No. 2 Wreath (Fig. 5, Pl. xv.).—As in previous examples the triangular section of the imaginary prism, whose plan is shown at C, D, E, Fig. 1, is produced by laying down the true length of the diagonal shown at j-e, Fig. 2, and describing intersecting arcs from its ends, with radii equal to the length of the tangents C-d and d-e, Fig. 2, then joining point D' so found to points C' and E', Fig. 5. In this case, however, the " centre " lies outside the prism, or, expressed otherwise, the prism we have to deal with in cases where the tangents are not at right angles in plan is a triangular prism of which the sides in plan are C-D, E, X, C, instead of a rectangular prism, as in the preceding examples. Therefore, the centre cannot be located by drawing parallels to the tangents on the face mould section. The centre can, however, be easily located by other construction. Referring to Fig. No. 2, page 18 and page 33, Ill. 23, it will be seen that there is a level line drawn across the plane to the two opposite angles of the square prism. The reason that the line is level will be obvious, the solid stands on a horizontal plane and the heights of the two ends of the line B-x are equal. The point x stands vertically over the centre of the circular plan curve, therefore it is the centre of the elliptic curves on the oblique plane of section; also we see that the line joining points B and x passes through the middle of the diagonal A-C. Now, referring to the geometrical development of this solid, No. 2, Fig. 1, it is seen that the tangents or edges of the oblique section are in a straight line, from which we deduce that when tangents of Type No. 2, i.e. of equal inclination, form an obtuse or acute angle in plan, then a line drawn from the salient angle on the section plane through the middle of the diagonal will pass through the centre of the elliptic curve. Taking advantage of these properties, we can at once locate the centre upon Fig. 5, because we already know that the length of a level line upon an inclined plane is equal in length to its plan. So if we draw the median line D-x, Fig. 1, we know that this is the plan of a level line on the oblique plane, also that it will be equal in length to that line. Then draw a line from D' in Fig. 5 through the middle of the diagonal (found by bisection) indefinitely. Mark off on this line from D' the length of D-x in plan, and point x' is the centre of the elliptic axes, and this point, joined to the ends of the diagonal, will determine the position of the springings upon the section. By another property of tangents, Type 2, we know that the major axis of the ellipse will be parallel with the diagonal, and the minor axis perpendicular.

To Find the Slide Bevel and the width of mould at the springings. Draw a line on the plan, through the centre of joint C, parallel to the tangent D-E, and lay off line h-i anywhere between them, equal in length to the perpendicular distance of the tangent D'-E' (produced) from the springing point at C'. On this line describe a circle equal in diameter to the width of the rail and draw lines tangent thereto, parallel with h-i, and cutting the line C-i. This shows the width required at each end of the mould, and a circle equal in diameter to that at i must be drawn on the tangents at each end of the face mould, and lines touching these, parallel with the tangents when drawn to the springings, provide the points from which the elliptic curves start. These are to be trammelled upon the two axes shown in Fig. 5, taking the length of the minor axis from point X, Fig. 2, to the inside and outside respectively of the rail in plan, and discovering the length of the major axis by marking the point upon the trammel rod where it crosses the minor axis, as described in earlier chapters.

The Face Mould for No. 3 Wreath is produced by means of **Level Ordinates,** and for convenience of illustration the section of the prism E-F-G-E is constructed upon one of its edges f-g, that is to say, it is folded up on this line into the vertical plane. To construct the section : with point f as centre and f-e as radius, describe the arc shown in full line, then with g as centre, and the length of the diagonal k-g as radius, describe an arc, cutting the first one in point E'. Join E' to g, which gives the position of the diagonal on the plane of section. Join E' to f, thus obtaining the remaining tangent. Next, the direction of a level line upon the plane of section is required, and the readiest way to obtain this is to find the horizontal trace of the oblique plane, by producing the upper tangent to the " ground level," which in this case is at point e. It so happens in this instance that the projection of the upper tangent and the line of development of the lower tangent e-f coincide, but that has no influence on the construction ; it merely prevents us showing the vertical trace separately. Join point e to E', which is a point at the same level when turned over into its normal position, therefore the line connecting them will be a horizontal trace, and all lines drawn on the plane of section parallel with it will also be level lines and equal in length to corresponding lines in the plan.

To find the direction of the corresponding lines on the plan. Draw the median line F-x, Fig. 1. It was seen in the view of the prism, No. 2, Ill. 19, page 18, that a line from the centre bisecting the diagonal of two equally inclined tangents was necessarily level, thus the line F-x becomes the " director of level lines " in plan. Divide the plan of the wreath into as many parts as desired and draw ordinates through the points parallel to the " director of level lines." Let the first and last ordinates pass through the extreme point of the joints inside, produce the ordinates through the tangents E-F and F-G, and rotate points 1, 2, 3, 4, 5 into the same plane as 6, 7, 8, 9, 10. Then project them into the elevation, as indicated by the dotted lines, to intersect the tangents in elevation at points 1', 2', 3', 4', 5', 6', 7', 8', 9', 10'.

Rotate the points 1′ to 5′ into the section on point *f* as centre, and draw parallels to the horizontal trace through them. Set off on these lines points at equal distances from the tangents, that the edges of the rail are in plan upon the corresponding numbered line, and draw curves through the points so found. Make the joints square with the tangents, through the angles of the ordinates 1″ and 10″, thus completing the face mould.

The Slide Bevel can be found by the method used for the No. 2 wreath by producing the upper tangent and drawing a perpendicular from the centre of the joint E′ to 2′, laying this distance down in the plan at *k*-2 upon parallels F-G and E-12. The width of the mould may be found as before upon this line, and used as a check upon the width obtained by the ordinates.

The Face Mould for No. 1 Wreath (Figs. 3 and 4, Pl. xv.) is shown produced both by the trammelling and the ordinate methods. Fig. 3 is the face mould obtained on the oblique section of the prism A-B-C-X-2, Fig. 1, and will need little description at this stage. The tangents and diagonal are obtained from the development, Fig. 2, and, as stated in a previous example, wreaths for mitre caps are, by this system, better obtained by considering the wreath as a quarter of a circle, and cutting the blank, if required, to the springing line A, which, after squaring, has the excess cut off to the mitre.

To obtain the position of the point of the mitre *m* on the mould, take the perpendicular distance of *m* from tangent A-B in the plan, and lay off on a level line from *b*, Fig. 2; draw a perpendicular from the point, intersecting the upper tangent in point *o*. Lay off the distance *b-o*, Fig. 2, upon the face mould at B′-*o*′, and draw a parallel to A′-B′ from *o* which will locate the end of the mitre in the centre line.

Fig. 4 indicates the procedure to obtain the mould by means of ordinates perpendicular to the tangents. Divide the curve in plan into any desired number of parts, which need not be equal, as 1, 2, 3, 4, 5. Draw through these points perpendiculars to the tangents, and project them to a parallel plane whose ground line is X-Y. Upon X-Y describe the triangle X-O-Y equal to the pitch of the tangent in Fig. 2; project the points to the line O-Y and at their intersection draw perpendiculars to the tangent O-Y. Make these equal in length on each side of the tangent to the corresponding distances in the plan. The mould, as shown in Fig. 4, should be cut out full to the lines to compensate for the slight error in length owing to the ordinates on the section being slightly inclined, as shown by the tangent *a-b*, Fig. 2. There is a theoretical error in this method, but the amount is so small that it may be disregarded in practice.

The Face Mould for the Landing Wreath No. 4 is shown in Fig. 6, Pl. xv. The method of drawing this will not cause difficulty, but there are points in the elevation that will need explanation. The common tangent from *e* is continued through the joint *g* to the tangent elevation I, to bring the rail at the required height over the landing, thenceforward to the joint, and the tangent becomes level. This will cause no difficulty either in the application of the bevel, which is the same at each end, or in the working of the wreath, but the usual method of finding the thickness of the wreath-piece will need to be varied. The curved centre falling section is made with the level end turned into the same plane. Then the top and bottom curvature of the rail is enclosed by parallels, as shown in chain lines, and the perpendicular distance between these determines the required thickness. To avoid obtaining a special slide-bevel for the shank joint, first cut the block off, as shown at P-P′, square with surface of plank, which, be it noted, is parallel with the tangent. Mark the centre and the bevel shown at G through it to obtain the new tangent. Slide the mould to this point and mark for bevelling, then mark down the depressed centre for the level shank and draw in the top and bottom square to the springing line, when the shank joint can be cut square to these lines.

Falling Moulds (Figs. 7, 8, 9, 10, Pl. xv.).—Falling moulds are now seldom used, except in cases where the rail is bent out of a true helical falling line by the introduction of ramps or knees; as little or no guidance in the shaping of these is to be obtained from the face mould, it becomes necessary when they are to be formed in a rail to obtain a templet by which to mark out their shape upon the side. This templet is deduced from the approved central falling section of the rail, and may be obtained for the inside or the outside surfaces, or for both, as may be considered necessary. Several examples of more difficult moulds are given in subsequent plates, but the details of the method of obtaining them can be more clearly explained in connection with this rail, which is relatively simple.

To avoid confusion of lines, a reproduction of the plan of the two lower wreaths is made in Fig. 7, and the stretch-out, or central falling line section of the rail, reproduced in Fig. 8. Of course in practice all would be done on the one drawing. On inspection of the falling section, it will be seen that a bend or knee occurs over the fifth step, and that the rail ramps down into the mitre cap with a swan neck easing over the second step. Between and beyond these points the developed falling line is straight. Therefore, it is only at the easings that moulds are required for shaping purposes, but the straight portions are required to keep the others in the correct position. Select a number of points on the centre line of Fig. 8, in the curved portions, as centres for a series of circles equal in diameter to the depth of the rail; draw the curves tangent to these circles, and complete the falling section. Next, drop projectors from the centres to the stretch-out M^2-E^2. These originating projectors are distinguished by full lines, the derived projectors by dotted lines. Having obtained their positions on the stretch-out as points 1, 2, 3, 4, 5, 6, 7, 8, transfer these points to the central plan line, Fig. 7, and draw through them radials from the centres of the plan curves, producing them to cut the outside curve of the rail. Lay down at convenient places in the development the stretch-out of the inside and of the outside of the rail, as at M''-E'' and M'-E', on these lines, lay down the radial points as they occur in the plan, and erect perpendiculars to meet corresponding horizontal projectors from the centres of the circles in Fig. 8. These intersections supply the required points for centres of circles on the falling moulds, which are drawn similarly to the central section.

Application of the Moulds.—After the wreaths are jointed and bevelled to the face moulds, bolt them together and apply the falling moulds to the respective sides, keeping the centres of the ends of the moulds at the same level upon each side, which is best done by squaring a line across the joint. These moulds may be got out of sheet zinc, ash veneer, or stiff cardboard, and should be tacked on the sides of the wreath, care being taken to drive the pins into waste wood; then the rail is " squared " by working it off to the two moulds.

CHAPTER XIV.

A SET OF WREATHS FOR THE INSIDE RAIL TO A QUARTER-CIRCLE WINDING STAIR.

(PLATE XVI.)

Where Joints are Placed—To Arrange the Tangents, locating their Heights—Construction of the Face Mould—View of the Containing Prism—Special Disposition of the "Slide Bevels," the Reason—A Bisector Joint—Obtaining the Bevels—Alternative Treatment of Landing Wreath—Wreath Covering more than a Quadrant—The Face Mould by Level-ordinate System—Locating the Mitre Joint.

THE rail shown in plan, Fig. 1, Pl. xvi., is the complement of the preceding set, redrawn here for convenience of reference. As in the last case, the number of joints to be used must depend upon the circumstances. It is always advisable to make a joint at a change in the direction of the curves, thus joints C and G are determined; another is placed at E, and others at I and K on the landing. The level rails on the landing are not dealt with in this article.

Having fixed on the position of the joints, draw them radiating from the centre of the curve in which they lie.

The tangents, in accordance with the general rule, are arranged square to the joints. Those in connection with the main curve, meeting in points D and F, produce pairs of tangents of equal length and similar obtuse angles. The first wreath comprised between the springing C and the mitre cap has also obtuse-angled tangents, thus providing a third method in conjunction with the two shown on Pl. xv. for obtaining the moulds for this type of wreath. The direction of the tangent A-B is determined by treating the end of the rail where it mitres into the cap as a square joint, radiating from centre X', and the tangent is made square to this line. The landing wreath provides a simple case of right-angle tangents of Type 2.

The various tangents are next unfolded into one plane and their elevation made in the manner described in the preceding example.

The Developments (Fig. 2). The stretch-out of the centre line of rail and the development of the tangent planes are superposed. The development of the stairs upon the centre line (shown in dotted lines) produces a straight falling line, the rail between points C and G forming a true helical curve. The elevation lines at the joint centres are distinguished by broken or dash lines and small circles are shown at their intersection with the centre line of the rail, which indicate the required height of the wreath at these points. These heights are projected to the corresponding lines on the tangent planes and the tangent is drawn through them, as shown by the full line. The first wreath also develops into a straight line with the upper tangents.

The landing wreath, having to correspond in height with that on Pl. xv., compels a break in the line of tangents at joint G, and this joint must be made to bisect the angle as described in connection with Pl. xi.

The face mould for No. 1 wreath (Fig. 3, Pl. xvi.) is constructed thus. Make A'-C'

(54)

PLATE XVI.

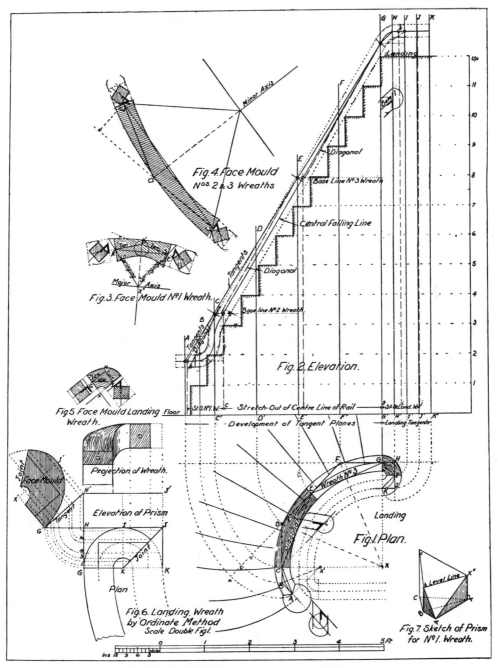

Fig.4. Face Mould
Nᵒˢ 2 & 3 Wreaths

Fig.3. Face Mould Nᵒ1 Wreath.

Fig.5 Face Mould Landing Floor
Wreath.

Fig. 2. Elevation.

Stretch-Out of Centre Line of Rail
Development of Tangent Planes

Projection of Wreath.

Elevation of Prism

Plan

Fig.6. Landing, Wreath
by Ordinate Method
Scale Double Fig.1.

Fig.1. Plan.

Fig.7. Sketch of Prism
for Nᵒ1. Wreath.

SET OF WREATHS FOR INSIDE RAIL TO A QUARTER-CIRCLE WINDING STAIR.

equal to the diagonal shown on the elevation, Fig. 2, and the tangents A'-B' and B'-C' equal in length to the tangents in elevation. To obtain the centre of the elliptic curves and points for the springing lines, bisect the diagonal A'-C', and draw a line from B' through the bisection. This is a level line passing through the centre required, therefore will be of the same length as its plan in Fig. 1. Take the length B-X', Fig. 1, and mark off from B, locating the centre X''. Draw the major axis through this point parallel with the diagonal and the minor axis perpendicular thereto.

Fig. 7 is a sketch of the imaginary prism formed by the tangents A-B-C, and the springing lines C-X' and A-X'; it shows clearly why the line B'-X'' is a level line on the oblique plane.

The disposition of the bevels as shown at the ends of the wreath-piece may not be clear, as it differs from that hitherto shown. It will be observed that in this case both bevels move outwards. This is due to the inclination of the tangents and the relatively small portion of a circle covered by the wreath in plan. The same thing occurs in the case of the Nos. 2 and 3 wreaths. The matter is fully gone into in Chapter XXVII., "Practical Work." As will be seen by the end sections, the face mould will be wide enough to line out the wreath-piece, but the latter should be cut full in the middle, i.e. upon the minor axis, for at this point the mould is the net width of the rail, as shown by the circle drawn in. The face moulds for No. 2 and No. 3 wreaths are exactly alike, as shown in Fig. 4, and are constructed as described for No. 2 wreath, Pl. x., but it must be remembered that the joint at G, in No. 3 wreath, will be slightly out of square with the surface of the plank. A bevel set to the bisector must be used instead of a square to make this joint; all the other joints are square to the plank.

The Bevels, as in the preceding example, are taken in the plan upon parallels to one or other of the tangents, and it may be explained that when the tangents are of equal length in plan it does not matter which is selected to take the bevel upon, but when they are unequal in length the parallel must be drawn to that tangent which is connected with the joint at which the bevel is to be applied. The reason is that by drawing parallels to oblique tangents we obtain the plan of the oblique prism, of which the tangents form the edge of the sections, and the bevel is obtained thereon in like manner to the procedure when the prism formed by the tangents is rectanglar. This is explained fully at page 33. It should be noted that although the bevel can be obtained on the development or elevation of the tangents when the plan of the prism is rectangular, it cannot so be found when the prism is oblique, and the special construction shown in this and the preceding example then becomes necessary.

The Face Mould for the landing wreath (Fig. 5, Pl. xvi.) is a simple case of type No. 1 tangents, and the method of producing these has been fully described at page 26 (Chapter V.). The bevel for joint I is taken between the development of tangents G-H. An alternative treatment of this wreath is shown in Fig. 6, Pl. xvi. (to larger scale); in this example the wreath, instead of making a butt joint at the springing K, is mitred to the level rail on the line X-J, the wreath in one piece covering nearly two-fifths of a circle, thus one joint is dispensed with.

The face mould is produced by a level-ordinate system, more suitable for this type of mould than the trammel method. Having drawn the plan of the prism G-H-I-J-K, Fig. 6, produce the tangent line H-J to G', make this equal in length to G-H, and draw thereon the pitch of the tangent G'-H', obtained from G-H, Fig. 1. Draw the line H-J', representing the level tangent and completing this elevation of the prism.

Divide the curves in plan into any number of parts, and project them perpendicular to the side of the prism H-G in points 1, 2, 3, 4, 5, 6, 7. Rotate these as shown to G'-H, thence project them to the tangent by perpendiculars to G'-H, and project them across the section by perpendiculars to the tangent.

Mark off from G'-H' on these lines points equal to the distance of the corresponding points in the plan from the side G-H and draw curves through these points. The joint is located in like manner.

CHAPTER XV.

A PAIR OF WREATHS FOR A QUARTER-PACE LANDING AND QUARTER OF RADIAL WINDERS BETWEEN REVERSE FLIGHTS, EASINGS IN THE WREATH.

(PLATE XVII.)

Typical Difficulties in Wreaths for Stone Stairs—Common Faults—The Correct Method—Summary of Setting Out—The Control Points—Joint Square to Pitch—A Bisector Joint—Finding the Elliptic Axes—A Peculiarity of this kind of Joint—Obtaining its Width—Blank Moulds—Danger of Generalising Intaking Bevels—The Falling Mould.

THE stair for which this handrail is required shows a common arrangement of the plan with stone stairs, and by having both landing risers in the springings provides a somewhat difficult problem for the handrailer. Its solution by the ordinary tangent system, wherein the pitch of the tangent is obtained by making a development of the tangent planes as laid down in the plan, then producing the rail centre lines to meet the cross tangents and joining these points by a straight line, which thereupon becomes the falling tangent, results in a wreath raised too high at the central joint, which is arbitrarily " corrected," but always remains an offence to the trained eye. The proper method is shown in Pl. XVII.

Commence by laying down the plan as in Fig. 1, Pl. XVII. (take no account of the dotted radials at present). Next, make a stretch-out of the centre line and the steps, as they occur thereon (Fig. 2). The methods of doing this and other details to follow that have already been described under previous examples will not be repeated. Draw the flyer rails resting on the nosings, and produce their centre lines to the springings. Draw the underside of the wreath parallel with the nosings of the winders and at any height it is desired to raise the rail thereon. Make its centre line parallel and ease off the angles at the intersection with the straight rails, as shown. The centres for these easings are indicated, but any other easing may be used.

The small circles at *a, c* and *e* locate the heights of the tangents (required to form this wreath) upon the tangent planes at A, C and E. Draw the development of the tangent planes (Fig. 3); you may or may not draw the steps as they occur thereon, they are indicated by dotted lines on the plate merely to show how useless they are for the purpose of discovering the pitch of the tangents. Having projected the controlling points from Fig. 2, draw the tangents through them to tangent lines B and D. From their intersections, draw lines to the centre point C, thus indicating the pitches of the two wreaths. The top wreath has a shank, and the joint is made square to the pitch. The joint at the centre for both wreaths is a bisector of the angle between the two pitches, and the bevel shown is used in place of a square for the side joint. Reversed, it answers for the top wreath. The bottom wreath is shown jointed at the springing for the sake of reducing the thickness of plant, but apart from the length of the face mould at this end, no variation would be needed if it were decided to use a shank here also. The diagonals are drawn in position for each wreath, and as all points are correspondingly lettered, no difficulty should be found in drawing the face moulds. The bevels and widths of the moulds are, for convenience, laid off upon the elevation instead of the plan as usual. Of course, the widths of rectangular prisms are alike in each projection, so that the same bevel would be obtained upon either with the given dimension.

As the location of each bevel is indicated thereon, no further explanation is considered necessary. In both wreaths the direction of the elliptic axes must be found either by trial or by geometrical construction, these being examples of Type 3 tangents. The method adopted on the drawing is by obtaining the horizontal trace upon the face mould, then drawing the direction of the minor axis parallel with it. The dotted lines at a''-b and p-d, Fig. 3, indicate the lengths to be added to the respective tangents on the face moulds to locate one point in the horizontal plane, points A and E furnishing the other points. The method is fully detailed at page 18. The shape of the bottom mould at joint A may need a little explanation. Owing to the acute angle between the tangent and the springing line—on the latter, of course, the width of the mould is set off—the joint, being made square to the tangent, cuts some distance within the convex curve, and a similar distance outside the springing at the concave curve. The former incident causes no difficulty, but the latter does, as there is no guide for the curve beyond the springing. Theoretically, another ellipse is here dealt with, and new axes and direction should be found, but the portion required is so small that in practice this is always ignored, the procedure being to mark off along the joint line from j, the point where the joint cuts the convex curve, the full width of the mould as shown at k and to continue the elliptic curve by an easy sweep to that point. This results in a slight excess of wood at the outside of the joint, which is flushed off exactly when the wreath is bolted to its adjacent wreath after bevelling.

Both of these wreaths will need special moulds for marking the blanks, as indicated by the dotted lines, and described in Chapter IX. The size required at each end is first set out, as shown, beyond the joint lines of the face moulds (Figs. 4 and 5), by drawing the enclosing rectangle which contains the wreath section (shown in these examples section-lined) arranged symmetrically upon its appropriate level. The method of obtaining the necessary thickness of the plank is shown at Fig. 6, where all the four sections are drawn for the purpose of demonstrating that it is not invariable for the most acute bevel or "twist" to require the greatest depth of plank. In this case the most acute bevel requires an $\frac{1}{8}$ in. less in thickness than does the bevel at the other end, which is only slightly less than a right angle. Admittedly, this is chiefly due to the relatively deep section of the rail, but it indicates the danger of generalising in the science of handrailing.

A Falling Mould, as shown in Fig. 7, Pl. XVII., will be useful for lining out the top and bottom edges of the wreath, after the sides are worked to the face mould, i.e. bevelled. The necessary lines for obtaining this mould are shown on the plan, Fig. 1, numbered 1 to 9, and on the stretch-out at X-X, these are projected to the centre falling line and projected thence to Fig. 7, as fully described in Chapter XIII., page 53.

PLATE XVII.

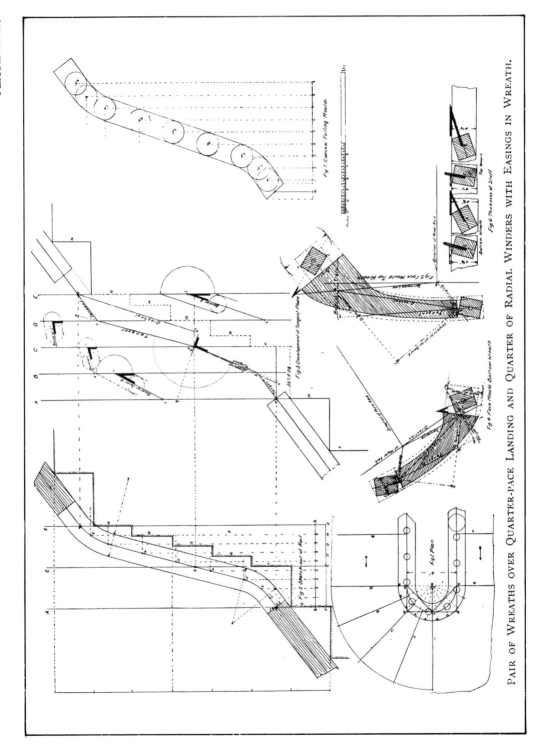

Fig 7. Convex Falling Mould.

Fig 6. Thickness of Stuff.

Fig 5. Face Mould Top Wreath.

Fig 4. Face Mould Bottom Wreath

Fig 3. Development of Tangent Plane

Fig 2. Stretch-out of Rail

Fig 1 Plan

PAIR OF WREATHS OVER QUARTER-PACE LANDING AND QUARTER OF RADIAL WINDERS WITH EASINGS IN WREATH.

PLATE XVIII.

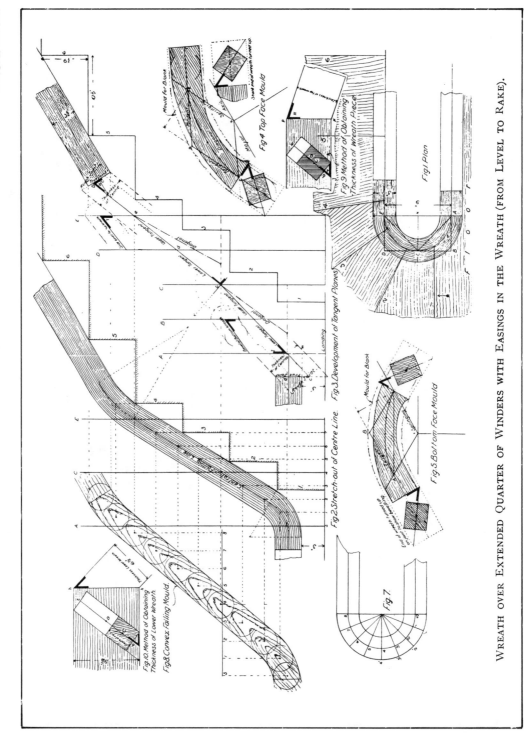

Fig.1. Plan

Fig.2. Stretch-out of Centre Line.

Fig.3. Development of Tangent Planes.

Fig.4. Top Face Mould

Fig.5. Bottom Face Mould

Fig.7.

Fig.8. Convex Falling Mould.

Fig.9. Method of Obtaining Thickness of Wreath Piece

Fig.10. Method of Obtaining Thickness of Lower Wreath.

Mould for Blank

WREATH OVER EXTENDED QUARTER OF WINDERS WITH EASINGS IN THE WREATH (FROM LEVEL TO RAKE).

CHAPTER XVI.

WREATHS OVER EXTENDED QUARTER-SPACE OF WINDERS AT BOTTOM OF FLIGHT, WITH EASINGS IN THE WREATH (FROM LEVEL TO RAKE).

(PLATE XVIII.)

Plan of Rail Rising from a Long Landing with Winders Spaced to Suit Falling Line—A Helical Wreath—Alternatives to Easings in Wreath—Broken Pitch Tangents—A Service Joint, Reasons for Use—Faulty Instructions in Certain Books—The Right Method to Ascertain Thickness of Plank—Displaced Centres—Method of Making the Joint—The Triangular Templet—Guide Line for Falling Mould—Locating Bolt-holes.

THIS plan, Fig. 1, Pl. XVIII., shows a flight of stairs making a half-turn from a long landing or floor, with three balanced winders in an extended quarter-space, the arrangement having been made to suit the desired falling line shown in Fig. 2. This, it will be observed, is a straight line between the springings, which will produce a true helical wreath clinging closely to the steps. This wreath could be most easily made by forming the easings upon the straight rails, but this would necessitate either two extra joints, through making the easings in separate pieces or extra thick plank, from which to cut the straight rails. For these reasons, the easings are shown on the wreath itself. None of the matters that have been dealt with in the more elementary examples will be repeated here; attention is confined to the new problems that arise in this particular construction. The developments in elevation are set out separately for ease and clearness of reference, but in the workshop all would be superposed on one rod. The only thing needing attention in Fig. 2 are the easings. The centres for these are found by measuring off from the angle of intersection of the centre lines of wreath and straight rails an equal distance along the centre line, and drawing perpendiculars to each pitch, which, at their intersection, locate the centres of the curves. The points where the falling line passes through springings A, C, E, determine the heights of the tangents on the corresponding line of the development, Fig. 3. Draw the tangents thereon, to pass through these points as shown, producing them beyond the springings to the predetermined joint-lines. Sufficient of the straight rails over the flyers and the landing, to obtain their pitches, must be drawn. Broken pitches to the tangents result in each case. We will consider the joint at the top end first. The line marked " true joint " is made square to the pitch of the straight rail. It might be made differently, but there is one practical reason for adopting this method. Many shops give out the straight handrails to the ordinary joiner for preparation, and it is better not to trust him with special joints, these should be manipulated by the handrailer, who thoroughly understands the setting out and is not likely to make mistakes. Moreover, a joint made square to the pitch of this tangent would look like a splice joint when in position, and would be difficult to bolt properly, also, as we shall see presently, it would require thicker stuff. If the student desires, he may obtain the down or edge bevel for this joint by the process described in Chapter VII., but the bevel shown at H will be correct for marking this joint on the side of the wreath *after it is bevelled*, and as this joint is not required until that stage is reached, the simpler way may be satisfactory.

It has been asserted by some writers on the subject that the thickness of the plank for

(59)

such wreaths as this may be determined by drawing on the development parallels to contain the extreme points of the easings, or, if this thickness is exceeded by parallels through the corners of the section pitched to the quickest bevel, that will be the thickness required. Neither statement is correct. The chain-line parallels drawn on Fig. 3 indicate the thickness required to form the easings, but is really only about three-quarters of the required depth ; such a section takes no account of the tilting of the corners, neither will the usual method, as described with previous examples, indicate sufficient depth. The correct method is shown in Figs. 9 and 10. In consequence of the break in the pitch of the tangents at the top joint, a displacement of the normal centre of the wreath occurs, and the difference between this point and the new centre required to coincide with that of the straight rail represents the amount of thickness to be *added* to that necessary to obtain the twist.

To Obtain Thickness of the Top Wreath (Fig. 9, Pl. xviii.).—Draw a horizontal line J-P', and upon it the angle J-K, with the slide-bevel T. Set off on this line symmetrically the squared section of the required rail (shown hatched). Mark the centre of the section point C, and set off above it the new centre D, which equals the distance between C and D upon the joint at H, Fig. 3. Next, mark off on the centre line point K at the same distance above D that point *b* is below it, draw the top edge through this point at right angles to the centre line, and complete the rectangle. Through the upper corner draw a parallel to J-P', and, if the joint H were " square to the plank," these parallels would show the required thickness of the wreath, but as it is not, draw a perpendicular at P', apply the bevel H to this as shown, and draw parallels at this angle from P and P'. The perpendicular distance between these lines show the required thickness of plank. From which we see that it is not always economical to use the square-to-plank joint.

Making the Joint.—Referring to Fig. 3, Pl. xviii., a dotted line marked rough joint will be seen, which is square to the surface of the plank ; this joint is necessary, because the slide-bevel T is, as in all examples save one in this book, obtained by measuring square to the tangent on the face mould, which means that the bevel must be applied in like manner if the correct angle is to be produced. Now, if the joint were at once cut as shown at H the bevel could not be applied square to the surface, hence the necessity of the temporary joint. Clean this joint off sufficiently to mark the centre of the depth and bevel thereon, and so obtain the new positions of the tangents for sliding the mould, as described in " Practical Work," page 90. When the wreath has been bevelled and the springing line marked across the side by aid of the face mould, gauge down a line at the centre of the thickness representing the tangent line *e*-D, Fig. 3. Upon this line mark off the exact distance point D is from the springing. Apply the bevel H at this point and cut in the joint line. After this joint has been made, prepare a templet to fit the triangle between the two tangents at H, and use this to mark the position of the depressed centre C on the side, or, if preferred, set a bevel to the straight-rail pitch from the joint and use this. We merely require to locate the position of the bolt-hole on the end of the wreath. Having secured this point, square a line through it across the joint, and use this line as a guide when applying the falling moulds to square the top and bottom edges. The shank joint on the bottom wreath is worked similarly, and is lettered in similar manner, so that the above direction will apply, the only variation being, that the joint here becomes plumb as the straight rail is horizontal, and the bevel to produce it is shown in the angle at I. This, of course, is merely a difference in position, and not in principle. The method of obtaining the thickness is shown in Fig. 10, the procedure being precisely as described for Fig. 9. The falling mould, Fig. 8, is produced by making a stretch-out of the convex side of the wreath, as shown in the auxiliary plan, Fig. 7 ; points in the centre falling line are projected from Fig. 2, and intersected by projectors from the stretch-out on Fig. 8, as described in detail at page 53.

PLATE XIX.

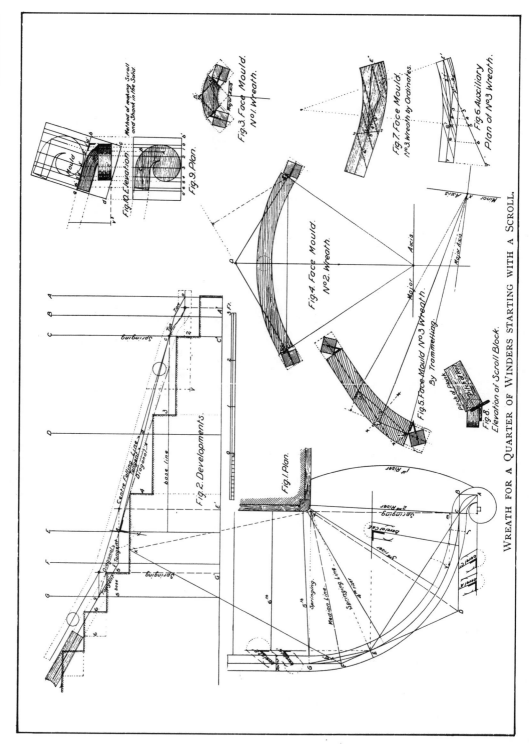

Fig.10. Elevation. Method of making Scroll and Stand in the Solid.

Fig.9. Plan.

Fig.3. Face Mould. No.1. Wreath.

Fig.7. Face Mould. No.3. Wreath by Ordinates.

Fig.6. Auxiliary Plan of No.3 Wreath.

Fig.4. Face Mould. No.2. Wreath.

Fig.5. Face Mould No.3 Wreath. By Trammelling.

Fig.8. Elevation of Scroll Block.

Fig.2. Developments.

Fig.1. Plan.

WREATH FOR A QUARTER OF WINDERS STARTING WITH A SCROLL.

CHAPTER XVII.

WREATH FOR A QUADRANT OF WINDERS STARTING AT BOTTOM OF FLIGHT. A CONTINUOUS RAIL WITH SCROLL FINISH.

(PLATE XIX.)

Typical Restaurant Stair—Setting Out the Plan—Developments—Determining Tangent Heights for Three Wreaths—A Difficult Face Mould—Methods of Obtaining it, by Tangent System, by Level-ordinate System—The Scroll Cap—Method of Jointing—Scroll and Shank in the Solid—Method of Obtaining the Mould—the Slide Line.

THREE wreaths are comprised in this quadrant, which makes a very graceful handrail. The ſtairs indicated in the plan, Fig. 1, Pl. XIX., are similar to one recently executed at a reſtaurant in London.

The commode ſtep faces the entry and the quadrant of winders turn the ſtair around a break or return wall. A dado framing rises above the wall-ſtring, which is merely indicated in the drawing. Owing to the peculiar disposition of the tangent planes, the produ&ion of the face mould presents difficulties not met in the preceding examples, therefore merit somewhat detailed treatment. The plan, Fig. 1, is set out by drawing the risers in the positions shown, spacing them equally upon the centre line of rail, and around the corner turning piece. The plan of the rail is ſtruck from a centre at the angle of the walls. The arrangements of the tangents, whilſt arbitrary, are the result of trials to obtain a suitable falling line. As mentioned in a previous case, they depend to some extent on the joints, and the obje& here was to get as long a wreath as possible at the ſtart; or, in other words, to avoid having joints low down in the rail. As will be seen in Fig. 10, Pl. XIX., this rail, which was made by one of the author's pupils, the scroll is cut in the solid without joint, but in the plan, joints occur at A, C, E and at the shank 9 ins. beyond the springing line G; with the exception of the laſt, they radiate from the respe&ive centres. The tangents are drawn perpendicular to the joints, and meet in points B, D and F.

The Developments of the centre line and the tangent planes (Fig. 2) are superposed, and they coincide at the springing C. The development of the central falling-line plane is drawn in dotted line, with the exception of the ſteps, which are in full line thereon and are se&ioned. The tangent planes are drawn in full lines and the two ſteps required to obtain the pitch indicated by dotted lines. The centre se&ion of the rail follows the nosing line of the ſtair closely, as obviously it would look ill to have any variation in the length of the baluſters in this position. The scroll cap is lifted 2 ins. above the firſt ſtep, and its centre line locates the height of the tangent on A. The rail is ramped down into the level part of the scroll, which commences at the joint A in the plan. A slight easing is made over the fifth riser to obliterate the jun&ion of the two pitches. The heights of the tangents are determined upon the joint lines A, C, E and G, by proje&ing level lines from the points shown in open circles, where the centre falling line interse&s the correspondingly lettered lines on the ſtretch-out. These produce in the firſt wreath tangents of different inclinations (Type 3),

(61)

in the second wreath tangents of equal inclination (Type 2), and in the third wreath tangents one level the other inclined (Type 1).

The first two wreaths need not be discussed—several examples of these have already been explained—but the third wreath introduces complications with which we will now deal.

The Face Mould (Fig. 5, Pl. XIX.).—The triangle E''-F''-G'' is drawn in the usual manner by obtaining the true length of the diagonal E-G, Fig. 1, on the elevation, where it is shown by the usual dot and dash line, and describing arcs upon its ends with the lengths of the tangents *e-f* and *f-g* as radii; joining up the points so found, produce the tangents sufficiently to obtain the length of shank, as shown in the elevation, also the perpendiculars with which to obtain the bevels.   Next, the centre of the elliptic curves must be found and, as in all cases of obtuse angles in plan, the prism containing the centre is a triangular one, whose base is represented by the tangents E-F and F-G and the springing lines E-*x* and G-*x*, Fig. 1. In previous examples, the median line F-*x*, Fig. 1, has been level, and its length, as in the case of No. 2 wreath in the present example, is also the length of the corresponding line on the face-mould section; this condition always applies when the tangents are equally pitched, but in the present case this is not so, one tangent being level, therefore another construction is required to ascertain the length of the line F'-*x''* on the face mould.   Proceed to draw the *direction* of the latter by bisecting the diagonal in point *b*, draw a line from F'' through this point indefinitely.   Return to the plan, Fig. 1: with point F as centre and radius F'-*b*, Fig. 5, describe an arc, cutting the diagonal in *b'*.   Draw a line from F through *b'* and intersect it at X' by a perpendicular on the line F-*x*.   Thus is obtained a section of the prism upon that line, and the line F-*x'* is the true length of the median line upon the oblique plane.   Set off this length from F'' in Fig. 5, and point X'' is the centre of the elliptic axes, also the point to which the springings are drawn.   The lengths with which to obtain the bevels are laid off between the tangent F-G and its parallel, drawn through the opposite centre of tangent and springing as shown, and the width of the rail described on these lines shows the width of the mould at the end of the tangent measured from, upon either parallel.   End sections of the wreath are shown at the ends of the face mould with the directions of the bevels.   It will be observed that in this case both bevels lie in one direction and cause the mould to slide outwards at each end.   This peculiarity is due to the small amount of the plan curve or cylinder which is embraced by the mould, the amount of " turn " in the tangents being insufficient to overcome the pitch of the inclined tangent.   A like effect is produced in the second wreath (Fig. 4), but No. 1 wreath, forming a quadrant in plan, the bevels lie in opposite directions, which of course is the most common condition.   In Figs. 6 and 7 has been shown a method of obtaining the face mould for No. 3 wreath by the **Level-ordinate** system, which in such cases as these will be found the more simple method of setting out in the workshop, because, to set this wreath out full size by the first method, a rod over 6 ft. in width would be needed, and two persons required to line it out, but it was thought advisable to show that such cases could be managed by the square-cut-and-tangent system, as the contrary has been stated several times.   It will be interesting to compare the moulds obtained by each method, which is best done by tracing the one and applying the tracing to the other.

The **Auxiliary** plan, Fig. 6, Pl. XIX., is redrawn in a convenient position and a series of ordinates drawn upon it, parallel to the tangent F'-E', which we know to be a level line (if it were not, we should simply obtain the direction of a level line, as described in Chapter XXI.). These ordinates are placed irregularly just where one pleases, or it is found they are needed; for instance, it was found necessary to obtain two points on the curve outside the tangent F'-E'.   Now as ordinates through these could not intersect that tangent, recourse is made to the top tangent, which is shown produced in dotted line, and measurements are taken therefrom.   To complete the plan, draw an elevation of the tangent G-F, upon its plan, obtaining the pitch from the development, Fig. 2. From the points of intersection of the ordinates with the plans of the tangents, viz., 1, 2, 3, 4, 5, 6, 7, draw perpendiculars, intersecting the elevation in points 1', 2', 3', 4', 5', 6. The section of the prism, Fig. 1, is obtained in the usual way by forming the triangle E''-F''-G'' upon the diagonal F''-G''. Transfer the above-mentioned points to the corresponding tangents, and draw parallels to F''-E'' through them; mark off on these parallels like distances from the tangents to those shown on the corresponding ordinates in the plan, and draw the curves through the points so found. It will be observed that the ordinates 1, 3 and 5 are so placed that they indicate the width of the mould at each end.

Draw the shank parallel with the tangents, and the joints square to the same, when the mould will be complete.

Fig. 8, Pl. XIX., is a front view of the scroll cap, with its shank wreath turned into the same plane to indicate the method of forming the joint between them; the one on the shank wreath is made square to the plank and the scroll piece bevelled to fit, with its bottom level. This method of jointing the scroll is the most economical in time and material, but sometimes it is preferred to make the scroll and its shank in one piece, so avoiding a joint at A. The method is shown in Figs. 9 and 10, and as we have already given the method of obtaining the shank wreath by means of tangents, for the sake of variety the ordinate method is here adopted.

Fig. 9 is the plan of the scroll redrawn, with a shank joint in the position marked at J in Fig. 1.

Enclose the plan within a rectangle, which represents the size of the piece of stuff needed to cut it from; the length of this cannot be known until the elevation is made, therefore proceed to draw the bottom line of the scroll a few inches above its plan; set up the thickness of the level portion and obtain the pitch as follows. Note that it is not the same as in the development, because the latter is a stretch-out, whilst this is a projection of the solid. At any convenient point V on the development, draw a perpendicular to the base line of the scroll shown in dotted line, cutting the elevation of the rail. Transfer the distance V-2 in the elevation to the plan at V-C by a series of steppings. Set off the perpendicular distance of point V' from the springing at m upon Fig. 10, measuring from the springing line C', erect a perpendicular at V², make it the same height as the back of the rail above point V, Fig. 2. Make C' the same height as 2-C in Fig. 1, and the line drawn through these points gives the correct pitch. Complete the elevation of the scroll by easing the pitch line into the level, draw the underside parallel, and enclose the figure within the rectangle a-b-e-d, which indicates the length and thickness of the block required. The plan shows the third dimension.

To Obtain the Mould, which is shown turned up on the front edge of the block, draw ordinates across the plan, as at 1, 2, 3, 4, 5, 6, project these points to the top edge in elevation, and at the intersections 1', 2', 3', etc., erect perpendiculars to the pitch, and mark off points in the curves upon these at like distances from the edge a-b that the scroll intersects in the plan when measured from a'-b'.

When this mould is applied at the top of the block the line O' is marked across the edge to the bevels shown immediately under; and this gives the slide line for applying the mould to the underside, also the direction of cut in forming the scroll. The sides of the shank are made square to the pitch and the joint is made radial to the plan curves, as indicated at J, Fig. 1.

CHAPTER XVIII.

QUARTER-TURN WREATH ON LANDING TO STONE STAIRS.

(PLATE XX.)

Reverse Flights—Pitches Rake to Level and Level to Rake—Requirements of Rails to Stone Stairs—Difficulties with Balusters—Drawings Required—Determining the Height of Rail—Alternative Treatment of Turns—Obtaining Size of the Blank.

Reverse Flights.—Pitches Rake to Level and Level to Rake.—The drawings on Pl. xx. contain no new principle, but vary considerably in detail from the earlier examples, and it will be necessary only to point these out.

The Plan (Fig. 1, Pl. xx.) shows parts of the landing and of the second flight of stairs therefrom. The dotted lines indicate the position of the nosings of the steps and landing, also the situation of the balusters, which are central with the rail. As usual, in landings to stone stairs, the junction between step and landing is at right angles, not turned off in a sweep as in wood stairs. Now the handrail has to be so turned and the problem is to place the baluster in the angle so that it shall lie in the centre of the turn. These two plans indicate different methods of accomplishing this. In the plan we are now considering the rail has an equal margin over the steps and the landing, the turn is made with a 6-in. radius, and the corner baluster is cranked out at the bottom, as shown in the elevation, Fig. 9, to bring into the middle of the rail. Of course, in so short a turn as is this, the necessity for making a stretch-out does not arise, and a development of the tangents, as in Fig. 3, is sufficient; the only data required to fix the tangents is the height of the rail over the landing. Assuming this is required to be 3 ft. to the back of the rail, and 2 ft. 8 ins. over the flyer-risers, the thickness of the rail measured perpendicularly is 5 ins., as shown at *h*, Fig. 3, therefore the lift of the rail must be 2 ft. 3 ins., and this lift over the landing is 9 ins. short of 3 ft., so the back of the rail must be drawn 9 ins. above the landing, and half its thickness shows the height of the tangent at A. Draw the pitch of the rail over the flyers and produce its centre line to the angle tangent B. Draw the second tangent from the intersection on B to the level of the centre of rail on the landing. In this case the tangents become a straight line when unfolded. The diagonal A-C is laid off on the base line and its true length ascertained as at D, Fig. 3.

The face mould (Fig. 6) is then constructed by aid of these three lines, as previously described. Fig. 7 is the face mould redrawn to larger scale, with the end sections of the wreath projected at their correct angles, showing the necessary size of the blank in dotted lines.

In the plan, Fig. 2, the rail is arranged with a smaller turn and is carried further in over the landing, thus the corner baluster is made to line with the landing riser, and so does not need cranking. In the development of tangents, Fig. 4, the lines A′, B′, C′ are drawn parallel, at the same distance apart that the points A, B, C are in the plan, and the steps and

PLATE XX.

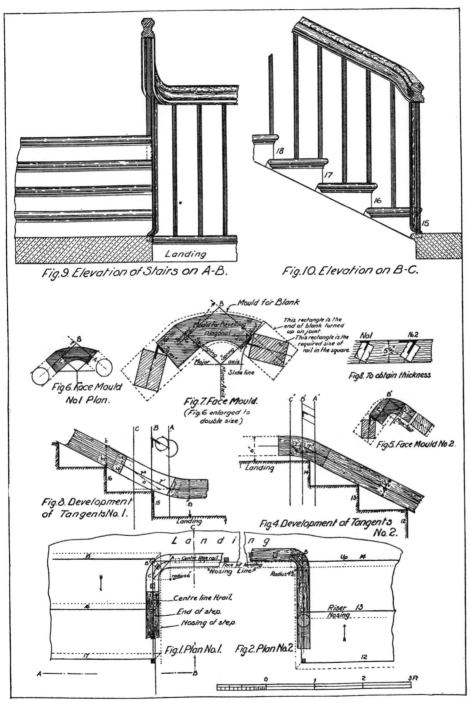

Fig.9. Elevation of Stairs on A-B.

Fig.10. Elevation on B-C.

Fig 6. Face Mould No 1 Plan.

Mould for Blank

This rectangle is the end of blank turned up on joint.
This rectangle is the required size of rail in the square.

No1   No 2

Fig 8. To obtain thickness

Fig.7. Face Mould.
(Fig.6 enlarged to double size.)

Fig 5. Face Mould No 2.

Fig.3. Development of Tangents No. 1.

Fig.4. Development of Tangents No. 2.

Landing

Centre line rail
Face for landing
Nosing Line
Centre line H.rail.
End of step.
Nosing of step.
radius 6
Radius 4½
Riser 13
Nosing

Fig.1. Plan No.1.   Fig.2. Plan No.2.

0   1   2   3 Ft.

WREATHS FOR QUARTER-TURNS ON LANDINGS. STONE STAIRS.

landing as they occur on the tangents in plan.   The back of this rail is drawn at 6 ins. above the landing, for the sake of variety.   Its centre line produces the level tangent, and the centre line of the flyer rail the inclined tangent.

Fig. 5 is the face mould constructed exactly as described in Chapter V., page 26, to which the reader is referred for further information.   The size of the blank in this instance is indicated in dotted lines outside the face mould.   Fig. 8 illustrates the usual method of finding the thickness of plank required, and Figs. 9 and 10 are transverse elevations of the stair that is shown in plan No. 1.

CHAPTER XIX.

A HALF-TURN WREATH FOR A STONE DOGLEG STAIR AND A WREATHED EASING TO A MITRE CAP.

(PLATE XXI.)

Typical Stone Stairs in Reverse Flights—A Difficult Wreath, Suggestions for Working—The Setting Out—The Face Mould—Finding the Horizontal Trace—Maximum and Minimum Thickness Required for Wreath—An Easing into a Mitre Cap—Two Methods of Obtaining the Face Mould—Obtaining Shape of the Mitre.

THE stair shown in plan and section, Figs. 1 and 2, Pl. xxi., is the usual type in stone stairs of reverse flights connected by a half-pace landing, and having the outer ends of the steps lying in the same vertical plane, approximating in this respect to the type of wood stair known as " Dogleg." As, however, in stone stairs newel posts are not necessary at the turns, the handrail is wreathed in a similar manner to that of an open or " geometrical " stair. There is not much difficulty in setting out the lines for this rail and obtaining its face mould, but the working of the wreath will test the handrailer's skill, for the " cylinder " or space between the rails must be kept very narrow to prevent undue encroachment on the stairs, and this renders the process of " squaring " the top and bottom edges somewhat difficult. The use of a pliable straight-edge, as described under " Practical Work," will render the task easier, or, if preferred, falling moulds may be used. The outside mould, which would probably be sufficient in this instance, is shown in Fig. 6. The method of obtaining these is described at page 53.

Setting Out.—The plan must be drawn as shown in Fig. 3, Pl. xxi., with the risers in the springings, and the centre lines of the rails produced as tangents to the wreath curve. To obtain the pitch of these, draw the development, Fig. 4 ; so far as obtaining the heights is concerned, a stretch-out is unnecessary, because we cannot depart from the generic pitches derived from the nosing lines of the steps. The centre lines of the two rails are made parallel with these, and produced to meet the landing tangent lines B and D. The intersecting points b and d are connected by a straight line, which indicates the pitch of the tangents over the landing, but the central falling section has been dotted in to make clear the shape of this rail, also to provide data for the falling moulds. It will be observed that the pitches of the centre falling line and of the tangents differ but slightly.

The Face Mould (Fig. 5, Pl. xxi.).—One only of these is required as, though the pitch of the tangent is reversed in the two wreaths, their length and amount of inclination are alike, therefore the same elliptic curves will be produced by either set of lines and, in applying the mould, its face side will be applied up on one wreath and down upon the other, and the sliding will, as usual, be in opposite directions. All the lines for producing the face mould are shown and their application has been described at page 24, Chapter IV.

The width at each end of the mould is obtained from the bevel lines laid off between the tangent lines A-B and B-C, Fig. 4, as previously described. These widths are laid off

(67)

on the tangent extensions upon the face mould shown at *c-c'*, Fig. 5, marked " width of mould," but remember when drawing the joint square with the tangent that it cuts the inside elliptic curve within the springing ; therefore the whole width as shown at *c-c* muſt be set off along the joint, obtaining point O, to which the outside elliptic curve muſt be continued.

The difference is not great in the scale drawing, but would be appreciable when drawn full size. The reference to one mould does not imply that it is inadvisable to use duplicate moulds when bevelling, as described in Chapter XXVII. The end elevations of the wreath-piece are drawn turned up on the joint lines for the twofold purpose of showing the direction of the bevels, and to ascertain width required in the blank. All of this has been previously explained, and the reader will readily follow the conſtruction. The direction of the minor axis of the elliptic curves is ascertained by first finding the horizontal trace of the oblique plane, done by laying off the length *c-a²*, Fig. 4, upon C-*a'*, Fig. 5, and drawing the trace, as shown, from the point to the angle at A. The minor axis is drawn parallel with this line, through the centre X. ·Fig. 7 indicates the maximum and minimum thickness required for the wreaths.

The Easing into Mitre Cap at the foot of the ſtair is shown in Figs. 8, 9, 10, Pl. XXI. The plan and development will need no explanation, but two methods of obtaining the face mould are shown in Fig. 10. The method already explained in connection with Chapter XIII. of treating the plan as a quadrant and cutting the mould out to point C may be used, and, to avoid the waſte of ſtuff incidental to cutting out the blank to the same size for the sake of obtaining the slide bevel at C, it is advised to cut the blank a little longer than necessary to make the mitre joint, mark the springing line across the face at A, and square this line over the inside edge of the piece. Mark the middle of its thickness thereon, apply the bevel through this point and draw parallels to the springing line upon the two faces of the piece at the points where the bevel line interſects these faces. Then, by moving the mould until *its* springing line lies upon the line juſt drawn, and keeping its tangent upon the tangent line A'-B', the mould will be placed in the correct position for lining out the ſtuff for bevelling.

Another way to obtain the face mould is indicated in dotted lines upon Figs. 8 and 10. Make A-*m'*, Fig. 8, equal to A-*m*, Fig. 9. Join *m'*-B and this line is the elevation of the tangent A-B. Project at right angles to A-B the extremities of the mitre, also its centre, to *m'*-B in points 1, 2, 3. Transfer these points to the face mould, Fig. 10, measuring from the springing at A'. From the points 1', 2', 3', draw perpendiculars to A'-B', make them equal in length to the corresponding ordinates in the plan, and draw the mitre and curves through the points so found.

Referring to the line X-S in the plan, this line is drawn from the centre of the plan curves, through the centre of the cap at O, and is produced to cut the tangent A-B in point S. Its object is to obtain the shape of the mitre, when the latter is taken to the centre of the cap, as described at page 8 ; project points O and S, Fig. 8, to the line *m'*-B in points 4 and 5. Transfer these to Fig. 10. Draw the line S'-X' and locate the centre upon it by a projector from point 4', the outside half mitre is indicated by the dotted line O'-1".

The method of obtaining the slide lines, in this case, would be as firſt described above.

PLATE XXI.

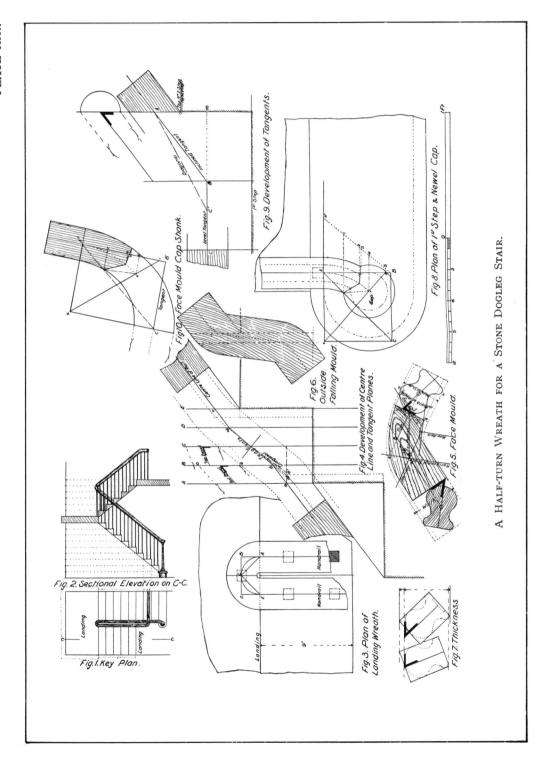

Fig.1. Key Plan.

Fig. 2. Sectional Elevation on C-C.

Fig. 3. Plan of Landing Wreath.

Fig.4. Development of Centre Line and Tangent Planes.

Fig.5. Face Mould.

Fig.6. Outside Falling Mould.

Fig.7. Thickness

Fig.8. Plan of 1st Step & Newel Cap.

Fig.9. Development of Tangents.

Fig.10. Face Mould Cap Shank.

A HALF-TURN WREATH FOR A STONE DOGLEG STAIR.

PLATE XXII.

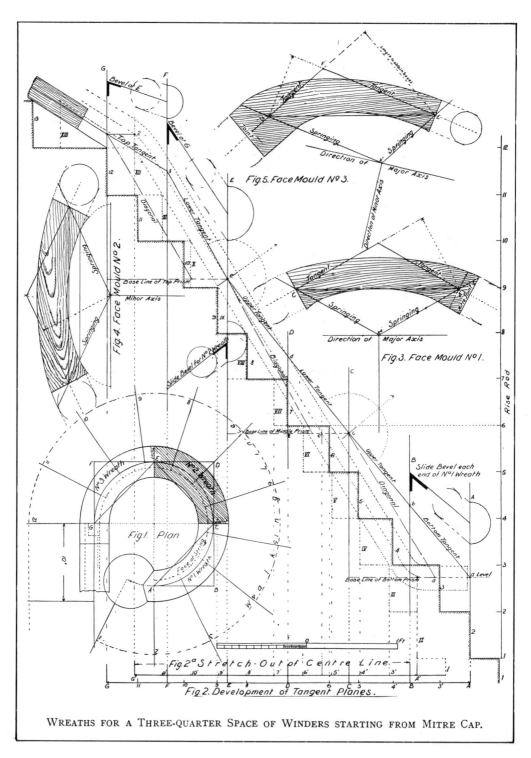

WREATHS FOR A THREE-QUARTER SPACE OF WINDERS STARTING FROM MITRE CAP.

A SET OF WREATHS OVER A THREE-QUARTER SPACE OF WINDERS, STARTING FROM A MITRE CAP.

(PLATE XXII.)

An Unusual Type of Plan for Restricted Floor Space—A True Helical Wreath composed of Three Differing Wreaths—Obtaining the Approved Section—Height of Mitre Cap—Face Moulds—Method of Conserving the Mitre Lines—A Bisected Joint.

This is a somewhat unusual arrangement of plan, but is very suitable for a restricted floor space such as occurs in restaurants and shops. The plan, Fig. 1, Pl. xxii., comprises eleven winders, covering slightly more than three-quarters of a circle and finishing with straight flyers or a landing, as may be required. Assuming space restricted, a small newel post, carrying a mitre cap, would be more suitable than a scroll finish; but the latter could easily be substituted if desired without affecting the setting out of the remainder of the rail. The width of the " well " is 1 ft. 2½ ins., and it is assumed the stairs will accommodate two lines of traffic, one up the other down. In such steep pitches as is this, the down traffic will hug the outside rail, therefore the winders are divided on a walking line about 7 ins. from the inside of this rail. They do not radiate from the centre, but are spaced equally around the centre line of the handrail. The centre line of the rail is enclosed by tangents set perpendicular to each other, and joints occur at the cap and over the fifth, eighth and twelfth steps, which is a convenient arrangement to suit the tangents. Thus there are three wreath-pieces, each different from the others in detail, but when built up, forming a true helical curve between the springings.

The Developments of the Centre Falling Line section and the tangent planes are shown superposed in Fig. 2 and Fig. 2a, the first-mentioned being in dotted line (which in the workshop would be set out with coloured pencil so that it would be readily distinguished by the architect or whoever had to " approve " the rod); the tangent planes are in full line, as are the steps, where they occur thereon; these are merely drawn that the reader may the better see their uselessness for the purpose of determining the proper heights of the tangents; that is to say, the suitable pitches of the plank within which may be contained the desired falling section.

The method of making this drawing need not be recapitulated, it has been repeatedly described in earlier examples, but possibly it may be necessary to point out that the two developments coincide on tangent line E, and the height points, to obtain pitches of the tangents, occur at the intersection of the centre falling line, with springing lines A', C', e' and g; these points, indicated by small circles, are projected to the correspondingly lettered lines on the tangent planes, which are the points where the centre line of rail in plan and the tangents coincide. Having obtained these points, draw the tangents through them. The height of the mitre cap is a matter of taste; here it is lifted 2¾ ins. above the second step, for the sake of obtaining an easy turn into the level. A similar easing is shown at the top end; the amount of easing is so small that it can be made in the wreath-piece without adding an extra thickness.

The Face Mould for the first wreath is shown in Fig. 3, Pl. XXII.; an extra length must be made at the end A′, in which to form the mitre shown on the plan; the blank must, of course, be cut in like manner, but until bevelled and squared, the end must remain square to the tangent, for the purpose of applying the bevel, also the section templet. When ready for moulding, a fine saw-cut should be run in at the mitre lines sufficiently deep to recover them after the moulding is worked. Personally, the author prefers to fill these cuts temporarily with a piece of pine, which enables the cut ends to resist the gouges, etc., without breaking off. The joints at C, also those at e, will not be square to the plank, but a bisection of the two pitches, as shown in dotted lines. These joints must be drawn on the elevation and a bevel set to them from the tangents, the same bevel answering upon each side of the joint, as described in Chapter XIV. The face mould for No. 2 wreath is shown in Fig. 4, and calls for no comment, being a common example of Type 2 tangents. The face mould for No. 3 wreath is shown in Fig. 5, and is a case of Type 3 in tangents, requiring the discovery of the direction of the elliptic axes, either by means of the " square " described at page 50 or by obtaining the horizontal trace of the oblique plane described on page 30, whichever method is preferred.

PLATE XXIII.

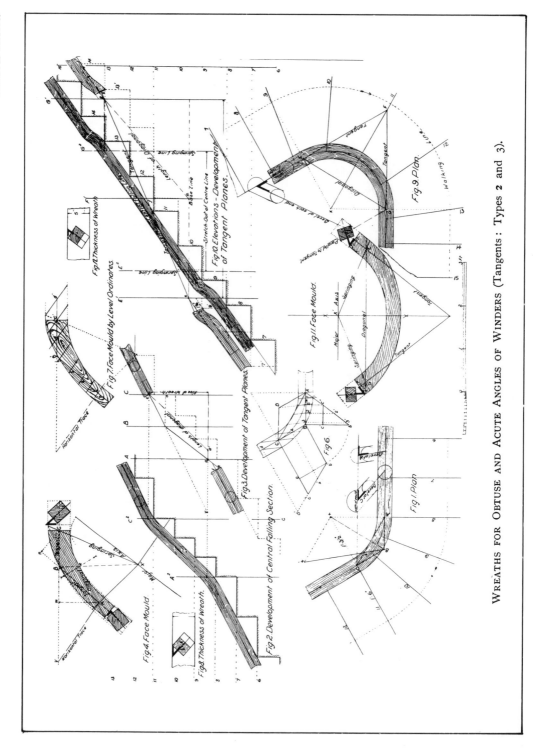

WREATHS FOR OBTUSE AND ACUTE ANGLES OF WINDERS (Tangents : Types **2** and **3**).

CHAPTER XXI.

WREATH FOR OBTUSE ANGLE OF WINDERS. CONTINUOUS FLIGHT WITH AN EASING IN THE WREATH.

(PLATE XXIII.)

Summary of Setting Out—Making the Rail Conform to Falling Line of Stair—Advantages of the Displaced Centre—Alternatives—Difficulties in Setting Out the Face Mould—How Overcome—Discovering the Length and Direction of the Elliptic Axes—Obtaining the Face Mould by Ordinate Method—Principle of the Ordinate Method—The Triangular Templet, its Use.
Wreath for a Continuous Rail over an Acute Angle of Winders—Description of the Drawings—Locating the Tangents and Joints—Forming the Ramps—False Sections, How Corrected—Remarks on the Face Mould—A Case of Displaced Centres – Marking the Wreath.

FIG I, Pl. XXIII., is the plan of the angle containing the winders, with two flyers above and below the springings. The centre of the wreath is at X, the radius of the centre line is 1 ft. 3½ ins. This line is enclosed with tangents formed by producing the centre lines of the flyer rails until they meet in point B. The diagonal A-C and the springing lines X-C and X-A complete the plan.

The Development of the Steps upon the centre line is given in Fig. 2, Pl. XXIII., with an appropriate falling section of the rail resting on the nosings. At the only two points, A and C, where the centre line and the tangent planes coincide, are located the heights required in the rail over the springings, and these points, marked by solid circles, are projected to the corresponding tangent lines in the development of tangent planes, Fig. 3. The steps as they occur on these planes are indicated in dotted lines. Draw the flyer rails resting on the nosings, and produce their centre lines, the lower to tangent line A, the upper to tangent line B. The lower tangent is drawn from the latter intersection to point *a* on the springing line, and continued until it meets the joint line at *e*. This arrangement causes a displacement of the centre from *e* to *f*, with consequent additional thickness in the wreath-piece, but it avoids an easing on the long rail, with an additional joint. Alternatively, a shank could be made at the top end of the wreath and the tangents drawn straight through from the springing, thus causing a similar displacement of the centre at that joint which would slightly reduce the thickness of plank required—as the latter increases with the steepness of pitch—but would require additional labour in making the joint. As a set-off to this, the face mould could be produced more readily. The most difficult arrangement is shown, as likely to be the more useful information.

The Face Mould (Fig. 4, Pl. XXIII.) is obtained so far as the triangular section of the prism A-B-C is concerned, as in all preceding cases, and no difficulty will be experienced with this part, but as in Chapter XIII. the centre of the elliptic axes cannot be found by drawing parallels to the tangents, as with rectangular plans. The construction required to locate the centre is in principle the same as described at page 50, and the reader is referred thereto, but in this case, the pitch of the tangent being unequal, a difference in detail is

(71)

necessary which will now be explained. Having produced the triangle A-B-C, Fig. 4, bisect A-C in point *e*. Draw a line indefinitely from B through *e*. This line will lie on the section exactly over the broken line B-X in the plan, but it will not be a level line ; hence the following construction to ascertain its length :—

Erect a perpendicular to B-X at point X, Fig. 1. Take the length B-*e*, Fig. 4, in the compasses, and describe an arc from B, cutting the diagonal in point *e'*. From B draw a line through *e'*, intersecting the perpendicular in point X'. Then B-X' is the real length of the line B-X upon Fig. 4, and X is the centre of the conjugate axes, also the point to which the springing lines must be drawn. The *direction* of the minor axis is parallel with the horizontal trace, found as described in a subsequent paragraph, and the *length* of the minor axis is obtained from the plan as usual, marking the rod at point X, when its end rests on the side of the rail desired. The joint at C, when made square to the tangent, cuts inside the springing, therefore reduces the width of the mould at the inside. The amount so reduced must be added along the joint line at the outside, and the curve continued thereto, as shown. The bevels are found by laying off the perpendicular distances A-*m* and C-*n*, Fig. 4, between the centre line of rail in plan, and a parallel drawn through the opposite springing point C, as shown on Fig. 1.

To further the usefulness of these instructions, an alternative method of drawing the face mould by means of level ordinates is illustrated in Figs. 6 and 7. Apart from the possibility of this method being more easy of comprehension by those unacquainted with geometry, it is of interest in affording proof of the correctness of each method, as the resulting mould obtained is the same by either construction.

An auxiliary plan is re-drawn at Fig. 6 simply to avoid confusion with the previous construction. The reader may be reminded that the principle of the ordinate system of drawing face moulds is based on the fact that level lines are of the same lengths as their plans, therefore level lines drawn on the oblique plane will be of the same length as corresponding lines drawn upon the plan. First draw parallels to the tangents A-B and B-C, meeting in D ; this is the location point for the " director of ordinates " and we have to find a point upon the tangent A-B, which shall be at the same height as the point D above the horizontal plane, therefore level with it. Draw elevations of the sides of the prism upon the base lines A-B and B-C, taking the dimensions from Fig. 3, that is to say, the development of the tangents is redrawn on the plan. On the perpendicular B-*b*, Fig. 6, set off B-C', equal in height to O-C, Fig. 3 ; project this point horizontally to cut the elevation of the tangent in point C''. Drop a perpendicular from this point into the plan, cutting the plan of the tangent A-B in point C''', join this point to D, as shown in dotted line, which indicates the direction of a level line upon the plane of section ; thereafter draw as many lines in the plan as may be considered necessary parallel with this line as at A, 1, 2, 3, 4, C, *d*, and project their points of intersection with the tangents A-B and B-C perpendicularly into the respective elevations, as shown at points 1', C'', 2', 3', 4', *c'* and *d'*, which latter point locates the end of the springing line on the mould. Next, construct the section of the prism as in Fig. 7, and transfer the aforementioned points to the appropriate tangents thereon, as indicated by the corresponding letters, and draw lines through these points parallel with the horizontal trace. The latter is found, as previously described (see p. 51), by projecting the upper tangent in Fig. 3 to the level of the lower one, at point V, the line V-*c* being then the vertical trace of the oblique plane upon a vertical plane, which contains the tangent. As obviously V and O are both points on the ground or horizontal plane, a line joining them will be a horizontal line, therefore make V'-C', Fig. 7, equal V-C, Fig. 3. Join V'-A', and the horizontal trace is obtained upon the plane of section. As in previous examples, the H.T. is indicated by a broken or " dash " line. Set off on each parallel, a distance from the tangent line equal to the length between the plan of the same tangent and the point of intersection with the curve lines in Fig. 6, and so obtain points through which to draw the elliptic curves. Make the joints square with the tangents and the shank equal in length to *a-e*, Fig. 3, and the mould is complete.

The method of ascertaining the requisite thickness for the wreath-piece is shown in Fig. 8, and has been fully described in Chapter XVI., page 60; it need not be repeated. The amount of displacement in this case is the distance of point *f* from *e*, Fig. 3, and a triangular templet of the dimensions shown thereon will be required to mark the centres on the side of the wreath shank after bevelling the same.

Wreath for a Continuous Rail Over an Acute Angle of Winders with Ramps to the Rail.

(PLATE XXIII.)

The plan, Fig. 9, Pl. XXIII., shows the portion of the stairs covered by the wreath, including one ordinary flyer, two diminished flyers, and four winders, spaced on the walking line and the centre line of the rail, the object of the arrangement being to obtain a continuous falling line with a constant length for balusters. If the latter point were immaterial, the construction could be simplified by raising the rail over the winders until it ranged with the common pitch above, dispensing with the top ramp, and increasing the bend of the bottom one. These are variations that can readily be made if the reader follows the construction here described. Having drawn the plan of the winders and centre lines of the rail over the return flights, produce the latter until they meet in point F, thus producing the acute angle described by the title. Draw the diagonal E-G and the springings E-X and G-E, also the median line F-X.

The Stretch-out of the centre plane, containing the central falling line and the steps as they occur thereon, is shown in full lines upon Fig. 10, the steps being in section. Superposed is the development of the tangent planes with the steps in dotted line. These two developments are not relatively adjusted to any particular point, being merely placed for convenience of illustration, but of course the levels are kept throughout. Having found the required heights of the tangents at the springings, as indicated by small circles at the intersection of the centre falling line with the springing lines E^2 and G^2, project these points to the corresponding springings on the tangent planes E' and G'. Draw a straight line connecting these points, which shows the true length and inclination of the pair of tangents *f-g* and *f-e*, produce the line at each end until it reaches the joints, which it is advisable in this instance to keep as near the springings as possible, to avoid complications. Next, draw the flyers and the straight rails resting upon them, when the amount of lift and depression respectively required to bring the rail in line with the wreath will be seen. The ramps are formed outside the springings, and may be made either in separate pieces or worked solid upon the straight rails as preferred, the side templets required for marking them being as shown on the development. As the joints of the wreath are made square to the plank, a bevel as at *g* will be required for use on the ramps. In all cases where the joint is not square to the plank, there is theoretically a false section produced on the joint which is not square, when the section templet is applied thereon, but this is automatically corrected when the joint is bolted together and the two sections are worked through, thus the aforesaid error is considered negligible in practice. A purist might get out the corresponding section for each side of the joint!

The Face Mould (Fig. 11, Pl. XXIII.) is obtained as described in Chapter XIII., this being a simple case of No. 2 type of tangents, where the line F-X becomes a level line on the section, consequently is of the same length as its plan, F-X, Fig. 9, and the minor axis of the elliptic curves lies in the same direction, the major axis being parallel to the diagonal. The end sections of the wreath-piece are drawn as if turned up on the joints of the mould, to indicate the direction of the bevels and the necessary width of the blank, which in this case would be sufficient, if cut slightly full to the face mould. The required thickness of the plank shown in Fig. 12 is found in the usual way for displaced centres, and is fully described at page 60. Referring to Fig. 10, the line T at the lower end, and *t* at the upper end, are the lines at which to apply the bevel when marking for bevelling, and the lines S and *s* are the corresponding lines to mark across the joint for the bolt centres. The construction to obtain the bevels is the same as in the last example, and will be readily followed on the drawing.

CHAPTER XXII.

A SET OF WREATHS AROUND A SQUARE NEWEL POST TO A DOUBLE FLIGHT OF STAIRS.

(PLATE XXIV.)

A Handrail to Railway Stairs—Description of the Wreaths—Avoiding a Ramp in the Wreath—Where to Place the Joints—A Departure from Orthodox Practice—Why a Stretch-out is Needless—How the Face Moulds are Obtained—False Economy—Finding the Width of the Blank.

THIS handrail occurs at the entrance to one of the London terminal railway stations, the wooden newel post enclosing a cast-iron column. The two parallel flights of stairs are separated by a glazed screen, which stands above the string marked on the plan, Fig. 1. Both sets of wreaths are exactly alike, therefore construction lines are shown only on the one side. As the most difficult wreath is the one formed at the junction of Nos. 1 and 2, this position is redrawn to larger scale in Fig. 8, Pl. xxiv. The piece of rail over the first step, as will be seen on the elevation, Fig. 6, is level and, following this on either side of the newel post, are three similar wreaths; thus, three-face moulds only will be needed for the six pieces. Nos. 3 and 4 wreaths are simple cases of Type 1 in tangents, and will not need explanation. The tangents, etc., are shown on the development, Fig. 2, at f, g, h, and the face mould in Fig. 5. To avoid having a ramp in the wreath, a joint is made between wreaths Nos. 1 and 2 at the point where the plan curves change in their direction; this joint radiates from the centre of the larger curve, and the springing line a-X^2 is made perpendicular to the straight rail. The centre for the curves of No. 2 wreath is situated at the angle of the newel, point Z. The curves being drawn, proceed to enclose them with tangents, by producing the centre lines of the straight rails to b and d. Rule-of-thumb followers of the tangent system would now connect these points by a straight line, which is *not* done here. The author considers the expert workman should be the master, not the servant, of a system, and consequently vary it, as to him seems best. There are advantages in having the tangents of equal length and controlling the curves as may be desired, which this arrangement secures; the only disadvantage is the purely theoretical one that the joint of No. 2 wreath will not be square to the tangent, needing the special bevel shown at C with which to make it. At this stage there will be no need to explain the method of making the development of the tangent planes, Fig. 2; the several tangent points marked in the plan are similarly lettered on the elevation, and should be easily followed. The height of the level rail and the pitch line of the flyers are the governing points in determining the pitch of the tangents. No stretch-out is needful in this case, because balusters are not used, and correspondence of pitch is not therefore imperative.

The Face Moulds (Figs. 3 and 4, Pl. xxiv.) do not differ in principle from others of Type 2 in tangents that have been already described, but as the combinations in the plan give some appearance of complexity, it may be useful to summarise the process of obtaining them. Taking the face mould for No. 1 wreath first, the diagonal A-C is made equal to a'-o, Fig. 2. A-B and C-B are made respectively equal to a'-b' and b'-c', Fig. 2. The centre

(75)

PLATE XXIV.

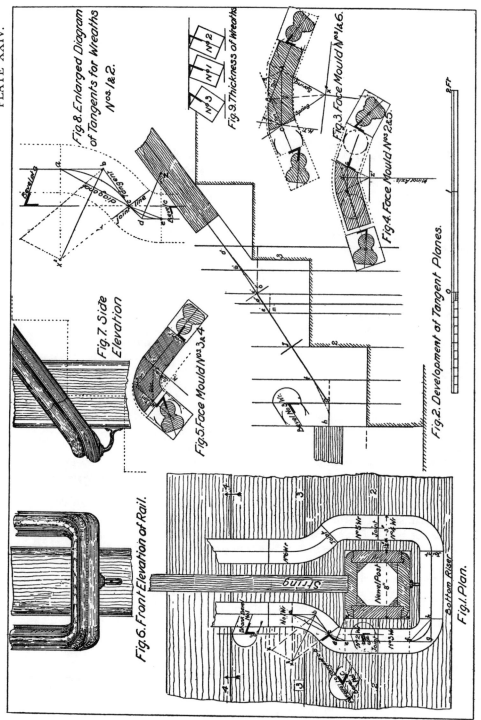

Fig. 8. Enlarged Diagram of Tangents for Wreaths Nos. 1 & 2.

Fig. 9. Thickness of Wreaths

Fig. 3. Face Mould No. 1 & 6.

Fig. 4. Face Mould Nos. 2 & 5.

Fig. 7. Side Elevation

Fig. 5. Face Mould Nos. 3 & 4.

Fig. 2. Development of Tangent Planes.

Fig. 6. Front Elevation of Rail.

Fig. 1. Plan.

SET OF WREATHS AROUND A SQUARE NEWEL FOR DOUBLE STAIRS.

of the elliptic curves is found by obtaining the true length of the line b-x^2, Fig. 1, as described on page 72 in connection with Chapter XXI., and setting it off, on the middle line B-X'', on the face mould. Draw the springings to this point, and the minor axis through it parallel to the horizontal trace; produce the tangents both ways and draw the joints square to them; that at C through the springings and the shank joint at the distance from a' indicated in Fig. 2. Obtain the bevels and widths of the mould at the springings by laying off the perpendicular distance from A and C, Fig. 3, between the tangents in plan and their parallels through C, as shown in Fig. 1, also as enlarged in Fig. 8. Describe circles of the required radius on the tangents of the face mould and draw, touching them, parallels to the tangents to intersect the springings. These give points in the elliptic curves which are trammelled in the usual way. Draw the tangent line produced, set off the required thickness as shown at Fig. 9, and through the middle of the depth draw the bevel line. Mark the section templet thereon, and so discover the required width of the blank, as indicated in dotted lines. It will be observed that there is an excess of stuff shown upon the inside at the shank end, and upon the outside at joint C. However, the amount of stuff to be saved by cutting the blank to the nett size would not compensate for the trouble of making the special mould needed to line it out and the necessary care to keep the " centre " line upon the right side.

Fig. 4 is obtained similarly to the last described, the finding of the position of Z' in this case being simplified as the tangents are at equal pitches, consequently the line d-z' is level, and of the same length as its plan d-Z, Fig. 1. The major axis of the ellipse is parallel with the diagonal. The only other point needing special attention is the joint at C, which is made to the bevel shown in the plan, as mentioned earlier; the joint of course is made square to the plank through its thickness.

Fig. 9 indicates the thickness of plank required in the several wreaths, as numbered, found in the manner now familiar to the reader.

CHAPTER XXIII.

A SERPENTINE WREATH TO STONE STAIRS WITH RETURN FLIGHTS TO A SQUARE LANDING.

(PLATE XXV.)

A Type of Wreath Assumed Unworkable by the Tangent System—A Ramped Wreath—Setting Out the Plan—Position of Joints—Making the Stretch-out—Types of Face Moulds Required—Obtaining the Horizontal Trace—The Inside Falling Mould—To Find the Various Thickness of Plank—Special Method Required for Ramped Wreaths.

THE handrail to a stair of the type shown in the key plan is a case that has been put forward as a poser to the advocates of the square-cut-and-tangent system. As the moulds herein shown are strictly obtained by that system based on the procedure described throughout this book, nothing further upon that point need be said. Admittedly this is a difficult case, needing careful setting out and exact working, but given these desiderata, the result will be satisfactory. The conditions are : Two flights of uniform pitch, at right angles, connected by a quarter-pace landing, with the fascias of the steps of one flight tangent to a 6-in. iron column, and the other abutting at the centre line of the column ; therefore the rail has to wind around the column, from which it must stand far enough for the hand to pass between. This brings the rail over the steps of the two flights and over the landing in different positions. Two treatments are possible, as herein shown : the rail is ramped over the landing riser No. 9, thus producing the double, or serpentine curve specified, which will need a falling mould for the purpose of lining out the edges of wreath No. 2.

The plan must be drawn as in Fig. 1, Pl. xxv., and the position of the rail located by means of the balusters, which are shown by the dotted circles, the centre line of rail coinciding with centres of balusters. The joints will radiate from the centres of the handrail curves, and be placed, one at each change of direction in the curve, one outside each springing, to provide shanks of sufficient length to take the bolts, and one over the landing in such a position that each pair of tangents will be of equal length, as this latter provision facilitates the setting out of the face moulds.

Next, the tangents to the curves are drawn square to the several joints, and the production of the centre lines of the straight rails will complete the tangents in plan. Draw the three diagonals and letter the several points for reference.

The Stretch-out of the centre line, Fig. 2, Pl. xxv., next claims attention. Starting from riser 8, step the compasses around the centre line in plan, marking off the distances as they are reached upon the line R-S of the points a', c', e', 10, g', h' ; set up a height rod of five steps, and with these data the development of the steps can be made ; draw the nosing lines and rails resting upon them. It is desired to raise the rail $3\frac{1}{2}$ ins. over the landing, therefore a knee ramp is introduced. The curves may be described by means of circular arcs or by freehand easings ; the latter is the method adopted in Fig. 2. Having decided the shape of the falling section, draw its centre line, and so obtain the heights of the tangents at points C, E, G and H. Proceed to make the development of the tangent planes, Fig. 3, and project the afore-

(78)

mentioned points to the corresponding lines, and draw the four pairs of tangents through them, as shown.

The Face Moulds (Figs. 4 to 6, Pl. xxv.) should offer no difficulties in construction at this stage ; in previous pages similar types have been dealt with fully. Nos. 2 and 4 wreaths are treated as obtuse angles in plan, No. 3 as an acute angle, and Nos. 1 and 4 are Types 3 in tangents, Nos. 2 and 3 are Type 2 in tangents.

Fig. 7, although in principle the same as in Chapter XXI., may need a word of explanation in consequence of the unusual position of the minor axis due to the obliquity of the pitch, and the small portion of the cylinder covered by the wreath. This is the mould for No. 1 wreath, and is produced as follows : Construct the section of the prism as usual, with the diagonal and two tangents shown between the three lines marked No. 1 wreath in Fig. 3. Bisect the diagonal A′-C′, Fig. 7, in point m, and draw a line from B′ through this point.

To obtain the length of this line upon the section, construct a triangle on its plan, B-X′, Fig. 1. With B′-m, Fig. 7, as radius, and B, Fig. 1, as centre, describe an arc, cutting the diagonal in point C. Draw a line from B through this point and intersect it at b by a perpendicular from X′. Make B-X, Fig. 7, equal to B-b, Fig. 1, and draw the springings to this point. To obtain the bevels and widths of the mould at each springing, lay off the perpendicular distances t and s, Fig. 7, upon the parallels A-B and C, Fig. 1. Upon these lines describe circles equal in diameter to the width of the rail, and tangent to these circles draw parallels to the bevel lines. The semicircles described on these points indicate the width of the mould at the respective springings. These are transferred in the usual manner, as shown in the drawing, Fig. 7.

To find the direction of the elliptic axes, obtain the horizontal trace by transferring the length c-v, Fig. 3, to the face mould at C′-V′. Draw a line through A′-V′, which will be the horizontal trace ; the minor axis of the ellipse is drawn parallel with this line through the centre X^2, and the major axis perpendicular to it.

The length of the minor axis is found as usual from the plan, where it equals the diameter of the circle formed by the rail. The length of the major axis is found automatically by marking the point where the trammel rod crosses the minor axis when its other point lies on the major axis and the end of the rod is at the springing point.

The great width of this mould in no wise indicates the required width of the blank, which is shown in dotted lines, and is ascertained in the manner that has been several times described.

The inside falling mould for Nos. 1 and 2 wreaths is shown in Fig. 8, and the auxiliary plan for determining it in Fig. 7a. The method is fully described at page 53, and does not require repetition.

The thickness required to cut wreaths Nos. 1, 3 and 4 is shown in Figs. 9, 10, 11, and the methods are explained in previous cases. These methods are not applicable to wreath No. 2, as this one is not a true helical curve, hence its thickness must be ascertained by a series of trials. Proceed to enclose the contour of the wreath, as shown by its greatest development, Fig. 8, within a parallelogram composed of the joint lines I-L and J-K as ends, and the chord line I-J and its parallel L-K as sides. At first sight the inexperienced workman might think that, as this development shows the greatest departure from the straight, the perpendicular thickness between I-J and L-K would be sufficient to hold the wreath, but the next step will prove this an error, and incidentally provide a warning against jumping to conclusions. The highest part of the wreath is at P, perpendicularly over point 2′, therefore draw a horizontal projector to Fig. 2, and locate point P′ directly over point 2 thereon. Next draw a line through this point, parallel to L-K, that is to say, at the same pitch as L-K in Fig. 8. Produce the joint lines to the same pitch shown in Fig. 3 to intersect this line, locating points L′ and K′.

Draw I'-J' from the lower end of the joint line parallel to L'-K, and, on measuring the perpendicular distance between these parallels, it will be found to exceed the first by $\frac{3}{8}$ in. Thus far we have obtained the thickness on the curved surfaces; we now require to know if the rectangular surfaces of the plank which are parallel to the tangents will require more. Take the height from the centre of the joint at either end to the surface, as at L' or K', and transfer this to the corresponding joint on the tangent planes, as at L''-K''; draw this line, which of course will be parallel with the tangent and represent the top surface of the plank. Next set off an equal amount below the tangent, as shown by the dotted line I''-J'', and it will be found the thickness is now increased by 1 in. We may, however, by careful marking, obtain the wreath out of the thickness shown by the full line at I''-J''. To do this, the centres, as shown at the face mould, Fig. 4, must be marked down from the face side, the distance shown in Fig. 3 at L'' and K''.

PLATE XXV.

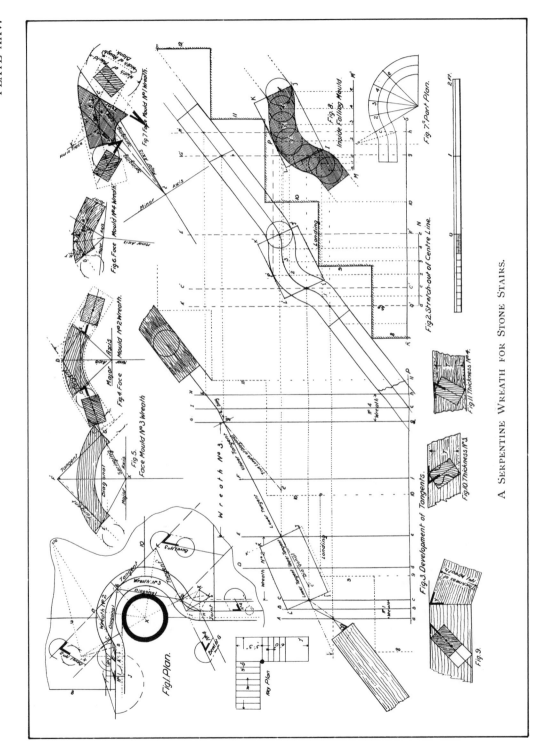

A SERPENTINE WREATH FOR STONE STAIRS.

PLATE XXVI.

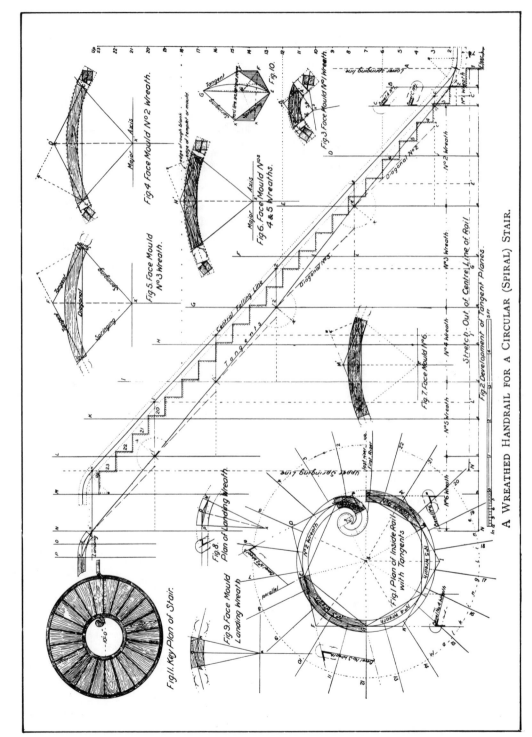

A WREATHED HANDRAIL FOR A CIRCULAR (SPIRAL) STAIR.

CHAPTER XXIV

A WREATHED HANDRAIL TO A CIRCULAR (SPIRAL) STAIR.

(PLATE XXVI.)

Arranging the Joints—What to Avoid—Developing the Tangent Planes—Square to Pitch and Bisection Joints—Face Moulds—Obtaining the Slide Bevels.

A KEY plan of the complete stair is given in Fig. 11, Pl. xxvi., showing the position of the inner and outer rails and their continuation around the landing. The inside rail only is dealt with in this plate, and a plan of this rail and portion of the stairs drawn to larger scale is seen in Fig. 1. Apart from the extent of the rail, which is a true continuous, or "geometrical" one, there is nothing of especial difficulty in rails of this class. As will be seen by their arrangement in plan, the several wreaths are treated as cases of obtuse angles with tangents of Type 2; the simplest form and several examples of these types have been already dealt with. The position and number of the joints is somewhat arbitrary; one must strike a happy medium between having the joints too numerous, which, apart from increasing labour cost, gives the rail a "spotty" appearance, and by having too few, thereby obtaining wreaths of such length that they become weak through the short grain at the middle, or, if this short grain is placed at the ends, it is liable to split off when bolting up. Obviously also, as the length of the wreath increases, so does the thickness of the plank from which it has to be cut. The longest wreath, as arranged in Fig. 1, will be about 3 ft. 3 ins. long, and the shortest about 2 ft. 6 ins. Having decided the number of joints it is intended to use, the next thing is to so arrange them that each pair of tangents shall be of equal length; it does not follow that adjacent pairs will be of equal length—such an arrangement could be made, but there is nothing practically to be gained by this disposition, and to do so would introduce an element of difficulty with the scroll joint, not an insuperable one, as we have seen in Chapter XXII., but it is foolish to add unnecessary difficulties, merely to gratify a desire for symmetry in a drawing. Draw the joints radially from the centre of the plan curves.

The Developments of the Tangent Planes and the central falling section are superposed in Fig. 2, Pl. xxvi., the point of contact of the two developments being at the lower springing A. The falling line is quite straight from the second step to the landing and forms, when bent around the cylinder, a true helical curve. The tangent heights are located at points a-c, e, g, i, l and n. These are projected to the tangent planes upon the correspondingly lettered lines and the tangent pitches drawn through them. Joints square to the pitch are obtained at a', c', i' and n', and bisection joints at e', g' and l'. The lines drawn at the latter joints show the edge bevels required to make them, which, of course, are reversible, as previously explained.

The Face Moulds (Figs. 3 to 7, Pl. xxvi.) are all clearly set out, and their construction will be quite familiar by this time to the reader. The sketch of the prism containing No. 3 wreath is given in Fig. 10 and shows clearly why the median line joining the intersection of the tangents to the centre of the elliptic curves is of the same length as its plan in Fig. 1.

The Top Landing Wreath is redrawn in plan at Fig. 8, Pl. xxvi., to avoid complication with the scroll, and its face mould is shown in Fig. 9. There is nothing in connection with these that has not been exhaustively dealt with under previous examples, to which the reader is referred if in difficulties. The slide bevels are all obtained between the tangents in the plan, and their respective parallels through the opposite springing centre, and their application to the wreath-pieces is shown in the end sections attached to the respective face moulds. The bevels for the wreath No. 1 can be found in the elevation because the tangents of this wreath are at right angles in plan.

PLATE XXVII.

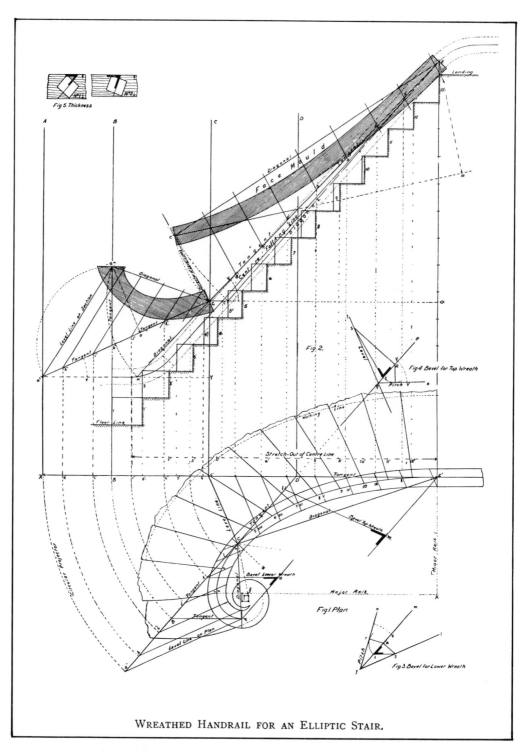

WREATHED HANDRAIL FOR AN ELLIPTIC STAIR.

CHAPTER XXV.

WREATHS FOR HANDRAIL TO AN ELLIPTIC STAIR. MOULDS BY ORDINATE SYSTEM.

(PLATE XXVII.)

Description of Drawings—Limitation of the Tangent System in Obtaining Face Moulds—Position of the Joints—Why Cross-grain is to be Avoided in Polished Rails—Finding the Foci of an Ellipse —Obtaining Face Mould by Level Ordinates—To Obtain the Bevels, Alternative Methods.

THE plan, Fig. 1, Pl. XXVII., shows a flight of stairs having winders starting with a commode curtail, and finishing at a straight landing, thus forming a quarter of an ellipse. So far as the construction of the handrail is concerned, the methods to be described would apply equally to a rail forming a complete ellipse in plan.

The tangent system has been adapted to meet the requirements of this case in ascertaining the pitches of the plank, direction of the joints, and in obtaining the bevels; but for reasons to be explained, the level-ordinate system is used to obtain the shape of the face moulds. Into the disposition of the risers it is not proposed to enter—as such minor details do not affect the principles—further than to say that the walking line and the centre line of the handrail are trammelled upon the conjugate axes shown, and the steps spaced out equally upon these, with, of course, the exception of the commode steps. As the centre line of the handrail is a true elliptic curve and the sides of the rail are drawn parallel with this line for obvious reasons, it follows that these latter curves cannot be truly elliptic, therefore cannot be trammelled, hence the necessity of using ordinates to obtain their shape upon the face moulds, as described in Chapter XIV., page 56. If the reader is not clear as to why elliptic curves cannot be parallel, let him refer to Ills. 16 and 17, page 15, where it will be seen that in the section of a hollow cylinder the internal and external edges form ellipses, having the same axes, but that the width of the section is greatest at the major axis, and least at the minor axis, and the space between the curves varies regularly between these points, whereas, were the two curves parallel, one of them would not be an ellipse. The position of the joints has first to be located. As in previous examples, this is a somewhat arbitrary proceeding, largely depend-ing on circumstances, and, whilst giving reasons for the positions adopted here, it does not follow these will be the best invariably. One has been placed over the landing riser at E to avoid a ramp in the wreath, another is placed at A, the point where the scroll starts level; for the convenience of the handrailer the third joint would be placed midway between these two, but such a proceeding would result in obtaining very cross grain in the lower wreath over the fourth step. Mostly these rails are furnished with an iron core, so this consideration may not trouble us on the score of weakness, but it is impossible to polish a rail having much cross grain in it, to a regular depth of colour or tone; therefore the perfect handrailer avoids these contrasts in grain as much as is possible, so the third joint is made just clear of the fourth riser at C. The joints are drawn normal to the curve, that is to say, perpendicular to a tangent to the curve at the point selected; the method is shown at joint C. Find the two focal points

(83)

on the major axis by describing an arc upon one end of the minor axis as centre, with the length of the minor axis as radius, cutting the major axis in points f-f', which are the foci of the ellipse. Draw lines from C to each foci (these are only partly drawn to indicate their direction) and bisect the angle between them.   The bisector is a normal to the curve.   The tangents are drawn square to the joints, these are lettered A, B, C, D, E, and their diagonals A-C and C-E.   The developments of the centre line section and the tangent planes, Fig. 2, are made similarly to those of circular stairs, and the heights of the tangents and length of the diagonals found in like manner.   All these matters will be familiar to the reader, and we pass on to those that are new.

The face moulds shown hatched in Fig. 2 are for convenience drawn in each instance as turned upon the upper tangent.   They could, of course, and would be generally in the workshop, drawn separately, but that method would not permit of such clear exposition of procedure.   As usual, the triangular section of the imaginary prism is first constructed. Dealing with the face mould of the lower wreath first, with b'', Fig. 2, as centre, and b''-a^2 as radius, describe an arc, intersect this in point a''' by another arc, described on point C with radius equal to the real length of the diagonal.   Join b''-a''' and a'''-c, completing the section with the other tangent b''-c already drawn.   Join points a'-a'', thus obtaining the director of level lines on the section.   Project points a^2 and a''' into the plan.   These projectors already exist, and need merely tracing; they occur at points a'' and A in the plan.   Join A-a'' and we have the horizontal trace of the oblique plane, or as marked—" the director of level lines in plan."   Next divide the plan curves into a convenient number of parts, and draw parallels to A-a'' through them, as at h, i, j, k, l.   Revolve these points into the vertical plane at h', i', j', k', l', and then project them to the tangents in elevation in points h'', i'', etc.   Through these points, draw parallels to a^2-a'', and mark off upon them points equal to the distance from the tangent of the corresponding intersection with the curve lines in the plan, or, if preferred, from the diagonal—either will answer; and draw the curves through the points so found.   The joints are made square with the tangents as usual.   Proceed in like manner with the upper face mould.   All the points are marked, and should be easily followed.

To Obtain the Bevels, take the perpendicular distance of the upper tangent b''-c from its opposite centre of joint, as at a'''-o, and lay this off between the tangent B-C in plan and its parallel A-O, as at k-o, and the slide bevel is disclosed in the angle.   The pitches being alike, one bevel answers for each end.   In like manner, the bevel for the upper wreath is found by laying off the perpendicular distance E-m between C-D and E-m in the plan, as at e-m.   The width of the mould can be found if desired in the usual manner by describing a circle equal in diameter to the width of the rail, drawing parallels to the bevel line touching this circle, and the width shown between them on the line E-m will be the width of the mould at the ends.   This construction is not necessary, as the width is already obtained by the ordinates.   Another method of obtaining the bevels is shown in Figs. 3 and 4; either method results in the same bevels.

Draw the line P-M parallel with, or in continuation of, the tangent.   At point P draw the line P-n at the pitch of the tangent as shown on the development, also draw the line P-l parallel with the level lines in plan.   At any point in P-m as at Q, draw lines Q-s and Q-r perpendicular to P-m and P-n respectively.   Make Q-t equal to Q-r, and join t-s.   The respective bevels are disclosed in the angles as shown.

CHAPTER XXVI.

THE FORMATION OF SCROLLS AND OTHER TERMINALS TO HANDRAILS.

(PLATES XXVIII., XXIX., XXX.)

Types of Terminals—Scrolls, Description of—Unpractical Advice—Requirements in Scrolls—Selection —Examples—A Large Terminal Cap—A Level Scroll, Method of Describing—Scrolls of Two or More Convolutions—Photograph of Scroll—To Describe a Scroll of any Given Width—To Describe a Small Scroll for a Small Rail—To Describe a Large Open Scroll for a Narrow Rail— Spacing of Grouped Balusters—A Small Open Scroll for a Large Rail—To Project an Elevation—Vertical Scrolls, where used, their Advantages—A Quoit Terminal—The Carved Volute —The Monkey Tail and Fist Terminals—The Turn-in—Preparing the Mould, Example of Bevel-cut Method.

MITRE caps and newel caps, which form the usual terminals to the rails of newel stairs, are dealt with in Chapter I. ; in this chapter the various terminals appropriate to geometrical or continuous handrails are considered. The commonest form of terminal to stairs of this class is the scroll in which the handrail is curved around quickly by a series of convolutions into an " eye " which is in effect the cap to the newel or, as is frequently the alternative, a group of balusters. A scroll may consist of one or more convolutions and its boundaries, that is, the sides of the rail approximate to spiral curves in plan, but the sides of the rail or the two contiguous curves are concentric, so that the rail remains of the same width throughout. Where, however, the two curves forming the sides of the rail run into each other, as they eventually do, the moulding hitherto parallel with the sides is gradually diminished in width and depth until it reaches the surface of the eye or cap. As it is, the two opposite sides of the rail which thus come together, the moulding is worked up into a solid mitre, which in plan forms the termination of the scroll. It is frequently advised in books that scrolls are best described, i.e. set out by freehand. Doubtless as regards their appearance in a drawing this is correct, but practically the advice is quite wrong, because curves that are not described geometrically cannot be reproduced accurately by any of the processes used by handrailers. They could, of course, be reproduced by carving, but the cost would be out of all proportion to the result. Moreover, the alleged " cripples " discernible in curves described geometrically at once disappear when the edges of the scroll are moulded, therefore this objection has no weight. Attention must be given, however, not only to the size of the scroll, i.e. its width, but to its inclination or pitch, and the several methods of setting out scrolls described herein are not merely alternatives introduced for the purpose of amplifying the book, but are necessary to meet the various requirements of pitch, space for the scroll step, width of the rail, and the section of moulding. The selection of method must be left to the reader's judgment ; too much space would be occupied in any attempt to specify the " best " in conditions that must necessarily be hypothetical, but a few guiding remarks are offered in each case.

Figs. 1 and 2, Pl. xxx., illustrate the terminal cap for a large handrail to a stair of Renaissance design, and would be appropriate in a stone or marble staircase. The cap is first prepared (turned) as a complete circular disc, then the handrail shank, shown in dotted lines, cut into it with a butt joint, the members of the moulding on the cap that rise above the bottom of the rail are scribed to fit the latter. The drawing of this terminal will prove an easier matter than its working.

The Level Scroll shown in elevation, Fig. 3, Pl. xxx., and in plan in full lines, Fig. 5, is suitable for the termination of a level landing rail; the scroll in this instance having one complete convolution. This method of construction is based on the width of the rail, the only other factor under control is the number of convolutions.

To Describe a Scroll when the width of the rail and number of convolutions are given. (a) With one convolution. Draw the springing line at O perpendicular to the rail. Divide the width of rail into four equal parts and set off eleven of these parts upon the springing line. Upon points 6-7 construct a square, as at a-b. The first quadrant of the scroll is described upon point 6, as centre, with radius 6-O. Draw the perpendicular 6-A; with point a as centre and length a-A as radius, describe the second quadrant to B. Draw B-a perpendicular to a-A. With point b as centre, radius B-b, describe the third quadrant to C. With point 7 as centre and C-7 as radius, describe the fourth quadrant, completing the scroll which intersects the outside of the rail at the springing. The line continued from this point into the eye or flat disc, surmounting the newel, is the mitre line between the two moulded edges, and is generally drawn freehand, because it is not a line worked to in practice, though useful as indicating the appearance of the cap. The mitre line really locates itself during the carving of the scroll, as the moulding is worked around, the railer using " drop-on templets " to ascertain if the cutting, as shown by the section lines, is taken down far enough. The flat or table of this rail is shaded, to facilitate recognition.

(b) To describe scrolls of two or more convolutions (Figs. 4 and 5, Pl. xxx.). To save space the previous drawing is utilised, the supplementary lines being dotted. By the method explained in the preceding paragraph, scrolls of any number of convolutions can be constructed, upon a series of proportional squares to the first square. Refer to Fig. 6 for the enlargement of the central parts of Fig. 5. From point X, midway between centres 6 and 7 on the springing line, draw lines through centres a and b, and produce them indefinitely. Make a-e equal to a-x and b-d equal b-x. Construct the large square f-e-d-c by drawing parallels to the sides of the smaller square, through the aforementioned points. These points, following round in alphabetical order, are the centres of the successive quadrants, and they may finish into the straight rail at points D or E, or, if a further convolution were necessary, by constructing a third square proportional to the second one, and continuing the scroll round to F.

Fig. 4, Pl. xxx., is the front elevation of the scroll shown at E, Fig. 5, running into the level at point C by means of two slightly differing pitches not shown. A scroll of this type of pitch is shown in the photograph (Pl. xxviii.) of the Georgian stair in No. 1 Lincolns Inn Fields, London, and is not so graceful in appearance as that at Fig. 4, Pl. xxx., where the pitch is continuous throughout the convolutions.

To Describe a Scroll of any given width (Fig. 7, Pl. xxx.).—This method is especially suitable for large scrolls to rails of heavy section. In the drawing, the rail section is 4 ins. × 3 ins., and the width of the scroll 22 ins., having one and three-quarter convolutions. Draw the springing line A-11 in suitable position in relation to the curtail step. Set off upon the desired width, as 22 ins.; divide this equally into eleven parts. From the sixth point as centre, with radius 6-A, describe the first quadrant to B. Draw the perpendicular B-6, and on it from B set off the length B-2, equal to five divisions of the springing. Point 2 is the centre of the second quadrant continued to C. We have next to find corresponding proportionals for the successive radii, and this is most readily done by triangular projection, as shown in the diagram on the left hand. Draw the line a-x parallel and equal to A-6. Make x-b equal to the second radius B-2. Draw X-M at any convenient angle with x-a. With x as centre,

PLATE XXVIII.

No. 1 Lincoln's Inn Fields.

PLATE XXIX.

THE HOME FOR AGED JEWS, STEPNEY GREEN, LONDON, E.

describe the arc b-1, draw the straight line 1-a and the line b-2 parallel with it. From centre x describe the arc 2-C. Then X-C is the third proportional to be set off on the line C-3, Fig. 7, as radius for the third quadrant. In like manner the radii 4-D, 5-E, 6-F, 7-G are found. There are no mitres in this scroll, the convolutions of the inner and outer spiral are continued until they coalesce at point H, and the members of the moulding are kept parallel throughout, as shown by the several sections on the quadrants taken on radials from each centre, and the mouldings are continued normally until they die into the edges of the disc. The eye, in this instance, is a complete circle struck from the centre of the smallest square, and may finish flat as shown, or be worked into a patera if preferred. The scroll can be extended by adding quadrants as desired by drawing further arcs, as indicated in dotted lines at a-m, and, by means of parallels to 1-a, obtaining the increased proportionals upon x-a.

To Describe a Small Scroll for a Small Rail (Figs. 8 and 9, Pl. xxx.).—This is a very simple method, yielding a good shaped scroll, but is suitable only for comparatively narrow rails with small central newel. The dotted circle in Fig. 8 indicates the position of the newel, and the dotted outlines the riser of the curtail step. Draw the springing line perpendicular to the handrail, set off thereon the required width of the scroll, which in the example is 9 ins., divide this width into seven equal parts. Make the radius of the first quadrant equal four parts. The second radius B-a equals three-quarters of the first radius, and successive radii equal three-quarters of the preceding radius, as indicated by the division points upon the enlarged diagram, Fig. 9.

To Describe a Large Open Scroll for a Narrow Rail (Figs. 10, 11, 12, Pl. xxx.).—The method used in this case results in a close approximation to a true spiral in plan, and if used in conjunction with a continuous falling line produces a very graceful scroll, as indicated in the projection, Fig. 11, but shown much more effectively in the photograph of the charming old stair to a house at Stepney Green (Pl. xxix.). The rail in this example is taken at 3 ins. wide, and the scroll measures 18 ins. over all, yielding a large cap 7 ins. in diameter to accommodate a group of balusters. If it were desired to reduce the size of the cap, it would be necessary by this method to reduce also the over-all width of the scroll; for example, if the latter is made 16 ins. in place of 18 ins., the resulting cap will be only $4\frac{1}{4}$ ins. diameter, with the same width of rail. Draw the springing line A, set off the required width thereon, and divide this into ten equal parts. Set off one of these parts upon the line 10-C, drawn at right angles to the springing line. Join points C, A and describe a semicircle tangent to this line upon point 5 as a centre. At point a, where the semicircle cuts the springing, is located the centre of the first quadrant A-B. Describe the quadrant and draw the perpendiculars a-B. Intersect this line by a perpendicular from C, locating thereon the second centre b_3, complete the quadrant. Next draw a perpendicular to A-C from point B, and through the intersection draw diagonals from the centres a and b, locating upon b-C the third centre c, and upon C-D, drawn perpendicular to b-C, the fourth centre, point d. The remaining centres are all located upon the diagonals, the points being obtained by drawing parallels to the preceding perpendiculars, as indicated by alphabetical lettering of the centres in the enlarged diagram, Fig. 12. Advantage is taken of this enlargement to indicate the spiral nature of the curve, which is continued in successively diminished convolutions until the "pole" or centre is reached. Of course, such reduction is impossible in the scroll proper, because the companion spiral on the outside of the rail will coalesce with it long before the pole is reached.

The proper spacing of grouped balusters, as shown in this drawing, requires considerable judgment to obtain the best effect. No definite rule can be laid down, because the circumstances of size, shape and design of the balusters, most important view-point, lighting, etc., need consideration. It is generally advisable to reduce the spacing by an accelerated gradation as the centre is approached, also to make each baluster in the interior row lie intermediate between those of the outer rows. Where a single row of square balusters is used, as in Figs. 5 and 13, their centre lines should radiate from the centre of the curve in which they lie, and their sides, of course, be parallel with this line.

To Describe a Small Open Scroll for a Large Rail, the position of the newel being given (Fig. 13, Pl. xxx.). Let O be the centre of the newel relative to the straight rail. Divide the distance between this centre and the inside of rail by $5\frac{1}{2}$, or, in other words, into eleven equal parts. Set off the half-part parallel with the rail, and draw the springing line through it perpendicular to the rail; lay off the $5\frac{1}{2}$ parts upon this line, with a half-part beyond as shown, locating point 8. Construct a square upon the side 5-8, and the angles in numerical order are the centres of the successive quadrants; the last quadrant is described upon point 9, half-way between points 5 and 8, that is, upon the centre line of the newel. The cap is described upon the axis of the newel O.

The riser of the curtail step is indicated in dotted lines, the curtailment being made just behind the point of junction of the inner and outer curves of the rail, which correspond to the lines of the tread not shown. This drawing is utilised to indicate the method of obtaining the projections of the rails shown in the previous examples, and the projection in Fig. 14 is of the rail in the square, the better to illustrate the method. All the arrises, however, are found in like manner. Commence by describing a centre line on the scroll, struck from the corresponding centres of the sides; divide this into any convenient number of equal parts as at a, b, c, d, e, and draw lines through these points radiating from the centre of the segment in which the division lies. Make a development of this centre line as in Fig. 15, its position being adjusted to meet the requirements of the proposed elevation, Fig. 14; that is to say, the pitch of the rail over the fliers is ascertained as shown, the height of the scroll cap above the lowest step decided, and the height at the springing and at the level of the cap projected to Fig. 15. A continuous falling line from the springing to point e, where the level of the cap starts, is shown, and the slight easing required at the junction of the two pitches is made. Then the seats of the points a, b, c, d, e are projected to the top and.bottom edges of the development.

Take point C' as an example; a perpendicular on the point cuts the rail edges in points C'' and C'''. Horizontal projectors are drawn from these points and are intersected by vertical projectors from the ends of the radial C in the plan, locating points C^2 and C^3 upon the inside of the rail in elevation, and corresponding points upon the outside edges, as indicated by the dots thereon. The remaining points are located in like manner, and the curves of the rail drawn through them. Fig. 15 supplies the necessary data in connection with the development of tangents to obtain the face moulds, as explained elsewhere.

Vertical Scrolls and Terminals of various designs are shown in Figs. 16 to 23, Pl. xxx. These terminals are chiefly used in public stairways, railway stations, public halls and the like, where space cannot be found for scroll steps, and where newel posts would be a source of danger to the traffic. The vertical scroll occupies no ground space, and the abrupt change in the falling line affords a useful warning to the passenger that he has arrived at the bottom step. The upturned " scroll " or quoit terminal, Figs. 20 and 21, is. an example of a simple and effective check of this nature, suitable for a wall rail, as is also the design shown in Figs. 16 and 17.

The carved volute shown in Figs. 18 and 19 is more suitable for an outside rail. The end baluster, against which the volute rests, is generally of cast-iron, and may be of similar pattern to the wood balusters, or be of a special design; the latter perhaps is the more appropriate. The method of fixing the foot of an iron baluster is shown in Fig. 9, Pl. xx. (also block in text, Vol. I., p. 72).

Fig. 24 is an enlargement of the scheme of centres used in describing the scrolls, Figs.

PLATE XXX.

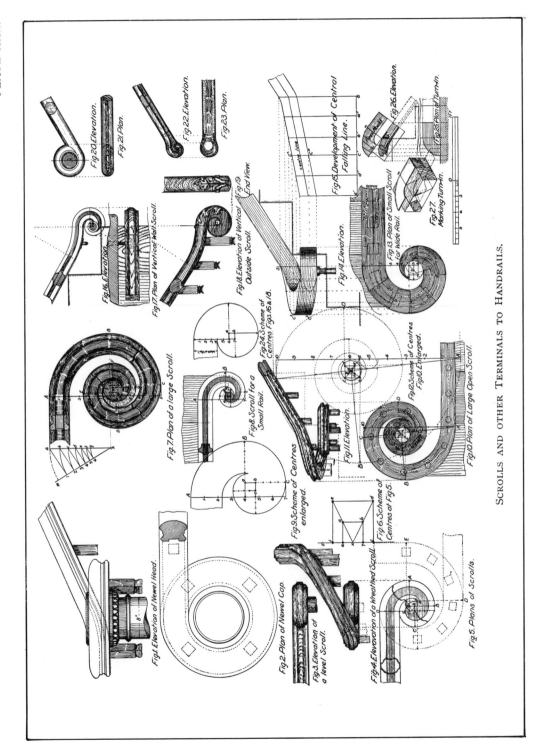

Fig.20.Elevation.

Fig.21.Plan.

Fig.22.Elevation.

Fig.23.Plan.

Fig.19. End View.

Fig.18.Elevation of Vertical Outside Scroll.

Fig.16.Elevation.

Fig.17.Plan of Vertical Wall.Scroll.

Fig.15.Development of Central Falling Line.

Fig.26.Elevation.

Fig.25.Plan of Turn-In.

Fig.27. Marking Turn-In.

Fig.13.Plan of Small Scroll for Wide Rail.

Fig.14.Elevation.

Fig.7.Plan of a large Scroll.

Fig.8b Scroll for a Small Rail.

Fig.24.Scheme of Centres Figs.16 & 18.

Fig.9.Scheme of Centres enlarged.

Fig.11.Elevation.

Fig.8.Scheme of Centres Fig.10 Enlarged.

Fig.10.Plan of Large Open Scroll.

Fig.1.Elevation of Newel Head.

Fig.2.Plan of Newel Cap.

Fig.3.Elevation of a level Scroll.

Fig.4.Elevation of a Wreathed Scroll.

Fig.6.Scheme of Centres at Fig.5.

Fig.5. Plans of Scrolls.

SCROLLS AND OTHER TERMINALS TO HANDRAILS.

16 and 18. The depth of the rail is divided into four equal parts upon the springing line, and three similar parts are added, making the length of the line equal to seven parts. A square is constructed upon the side 6-7 and its angles 6-*a*-*b*-7 provide the successive centres. The design shown in Figs. 22 and 23 may be produced with the width of the rail constant around the scroll, in which form it is known as a monkey-tail terminal, or whatever section is used for the rail, the end may be swelled out as in Fig. 23. This form is known as the " hand " or " fist " terminal.

The Turn-in, Figs. 25 to 27, Pl. xxx., is a terminal to the wall rail of a flight of steps finishing at a landing. It may, of course, be at either end of the rail, but in Fig. 25 it is shown at the top end; if used at the bottom the wreath would be simply turned over. These terminals are, in fact, simple quarter-turn wreaths, as described at page 24, but requiring a turn-in or level end for fixing in the wall, they are more conveniently set out as shown here than by the tangent system. The dotted line rectangle in Fig. 25 indicates the width of block required, and the fine line rectangle in Fig. 26 its thickness and length. The face mould, Fig. 26, is found by means of level ordinates, as described at pages 51 and 56, and the method will readily be followed here upon inspection of the projectors. Fig. 27 is an isometric sketch showing the method of marking the block by sliding the mould. The face mould is shown shaded on top, with its joint-end flush with the end of the block, duly squared. The dotted outline underneath indicates the position of the mould when slid back to coincide with the springing line marked across the side by the bevel A, as shown. The lines for bevelling and squaring the turn-in are also shown; the latter of course are not revealed until the blank has been cut out from the block, which in this instance is done by the bevel-cut method.

CHAPTER XXVII.

PRACTICAL DETAILS OF WREATH-MAKING.

(PLATE XXXI.)

Principles—The Evolution of a Wreath Illustrated—Preparing the Moulds—The Face Mould—How Made, Materials—What the Mould must Contain—Falling Moulds, Where Used—Materials—Section Templets, Their Uses, Materials—Setting Out—Marking the Blank, to Line in the Tangents—Marking the Slide Bevels—Rules to Ascertain Right Position—Applying the Mould—Bevelling the Wreath—Fixing the Moulds—Methods of Removing Surplus Wood, Tools—Squaring the Wreath—Boring Bolt Holes, when to Bore for Dowels—Usual Method of Squaring, its Drawbacks, Author's Method—Marking the Falling Lines—Applying the Square—Order of Work—Trying the Joints—Uses of the Well Gauge—Moulding the Wreath—Gauging, Grooving, Sinking—When to Paper-Off—Sliding of Moulds—Rules and Characteristics—Applying Falling Lines.

A FEW remarks upon the applications of moulds and the marking and shaping of wreaths have already been made incidentally in the preceding chapter in connection with certain examples. These may be considered particular cases, requiring some departure from the usual procedure. The instructions given in this chapter may be looked upon as general principles applicable in all ordinary cases, therefore not in conflict with, but supplementary to, the aforesaid remarks.

The Evolution of a Wreath (Figs. 1 to 8, Pl. xxxi.).—Preparing moulds—The face mould. This templet, used singly or in duplicate, as the difficulty of working the wreath requires, is usually cut from a piece of thin dry pine, free from knots and shakes ; ⅛ in. thick is ample. In cases where there are several wreaths to be made to the same templet, it is preferable to cut the mould from sheet zinc. The curves may be trammelled directly on the templet or be traced from the rod and the tracing then glued or pasted on the stuff. The tangents and springing lines must be drawn on both sides, and be made to coincide exactly. In the method of marking advocated in this book, the " diagonal " line is not needed either on the templet or the wreath, although indispensable on the drawing or rod. The ends of all lines should be squared across the edges and two lozenge holes stabbed through the mould with a scribing gouge directly on the tangents, as shown at No. 4, for the purpose of observing the tangent line underneath when adjusting the mould upon the blank.

Falling Moulds, in the strict sense of the term, are used only where the curves of the wreath are bent out of a true falling line, that is to say, when a ramp or a knee is worked in the wreath itself. Several instances are shown in the examples where they would be required, also instructions given to obtain their shape, and all that need be said here is that they should be prepared from either stout, tough veneer that will bend without splitting, or of tough cardboard or sheet zinc.

Section Templets are used at the joints for the purpose of outlining the moulding, also to locate the centres of the dowel and bolt holes. They are best made of zinc, but are frequently made of stout cartridge paper, which, after cutting to shape, is brushed over with thin glue or gold size to add to its stiffness. The templet must, of course, be the exact size and shape of the required moulding, and is best set out by marking a centre line across both

(90)

PLATE XXXI.

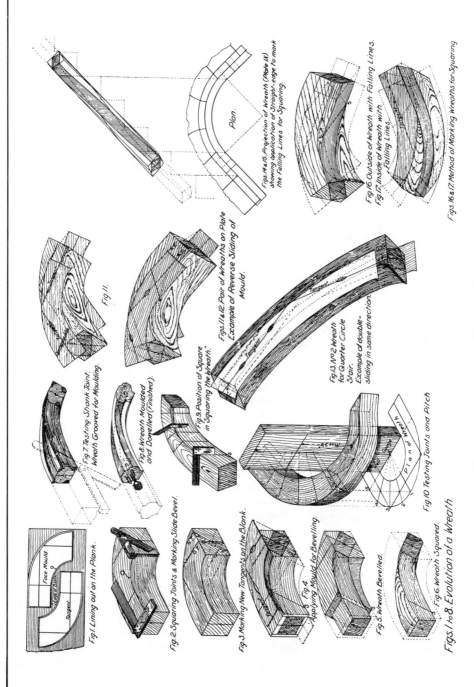

Fig.1. Liming out on the Plank.

Fig.2. Squaring Joints & Marking Slide Bevel.

Fig.3. Marking New Tangents on the Blank.

Fig.4. Applying Mould for Bevelling.

Fig.5. Wreath Bevelled.

Fig.6. Wreath Squared.

Figs.1 to 8. Evolution of a Wreath.

Fig.7. Testing Shank Joint. Wreath Grooved for Moulding.

Fig.8. Wreath Moulded and Dovetiled (Finished).

Fig.9. Position of Square in Squaring the Wreath.

Fig.10 Testing Joints and Pitch

Fig.11.

Figs.11 & 12. Pair of Wreaths on Plate Example of Reverse Sliding of Mould.

Fig.13. Nº2 Wreath for Quarter Circle Stair. Example of double-sliding in same direction.

Plan.

Figs.14 & 15. Projection of Wreath (Plate IX) showing application of Straight-edge to mark the Falling Lines for Squaring.

Fig.16. Outside of Wreath with Falling Lines.

Fig.17. Inside of Wreath with Falling Lines.

Figs.16 & 17. Method of Marking Wreaths for Squaring

PRACTICAL DETAILS OF WREATH MAKING.

sides, taking a tracing of half the section with a centre line drawn on. Make the centre line coincide with that on the templet and mark the half outline, then turn over and mark the other half, which ensures both being alike; this direction applies naturally to symmetrical mouldings only. In the exact centre of the templet pierce a pin hole, also two or more pin holes as required for the centres of dowels. Mark a " face " line on the templet, and in applying to the joints take care to reverse the templet on the opposite joints, otherwise the dowel holes may not coincide, prick the centres through with a needle-point bradawl, and adjust the twist bits to them. As a general rule, the section templet is applied with its centre line directly upon the " bevel " line of the joint, and its centre hole exactly in the middle of the thickness of the stuff. There are exceptions to this in wreaths with " displaced " centres. In machine shops the straight rails are frequently machined first and the handrailer is expected to make his wreaths to fit this section, consequently a thin section of the rail is sometimes used as a section templet, but the dowel centres cannot be accurately marked with these, wherefore a square section templet is used in addition, for the latter purpose.

Marking the Blank.—The " blank " is the wreath-piece cut roughly to the shape of the mould, and ceases to be a " blank " when it is bevelled. One is shown in the sketch, Fig. 2, Pl. XXXI. Fig. I shows the method of lining out a pair of blanks on the plank. The face mould is reversed in the operation and the blanks are lined out about ⅛ in. full all round. They are then cut out square to the plank, faced-up and planed to a thickness next the tangents and springings drawn upon both sides, as in the view No. 2. The best method of lining out the tangents is to prick them off at each end of the·mould upon the face side, then to square the joints, as shown at the shank end of No. 2, making them square to the tangent in one direction, and square to the face in the other. When this is done, square the ends of the tangents across the joints, tack a straight-edge along the line, turn the blank over and apply another straight-edge to the squared over end of the tangent and take it out of winding with the first straight-edge, then line in the tangent on this side. The next operation is the marking of the slide bevel across the joint, to obtain new positions for the tangents. Run a gauge from the face across the middle line at half the thickness of the stuff, thus obtaining the centre of the wreath-piece at the joints. Draw the slide bevel through this point, as shown in No. 2. The direction of the bevel is shown in most of the preceding examples, but generally the direction can be decided by holding the blank up in approximately the position it will occupy when finished, and the bevel line then should be upright. If it lies horizontal, the bevel has been applied on the wrong side of the centre line. Another fairly general rule is that in the case of wreaths having tangents at right angles in plan, and with one pitch only, will require the mould to slide upwards in bottom wreaths, and to slide downwards in top wreaths. Wreaths having tangents of two pitches will require their moulds to slide upwards and outwards in bottom wreaths, and upwards and inwards upon top wreaths, that is to say, they move in opposite directions on each side of the cylinder. Although this may not be clear by the wording the significance of the direction will become apparent, when the workman has the wreath in hand. The above instructions refer to the *face* side of the wreath : the operation will, of course, be reversed upon the under side. Having marked the bevel line, as shown in sketch No. 3, scratch over the original tangents marked O.T. in the figure, and draw new tangents on each side of the blank, parallel with them, through the intersection of the bevel-line and the faces of the stuff as shown at N.T. As the pair of wreaths illustrated have only one tangent pitched, the other one being level, no bevel appears upon the shank joint, and the mould merely slides along the original tangent at this end.

The position of the mould when applied for marking the blank for bevelling is illustrated in No. 4. The tangent lines on the mould are made to lie exactly over the tangent lines on the blank, and the advantage of the sight holes for locating these will be apparent.

Mark the outline of the moulds so far as possible on each side, also prick in the ends of the springing line. This line, marked S-S in the sketch, is only shown there to make clear its position, which must be located; it need not be drawn on the wreath until the latter has been bevelled, but it is an important line, as we shall see presently. The square section of the wreath-piece is shown hatched upon each joint; this is rarely done in the workshop, but is added here for the sake of clearness. The dotted line underneath the blank in No. 4 indicates the position of the mould on that side, and the dotted projectors from the ends of the top mould to the corresponding ends of the bottom mould will be seen to be parallel to the springing line S-S.

Bevelling the Wreath.—Sketch No. 5, Pl. xxxi., illustrates the wreath after bevelling, and we may now describe the steps taken to reach this stage. Assuming one mould only to be used (beginners will find it advantageous to use two, one on each side of the blank), tack the mould in the position shown by the dotted lines in No. 4, of course driving the pins or screws into the waste wood and fix the wreath in the bench screw, hollow side up— always work the outside of the wreath first as being the more important side. Next cut away the surplus wood lying between the curved line marked on the top side and the edge of the mould upon the bottom, driving the gouge or chisel across in the direction of the springing line S-S.

Expert handrailers would cut this out with a frame saw and finish off with a flat round, but the beginner usually prefers chipping the core away with a gouge, and finishing with a spokeshave. The important thing to do is to make the tools work parallel with the springing and bevel line on the joint throughout, so that when the wreath is pitched up this side becomes quite vertical, and if placed against a cylinder of the diameter of the well, would fit its surface closely.

The inside, that is the convex side of the wreath, is finished similarly, but in this instance the mould must be tacked upon the top side of the piece to provide the missing edge required as a guide for the tools. Should duplicate moulds be used, their edges would need bevelling off to the underside, where they come in the way of the tool or straight-edge. The shank surfaces can be gauged from the face of the blank and cut away, as shown, up to the springing line. The dotted line at the springing in No. 5 indicates the original line before the stuff was removed; the bottom of the cut, which is the true springing line, is drawn full.

The next step is **the Squaring of the Wreath.** The full lines in the sketch, No. 6, Pl. xxxi., show the shape of the wreath after squaring; the dotted lines indicate the portions to be removed, and as it appears after bevelling. Before commencing operations, it will be best to bore the holes for the bolts, because the tangent lines can be used as a guide to their direction. If the bolt holes are not made exactly square with the joint in each direction it is almost impossible to pull up the joint tightly all around. It is not advisable to bore or mark the dowel holes at this stage, because once these are bored no alteration can be made in the joint, and, although theoretically no alteration should be needed, there are times when the most skillful will need to correct their work, and nothing is lost by the delay.

The usual process of squaring the wreath is shown in the sketch, Fig. 9, and consists in cutting the surplus wood away gradually with the chisel or saw, until a try-square held in the various positions indicated by the lines drawn on the wreath will sit squarely across the top and bottom surfaces, and its stock, held vertical, that is parallel with the springing line, will fit tightly against the outside surface. Obviously this method has its dangers, especially in the hands of the inexperienced. Practically there is no guide to the falling line, and this must be obtained with more or less accuracy by the negative process of " not taking off too much." The method now to be described and practised by the author gives entirely satisfactory results, and in much less time than occupied in the process of " squaring." Procure a very pliable straight-edge about 12 ins. to 18 ins. long and 2 ins. wide—the one used by the author is made of xylonite, a material very similar to celluloid, but more pliable and less inflammable than the latter. Failing this, a thin steel band will answer the purpose. Having bevelled the sides of the wreath, mark the corners of the required rectangle on the sides at the joints, carrying the shank lines parallel to the top surface up to the springing. Now fix the wreath in the bench screw with the straight-edge held correctly, say to the top line at the springing, and nip it in the screw whilst the other end is bent round closely to the surface and adjusted to the angle at the opposite joint. The process is shown in Figs. 16 and 17, the shaded bands representing the straight-edge bent respectively around the outside and inside of a wreath. The straight-edge must be made to bed firmly to the surface all round ; when this is secured and the two ends adjusted at the proper points, pencil-line the edge from end to end, and an absolutely correct falling line will be obtained. Repeat the procedure at each edge, and the excess stuff may then be cut away to the lines with freedom and celerity. It will, however, still be necessary to apply the square across the wreath in a radial direction to obtain a correct surface. The reason for this will be realised by referring to the sketch, Fig. 10. A further purpose of this drawing will be explained presently ; for the moment consider the line A as the axis of the imaginary cylinder, of which the outer surface of the wreath forms a part ; the lines 1, 2, 3, 4, 5 in the plan radiate from the centre at A ; if these lines are considered as plans of vertical sections of the rail above them, these sections will be rectangular, that is to say, the top and bottom surfaces will be square with the sides. The direction of these section lines on the top surface or back of the wreath are continued to the axis by dotted lines, and it will be observed they fall in regular steps thereon. Thus, to obtain " square " sections to the wreath the try-square must be applied in radial directions as indicated. Returning to the description of the order of work, when one surface has been squared—usually the under one—gauge the other from it to ensure parallelism in the moulding members. Next try the joints for correctness of pitch. The shank joint is tried, as indicated in No. 7. The straight rail is squared off and bolted to the wreath and the slide bevel applied as shown at the side. Usually a long wood bevel is necessary ; when the joint is correct the blade should lie exactly along the springing line S-S and the sides of the shank line accurately with the sides of the straight rail. Assuming this joint correct, separate and bore for dowels, rebolt with the dowels in, and mark the outline of the moulding on the joint. Some railers prefer to cut in the shape for about $\frac{1}{4}$ in. up the shank. Unbolt and try the centre joint. For this purpose a " well gauge," as shown in sketch, Fig. 10, should be used. This is made of a length of board from 1 in. to 2 ins. thick, according to the length of shanks, gauged to the exact width between the outsides of the wreath in plan. For greater clarity the gauge is drawn standing on the well rod, but of course this position is not imperative ; mostly it is fixed at the bench end. Gauge a central line A through the face and square across at a convenient height two lines representing the " rise of the wreath." This height is specified on each example on Pls. VI., VIII., XII., and XVII. ; in the present case it is taken as $9\frac{1}{2}$ ins. Having bolted the wreaths together, slip them on the gauge as drawn, adjusting the centre line of the shanks at the springings to the aforesaid squared over lines. If the joint is correct, these points will coincide and the sides of the shank will fit neatly to the edges of the gauge ; if not, then correction of the joint as required is necessary. If the moulds have been set out correctly, this correction seldom requires more than a shaving at one or other side, but with the use of the gauge it is impossible to get the pitch wrong. It is perhaps superfluous to mention that if correction is necessary it will be advisable to fix the wreath not operated on with a light bench cramp, or large handscrew, and a couple of fillets bradded to the edges of the gauge under the rail to the correct pitch facilitates the trying up. The joint being passed satisfactorily, dowel and mark the wreath for moulding as in No. 7, where the white sections represent the moulding templet.

Moulding the Wreath.—The lines of the members should be pencil-gauged all round, then grooves and sinkings made in suitable positions, as shown in Fig. 7, Pl. XXXI. Great care must be taken with these sinkings, as no correction of them is possible without alteration of the moulding section. The grooves are made with the quirk router illustrated on Pl. XLIII., Figs. 10, 11, page 94, Vol. I. Where possible a chamfer, as indicated at the left-hand of the figure, should be made, just touching the moulding. Finish up with thumb planes, as illustrated on Pl. XLIII., Figs. 13-18, Vol. I. When finished, the wreath will appear as in Fig. 8. It should not be papered up until bolted up completely to the rails. For further instructions on moulding refer to Chapter I.

The Sliding of Moulds to obtain the plan curves of wreaths has been incidentally referred to in a preceding paragraph dealing with application of the bevel. To those remarks may be added that there are three varieties, or types of sliding, the first—illustrated in Fig. 4, Pl. XXXI.—occurs when one only of the tangents are inclined; the mould therefore in this type slides in one direction only, the other tangent is kept in line with the tangent on the wreath. In the second type, the mould slides in two directions, and these directions are reversed on the opposite wreaths. The process is illustrated in Figs. 11 and 12, which are views of the pair of wreaths shown on Pl. XII., and the duplicate moulds are drawn in their relative positions for bevelling the wreath. In the third type, exemplified in the quarter-circle stair, Pl. XV., the mould slides in two similar directions, that is to say, the bevel is applied across the joints at each end in the same direction. The latter peculiarity is due to the relatively small portion of a circle covered by the wreath-piece.

Figs. 15 and 16 are the plan and elevation of the wreath shown on Pl. XIV., illustrating the method previously described of applying a pliable straight-edge to the bevelled wreath to obtain the correct falling lines. The shaded portion represents the straight-edge, which in this instance is assumed to be reduced to the required width that both edges may be marked at once. Figs. 16 and 17, Pl. XXXI., are further illustrations of the wreaths in Figs. 11 and 12, showing application of moulds and straight-edge which is described in an earlier paragraph.

CHAPTER XXVIII.

THE CYLINDER METHOD OF MAKING WREATHS.

(PLATE XXXII.)

Reasons for Introducing the Method—Period of its Use—Chief Objections—Advantages of the Method—Early Method of Building up the Wreath-piece—Forms of Joint that may be Used—Making the Cylinder—Setting Out the Rail thereon—Obtaining the Thickness of Plank—Scribing the Wreath—Bevelling—The Compass Jack Plane—The Grasshopper Gauge—Suggested Use of a Falling Mould—Marking the Joints.

A CLOSE search through a large number of books relating to the subject of stair construction, published since 1700, has failed to reveal any but a passing reference to the cylinder method of handrailing, and it would seem appropriate in a work in which the whole subject has been attempted to place on record some illustration and explanation of this interesting forerunner of the tangent or " geometrical " system of handrailing, which was falling into disuse when the author entered the trade over half a century ago.   Although, as then practised, a somewhat tedious and comparatively expensive method of producing wreaths, that is not now likely to replace the more scientific system advocated herein, it must be confessed that some of the abortions that nowadays pass for handrail wreaths would never have been possible had the cylinder been used, for with the aid of this apparatus it is practically impossible to make a rail that does not follow the lines of the stair.   The chief objection to the method is the necessity of using excessively thick plank, because, unless he starts to make drawings and developments to demonstrate suitable pitches, the user of this method must be content to pitch his plank in one direction only, consequently the plank must be thick enough not only to cover all the bends of the wreath, but to include in addition sufficient for the winding or twist that occurs therein, and, if the aforesaid drawings are made, they might just as well be completed as herein described, when he has at once the data for the tangent system which, as has been pointed out already, is simply a scientific method of ascertaining the " pitch of the plank."

There are two advantages possessed by this system not available in any other ; first, the wreath can, and generally was, made in one piece, that is to say, there were no joints inside the springings.   Of course, with a half-turn wreath, this involves enormous thickness of plank, but it will be found in the majority of cases of rails executed before 1820 that pieces were glued on the face of the plank as it lay on the cylinder, sufficient in thickness to cover the rises and drops in the curves, and, where possible, the plank surface was kept to the highest point at top, so that the added pieces were underneath and require looking for to find them ; possibly it was to assist this device that about that period the sections of the rails took on the ogee shape, with the width much reduced at the underside, a type of moulding which has prevailed more or less until the present time.   Previous to this, rails were more nearly rectangular in section.   The second advantage is, that practically any form of joint can be used ; in the earliest examples a mortise and tenon sometimes occurred, but chiefly the splice or vertical joint was used, so that the parts could be fastened together with wood screws.   About 1850 the handrail-bolt was invented, and thereafter joints became square or butt.   The first thing done by the cylinder handrailer was to lay down a plan of the winders and rail full-

(95)

size, as shown in Fig. 1, Pl. XXXII., then to make a " cylinder " or drum, as also shown there, to fit the outside of the rail.   The length of the cylinder depends on the number of steps or rises in the well, and is shown by the dotted outline in Fig. 2, which, by the by, is a suggestion of the author's, and will be referred to presently.   Having built the cylinder, which is shown complete in the view at Fig. 3, the usual practice was to stand it up end on the rod or bench to square up the risers off their plans, also the springing lines, then by aid of the pitch-board, which was usually made of zinc, so that it might be bent around, the treads were lined in as shown on Fig. 3.   The nosing line was then drawn in by aid of a thin strip, bent around the cylinder, and sundry easings made freehand, with a section of the rail drawn likewise above it, as shown.   This was the only " working drawing " used.   Next, after measuring between parallel straight-edges, laid so as to cover the drawing, the thickness of plank was ascertained and estimate made of the amount required for twist.   The appropriate piece of plank was then fixed against the cylinder, as shown in Figs. 4 and 5, the cylinder itself being screwed to the bench.

The plank, of course, needed several trial pitches to find which covered the bends best ; when this has been found, a rough brace, cut to the pitch, was fixed beneath it, also a screw raked into the cylinder through the waste, then a pair of compasses set to the greatest extent of the edge from the cylinder, was either scribed down, or, what is perhaps easier, a series of

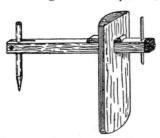

ILL. 25.—GRASSHOPPER GAUGE.

points pricked in with the compasses held in the direction of the dotted lines in Fig. 4, that is to say, at right angles to the edge of the plank (see also Fig. 5).   These points are afterwards joined up into a fair line.   A similar series is marked on the underside, the plank removed, and cut away to the lines, when its appearance will be as in the sketch, Fig. 6.   Nowadays this bevelling would be done by means of a band saw, but in the time referred to it was done with a large two-handed frame saw having a blade 1½ ins. wide. If properly marked and cut, very little cleaning up was required, but also very often correction had to be made with a handrailer's compass plane, a tool now seldom seen.   This was a kind of short Jack-plane with a rounded sole, made to fit the job in hand, and was traversed across the edge until the plank fitted the cylinder closely, when it would lie as shown in the dotted outline in Fig. 4.   Next the plank was gauged to a width by means of the grass-hopper gauge, shown in Ill. 25, and the wreath cut out to this line ; it was then applied to the cylinder in the original position and a pencil run down its face to mark the outline on the cylinder ; any required number of points were then ticked off on the face, also on the cylinder, and the wreath removed, when the distances between the edge line of the wreath and the edges of the rail section taken in the compasses were pricked off on the inside of the wreath, as shown in Fig. 6.   The outline of the rail was then drawn through these points. In the author's opinion, a better method than the foregoing would be, first, to make a stretch-out of the face of the cylinder on a large sheet of paper, as shown in Fig. 2, obtain the desired outline of the rail thereon, and fix this on the cylinder by tacks at the back edges, where it would appear as in Fig. 3.   When the stage was reached for marking the thickness, remove the paper and cut out to the outline of the rail as drawn thereon.

Use this as a falling mould to apply to the concave side of the wreath, and cut out square to the bevelled surface.   The joints are made square to the pitch and perpendicular to the face of the cylinder, marking them on the wreath by means of a set square, which was usually the pitch-board.

The dotted outline drawn in Fig. 3 represents the outer edge of the wreath after squaring and when ready for moulding.

PLATE XXXII.

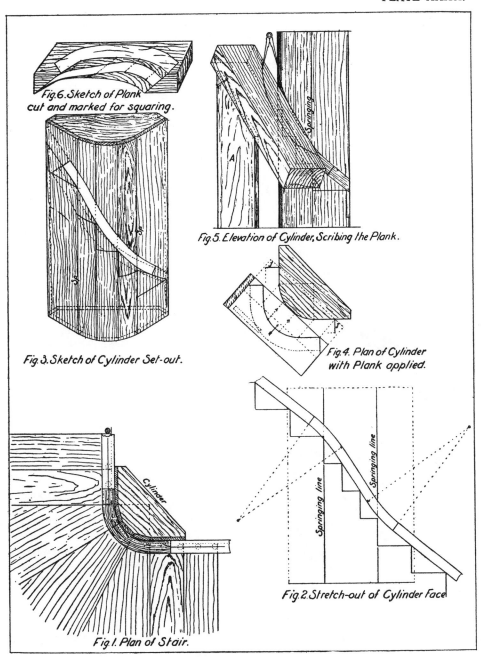

Fig.6. Sketch of Plank cut and marked for squaring.

Fig.3. Sketch of Cylinder Set-out.

Fig.5. Elevation of Cylinder, Scribing the Plank.

Fig.4. Plan of Cylinder with Plank applied.

Fig.2. Stretch-out of Cylinder Face

Fig.1. Plan of Stair.

THE CYLINDER METHOD OF FITTING HANDRAILS.

During the first half of the eighteenth century, the woodworkers of this country had attained a high state of perfection, and considerable ingenuity was displayed in the production of particularly difficult pieces of work.

The designs of this period called for a very high standard of worksmanship.

This was especially noticeable in the execution of many of the elegant staircases of the period, and before the introduction of the tangent system of handrailing numerous methods or "systems" for the production of continuous handrails for geometrical stairs appear to have been attempted.

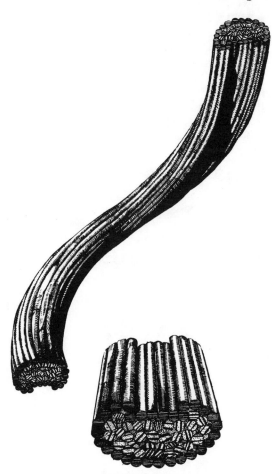

In the old Polytechnic, Regent Street, London, there was an old handrail built of pine wood around an iron core; all jointing was made with the grain of the wood, that is to say there were no "butt" joints. The handrail had obviously been constructed *in situ* over iron balusters reaching from the basement to the top of the rear portion of the building. The pine wood was carefully moulded and then covered with figured Spanish mahogany which was at no point less than $\frac{1}{4}$-inch thick. The joints in the veneer were formed like the teeth of a saw; the "fingers" or teeth being about 3 ins. long and were practically invisible even when the surface had been scraped. This stair was demolished in 1910.

Another remarkable stair-rail [Ill. 26] which came under the writer's notice was one in a house which was constructed some time in the late eighteenth or early nineteenth century and was situated in the Euston Road between Stanhope Street and Tottenham Court Road on the site now occupied by the extensive premises of Messrs. Buck and Ryan, the well-known tool-makers, to whose courtesy we are indebted for the portions of the continuous handrail [Ill. 26] which was originally fitted to a geometrical staircase extending through four floors.

ILL. 26.—A CONTINUOUS HANDRAIL CONSTRUCTED OF LONG RODS OF PITCH PINE.

The rail was constructed of long strips of pitch pine rounded like dowels about $\frac{1}{4}$ in. in diameter; these appear to have been laid side by side direct on to the square balusters and secured by nails about 1 in. in length; successive layers of these dowels or reeds were glued around the first layer, until the whole was about 2 ins. in width by about $1\frac{1}{2}$ ins. in thickness when a final layer of mahogany "reeds" was glued on; the completed rail had a very pleasing appearance as though continuously reeded, as will be clearly seen in the photograph. A portion of this rail may be seen in Geffrye Museum, London, E.

GLOSSARY OF PHRASES AND TERMS USED IN HANDRAILING.

A.

ARRISES.—The sharp or salient edges of the members of a moulding.

B.

BALANCED WINDERS.—*See* "Balanced Steps." Glossary, Vol. I.

BEVELLING A WREATH is the cutting away of its square sides until they become vertical when the wreath is in the true inclined position over its plan.

BEVEL CUT.—A system of preparing wreaths in handrailing in which the sides of the wreath-piece are shaped by vertical cutting when the plank from which they are cut is placed at an inclination parallel with the pitch of the stair.

BLANK, THE, is the first stage of a wreath before it is shaped or set out. *See* Pl. VIII.

BRACKETED HANDRAIL.—A wall rail carried on metal brackets. *See* Figs. 6 and 7, Pl. XXIV., and Figs. 16 and 17, Pl. XXX.

C.

CAP MITREING BLOCK.—An appliance for ensuring the correct centering of a mitre cap to the extremity of a handrail, and a guide to the saw when cutting the mitre. *See* Ill. 11, 12, 13, p. 8.

CYLINDER SYSTEM.—In handrailing is a method of forming, or lining-out wreaths by applying the "blank" directly to the drum, or centre; generally called a "cylinder," although it may be of other shape, and scribing on the upper and lower surfaces of the blank, lines parallel or equidistant from the surface of the "cylinder," so obtaining the true shape of the wreath sides. For full details *see* Chapter XXVIII. and Plate XXXII.

D.

DISPLACEMENT OF CENTRES IN A WREATH.—That is to say, arranging the centre of the bolt on one side of the joint higher or lower than the centre on the other side. This device is used to avoid excessive thickness in the wreath-piece. *See* Fig. 10, Pl. XIII. ; *also* Fig. 9, Pl. XVIII.

E.

EASINGS are the curved junctions made in a handrail to bring parts at different levels into one flowing curve. They are seldom regular or geometrical curves, being mostly produced freehand. *See* Fig. 16, Pl. IV.

EASING BOARD.—A mechanical contrivance for readily drawing curves of regular, or of varying flexure. *See* Ills. 6, 7, 8, 9, p. 7.

F.

FACE MOULD.—A templet for lining out the shape of a wreath-piece upon the " blank " (*which see*).

FALLING COMPASSES.—An instrument formerly used for describing the elliptic curves of the sides of a handrail directly upon the plank.   *See* Ill. 22, p. 20.

FALLING LINE is the contour (usually taken at the centre) which a wreath assumes whilst in "the square" actual or imaginary.   *See* Chapter XI., Fig. 2, Pl. XIII.

FALLING MOULD.—A templet for marking the side curves of the wreath-pieces upon the plank.   *See* Plate XV., Figs. 8, 9, and 10, Chapter XIII., p. 53.

G.

GRASSHOPPER OR HANDRAIL GAUGE.—A tool which enables lines to be marked on the offside of the work, the pointer, slider and scriber being adjustable for width and depth.   Particularly to hand-railing, the grasshopper is used in wreaths for marking the depth of sinkings in the moulding that are much below the crown or back of the rail.   *See* Ill. 25, p. 96.

K.

KNEES.—A knee is primarily a vertical abrupt bend in a handrail whose purpose is to convert the inclined pitch of the rail over the step into a level one where it enters a newel post.   *See* Figs. 1 and 9, Pl. IV.   When a joint is made in a knee it is generally a mitre, and if worked in the solid the mitre is also solid.   By an extension the term is also applied to a curved easing (*see* D and J, Figs. 12 and 14, Pl. IV.), this, however, is not strictly correct.   See also amplified description, p. 2, Chapter I.

KNEELINGS are the reverse of knees, that is to say, are concave on the upper side and are made at the lower ends of handrails.   *See* Figs. 3 and 7, Pl. IV.

L.

LEVEL-ORDINATE SYSTEM, THE, is one in which the true shape of a face mould is found by locating on the plan sundry points which are projected perpendicularly to the plane of inclination, and the distance of the several points from an arbitrary line made to correspond with the like points in the plan, through the intersections ; the curves of the mould are traced.   *See* Fig. 6, Pl. XVI., Chapter XIV.

M.

MITRE CAP.—A mitre cap is a flat circular terminal, connected to the handrail by a mitred joint at the top of a newel post.

MONKEY TAIL.—A handrail terminal formed by carving the back portion of a handrail moulding into a vertical scroll.   *See* Fig. 22, Pl. XXX.

P.

PROFILE BOX.—A square ended box templet, the inside of which is shaped to fit a moulded rail or similar object for the purpose of marking shoulders and straight lines on a curved surface.   *See* p. 5, Chapter I.

Q.

QUOIT TERMINAL.—A vertical disc-like finish to a handrail.   *See* Fig. 20, Pl. XXX.

R.

RAMP, THE, is an extensive easing in a handrail, connecting a horizontal part to an inclined part.   *See* Figs. 9 and 10, Pl. IV.   Ramps are usually made in the solid, but in large rails may be built in several pieces.   *See* Figs. 1 to 9, Pl. V.

S.

SCRIBING THE PLANK.—Old method of marking wreaths by application to a solid cylinder. *See* Fig. 5, Pl. XXXII.

SCROLL.—The terminal of a handrail worked into a spiral curve. *See* Pl. XXX.

SHANK, THE, of a wreath is a short length of straight moulding worked at the end of the curved portion of a wreath to correspond in section and direction with the straight rail, its purpose being to receive the handrail bolt perpendicularly to the joint.

SHANK JOINT is the joint between the shank of a wreath and the straight part of a rail.

SPLICE JOINTS.—In handrails are of two classes : (*a*) the commoner, also known as a bevel joint, is a plumb joint when the rail is inclined at the same pitch as the stairs (*see* cylinder method P). (*b*) This joint, also called "dog's tooth" and "zig-zag," is formed by cutting one end of the jointed piece into a series of semi-lozenge shaped projections, their points running parallel with the sides of the rail. The opposite piece is notched in reverse, and when the two are brought together and drawn up by a screw bolt, or a double ended wedge, the joint becomes practically invisible and is very strong. I have seen rails over 150 years old with joints as close as on the day they were made. They would, of course, not be appreciated by the jerry-builder of to-day.

SPRINGING.—In architecture the point at which an arch commences, or leaps across an opening (particularly to handrailing), a line drawn on the face mould from the centre of the cylinder or intersection of the axes to the end of the diagonal. *See* Chapter IX., Fig. 4, Pl. XI.

SPRINGING LINE is a horizontal line connecting the ends of an arch. *See* p. 18, Chapter III.

SQUARE-CUT SYSTEM.—One in which the joints in the handrail are made square, or perpendicular to the surface of the material from which the wreath is cut, so producing "butt joints." *See* "Tangent System."

STRETCH-OUT, A, is a drawing of the development of a curved surface upon a plane.

SWANS-NECK.—A compound vertical curve of contrary flexure in a handrail, formed by uniting a "ramp" and a "knee" (*which see*) in one solid piece of handrail. *See* Figs. 12 and 14, Pl. IV.

T.

TANGENT.—A tangent in geometry is a line, or plane, touching a curve, but not cutting into it. Tangents in handrailing are the various planes on which the constructive lines and curves are drawn or developed. *See* Chapter III., Ill. 18, and Chapter X., Pl. XII.

TANGENT SYSTEM.—A modern geometrical method of describing face moulds for handrails without the aid of a cylinder, in which the basic lines are drawn on plane surfaces ; these surfaces being made tangent to the plan curves of the handrail at three points in each wreath. For details *see* Chapter II., p. 12, also Chapter III., p. 16.

TRAMMELLING SQUARE.—An appliance for drawing ellipses of various dimensions, used chiefly in setting out handrail moulds.

TURN-IN is a small horizontal curve in a handrail to carry it into a newel or a wall. *See* Figs. 25 and 26, Pl. XXX.

W.

WELL GAUGE.—An appliance made by the railer himself to suit the particular job in hand. It is shown very clearly at Fig. 10, Pl. XXXI. Its use as described ensures correct joints in the wreath and consequently correct pitch in the rails on each side of the well.

WREATH.—That part of a handrail or of a string which is curved both in plan and elevation. *See also* Glossary, Vol. I.

WREATHED HANDRAIL.—One with a portion rising over and around a circular or elliptic plan. *See* Chapter III., Ill. 15, and Pl. VI., Figs. 6 and 7.

INDEX TO ILLUSTRATIONS.

(For Index to Subjects in Text see page 105.)

The references in *Roman* numerals are to *Plate* numbers ; text illustrations are indexed under the numbers of the pages on which they occur.

INDEX TO TEXT.

(For Index to Illustrations see page 102.)